WASHINGTON, D.C.

THEN AND NOW

Pavilion
An imprint of HarperCollins*Publishers* Ltd
1 London Bridge Street
London SE1 9GF

www.harpercollins.co.uk

HarperCollins*Publishers*
Macken House
39/40 Mayor Street Upper
Dublin 1
D01 C9W8
Ireland

10 9 8 7 6 5 4 3 2 1

First published in Great Britain by Pavilion
An imprint of HarperCollins*Publishers* 2024

ISBN 978-0-00-865899-1

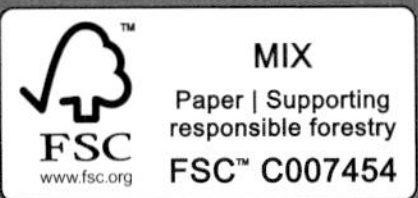

This book contains FSC™ certified paper and other controlled sources to ensure responsible forest management.

For more information visit: www.harpercollins.co.uk/green

Publishing Director: Laura Russell
Commissioning Editor: Frank Hopkinson
Editorial Assistant: Shamar Gunning
Designer: Cara Rogers
Junior Designer: Lily Wilson
Production Controller: Louis Harvey
Photographer: Karl Mondon
Proof-reader: Molly Price
Indexer: Colin Hynson

Printed and bound by RR Donnelley in China

ACKNOWLEDGMENTS

I am so grateful for my family and friends for their support of me during this project. Mom, Dad, Liam: thank you for all that you do and have done for me, and for those early family vacations to D. C. that made me fall in love with this city. To Megan, Abby, Christine, Kayla: thank you for keeping me caffeinated and for always picking up the phone when I needed to work out an idea or string together a sentence. Lastly 9 Logan Circle: my first home in Washington, D.C., which showed me how endless the history is in this great city (and also that landlords have no obligation to update kitchen appliances from 1983). I love you all very dearly, and couldn't have done this without you. I'd also like to thank WETA's Boundary Stone's website: I learnt so much from browsing their records, and was inspired to include some locations within these pages, picked from the highlighted works of fellow WETA intern alum.

PICTURE CREDITS

"Then" Photographs:
All photos are supplied by the Library of Congress archives except the following.

Wikimedia Commons pages 8 main image, 53 left, 68 left, 86, 90
Alamy pages 17 top left, 20, 22 bottom, 30, 52, 55 left, 60, 70, 75 left, 92, 104 below, 118, 126, 128, 142, 143
Lincoln Theater page 24 top
Naval History and Heritage Command page 34
Heurich House Museum page 37 bottom
Getty Images pages 110, 111 left
DC Public Library pages 112, 114
National Archives page 62

"Now" Photographs
All photos were taken by Karl Mondon, except for images listed below.

ACM Archives, Smithsonian page 143
Alamy pages 7, 19, 89 (both), 143
Wikipedia Creative Commons page 11 left
Hay-Adams/CN Traveler page 61 below
Getty Images pages 85 below, 129

WASHINGTON, D.C.

THEN AND NOW

EMMA TANNER

PAVILION

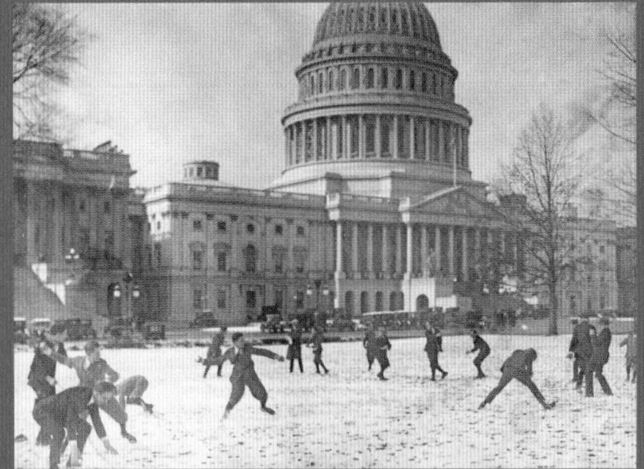
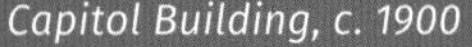

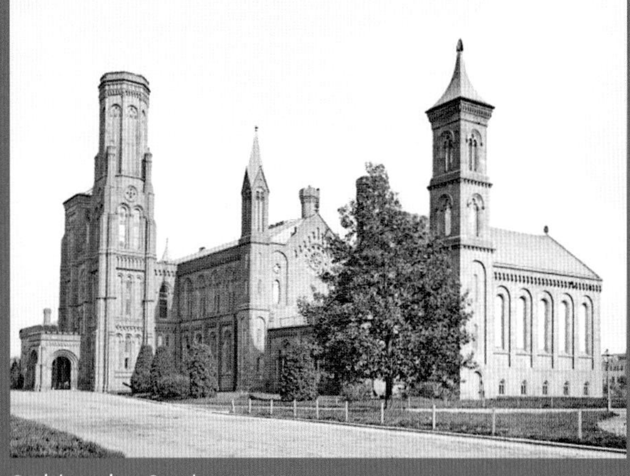

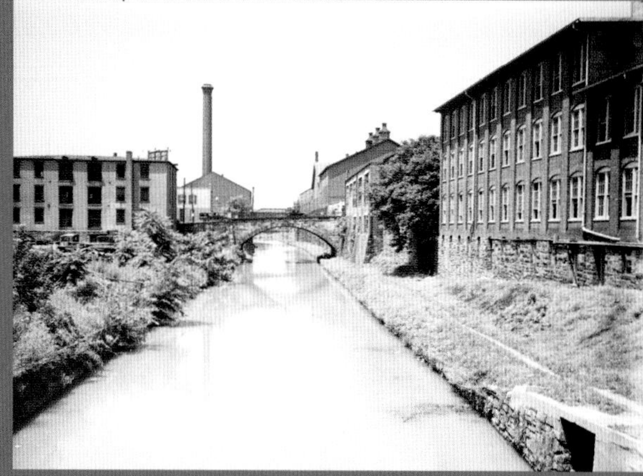

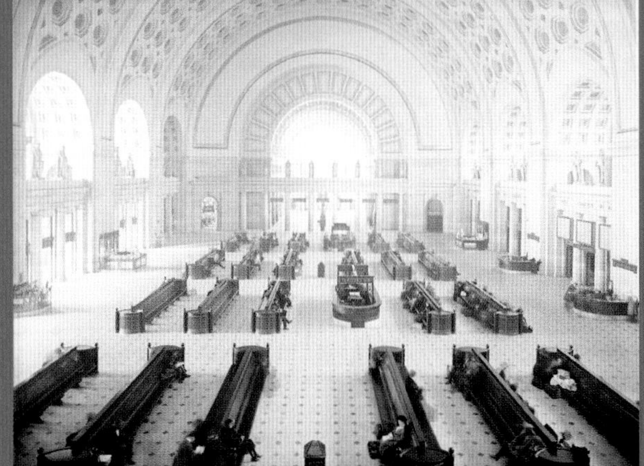

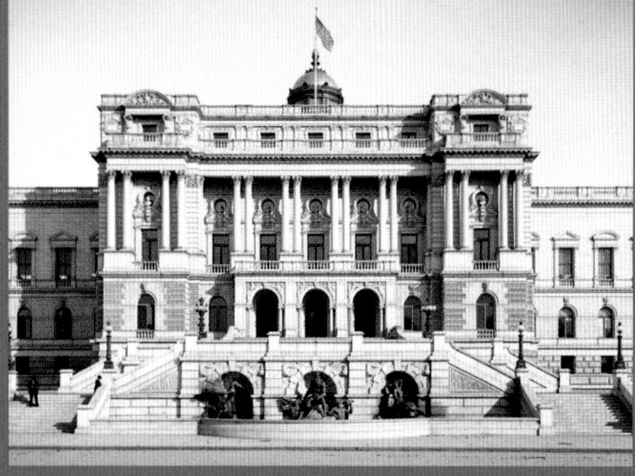

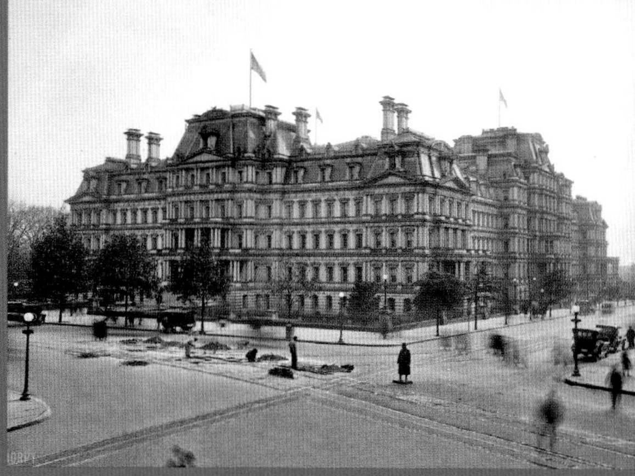

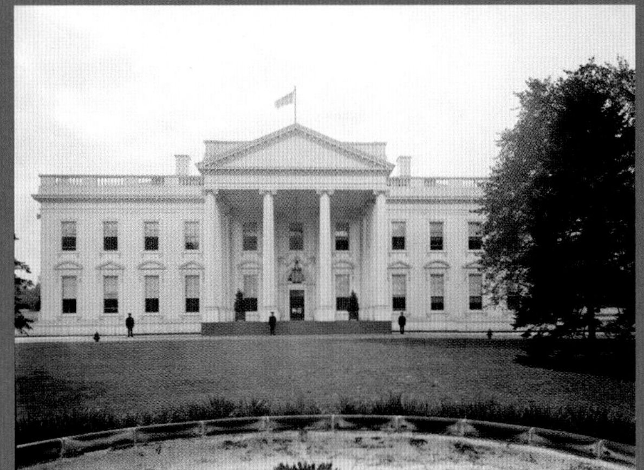

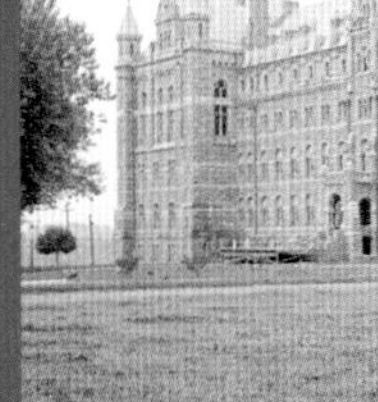
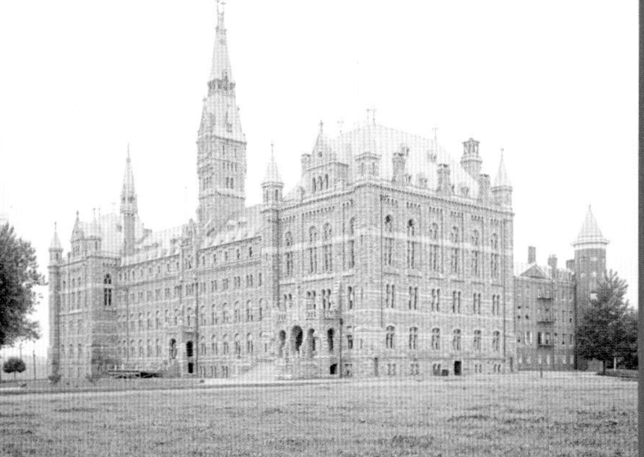

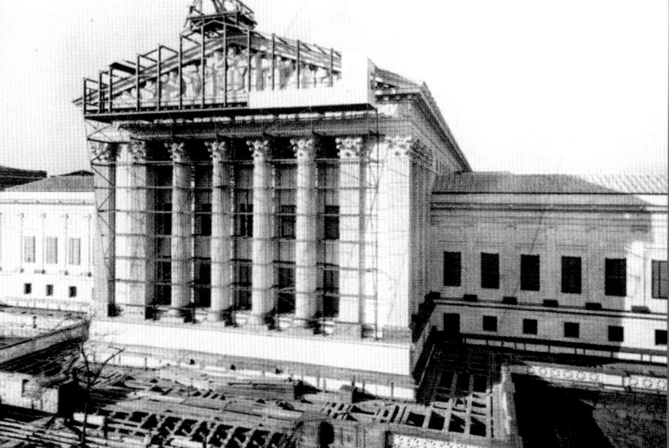

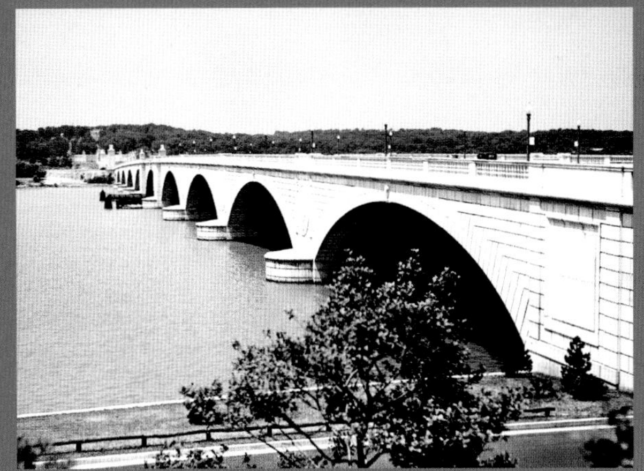

Arlington Memorial Bridge, 1934 p. 92

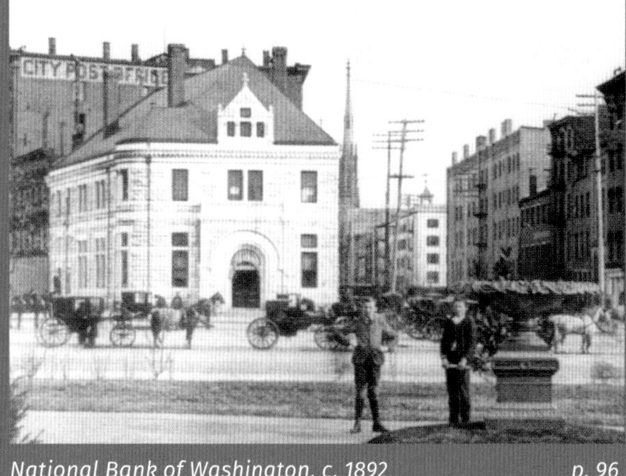

National Bank of Washington, c. 1892 p. 96

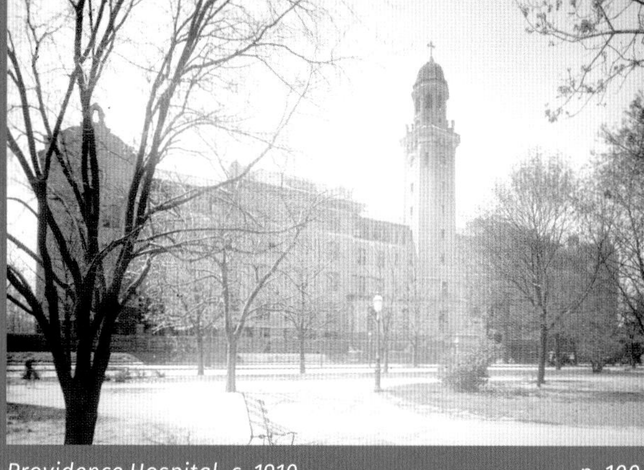

Providence Hospital, c. 1910 p. 100

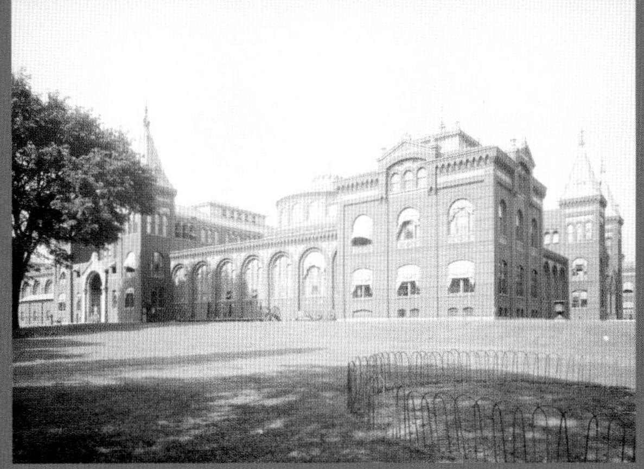

Old National Museum, c. 1900 p. 104

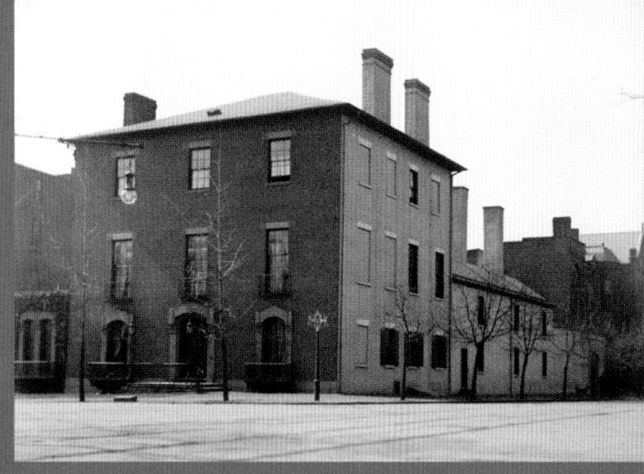

Decatur House, c. 1918 p. 106

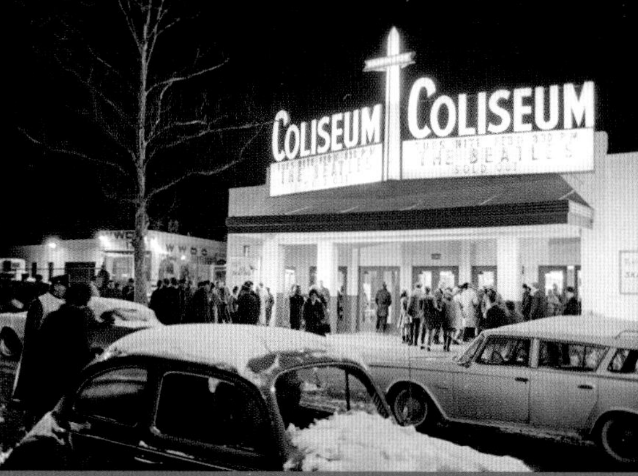

Uline Arena, 1964 p. 110

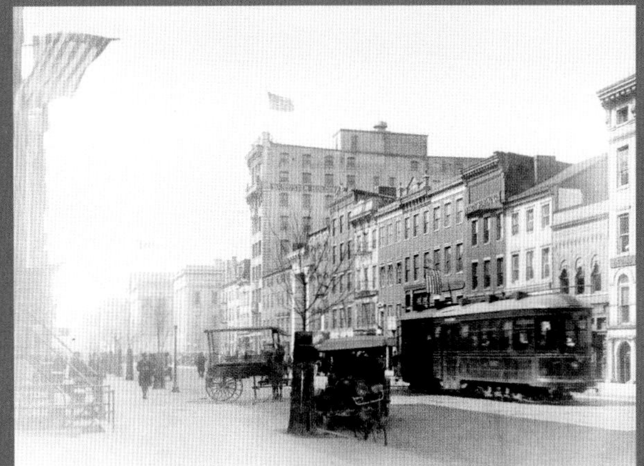

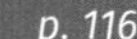

Commercial Shopping Street, c. 1909 p. 116

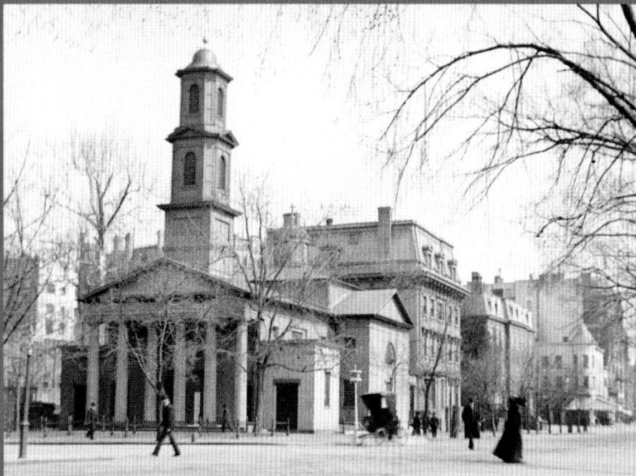

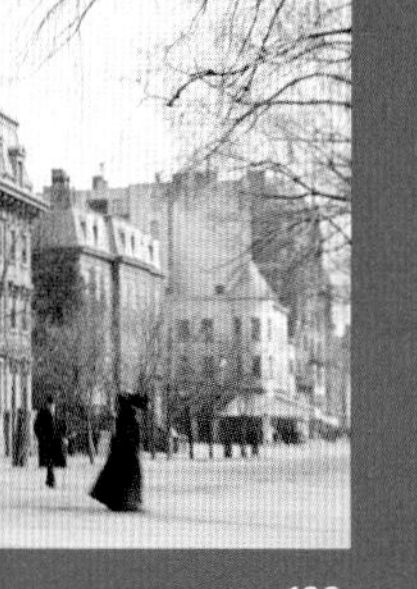

St John's Church, c. 1918 p. 122

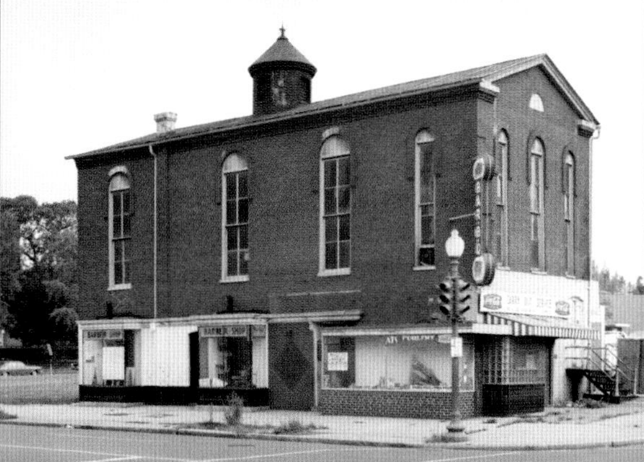

Ada's Israel Synagogue , 1969 p. 130

WASHINGTON, D.C.

THEN AND NOW INTRODUCTION

What is often forgotten about the grandiose city of Washington, D.C. is that it is a home to many. Alongside stately buildings, and presidential homes there are ordinary people born and raised in D.C., who continue their family's long-standing legacies in the nation's capital. Others travel from elsewhere, adopting the title of "transplant", and arrive hoping to influence the historic decision-making process in the capital of the United States. No matter how one ends up in the District, any who live in its 131 neighborhoods – the exact number is debated – call this quasi-diamond shaped town their home. It is those stories which we endeavor to tell within this book, illuminating the hidden lives, and histories of the streets of Washington, D.C.

The District of Columbia was not always brick row houses and brutalist architecture. In its earliest years, the land was occupied by several Native tribes. Around the Anacostia and Potomac Rivers; the Chesapeake Bay; and in the nearby states of Maryland and Virginia; there were over a dozen indigenous groups who made their home on this land. There were three primary Native tribe villages in the Washington area, the largest being that of Nacotchtank, from which the word Anacostia is derived. The access to rivers and wilderness that made up Washington at this time provided many resources for these communities.

The arrival of European settlers to the area in 1608 changed life for the people there. While these early Europeans and their descendants are often referred to as "the first Washingtonians," this is not an accurate reflection of the make-up of this land. Captain John Smith was the first documented European to reach the Potomac River, who recorded his interactions with those who lived there already. After forty years of contact, both hostile and friendly, the population of Native Americans in the area was reduced to a quarter of its original size.

While tobacco farmers and plantation owners lived in this area throughout the seventeenth and eighteenth centuries, it was not until the Residence Act of 1790 that Washington, D.C. was officially chosen to be the nation's capital. With plans due to be completed by 1800, rapid and ingenious work was needed to prepare the city for its congressional arrival.

French-born Pierre Charles L'Enfant was going by Peter after his move to the new United States, after a career in the Revolutionary War. He offered his architectural services to President George Washington and embarked upon a city which mixed traditional European features and solutions to the needs of a modern democracy. The new city took parts from Maryland: their town named Georgetown, and Virginia: their 'across the river' town, Alexandria to create its diamond shape. Although both the diamond shape and Alexandria's inclusion in the city were only temporary, these elements of the original plan bear a mark on the city today.

In the early 1900s infrastructural changes were much needed in D.C., with an influx of new residents to the Federal City. In 1902 , Senator James McMillan sat at the head of a congressional committee in charge of improving the infrastructure of Washington and so came The Report of the Senate Park Commission, also known as the McMillan plan, detailing artistic improvements. From large monuments such as the Lincoln Memorial to a central transportation hub called Union Station, the McMillan Plan brought architectural consistency to Washington, and is reflected in many of the white sandstone buildings seen within the District today.

Throughout the twentieth century, American involvement in the World Wars created a need for federal support and, with it, more jobs for those in Washington. After World War II the population in D.C. peaked, nearing a million in 1950 and in the decades following many Washingtonians who were financially able, primarily white residents, moved their lives to the new and developing suburbs. By 1957, Washington became the first major city with a majority Black population, which continued to grow throughout the 1960s. This decade saw a large amount of Latino migration into D.C. and tensions rose between communities, much of which persists in the still-political city today. In the second half of the twentieth century, Washington experienced a period of regrowth from which it emerged the triumphant and thriving capital of the United States.

This book documents the architectural changes of Washington, showcasing how these structures represent the lives of those who have made their home in the city. Buildings and monuments physically make up this city, but the stories of those who lived here and their experiences are what make Washington, *Washington*. We hope this book encourages those visiting to venture off the well-trodden National Mall and experience some of Washington's local history, or inspires local residents to try sightseeing for a day as they visit Washington's popular locations. Who knows, you might just learn something new.

RIGHT: The Capitol building, built in the eighteenth century, can be seen in the water of the Lincoln Memorial Reflecting Pool in Washington, D.C.

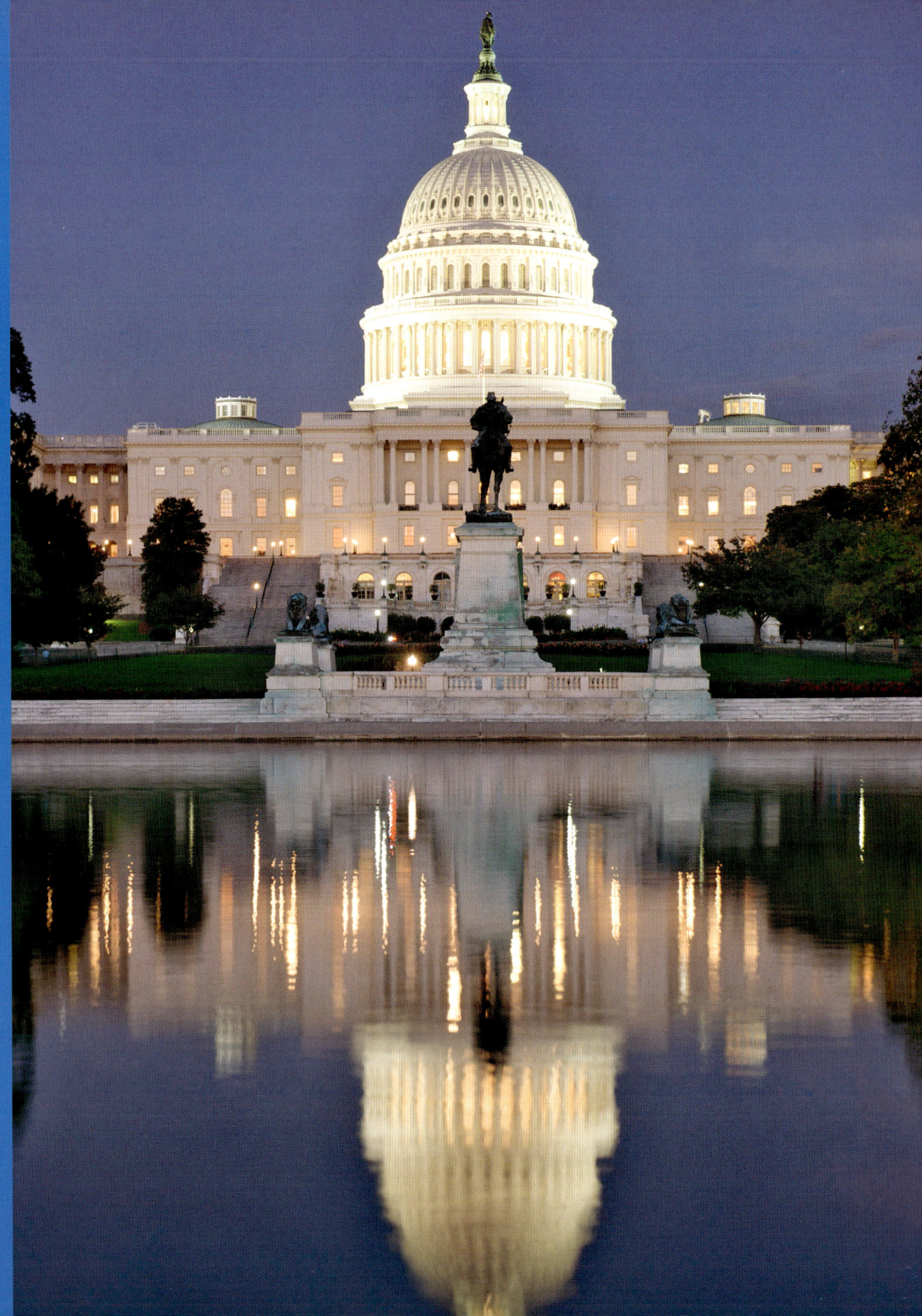

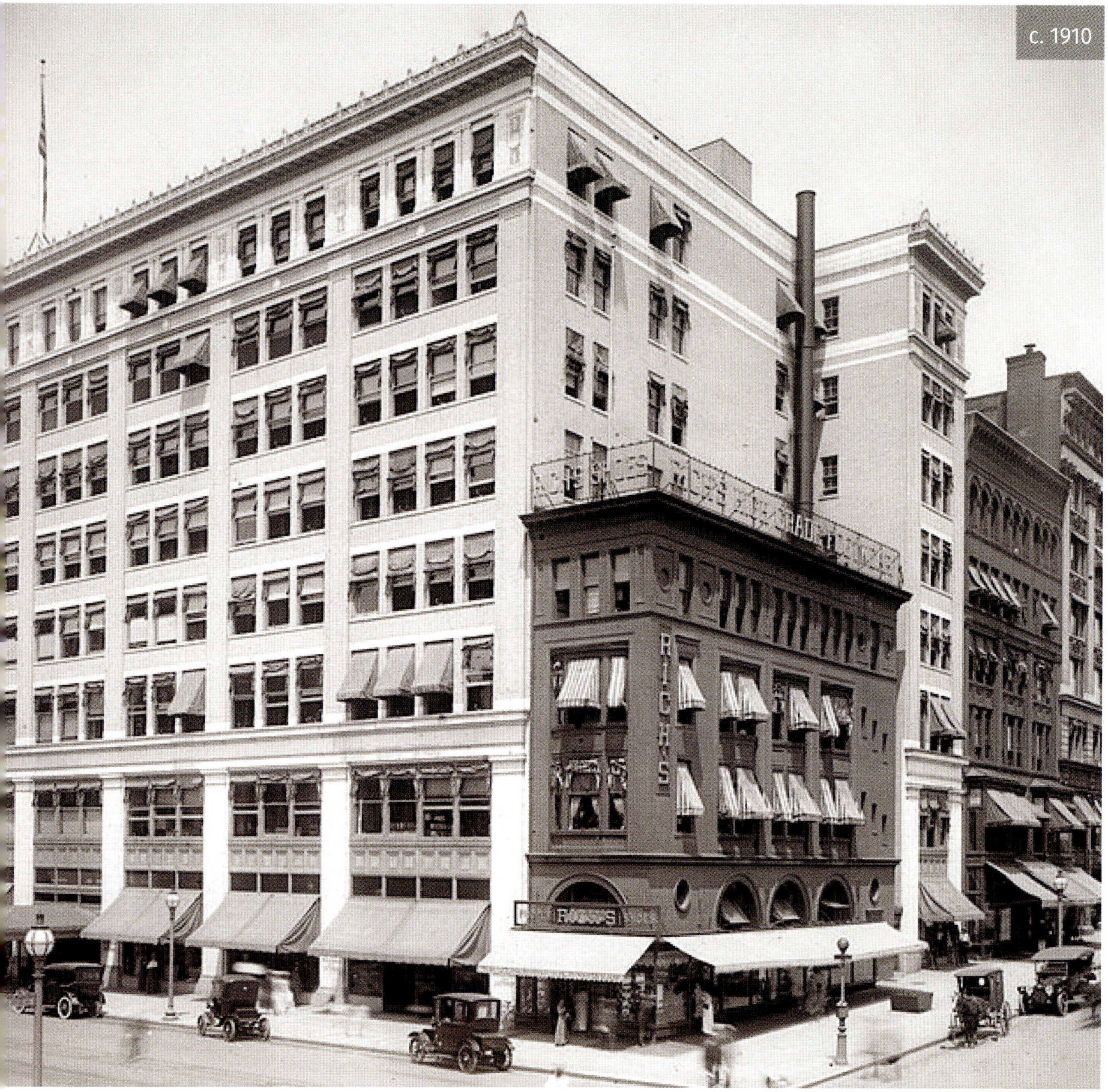

c. 1910

THEN: In the years following the Civil War to the early twentieth century, downtown D.C. saw the onset of a major commercial advancement: the department store. One of the very first stores in the District lived in this building, known as Woodward & Lothrop or "Woodies" as it was called by loyal customers. In 1886, business partners Samuel Walter Woodward and Alvin Mason Lothrop opened this flagship location on the corner of 11th and F Streets NW, and carried various products to suit D.C. shoppers' needs. Soon after they arrived in D.C., their business absorbed other buildings, dominating the entire block, adding floors and other businesses such as Rich's Shoes as time went on. However, Woodies didn't just change the physical landscape of D.C.; it changed how Washingtonians shopped altogether. The store instituted a "one price" policy, eliminating the haggling that had been standard at the time, and accepted returns for a cash repayment instead of just store credit. Eventually, Woodies became one of the most popular department stores in D.C., with customers including the White House.

BELOW: Woodies was not just known for its revolutionary shopping policies, but for its elaborate displays and promotions. These included eye-catching window displays. Most popular were their holiday displays, which even included live penguins from the Smithsonian's National Zoo one year.

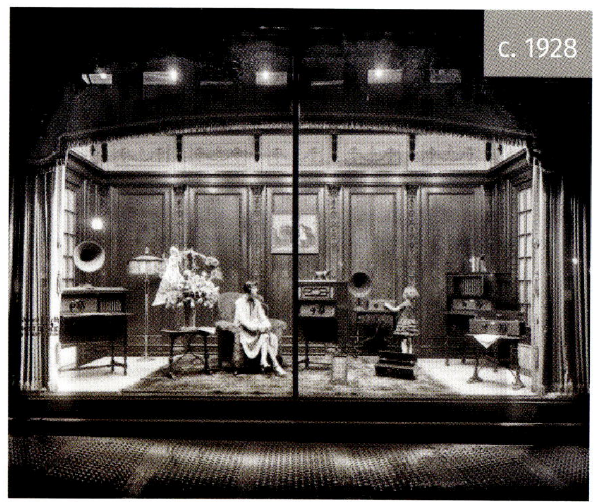

c. 1928

WOODWARD & LOTHROP

Changing the way Washingtonians shopped

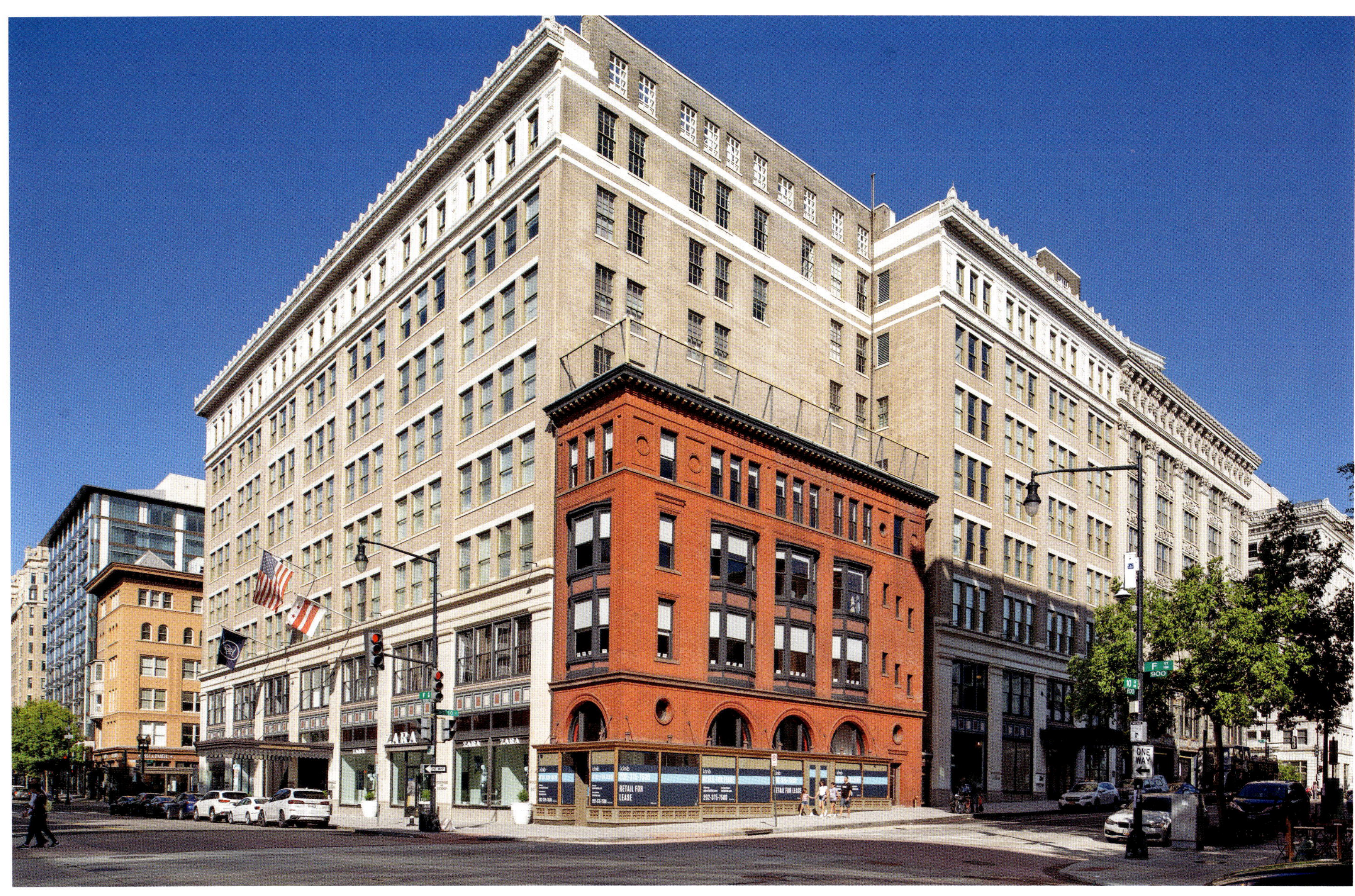

NOW: While Woodward & Lothrop stood out for changes it made to shopping for Washingtonians, they implemented aggressive policies of racial discrimination that were common in D.C. at the time. After World War I, they fired all Black employees in order to make room for white soldiers returning back to the District. The store practiced segregation, sometimes not allowing Black customers into the store at all. These policies received strong pushback from local civil rights activists, led by Mary Church Terrell who eventually had the policies overturned. Woodies continued its expansion with stores in D.C.'s growing suburbs, however by the mid-1980s, the local favorite faced a loss of family ownership and increasing competition from national retailers like Macy's. Since the store's closure in 1995, the flagship building has changed hands several times, but the Beaux-Arts style building will remain on its corner as a D.C. Historic Landmark.

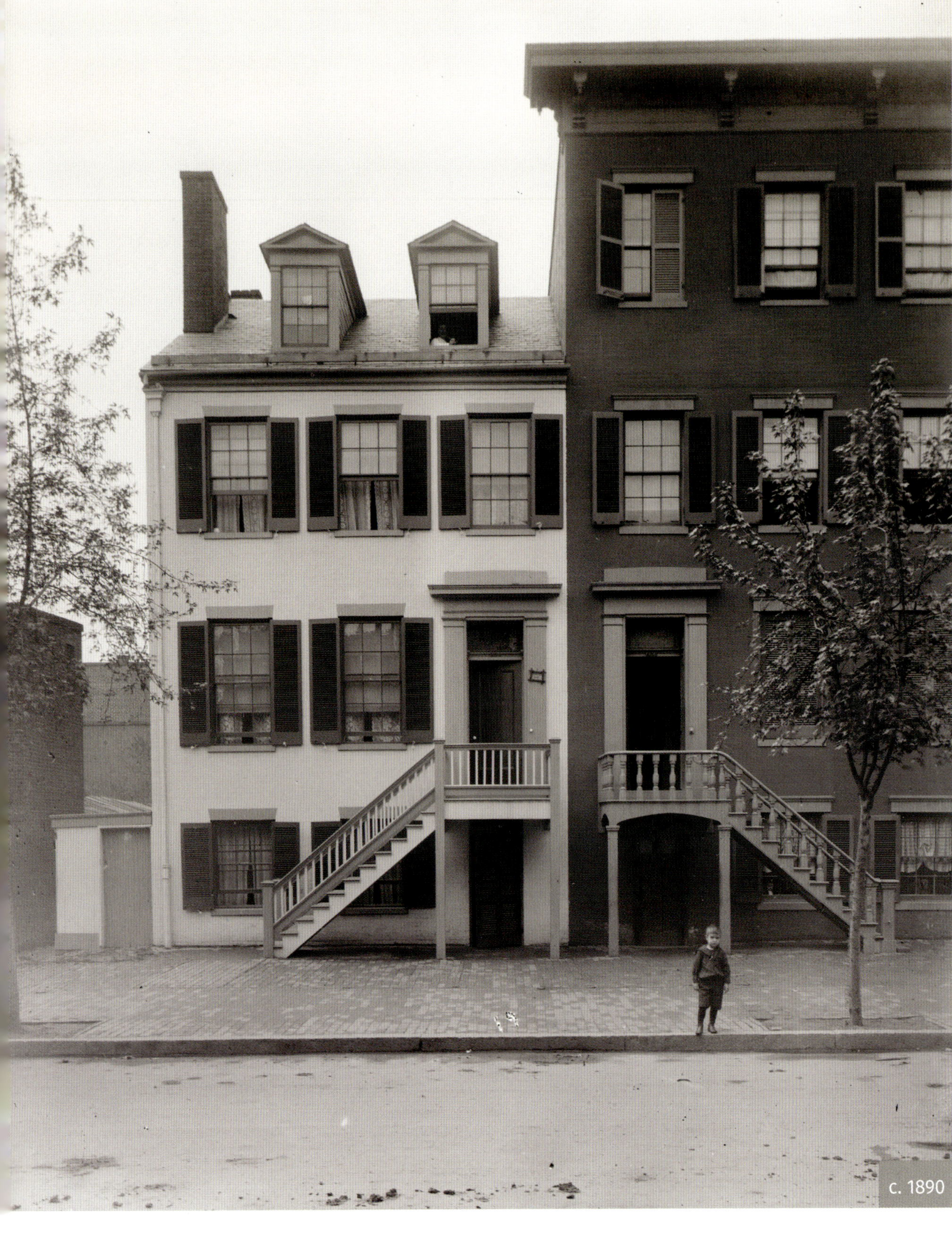
c. 1890

MARY E. SURRATT BOARDING HOUSE

The site where the Lincoln assassination was planned

THEN: President Abraham Lincoln's assassination was a significant moment in Washington, D.C.'s history, with Ford's Theater positioned at the forefront of this horrific event. However, another building in the District holds equal significance to the assassination: the Mary E. Surratt Boarding House. Built in 1843 in an Early Republic (or Federal) style, this pre-Civil War brick building operated as a boarding house from 1864 to 1865 by the Confederate sympathizers, Mary Surratt and her son, John Surratt, Jr. Throughout these final years of the Civil War, the building hosted several guests. One notable visitor at this time was John Wilkes Booth, the man responsible for President Lincoln's assassination. In his visits to the house leading up to the attack on the President, Booth met with his co-conspirators George Atzerodt, David Herold, Edmund Spangler, Samuel Arnold, Michael O'Laughlen, and Lewis Powell at the Boarding House to plan the details of the assassination. Involved in these conversations and supporters of Booth's plan were Boarding House proprietors Mary Surratt and John Surratt, Jr. Right before travelling to Ford's Theater to carry out his deadly plan, Booth stopped by the Boarding House to speak privately with Mary Surratt.

NOW: The plan to assassinate President Lincoln was successful although Booth and his co-conspirators were eventually discovered. Booth made it out of Washington, D.C., but was found and died resisting capture while several of his co-conspirators were arrested for their crimes. Mary Surratt was included in this group, and was arrested at her home, which was subsequently searched. In this search, several implicating items such as bullet molds and confederate flags were discovered. Following her trial, Mary Surratt was discovered to be guilty of conspiracy to assassinate the President and became the first woman to be executed by the Federal Government. After Mary's death, the building continued to operate as a boarding house, yet changed hands frequently and eventually was left unused by the 1920s. In 1925, the building was purchased by Irvan Schwartzman who made significant renovations to the building and converted the first floor to a commercial space. Changes in the area continued into the 1930s as Chinese immigrants moved into the neighborhood after being forced out of their previous housing units due to the construction of new federal buildings. The site is now a karaoke bar called Wok & Roll and exists in what is considered D.C.'s Chinatown.

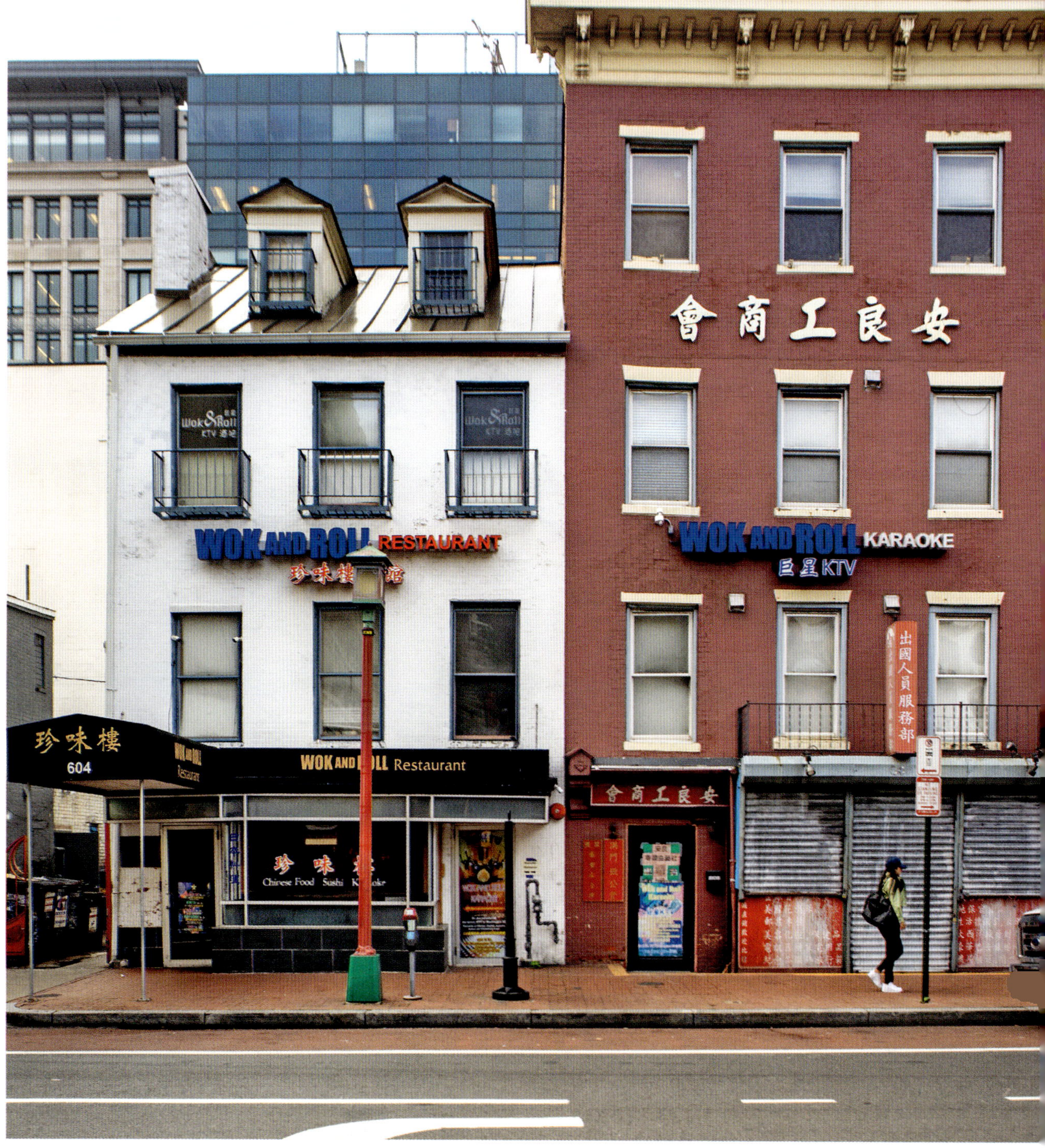

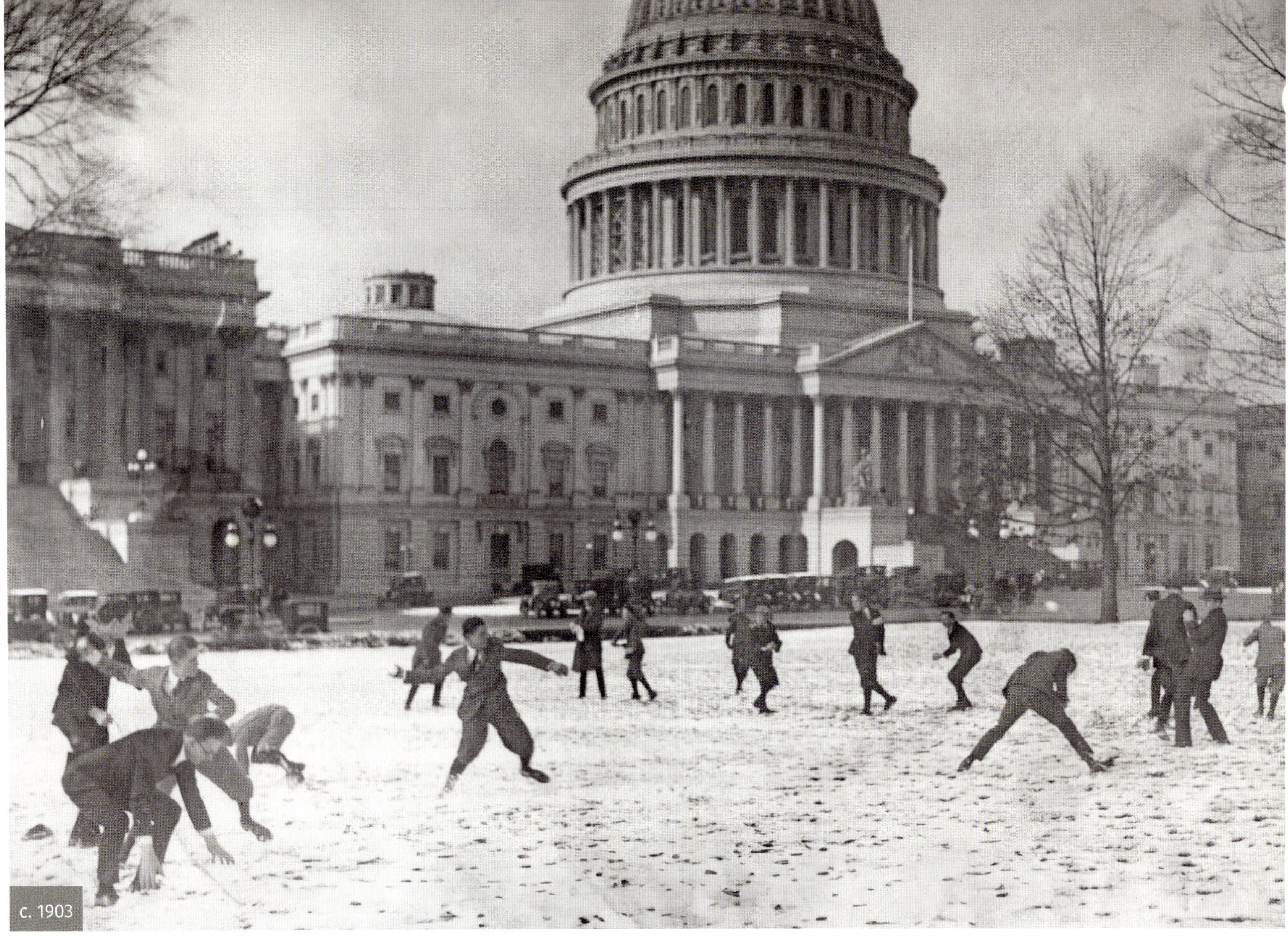

c. 1903

THE CAPITOL BUILDING

The ever-growing seat of American democracy

THEN: When city planners began work on the new capital of the United States, they needed a home for the legislative branch to sit. As early as 1793 the location was selected, and President George Washington laid its cornerstone on the southeast corner of the Capitol Building's eventual foundation. Unsure of who to hire for the job, the new United States Congress held a competition for the best architectural design which was won by Dr. William Thornton, a relatively new architect in Washington, D.C.

The expected move-in date for the new legislative branch was 1800 and the architectural plans proved to be overly ambitious. By the time Congress arrived in Washington, only the Senate wing had been completed. Construction continued to face early challenges throughout the nineteenth century when in 1814, British

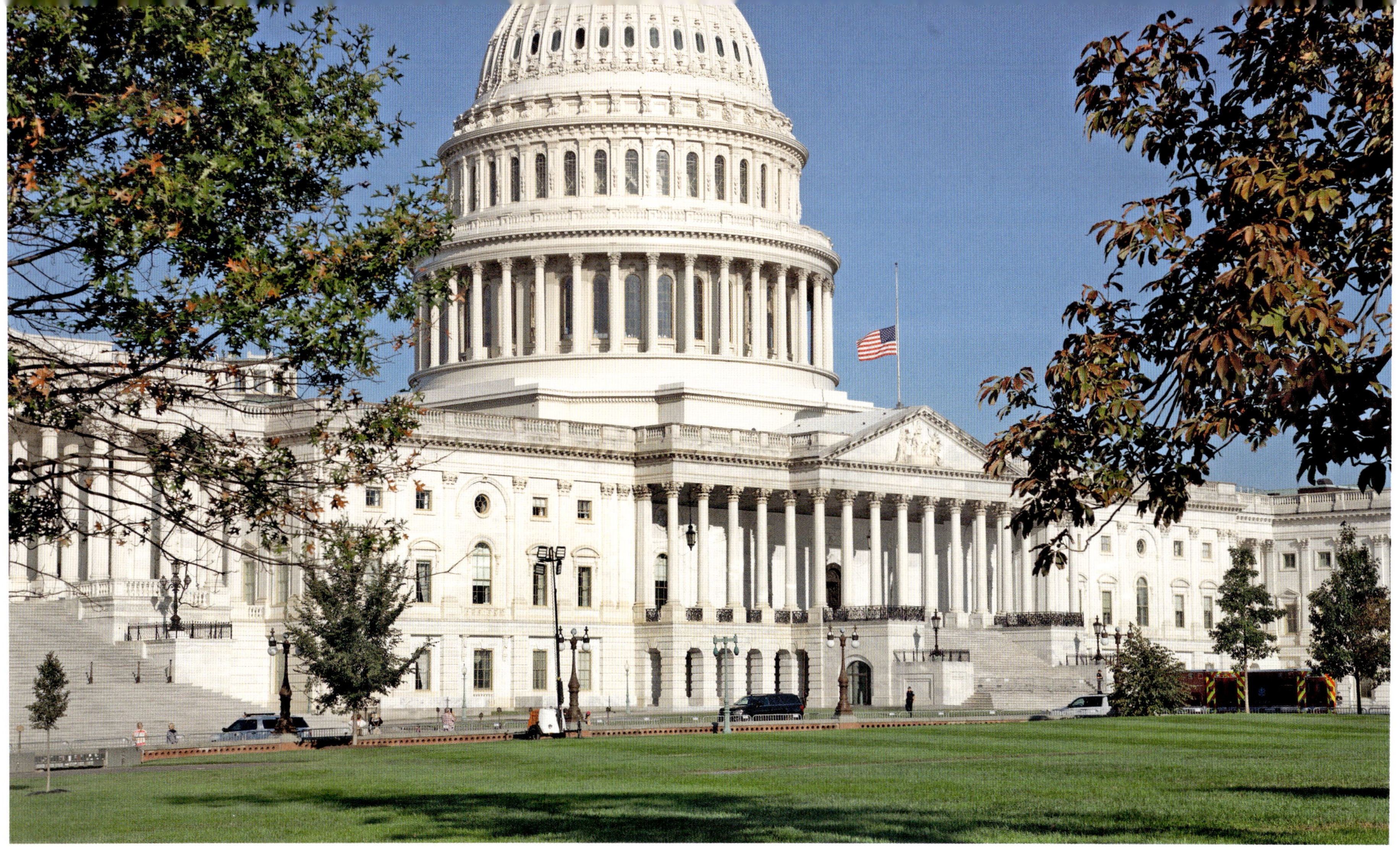

troops invaded the new capital city and set the District aflame; including the Capitol Building. A rainstorm prevented the structure's complete destruction, but the building ultimately required improvements. As the country expanded westward, more senators and representatives were needed for the growing number of seats which meant the initial chambers constructed in the Capitol Building became overly crowded. The building was already overfull with its reference library, the Library of Congress, and permanent tenant, and the third branch of the American government, the Supreme Court.

Construction stopped during the Civil War to provide support for the soldiers. The Capitol Building was used as military barracks, a hospital, and at one point, a bakery. The Capitol Building had been a relatively flat building with no distinguishable top feature but finally gained its iron dome in 1863. Constructed with almost nine million pounds of ironwork joined together, the dome topped with the *Statue of Freedom* is one of the most recognizable symbols of the American government today.

NOW: The Library of Congress was eventually granted its own building to free up space for Congress, and in 1935 the Supreme Court left the legislative branch for a building of its own, right behind it. The twentieth century brought with it technological advancements and expansions, such as separate buildings for office space and committee rooms for both the House and the Senate. To get around the District and into the Capitol Building more easily a senate terminal was added right under the Senate steps, and Congress continues to have its own small train to transport the congress people from building to building.

In 2008, the U.S. Capitol Visitor Center was completed, and includes an exhibit about the Capitol's unique history not only in American politics, but as a recognizable feature on the Washington, D.C. skyline.

The Capitol's congressional steps have seen presidential inaugurations, influential speeches, and moments of protest. In recent memory on January 6th, 2021, the Capitol Building was beset by a group of politically motivated individuals whose actions led to a breach of Capitol security and several related deaths, which continue to affect Washington and the U.S. political landscape.

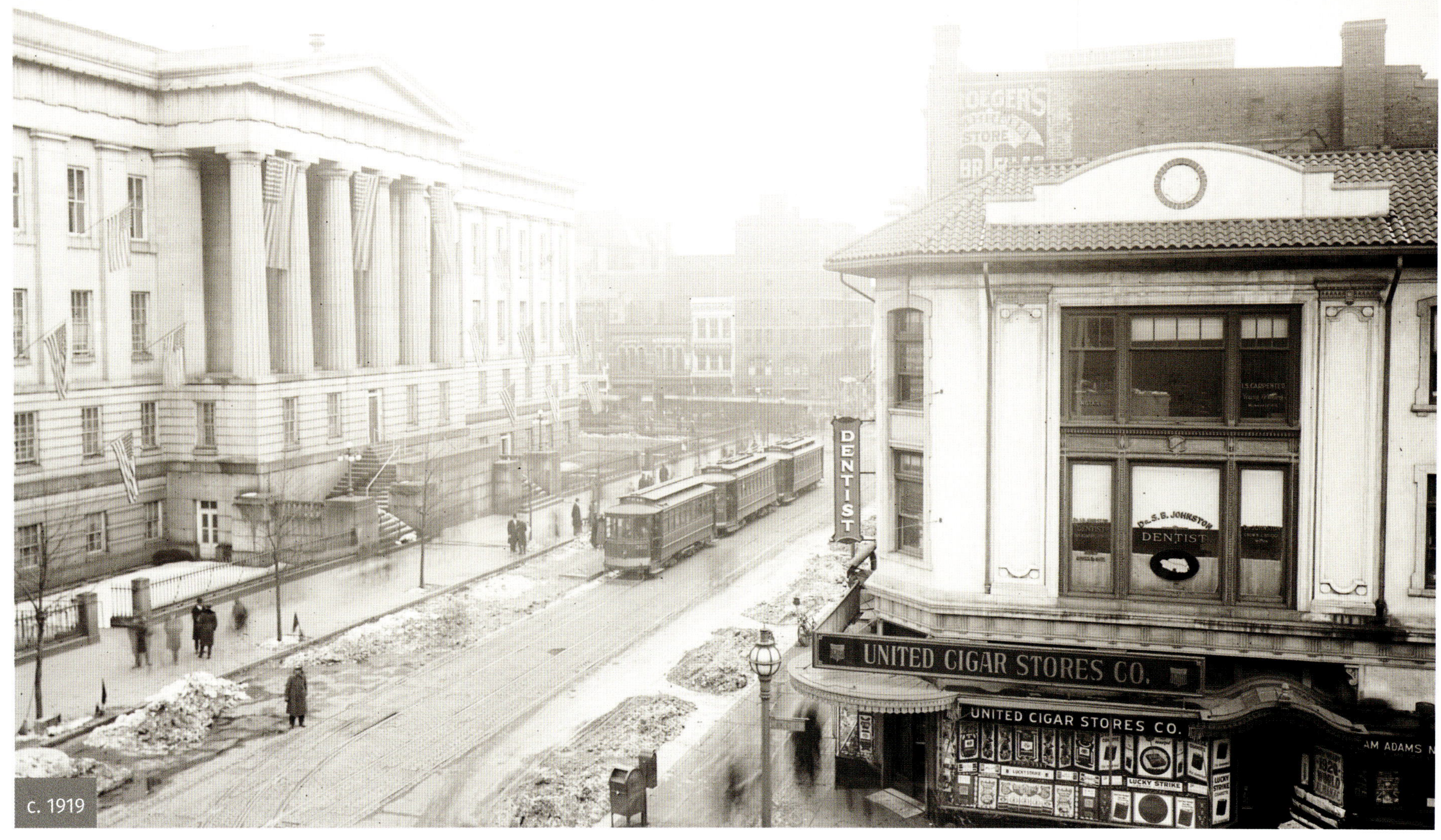

c. 1919

U.S. PATENT OFFICE

“That noblest of Washington buildings”

THEN: In his plan for the new capital, Pierre Charles L’Enfant set aside a location between the White House and the Capitol building on 8th and F Streets to be a monumental structure. He envisioned this to be a nondenominational church, or even a Pantheon to celebrate America’s heroes and accomplishments. In a way, L’Enfant’s vision came true when the site became the United States Patent Office, a building that housed the innovations and original models of America’s greatest inventors.

Popular Washington architect Robert Mills began construction on the building in 1836, including modern structural advancements such as brick vaults, balanced with more graceful details such as the rounded staircases. However, Mills fell out of favor with Congress, who questioned his competence and instead changed leadership of the project to Mills’s greatest critic, Thomas U. Walter. Completed in 1868, the building was considered to be one of the greatest examples of Greek Revivalist architecture in the United States and was donned “that noblest of Washington buildings” by famed poet Walt Whitman.

The Patent Office opened during its lengthy construction period and grew exponentially in the number of patents it received. It received over 200,000 patents in the 1880s, a significant increase compared to the 6,000 received in the 1840s. An increased number of patents meant a demand for more staff, and the office faced backlash when in 1853 the Commissioner of the office hired women to work alongside men and receive equal pay for their work – although this was short-lived. In 1854, Clara Barton, founder of the American Red Cross, worked in the Patent Office. She returned to the Office during the Civil War to care for injured Union soldiers, alongside Walt Whitman during the time when the Patent Office served as an important space for Union operations during the conflict.

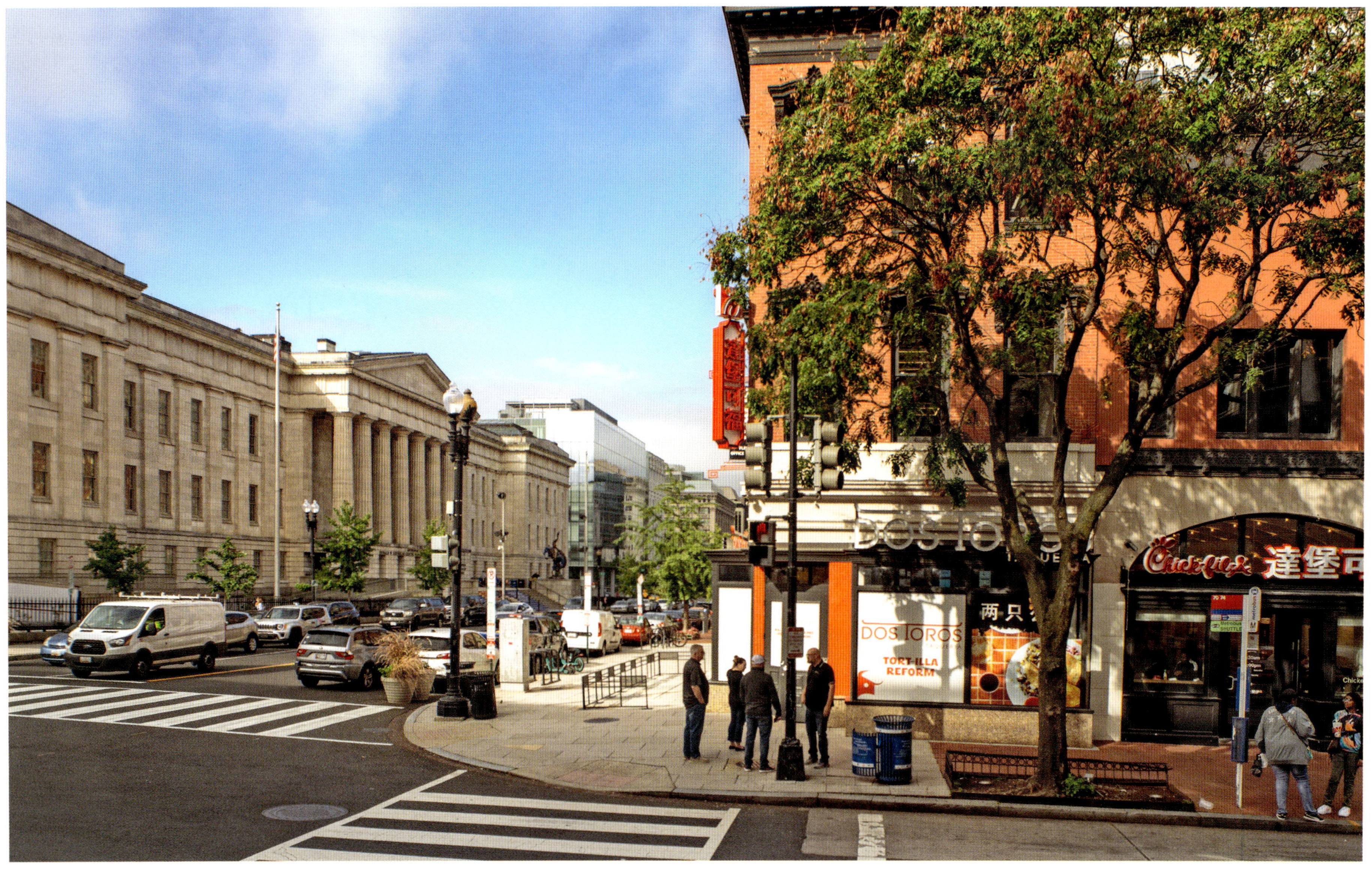

NOW: Architects Robert Mills and Thomas U. Walter promised their constructions were fireproof, which proved to be false. In 1877, the largest fire in Washington, D.C. history broke out in the building. The structure was later reconstructed, but by 1932 it no longer suited the needs of the Patent Office. Following the Patent Office's departure, the building fell into the common federal building fate in D.C. of hosting various offices, such as the Civil Service Commission. In the 1950s the building was recommended for demolition for the construction of a new parking garage, however local preservationists fought for the building to remain and with the intervention of President Dwight D. Eisenhower the building found a new purpose. In 1958 it was transferred to the management of the Smithsonian, and in 1968 opened as the dual home of the Smithsonian American Art Museum and the National Portrait Gallery. Although it is not the Pantheon L'Enfant intended, the building continues to maintain its long history of celebrating American achievement.

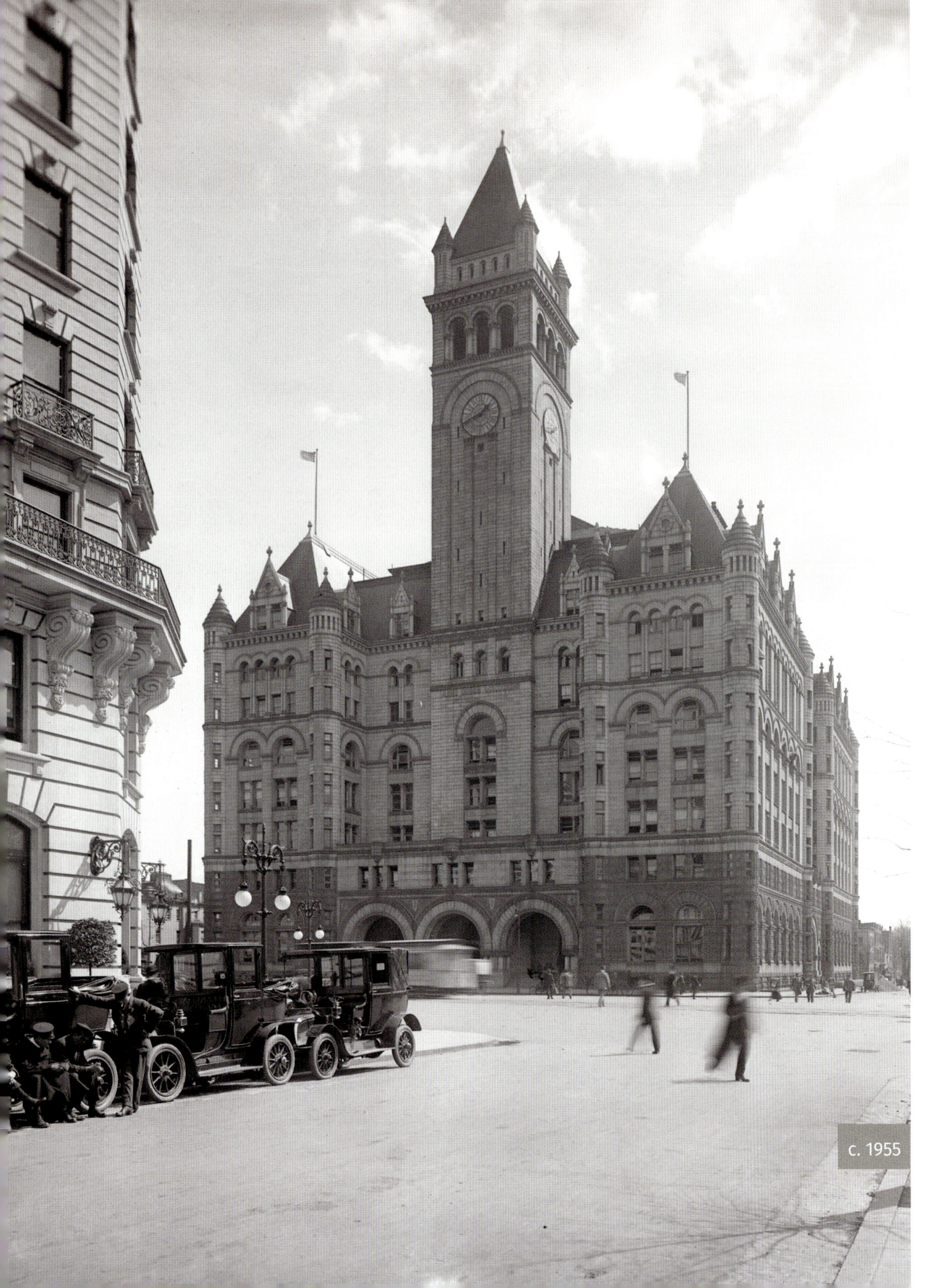

c. 1955

OLD POST OFFICE PAVILION

A commitment to conservation

THEN: In the years following the Civil War, Washington, D.C. saw a growing population and, in turn, an increased need for more efficient local and government buildings. One of these necessities was a post office. In the late nineteenth century, Washingtonians lacked a physical post office for their growing city. After more than twenty-five years of congressional debate about an adequate location for such an institution, a plot of land on Pennsylvania Avenue was finally determined. In 1892, construction had at last begun on the stylish Romanesque Revival building that would stand as one of the tallest buildings in the District, second only to the Washington Monument. Throughout the construction process a large clock tower was added to the building as D.C. lacked a prominent clock visible from long distances. At the building's completion in 1899, D.C. could finally proclaim it had not only a city post office but also a post office headquarters, for general postal needs—or so they thought. Within a year of the building's finalization, there was growing discontentment with the outdated design of the structure, which had been built in a stylistically transitional time. The *New York Times* went as far as to call it "a cross between a cathedral and a cotton mill." There were also increasing complaints about the poor design of the interior, as there was limited space for the federal offices it had intended to host. In 1928, less than thirty years after the building was opened, it was destined for demolition.

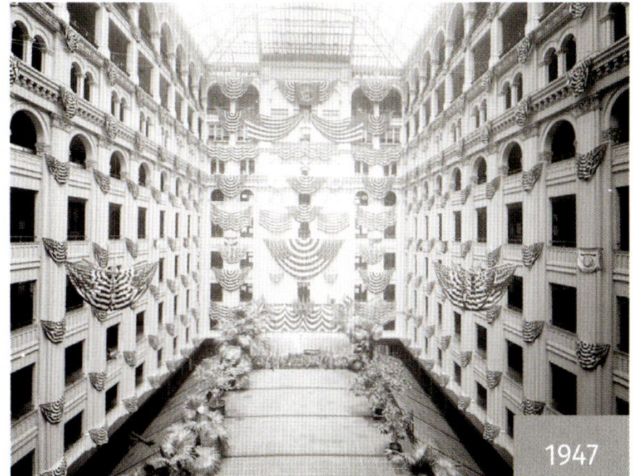

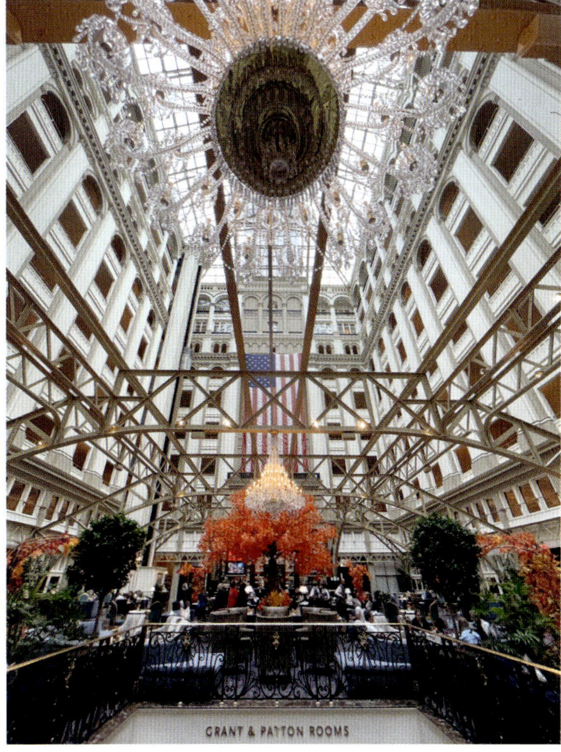

TOP AND ABOVE: A large skylight sits atop a court that was once the largest uninterrupted interior space in Washington. Today, visitors can visit the site as it functions as a hotel, and take an elevator to the building's observation deck for a bird's eye view of the city.

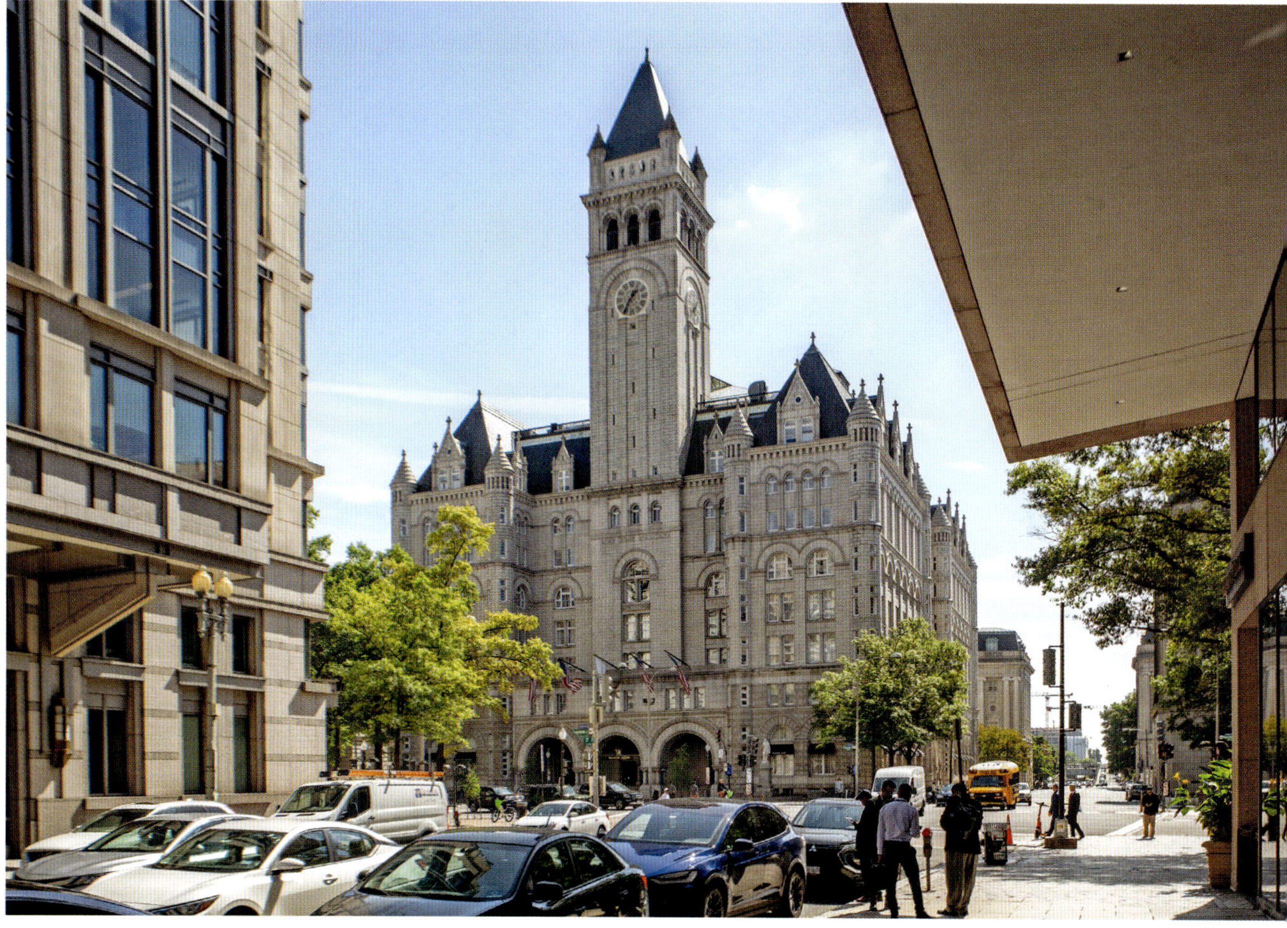

NOW: The fate of the Post Office building found a stroke of luck in one of America's darkest times: the Great Depression. Due to a lack of funds, the building evaded demolition. Unfortunately, the building's luck was not long-lasting. In the 1930s, the Post Office moved out and several agencies occupied the structure and, by 1964, the building lacked a permanent resident and showed signs of serious deterioration. The decision was made that all but the clocktower were recommended for demolition. This time, however, a group of preservationists and the National Endowment of the Arts, led by Nancy Hanks, stepped in and convinced Congress to reverse their decision, and the building was saved once again.

In 1983, the Post Office Pavilion was renamed the Nancy Hanks Center, in celebration of her dedication and community conservation efforts. Since then, the building has become a mainstay on Pennsylvania Avenue and currently functions as a hotel. The Old Post Office serves as a reminder to D.C. residents of how a commitment to conservation can bring the old into the new.

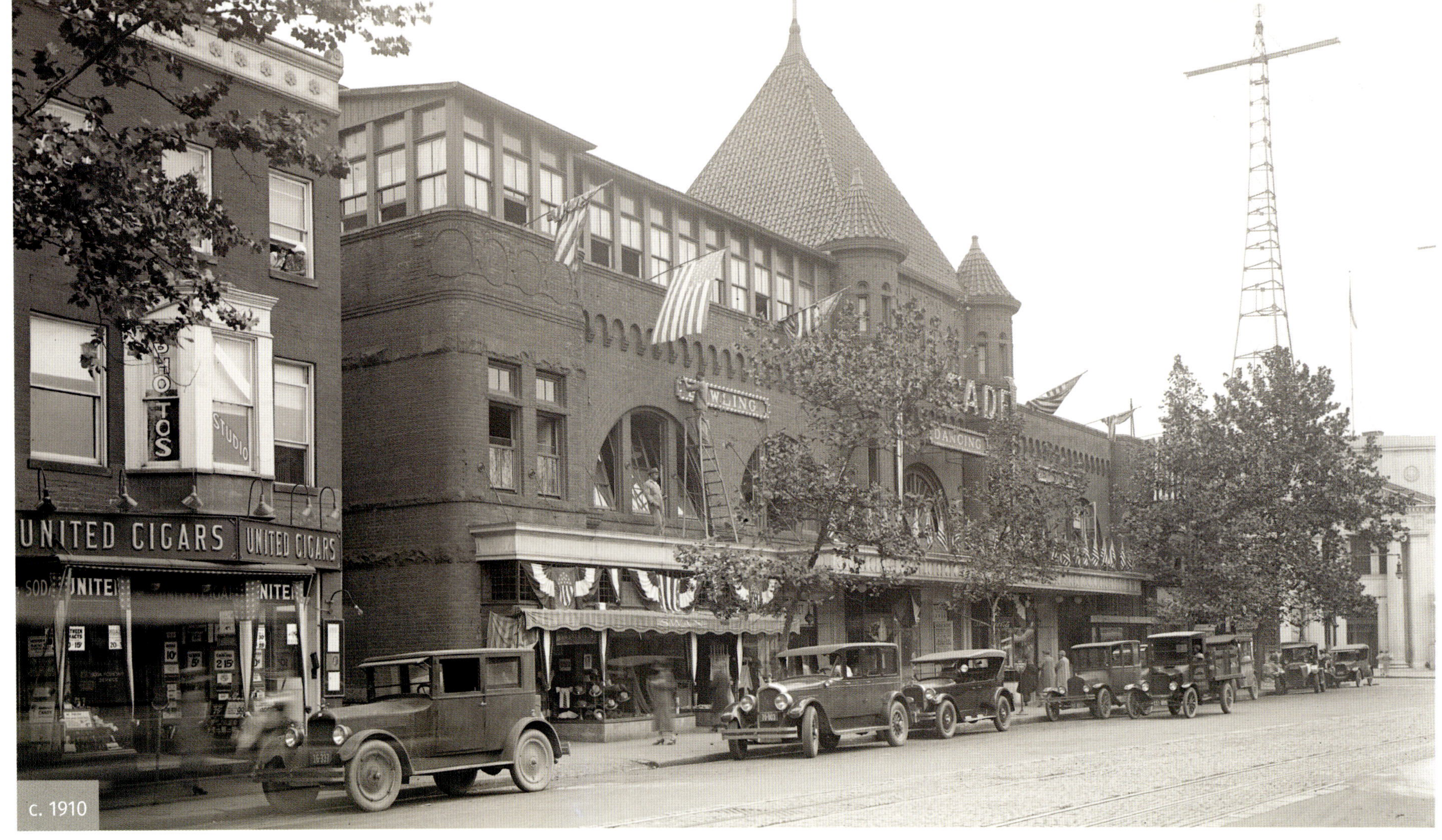

c. 1910

COLUMBIA HEIGHTS/14TH AND IRVING STREET NW

Farmland turned commercial shopping hub

THEN: Before Northwest Washington became one of the city's most populated quadrants, it was largely made up of sparsely populated farmland and sprawling estates. This is especially true for Columbia Heights, a neighborhood in D.C. that was once considered to be outside the city of Washington.

Although located within the boundaries of the District of Columbia, the steep hill in Northwest Washington where the neighborhood now sits, remained largely undeveloped throughout the nineteenth century. In 1822 Columbian College, which was the foundational college of the George Washington University that is located in the Foggy Bottom neighborhood, sat atop the hill alongside the Holmead estate. The area was quiet, with city folk occasionally making their way north to the neighborhood and farmers bringing their wares down the hill into the city.

However, as Washington's population grew in the years following the Civil War and transportation opportunities brought new Washingtonians into neighborhoods that were considered outside the central city, Columbia Heights population began to take off. As Washington, D.C. became one cohesive city, new residents began to take pieces of this once farmland region and transform it into a residential suburban solace, away from downtown. It was with this suburban perspective in mind that Senator John Sherman purchased land in the new neighborhood and named it Columbia Heights after the nearby college, soon lending its name to the entire neighborhood.

As streetcars made their way into Columbia Heights, parts of the region began to develop from residential solace into a commercial center. 14th Street NW which sat towards the western side of the neighborhood began to fill with new businesses, including the Arcade pictured here, which consisted of an indoor market, a sports facility, and a general amusement center. The neighborhood defined itself as a gathering place, with various churches, social clubs, and corner markets making a neighborhood in a metropolis into its own tight-knit community.

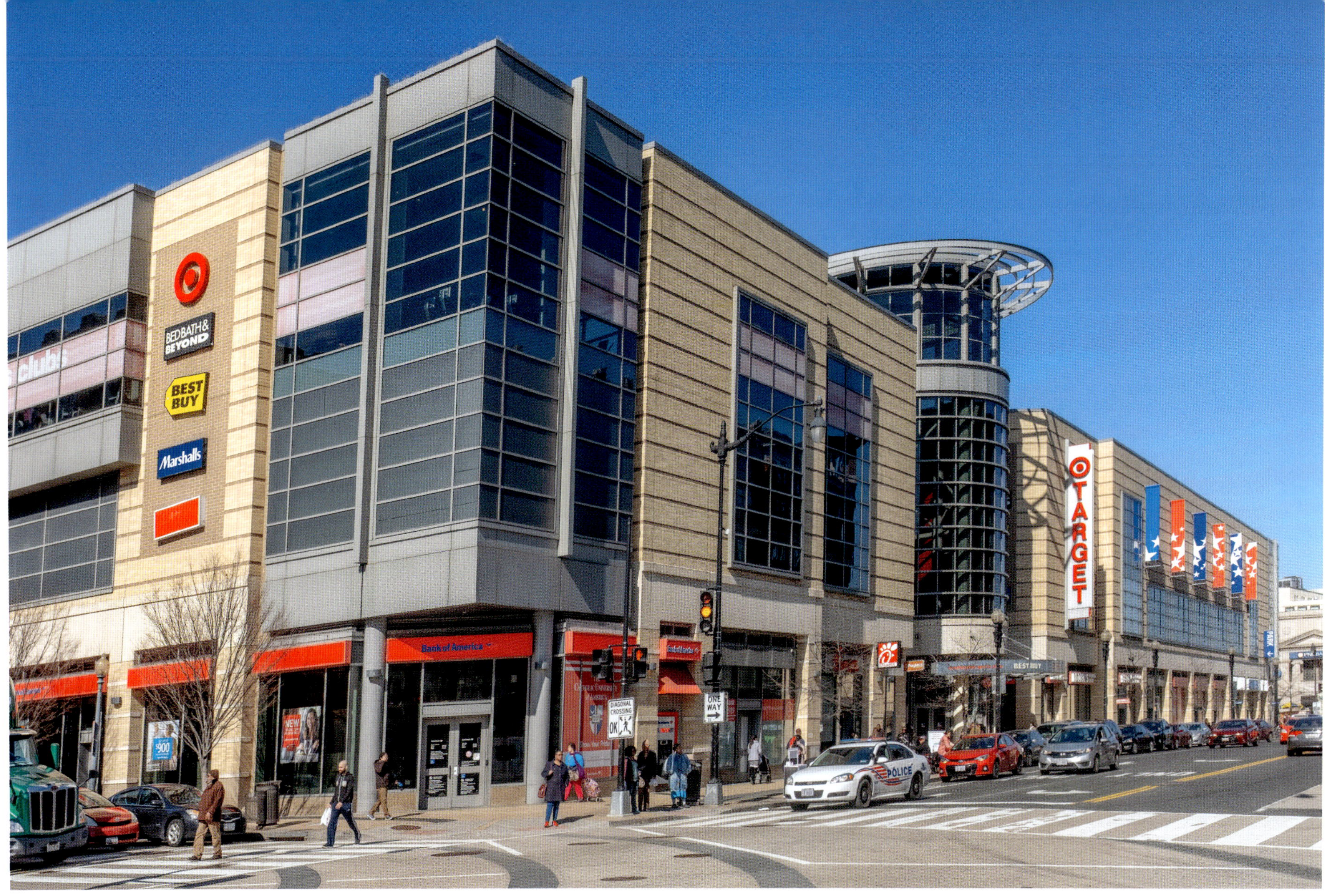

However, by the twentieth century, Columbia Heights was a predominantly white, upper-middle class neighborhood. At this time racial segregation was rampant in Washington, and restrictive housing and school segregation divided the neighborhood. Many schools in Columbia Heights became schools designated for Black students, such as the once Central High School which eventually became the segregated Cardozo High School, with notable alumni including Marvin Gaye.

By the mid-twentieth century, racial segregation had formally ended, but the neighborhood experienced a fate similar to nearby U Street. Neighborhoods saw white residents leaving for nearby Virginia and Maryland suburbs. The assassination of Martin Luther King Jr. saw riots throughout Washington, especially prominent on U Street and 14th Street in Columbia Heights.

NOW: Since the 1968 riots, the neighborhood on the hill has seen many changes and continues to grow. What was once a commercial center and arcade on 14th Street has become a popular mall. The street cars that brought the city folk into a residential area have been replaced by the Metro. In the 1970s, the neighborhood became popular with those who emigrated from Central America, making the region an important gathering place for these new residents. What was once sprawling farmland now makes up a diverse population of Washingtonians who call this neighborhood home.

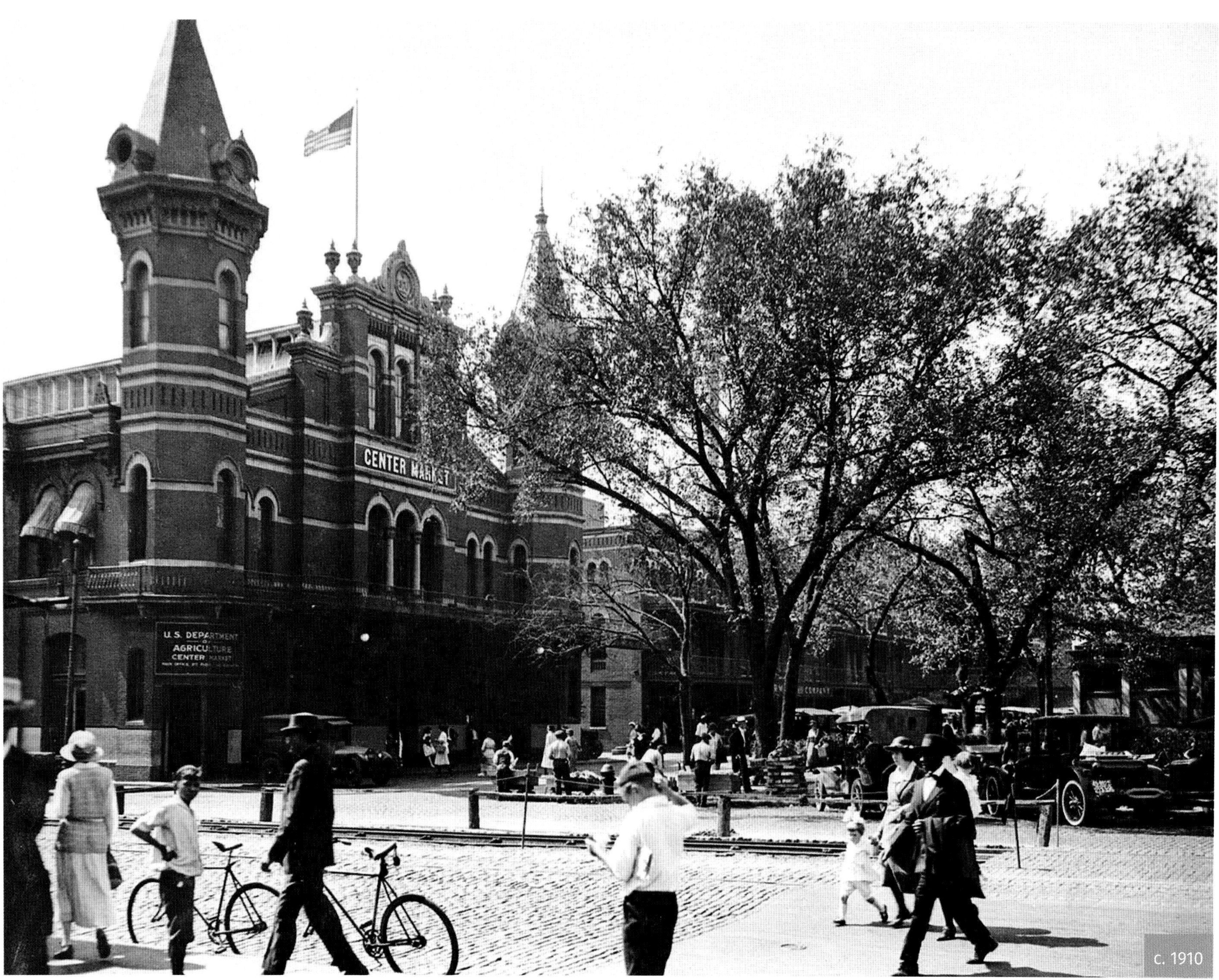

c. 1910

CENTER MARKET

The city's largest market, a commercial and social center in the heart of D.C.

THEN: Center Market began as more than just a commercial center for Washingtonians, but a social hotspot as well. At the beginning of the nineteenth century the first iteration of Center Market opened along the Washington City Canal, which is now Constitution Ave, for easy transportation of produce and market goods. As the market grew in popularity it expanded into the nearby swampland, earning it the name "Marsh Market." The market was immediately an important fixture in the landscape of the D.C. commercial scene; also playing a role in the city's trade of Enslaved people until the abolition of slavery in D.C. in 1862. In the following years, the market became an integral place of business for Black citizens, some of whom were previously Enslaved, to rent their own stalls and sell goods.

Although a popular center of commerce, the market structure itself was deemed to be a health and safety hazard due to its poor construction. A new, more formal building was constructed in 1872, which featured over 600 stalls and covered 60,000 square feet. This market had state-of-the-art refrigeration, ventilated skylights, and other technology to improve the market experience. Eventually, Center Market fell victim to the McMillan plan, a Congressional effort to improve downtown D.C. and unify the city architecturally, as well as to the rise of corner stores. Despite public protest, the building was torn down in 1931.

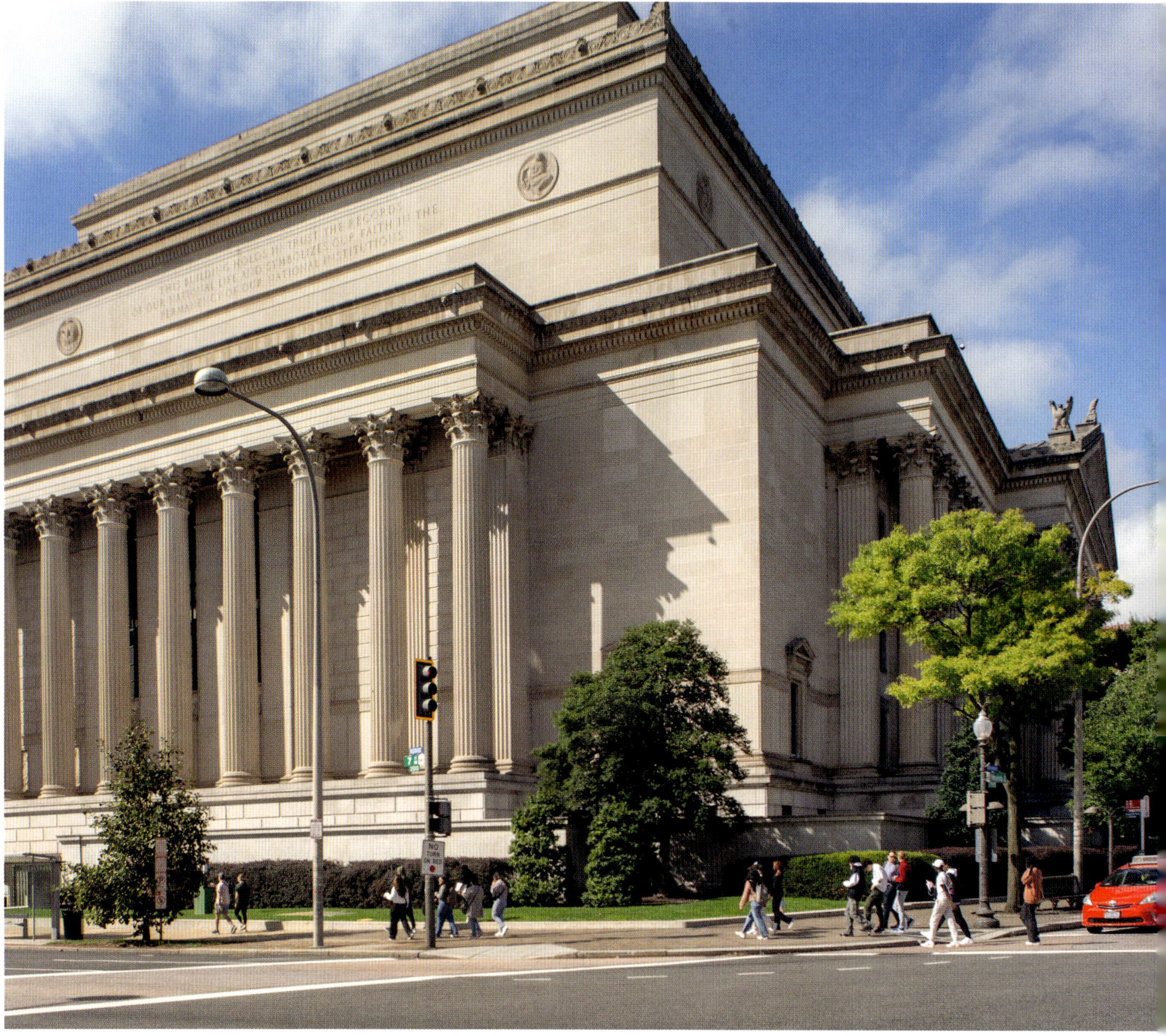

NOW: In the years immediately following Center Market's destruction, the National Archives and Records Building was constructed. Instead of a social and commercial center for Washingtonians, the land that originally held Center Market is now the center for American ideals and foundational documents. While D.C. lost its primary market, the market system in the District still exists. Eastern Market in Capitol Hill has been functioning from its current location since 1873. This market was threatened by the rise of supermarkets and other challenges; however, it currently provides locals with the commercial and social experience intended with D.C.'s original market system.

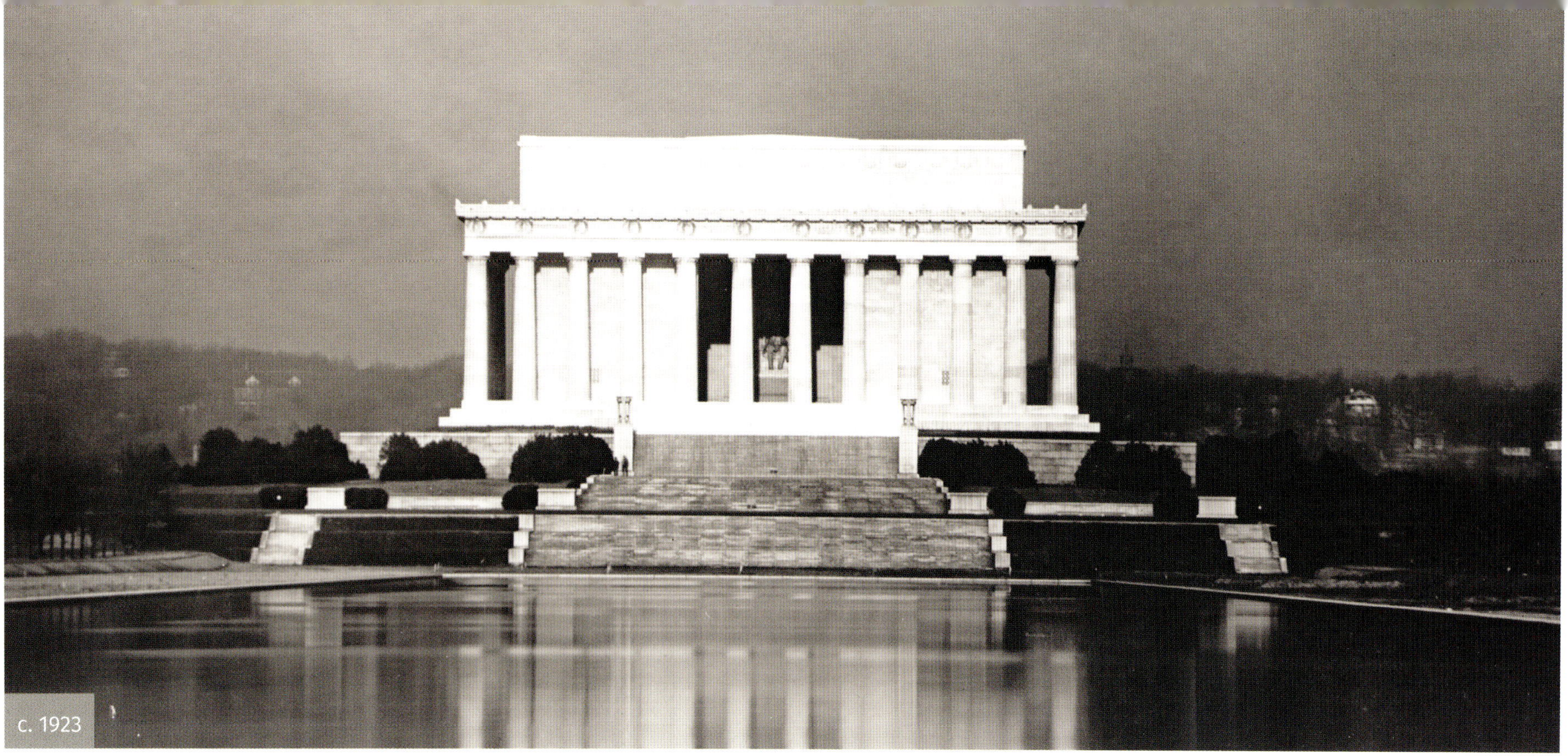

c. 1923

LINCOLN MEMORIAL

Lincoln "enshrined forever"

THEN: As early as 1867, just two years after President Abraham Lincoln's assassination, Congress began introducing bills to create a memorial in honor of the famed leader. While there was much congressional support the fruition of this idea took some time and it was not until 1911 that the Lincoln Memorial Commission was created by Congress.

The creation of the Lincoln Memorial aligned with the implementation of the McMillan Plan, also known as the Senate Park Commission, which was instrumental in developing various monuments to improve the overall design of the city. The McMillan Plan put the National Mall at the core of the city, proposing major developments including a spot for the future Lincoln Memorial at one end of the large park. Although a spot was chosen at the west end of the Mall, this was not the Lincoln Memorial Commission's first choice. The western side of Washington near the National Mall and the Potomac River was not structurally sound, and had swamp like ground.

Despite structural challenges, construction began on the Lincoln Memorial. The structure of the memorial was designed in a neoclassical style by architect Henry Bacon, and Daniel Chester French was commissioned to create the large statue of Lincoln. Building work started in 1914 and was a lumbering process from the start. The site the large memorial was planned for had to be drained and filled to accommodate the sheer weight of the structure. Eight years later, on Memorial Day 1922, the Lincoln Memorial was completed with President William Howard Taft proudly showcasing the new monument. Aside from the President there was another special guest at its opening: Robert Todd Lincoln, Abraham Lincoln's only surviving son.

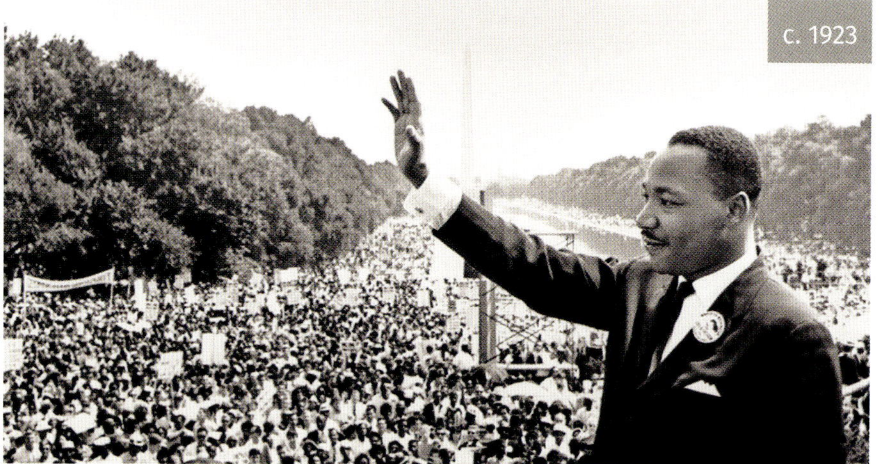

ABOVE: In front of Lincoln's statue stood Martin Luther King Jr. who delivered one of the most recited pieces of American rhetoric, his famous "I Have a Dream" speech in 1963. The location where Martin Luther King Jr. stood is marked in the steps of the Lincoln Memorial today.

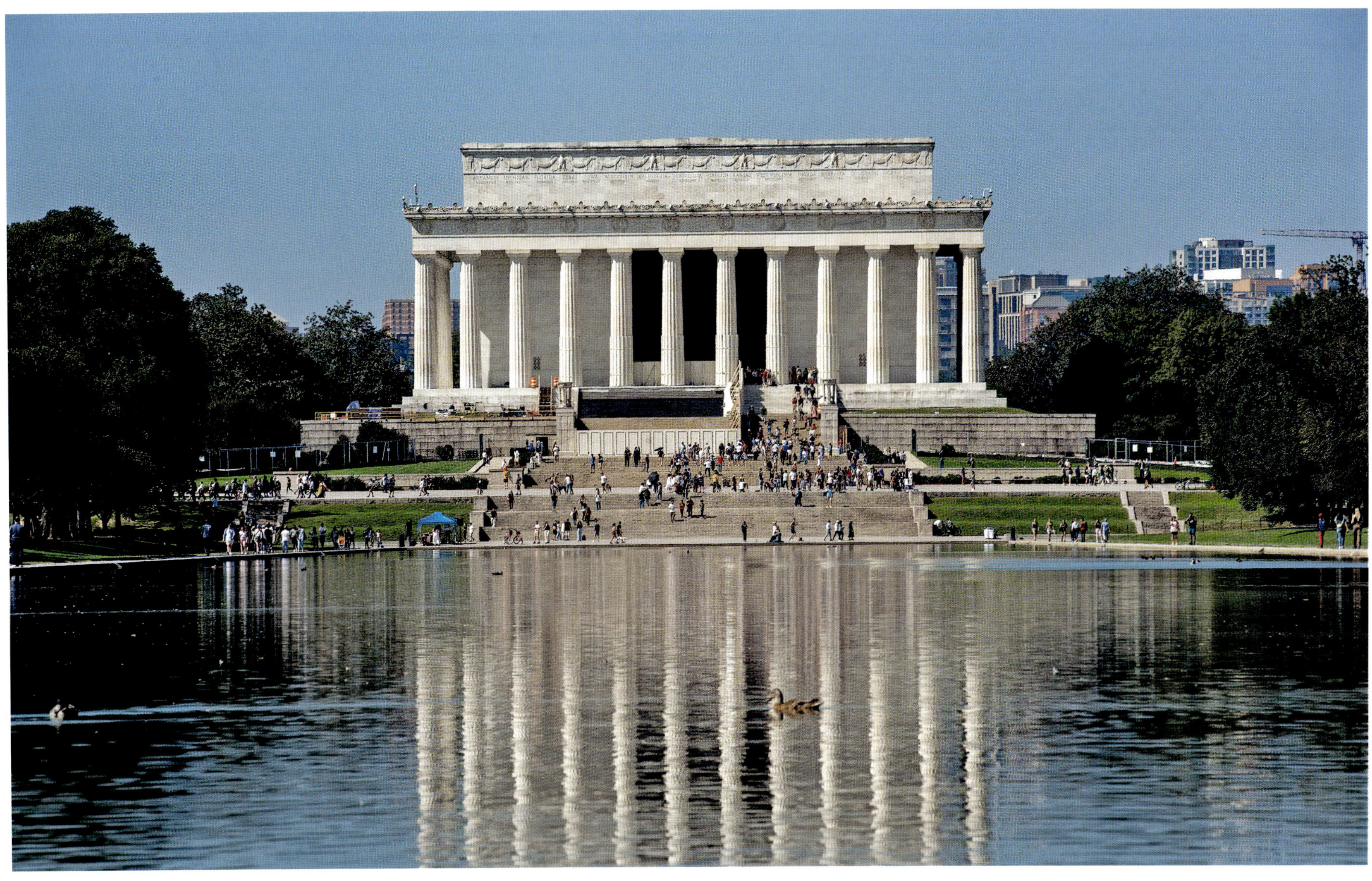

NOW: The Lincoln Memorial's importance and involvement in Washington, D.C. does not end with its foundation nor its current status as a tourist attraction. In much the same way, Lincoln's representation in the fight to unite the country did not end with his assassination. Throughout the twentieth century, the Lincoln Memorial served as an important site for Civil Rights activism. In 1939, Black musician Marian Anderson was refused from performance venues in Washington, D.C. but with the support of the First Lady of the time, Eleanor Roosevelt, the singer was able to perform on the steps of the Lincoln Memorial. The performance attracted a live audience of 75,000 people and nationwide radio listeners.

On August 28, 1963, another landmark moment for the Civil Rights Movement happened on the steps of the Lincoln Memorial. As a result of the March on Washington for Jobs and Freedom, 250,000 people gathered around the Reflecting Pool, standing in front of the statue of the late President and author of the Emancipation Proclamation to hear Martin Luther King Jr. give his iconic "I Have a Dream" speech.

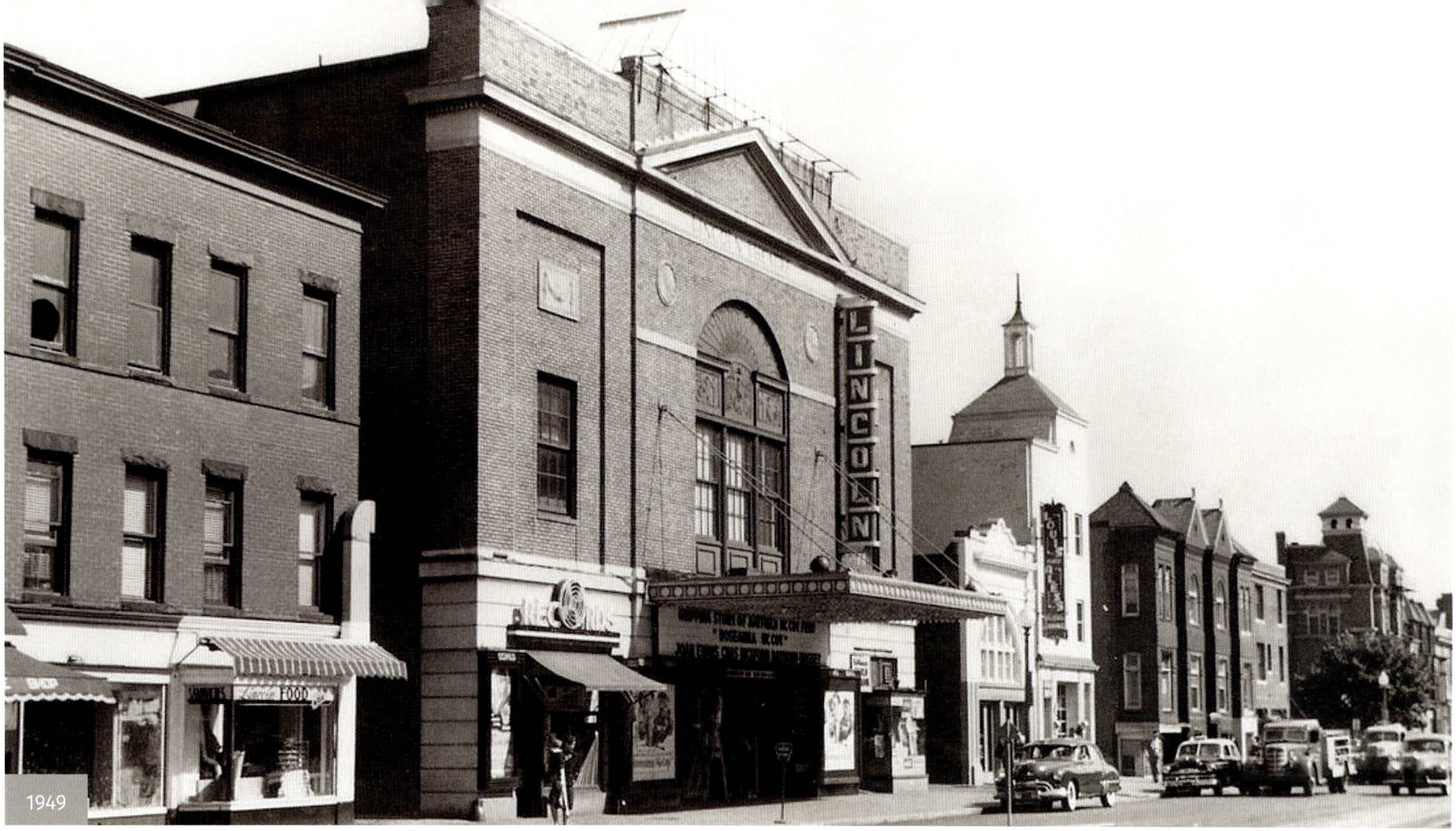

1949

THE LINCOLN THEATER

The heart of "Black Broadway"

THEN: Located in the heart of U Street, the Lincoln Theater is a reminder of an era of silent movies and the birth of jazz movements, as well as D.C.'s more troubling history. Opening in 1922, this neoclassical building was a "first run" movie theater, or a theater that was a common gathering space for its immediate neighborhood. On U Street this held greater significance as a neighborhood of predominantly Black residents. In a segregated Washington, the Lincoln Theater was boldly unsegregated and provided an important and accessible space for Black community members.

As the Theater grew in popularity, the building expanded to include a dance hall known as the Lincoln Colonnade in 1928. This dance hall hosted groundbreaking performances from some of America's greats including Duke Ellington, Billie Holiday, Nat King Cole, and Ella Fitzgerald. The dance hall was also a popular destination for various celebrations, including President Franklin Delano Roosevelt's birthday parties. Considered the "Crown Jewel of U Street", in an era when U Street was known as "Black Broadway," the Lincoln Theater played a vital role in the popularity of jazz music and served as an important community space for the immediate neighborhood.

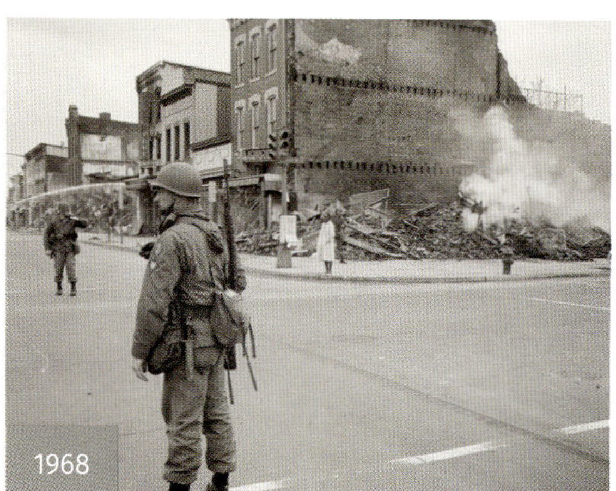

ABOVE: The 1968 riots began with violence at the corner of 14th and U Streets, NW. Stores, theaters and other businesses within the area sustained heavy damage.

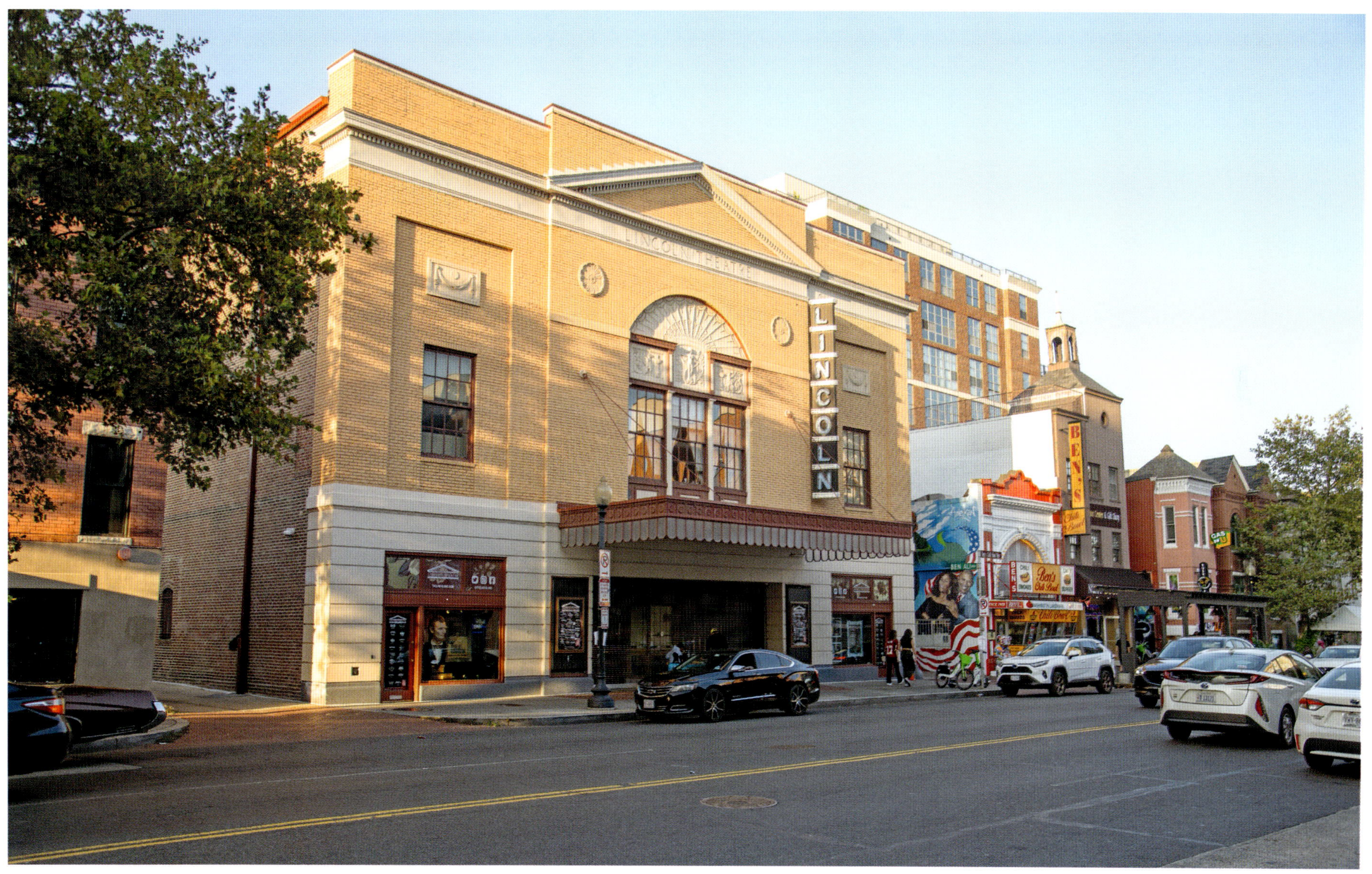

NOW: Despite the Theater's early success and popularity, the latter half of the twentieth century brought with it new hardships. As segregation formally ended in the 1950s, competition increased from venues that previously restricted the inclusion of Black residents. The U Street neighborhood additionally saw significant damage during the 1968 riots which followed the assassination of Martin Luther King, Jr. Following the damage, the Lincoln Theater underwent changes to keep up with the needs of the neighborhood before eventually closing for restoration. In 1994 the Lincoln Theater reopened to the public, restored to some of its former eclectic glory. The Theater is now managed by I.M.P., who also run another venue of musical significance in the U Street neighborhood: the 9:30 Club. While U Street has changed significantly in the years since the Lincoln Theater's opening, the venue stands alongside other noteworthy Black-owned businesses such as Ben's Chili Bowl and Lee's Flower Shop, a reminder of the neighborhood's resilience.

DEPARTMENT OF TREASURY, 15TH ST NW

Washington, D.C.'s de facto financial district

THEN: In the mid-nineteenth century, the Department of Treasury was built to the east of the White House. Its construction broke the mutual view and physical connection of the Executive Mansion and the Capitol Building, originally shared through Pennsylvania Avenue. The novel addition of this building heralded a new era in the identity of D.C.'s downtown, now as a thriving financial district. Throughout the nineteenth and twentieth centuries, banks began to cluster around the Treasury Building especially along 15th Street. There is a red brick building with a clock tower, which belonged to the National Savings and Trust Company. Just north of the columns of the Treasury Department Building sit the Riggs National Bank and the American Security and Trust Company. These buildings were designed as an impressive showcase of Beau-Arts style architecture. This style was chosen as it represented the "idealism and cosmopolitanism of the moneyed class," and was a direct response to Congress's McMillan Plan, to update the architecture of the city. The design of these buildings was ornamental inside and out, with some hosting marble wood paneling and ornate floor-to-ceiling fireplaces inside. The addition of these financial powerhouses and the developing private sector contributed to Washington's economic growth throughout the early twentieth century.

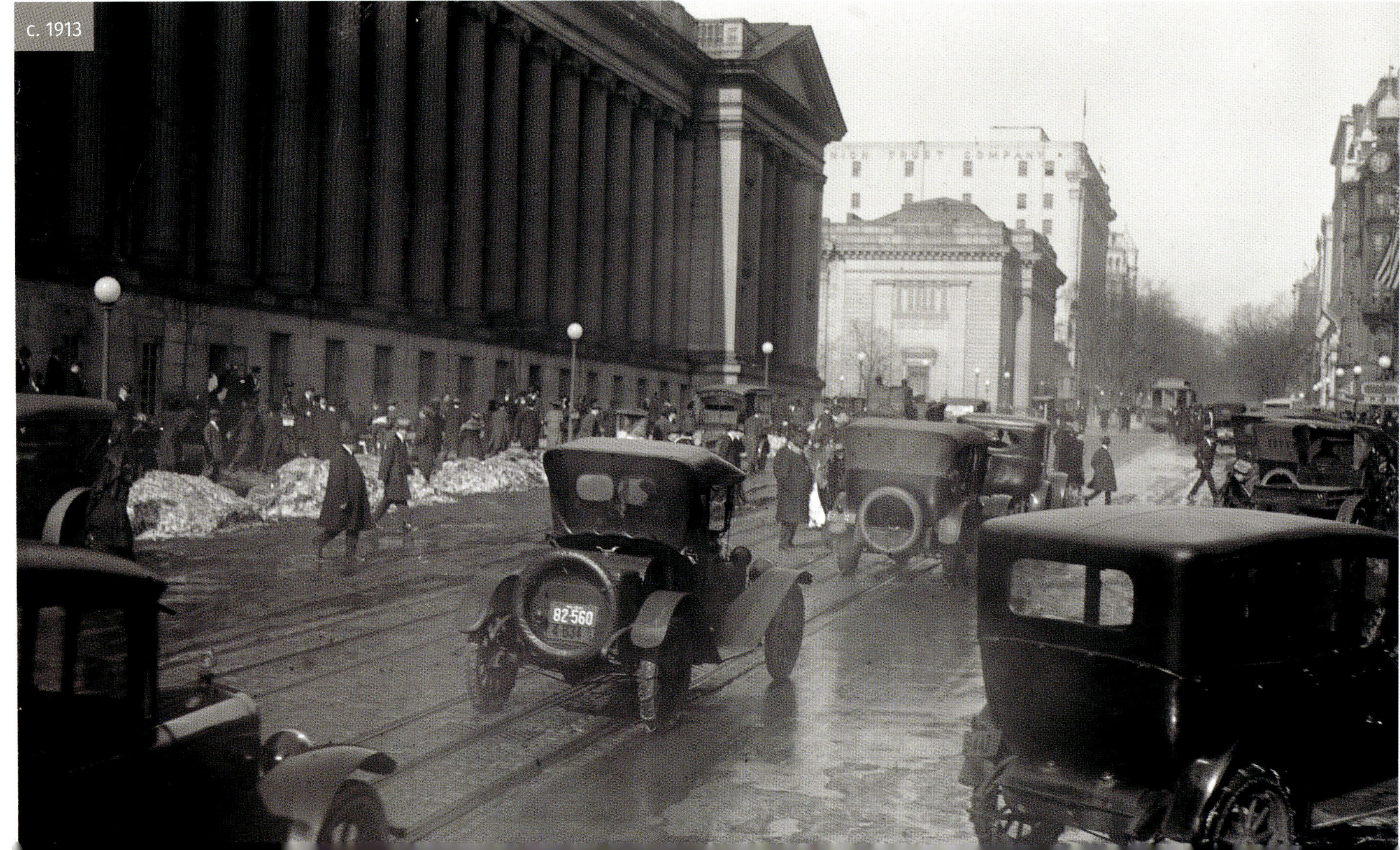

c. 1913

NOW: Many of the banks included in the financial district, such as the Riggs National Bank, hold great significance in the history of not only D.C. but of the nation. Facing the Treasury Department Building, Riggs National Bank was known as the "Bank of Presidents," with more than twenty U.S. presidents banking with them. The bank also funded monumental ventures throughout history, including the United States' purchase of Alaska, the expansion of the United States Capitol, and Robert Perry's first expedition to the North Pole. Remaining open for over a century, the bank eventually closed due to reports of money laundering and transferred its ownership. Today, the area surrounding the Treasury Building is the Financial Historic, serving as a testament to shared financial responsibility to the nation's constituents.

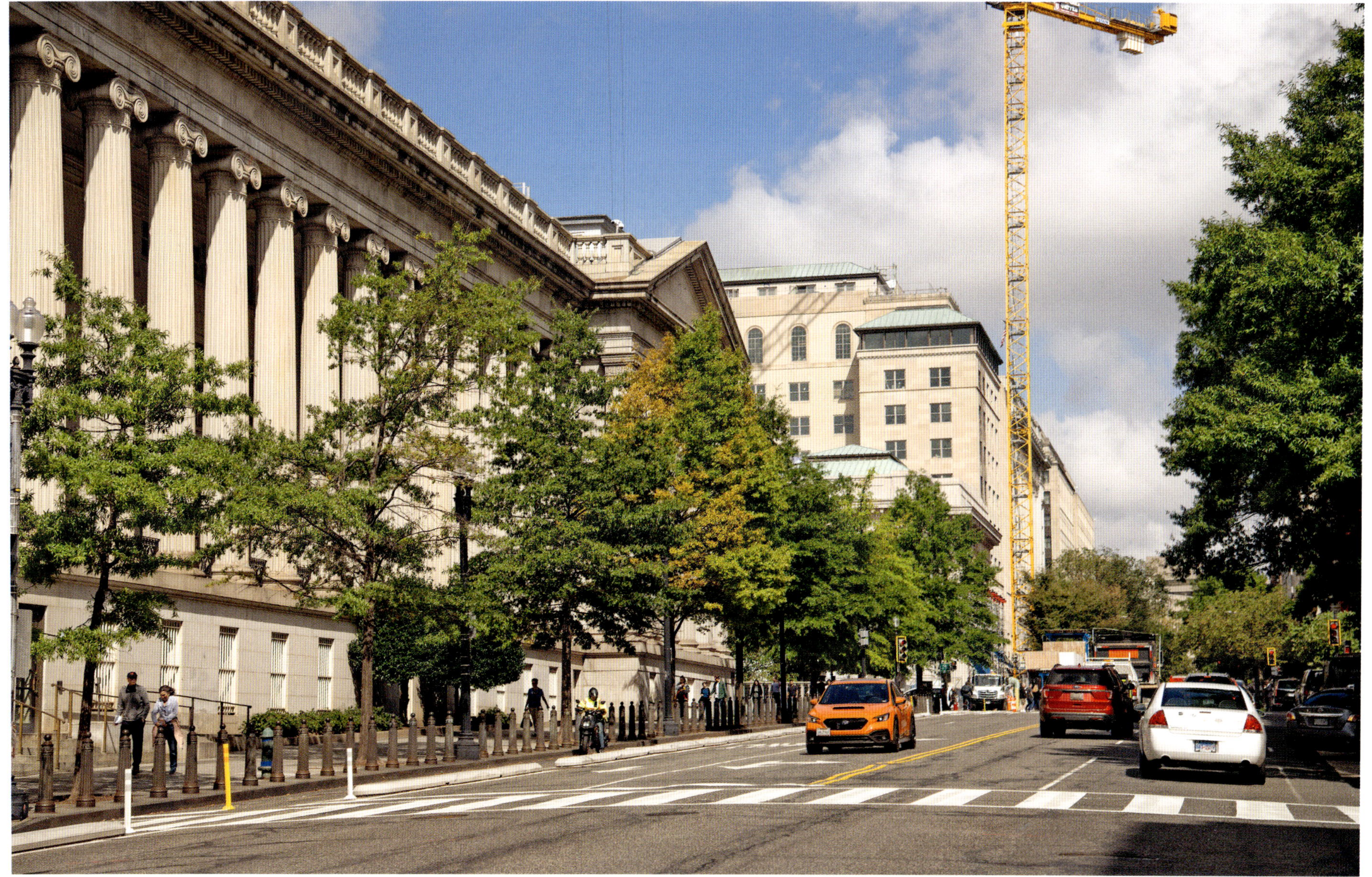

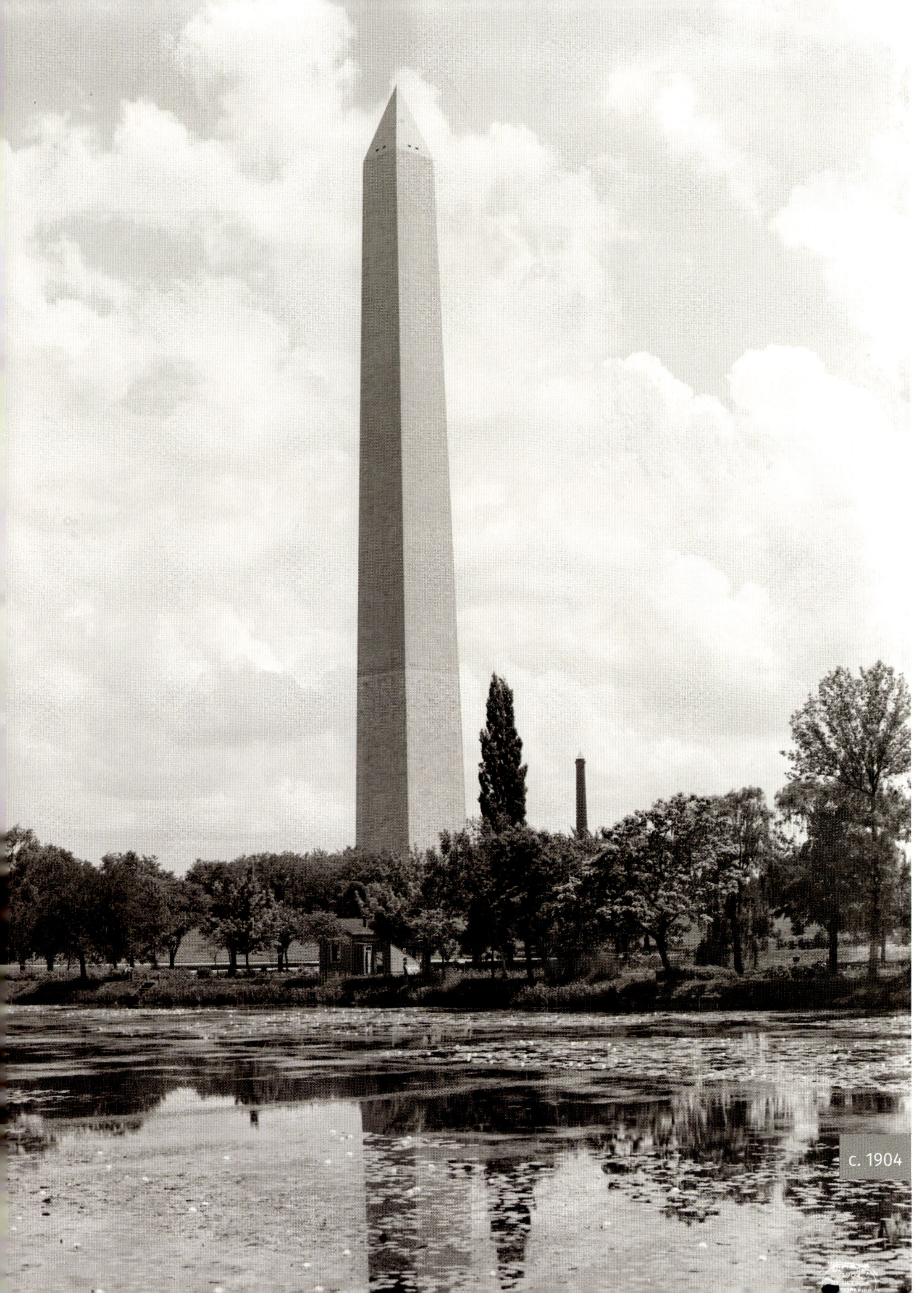

c. 1904

THE WASHINGTON MONUMENT

A Presidential monument in two parts

THEN: Even before his death in 1799, George Washington was a beloved figure of great significance, and a monument to his leadership was being planned. In his original plan for Washington, urban planner and designer Pierre Charles L'Enfant marked the location of a monument dedicated to the nation's first president. Designed by Robert Mills, the monument began construction in 1848, supported by fluctuating private funds. Eventually construction halted, owing to growing hardships caused by the Civil War and the involvement of the Know-Nothing Party, an unpopular political party in America during the mid-nineteenth century. The base of the monument constructed using the labor of Enslaved people, remained unfinished for over twenty years. In 1876 the construction of the monument finally continued, this time with public funds and congressional support. The structure was ultimately changed from Mills's elaborate design to a simple obelisk style. The type of stone also changed, causing a distinct line in the structure of the shades of marble, granite, and bluestone. When it was completed in 1884, the Washington Monument was the tallest manmade structure in the world, standing at 555 feet and 5 ⅛ inches. The monument was first accessible to the public in 1886 through a staircase, and reopened in 1888 with a public elevator, making the trip to the top of the monument more convenient.

NOW: Since its full construction, the Washington Monument has undergone various restorations and repairs, most notably the repair following the 5.8 magnitude earthquake that shook the District in 2011. Apart from intermittent closures, the monument has remained open for the public to ascend for an aerial view of the nation's capital. Inside the monument is a small museum of commemorative stones from different states, countries, and organizations that wanted to honor the legacy of the nation's first president. Although it is no longer the tallest building in the world, the Washington Monument remains the tallest stone structure in the world and the tallest structure in Washington, D.C., serving as a directional for locals making their way through the city.

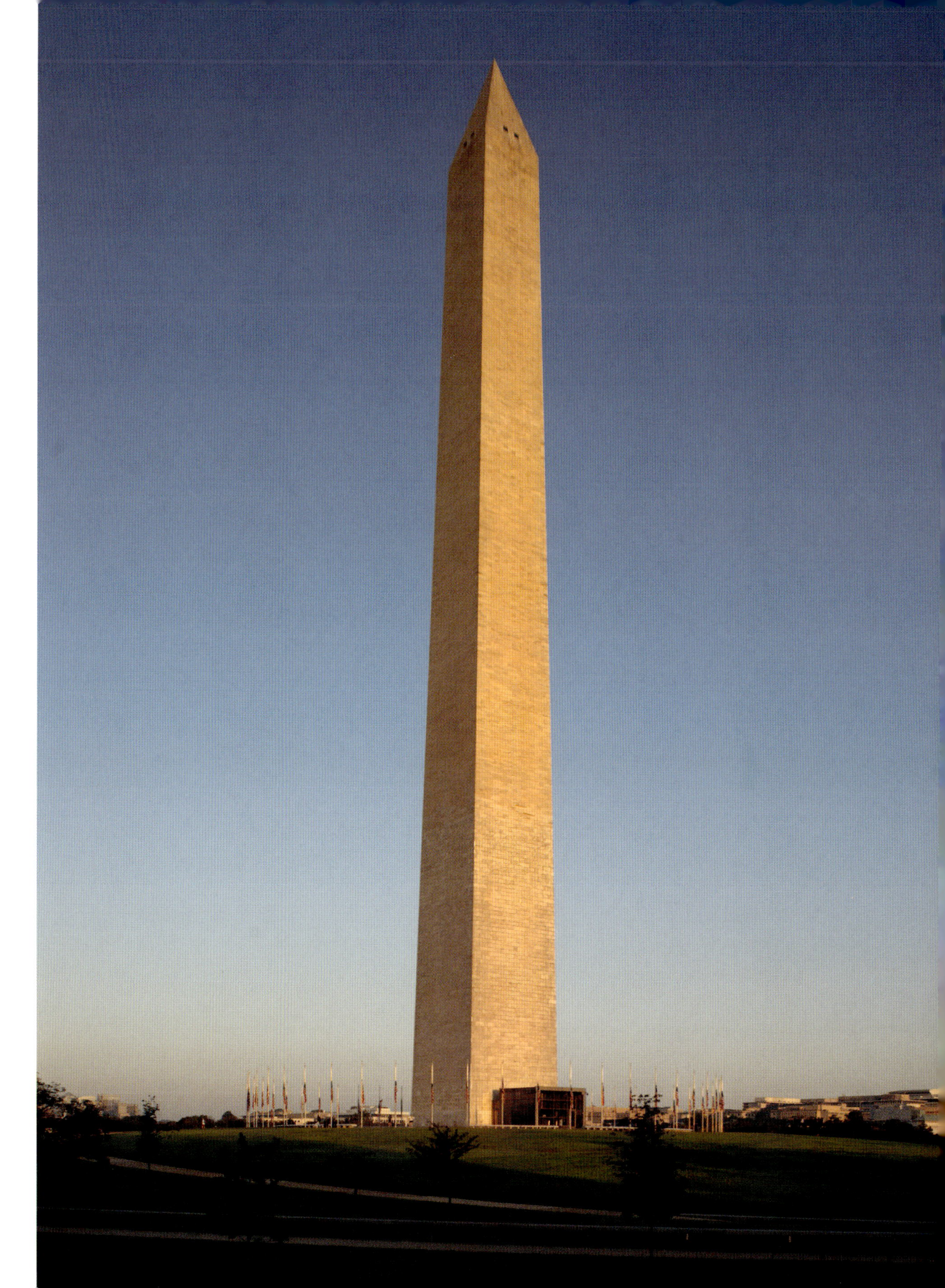

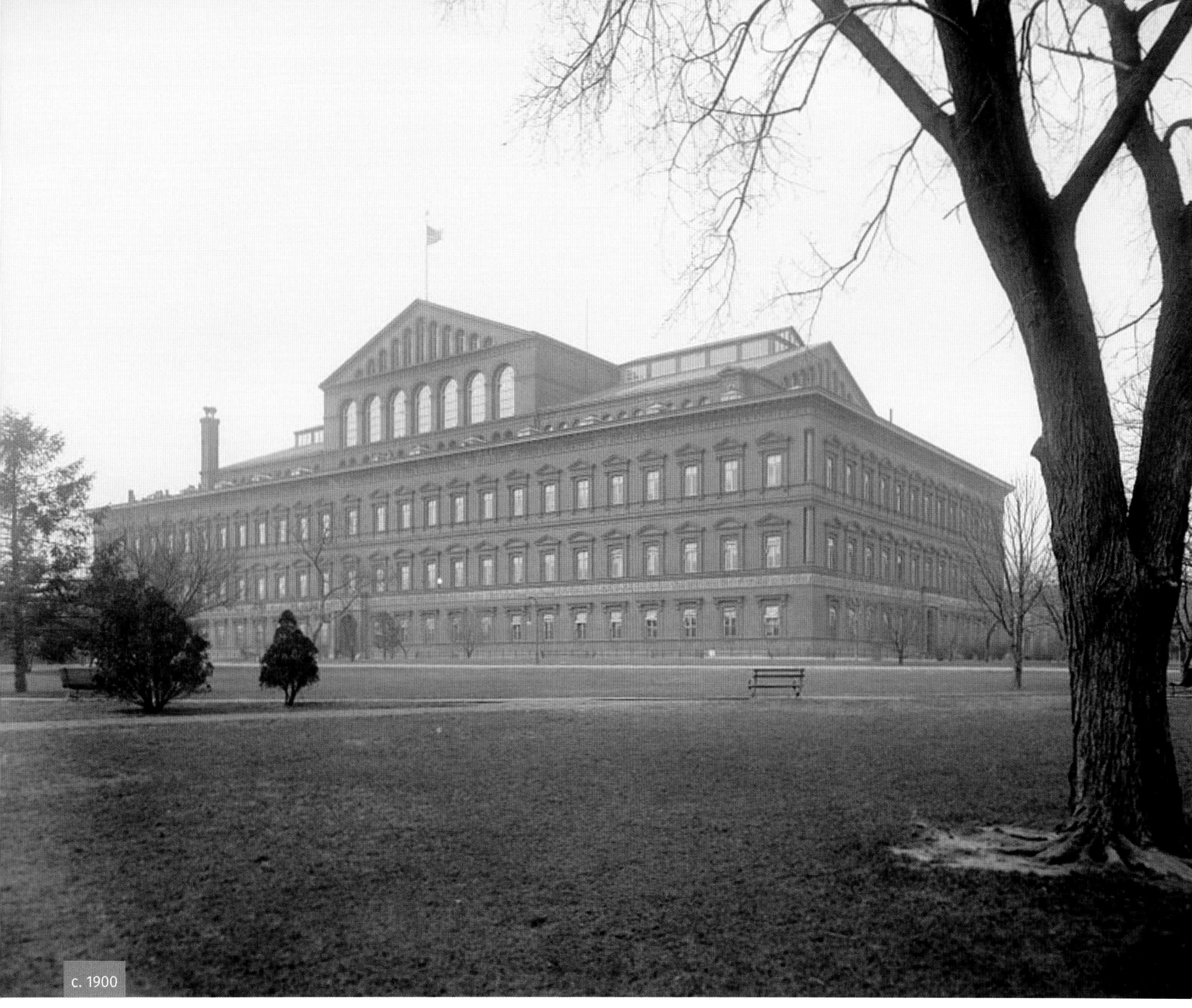

c. 1900

U.S. PENSION BUREAU

From veteran's pensions to architectural celebrations

THEN: By the end of the Civil War, the United States saw an increased number of veterans in need of support. Until this conflict, pensions were paid by state governments, as military personnel had typically served for their state militias. However, the Civil War added over 250,000 pensioners to the list of those collecting on behalf of veterans, deceased, or injured from wars prior. To meet this need, Congress commissioned the Pension Building in 1881. Designed by Army Quartermaster General Montgomery C. Meigs who was inspired by Roman palaces, the Renaissance Revival style not only served to house a federal office but also acted as the Civil War generation's memorial to the commitment of Union soldiers. On the building's exterior is a frieze that wraps around the entire structure, showing images of infantrymen, cavalry, and the navy, as well as nurses and medical units.

By the completion of the building in 1887, the building had over 1,500 clerks, and less than twenty years after the war almost 900,000 pension claims had been filed on behalf of the killed or the wounded, although not all of these were approved. Throughout the 1880s, pensions made up about one-third of the federal budget. These new pension applications were limited to Union soldiers, as the states that had separated from the Union were solely responsible for supporting Confederate pensions. In 1958 the federal government changed their stance on the pension eligibility of Confederate veterans and their dependents.

NOW: The primary purpose of this construction was to support the increased demands for pensions; yet, the building also served an additional purpose as a popular event space. In 1885, President Grover Cleveland held the first inaugural ball in the Pension Bureau, and many presidents followed his example. These inaugural balls were ticketed but ultimately open to the public for widespread celebration in a space of architectural inspiration. While some presidents did not participate in the precedent, President Richard Nixon repopularized the tradition, and Presidents as recent as Barack Obama and Donald Trump have held inaugural celebrations in the building's Great Hall.

World War I ultimately brought changes to the Bureau, and the responsibilities of pensions and veterans were moved to other agencies within government. The building served as an office space for the federal government throughout the 1960s. From its inception, the architectural style was criticized for not aligning with other buildings in Washington, and in the latter half of the twentieth century the building was almost demolished. Due to the support of interested preservationists and government offices, the building was saved and in 1980 an Act of Congress designated it as the new home of the National Building Museum. Opening in 1985, the National Building Museum serves as America's "premier cultural institution" that highlights great feats of architecture, design, and construction from around the world.

BELOW: Inside the building are vast Corinthian columns, widely considered to be some of the tallest columns in the world.

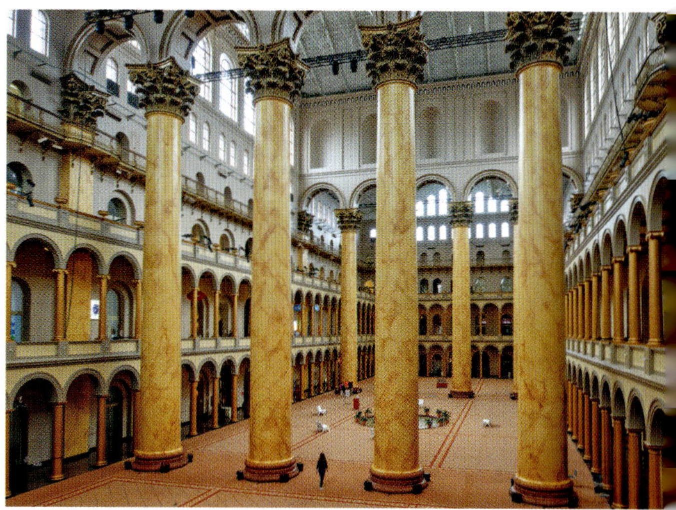

SMITHSONIAN CASTLE

More than just a museum

THEN: When English scientist James Smithson passed away, he left a bequest of $550,000 to the United States for the creation of "an establishment for the increase and diffusion of knowledge." The United States, although excited at the prospect of creating such an institution, was unsure of the best way to achieve Smithson's wish. Upon receiving the bequest in 1835 the United States welcomed a decade of debate on what "the diffusion of knowledge" meant, and how it could best be achieved. A university in Smithson's honor was suggested, as was a scientific research institution, a national publishing house, and a museum; all establishments connected with knowledge and education. With everyone from scientists to congressmen and the public weighing in with their suggestions, it became clear that just one of these

c. 1860

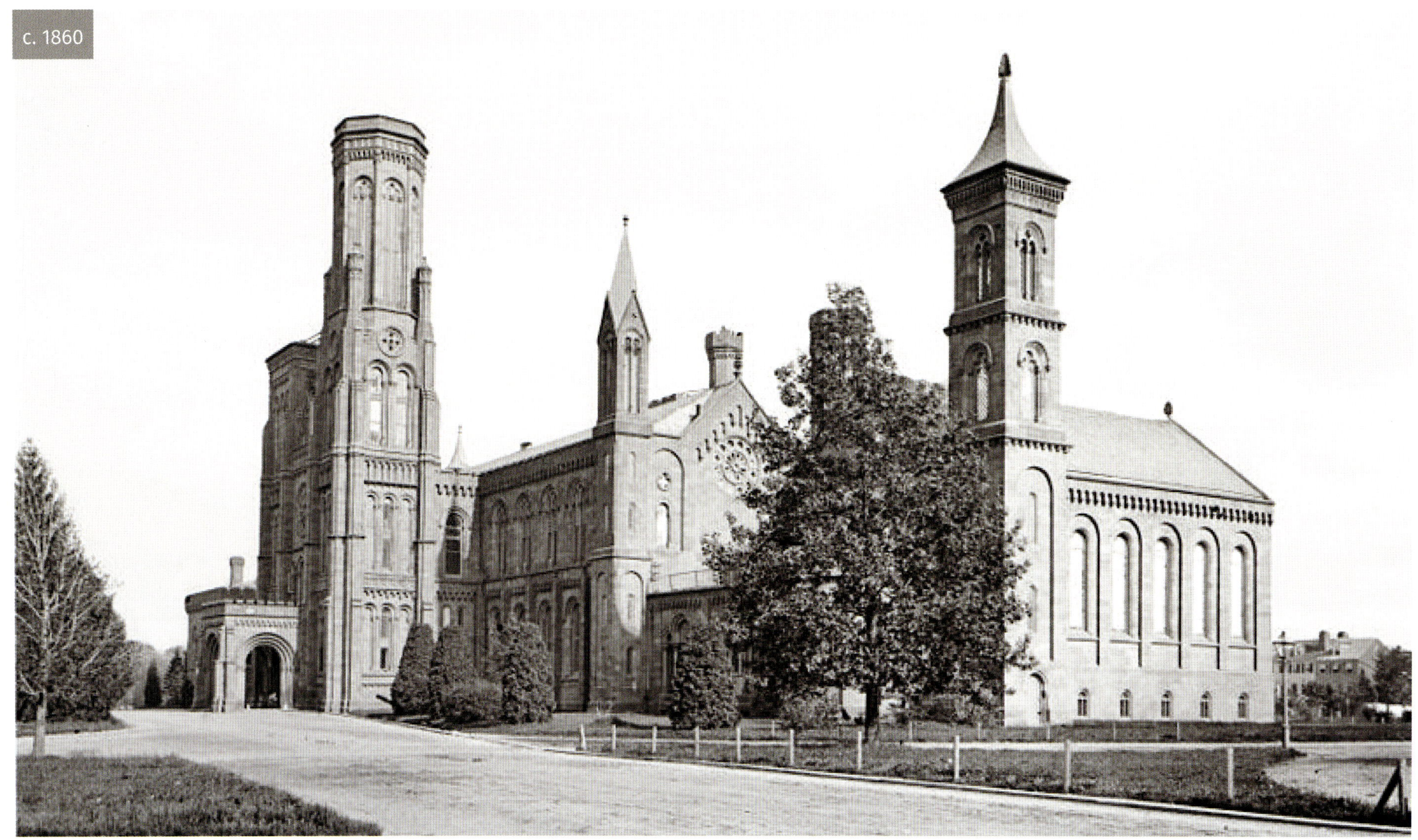

institutions wasn't going to be satisfactory. On August 10, 1846, Congress passed legislation that was immediately signed into law by President James Polk. While the two branches of government worked swiftly and in unison that day, this decision had been over ten years in the making. This was the creation of the Smithsonian Institution.

Eventually, with the legislation's passage in 1846, the Smithsonian Institution was founded as a combination of the many ideas suggested, including the scientific research center, an educational publication source and a museum. With the decision made, this federal educational institution could finally find its home.

Designed by James Renwick, Jr. and completed in 1855, the Smithsonian Institution Building, now known as the Smithsonian Castle, was created to house the United States' collection of scientific research and historical artifacts. Made of red sandstone from nearby Maryland and in a late Romanesque and Gothic style, this building has been a mainstay of the National Mall since before the Civil War.

c. 1889

ABOVE: Before the National Zoological Park in Rock Creek Park and Washington's beloved pandas made their way to D.C., paddocks were stationed around the Smithsonian Castle in the South Yard. These two buffalo were once a part of the National Museum's Department of Living Animals, which soon became what Washingtonians now know as the National Zoo.

NOW: The Smithsonian Castle has had many different responsibilities in its lifetime. In its earliest years, the Secretary of the Smithsonian, visiting scientists, specimens, and more all resided under its roof. In the 1880s, the yard around the building was used for the National Zoo, and in 1901 the first children's museum was in the Castle. Since its beginnings as a debated idea and a multipurpose educational facility, the Smithsonian Institution has expanded greatly. The institution now includes many different avenues of education including twenty museums (with more on the way), a national zoo, more than 150 million objects varying from scientific specimens to artistic masterpieces, and an astrophysical laboratory. Now used for administrative support, the Smithsonian Castle continues to represent the United States' successful attempt to fulfill Smithson's last wish.

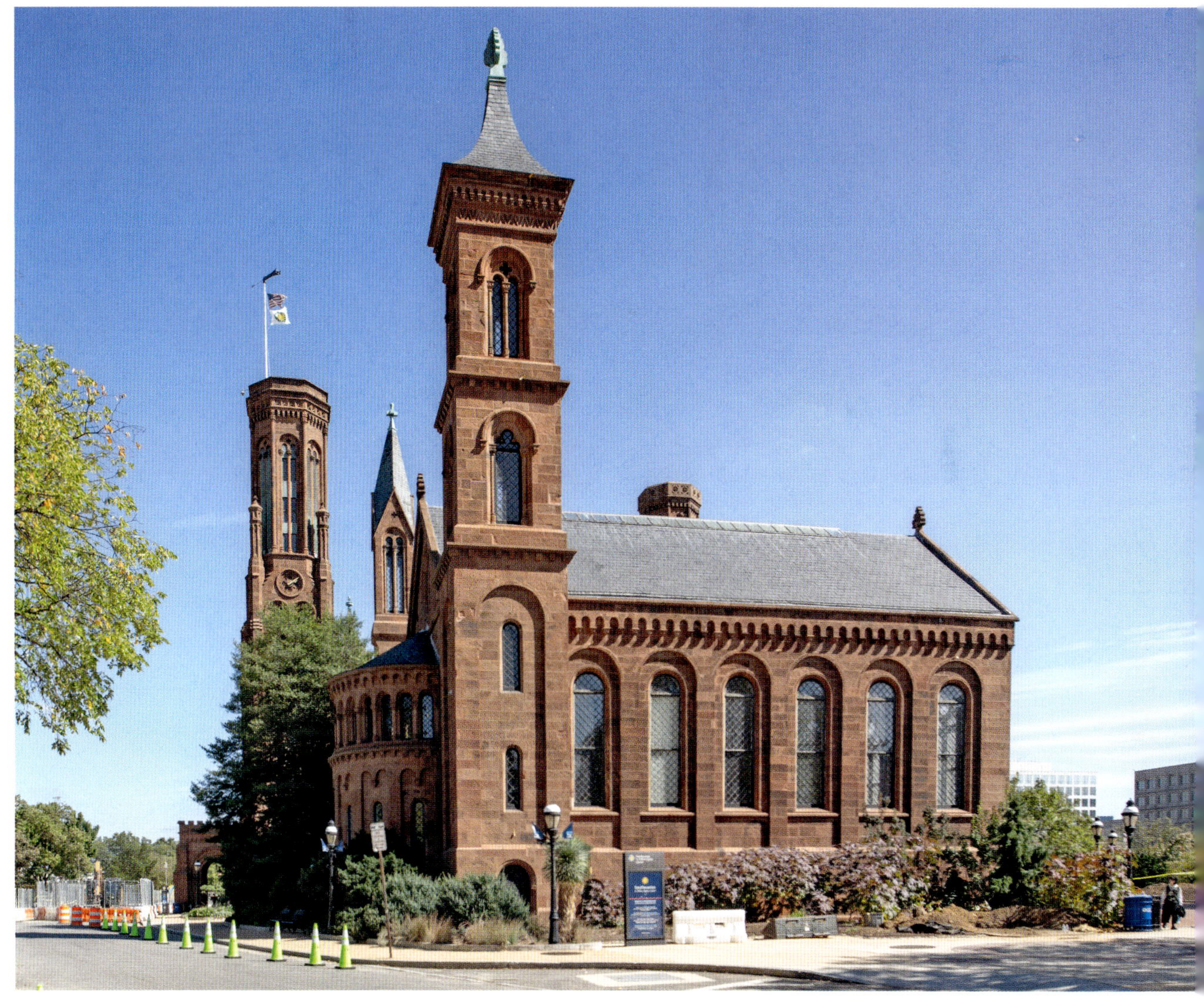

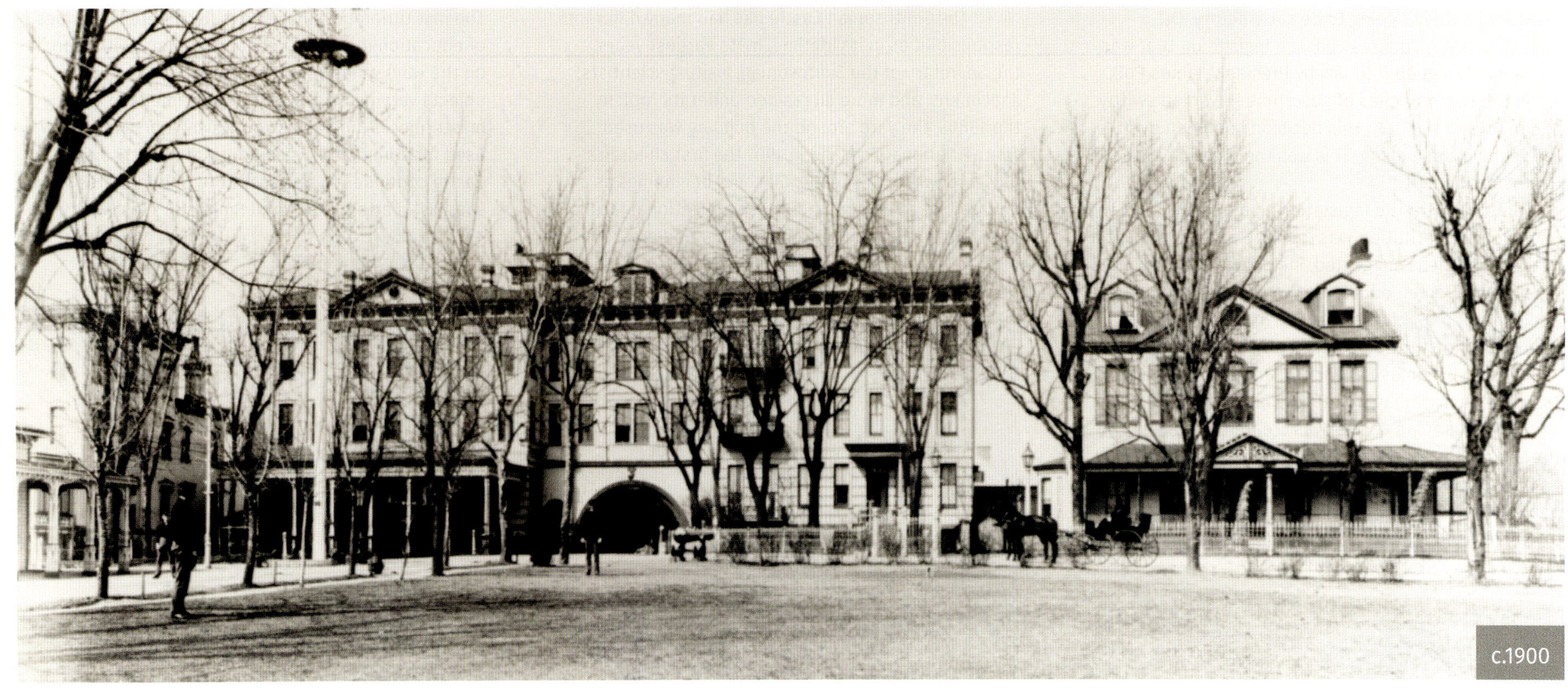
c.1900

LATROBE GATE, WASHINGTON NAVY YARD

A symbolic entrance into the capital city

THEN: The early years of Washington, D.C.'s status as the United States' capital city brought many changes, including the bolstering of local military resources. The city's proximity to the Potomac River which reaches the ocean, along with other convenient bodies of water such as the Anacostia River, made it an important location for naval operations. President Thomas Jefferson saw this opportunity, and in 1804 commissioned Benjamin H. Latrobe to design a dock and ship repair facility in a region of strategic significance. A prominent architect of the time, Latrobe accepted this responsibility along with his new title as "Engineer of the Navy Department" and began working on his plan for the barren Washington Navy Yard.

In 1806, the Main Gate, now known as the Latrobe Gate, was completed as the official entrance into the navy yard. At the time the Greek Revival style that the structure was designed in had not reached widespread popularity, and critics such as William Thornton considered it a "monument to bad taste and design." The building is now considered one of the oldest examples of Greek Revival architecture in the country, and the style itself has become symbolic of the connection between the ancient democratic ideals that America was founded on. Latrobe continued his career, rebuilding the U.S. Capitol Building in the years following the War of 1812 and designed the porticos in the White House under the Madison administration.

Since its creation, the Latrobe Gate has stood as a symbol of United States naval operations. In its earliest years, the Washington navy yard was the navy's largest shipbuilding and ship lifting facility, with the construction of twenty-two vessels, ranging in size. During the War of 1812, the yard acted as a support facility, but also played an important strategic role in defending the District. During the war, British forces made their way through Washington, burning buildings of significance such as the White House and the United States Capitol. To avoid the capture of this important military target, Commodore Thomas Tingey intentionally lit the navy yard ablaze. Few structures survived this destructive defensive move, but the Latrobe Gate remained standing.

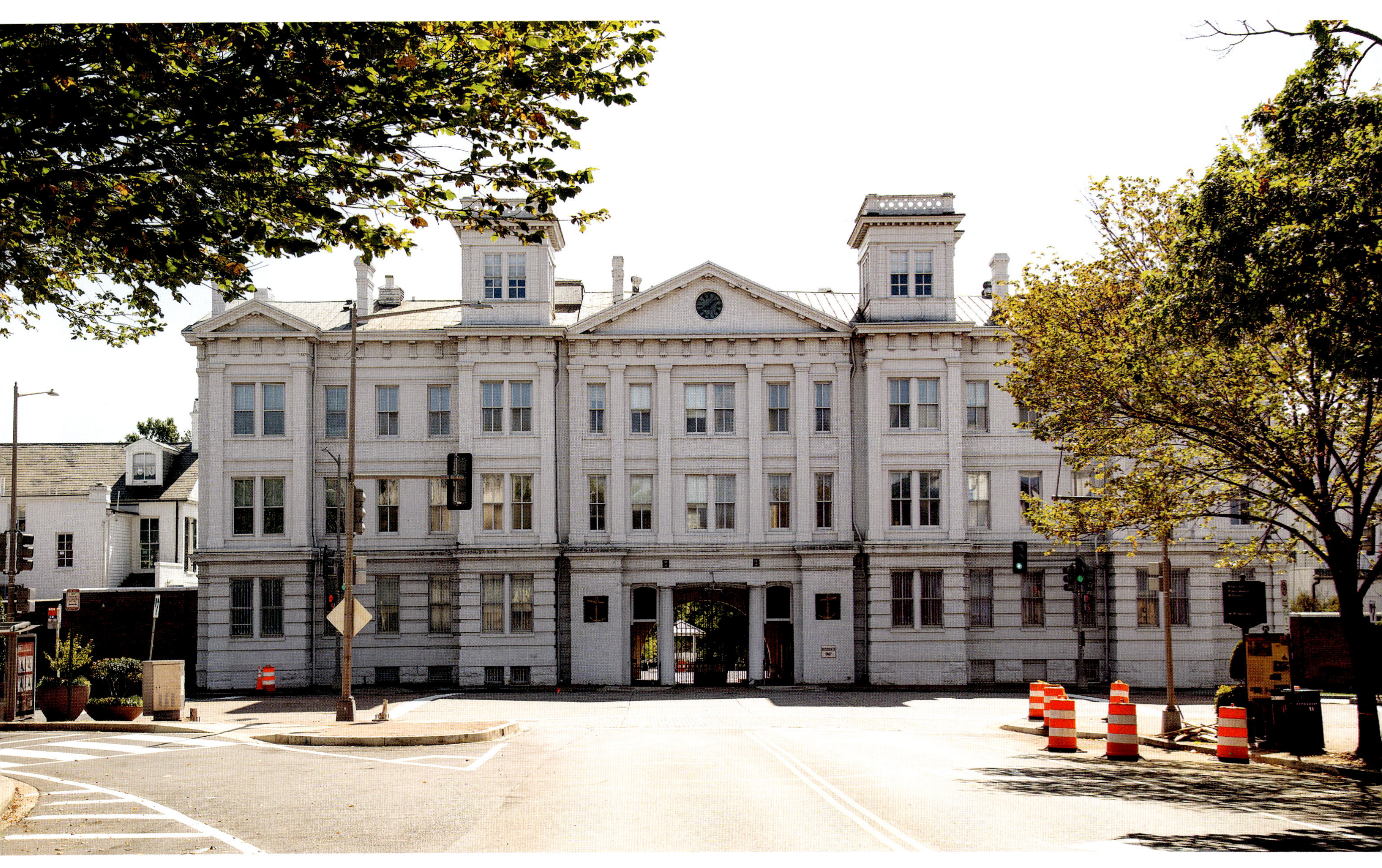

NOW: Following this war, the Washington navy yard was no longer a productive site for ship construction. The yard remained important through many American conflicts as a base to create military ordnance, although by the 1960s its work creating ammunition and supplies had slowed significantly. The area was redesignated as naval headquarters, becoming more ceremonial in nature. This included the Latrobe Gate, which was updated in 1881 with a large three-story Victorian building constructed over it, to serve as barracks and additional office space. The Latrobe Gate is the oldest continuously manned marine guardhouse in the United States and serves as a reminder of when Washington's naval operations and ship construction occurred in the nation's capital.

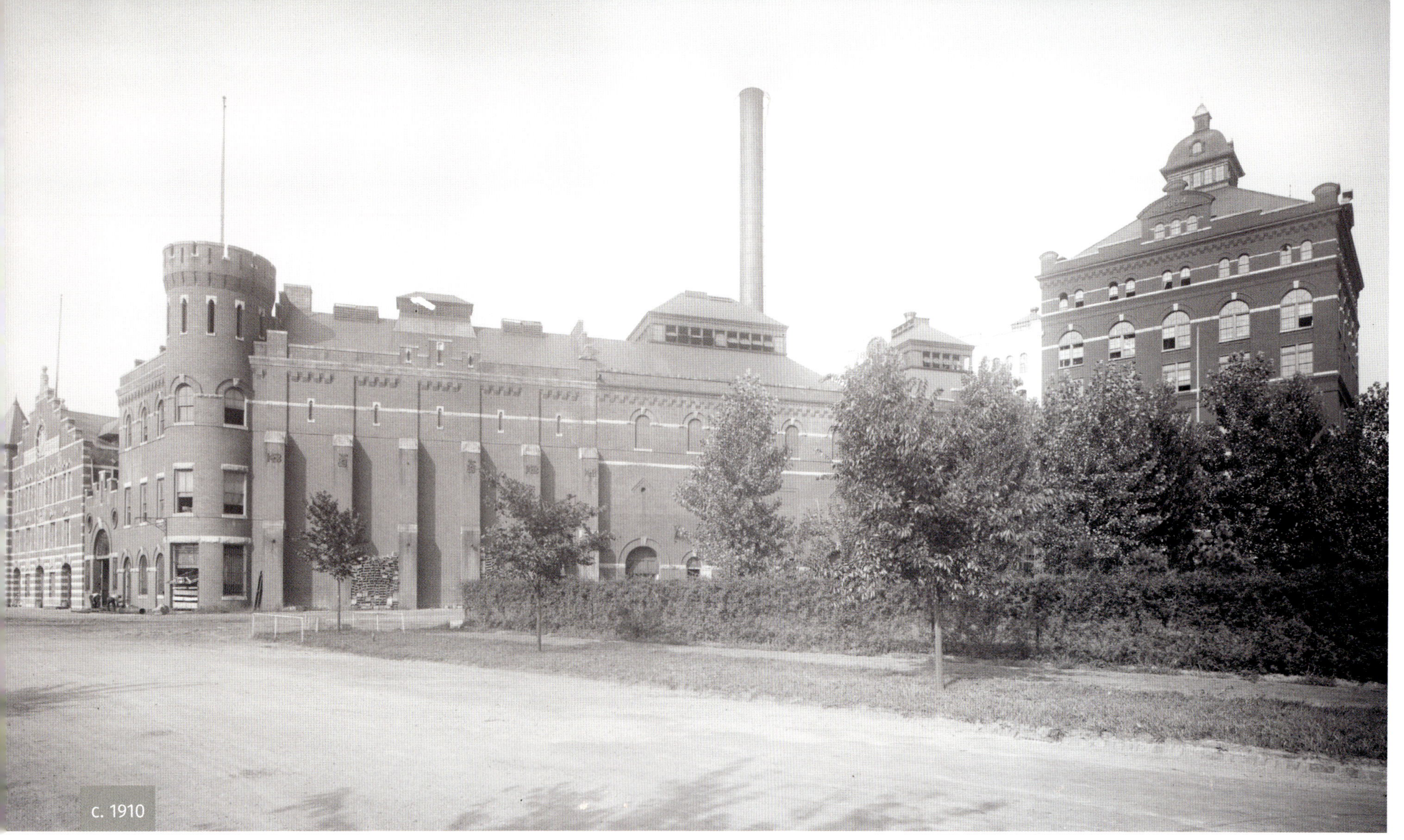
c. 1910

CHRISTIAN HEURICH BREWERY

D.C.'s biggest brewmaster and his lasting legacy

THEN: One historical resident of Washington, D.C. was Christian Heurich, a German brewer who saw D.C. 's urban developments following the Civil War as an opportunity for his new business. The brewer made his way to Washington and began a small brewery and biergarten, but soon demand for his popular product, and damage caused by local fires, required a new space.

In 1895 Heurich's new brewery was finished, located along the Potomac River in what would be known as the Foggy Bottom neighborhood. The building was an upgrade from Heurich's previous space, with a capacity of 500,000 barrels, an ice plant that could make 150 tons of ice daily, and eventually a bottling facility to streamline his brewing industry. Heurich soon became the largest brewer in Washington, with his numerous clientele including the White House. Very little could slow Heurich and his D.C. success down, that is until the start of Prohibition.

The constitutional amendment that prohibited the sale of alcohol meant Heurich and his brewery needed a new product to keep the business alive, and his workers employed. He decided to capitalize on one part of his large facility and began selling ice. With clients including the Supreme Court and Congress, Heurich was able to keep his company afloat. When Prohibition was eventually repealed, the brewer and savvy businessman who was by now in his nineties, saw the new demand for alcohol and decided to continue his brewing empire.

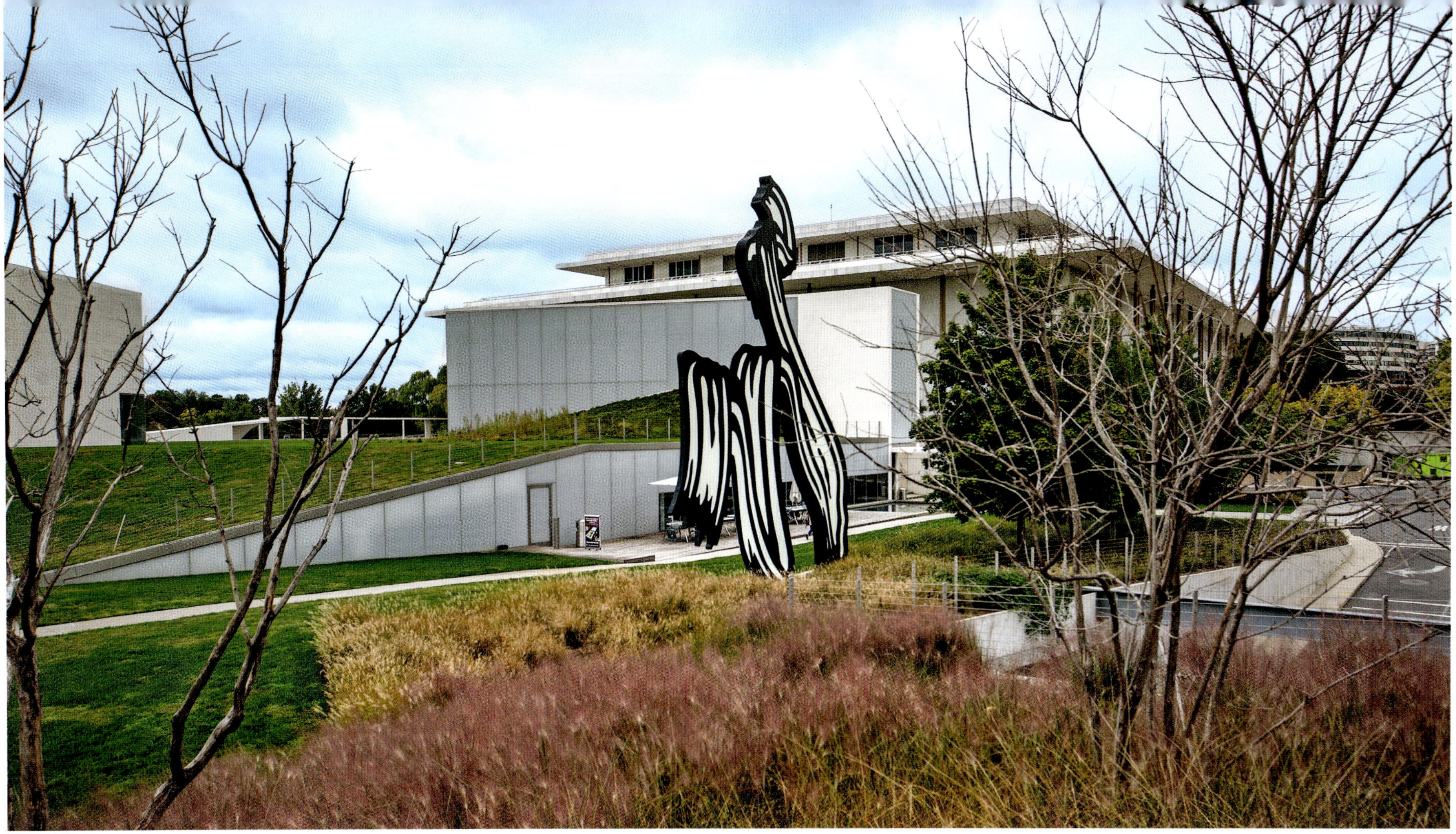

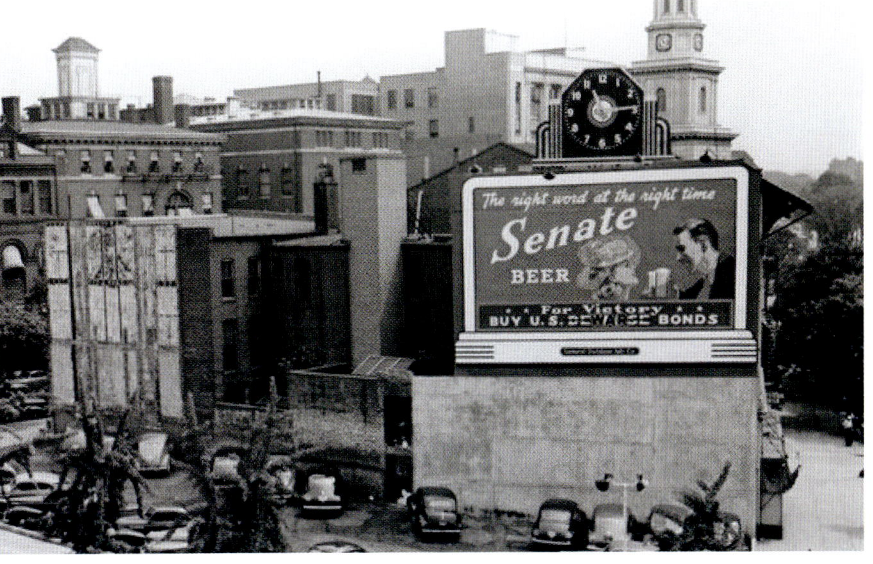

NOW: Before his death at the age of 102 in 1945, Christian Heurich was one of the largest employers in Washington. He also was one of the largest landowners in Washington, D.C., second only to the federal government. Following Heurich's passing, his son Christian Heurich, Jr. attempted to continue the family business, but was ultimately unsuccessful and the brewery was demolished in 1962. The location now hosts the John F. Kennedy Center for the Performing Arts, one of D.C. premier sites for theater and performing arts. In 2019, the now Heurich House Museum and D.C.'s Right Proper Brewing Company released a historically accurate recreation of Heurich's famed recipe, 'Senate Beer'. The beverage can be found across Washington, from baseball games at National Stadium to the museum's biergarten that sells products local to the Washington area.

LEFT: An advertisement from the World War II showcases the popularity of Senate beer. The drink has since been revived and is considered one of the most historically accurate beer recreations, based off of Heurich's recipe.

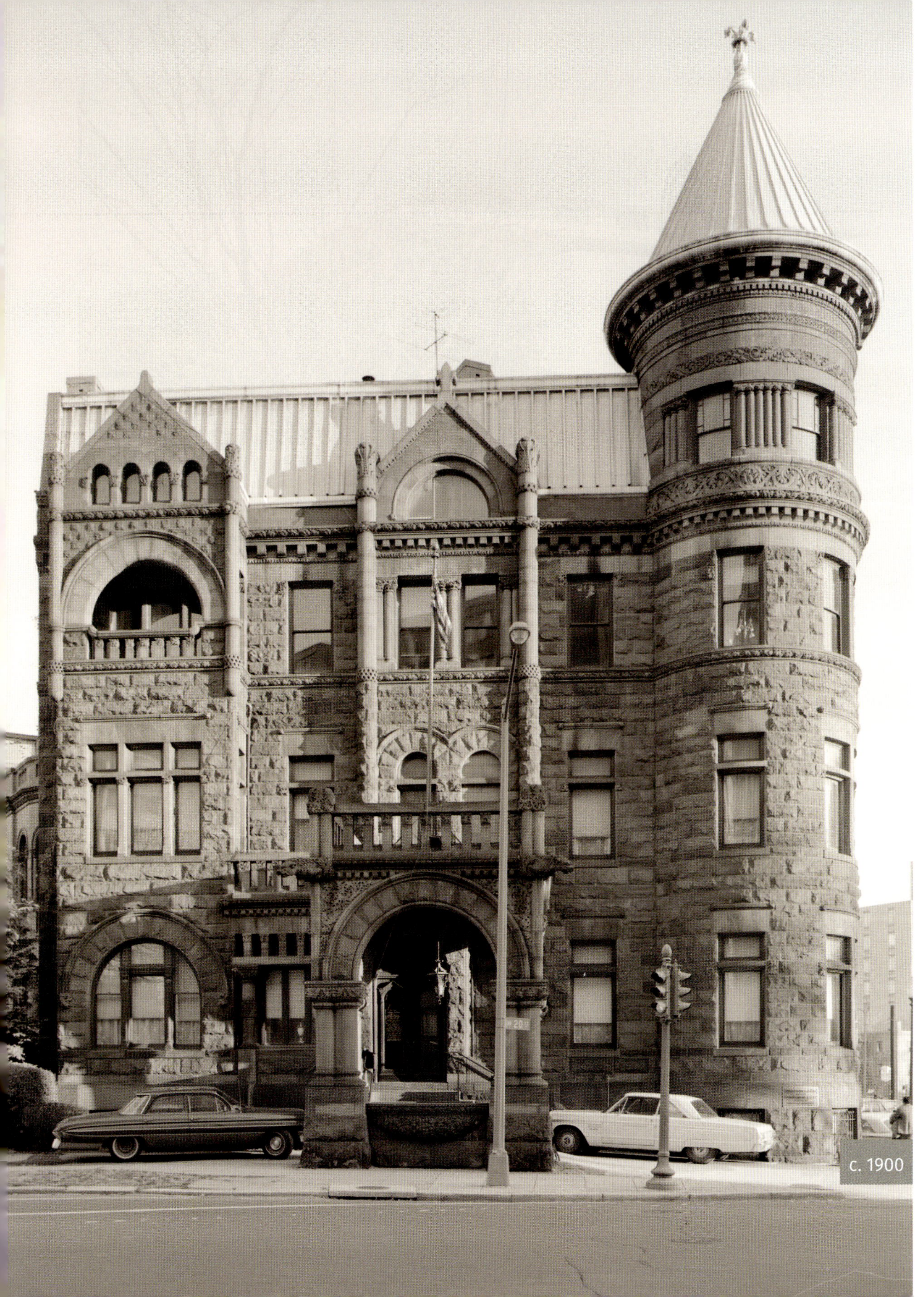
c. 1900

HEURICH HOUSE MANSION

From brewer's castle to collective action

THEN: Built in 1890s for Christian Heurich and his family, this example of Richardsonian Revival residential architecture still stands in D.C.'s Dupont Circle. The interior of the mansion is impressive, with the designs and decor completed by German-American craftspeople requested by Heurich himself. The house included many technological advancements for its time, such as electric lighting and alarms for intruders. Construction occurred from 1892–94 and was designed by John Granville Meyers. The house remained in the Heurich family until the late 1950s, with Heurich living until the age of 102 and becoming the "world's oldest brewer." After his death, Heurich's widow left the property to the Historical Society of Washington who maintained the property for the next few decades. In 2003, the house was placed on the market by the society, which was then bought by the Heurich House Foundation for preservation.

NOW: The mansion houses the Heurich House Museum and provides visitors with a glimpse into what life was like at the turn of the twentieth century. The museum highlights not only the extravagances of the Heurich home, but also what life was like for the household staff and their contribution to making sure the home functioned smoothly.

The museum continues to honor Heurich's legacy by supporting local small businesses through the Heurich Manufacturing Incubator, which looks to provide economic opportunities to local small businesses. Additionally, the museum's annual Christmas Markt, intentionally spelt this way, hosts local vendors in the mansion's backyard for local Washingtonian holiday shopping.

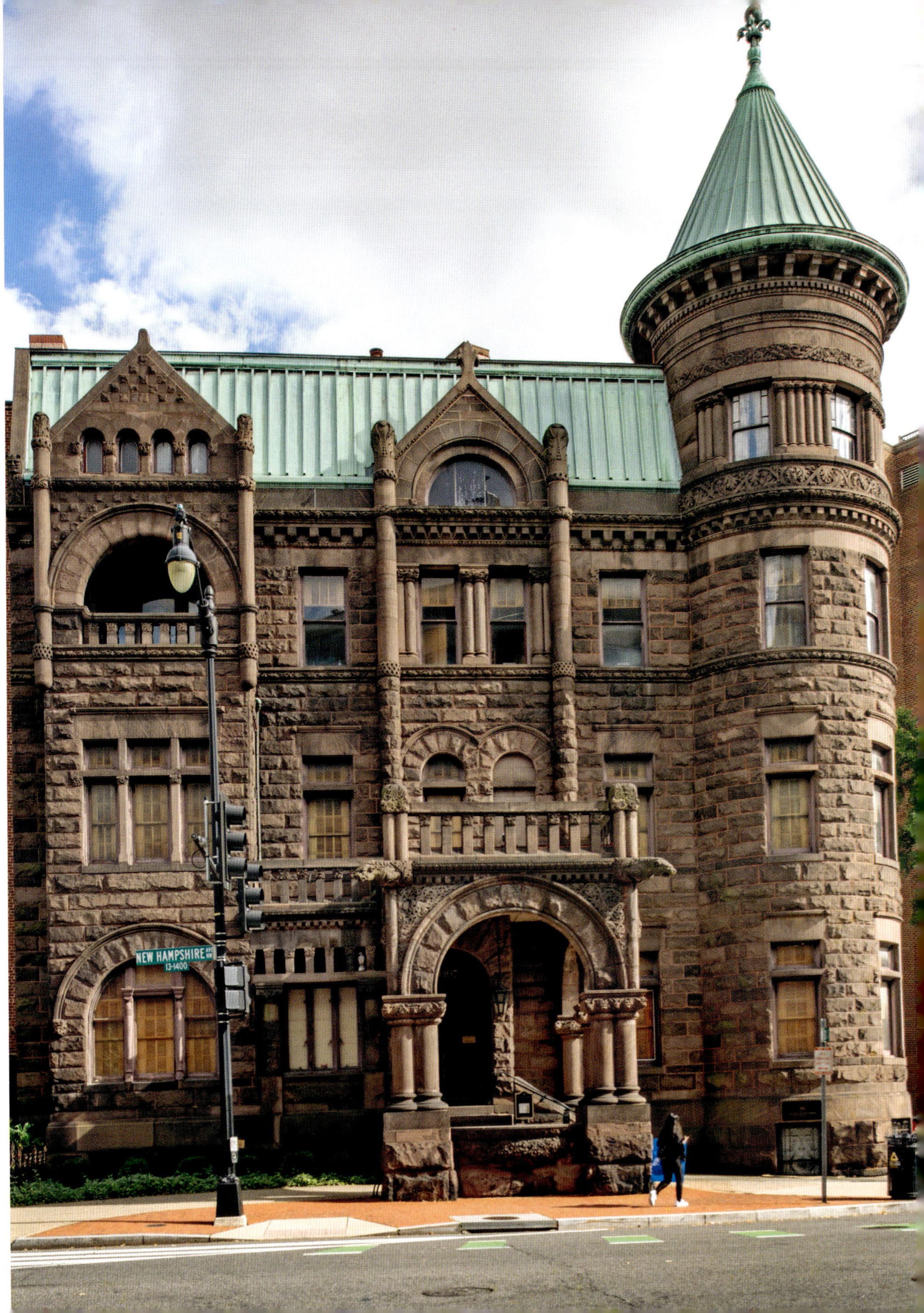

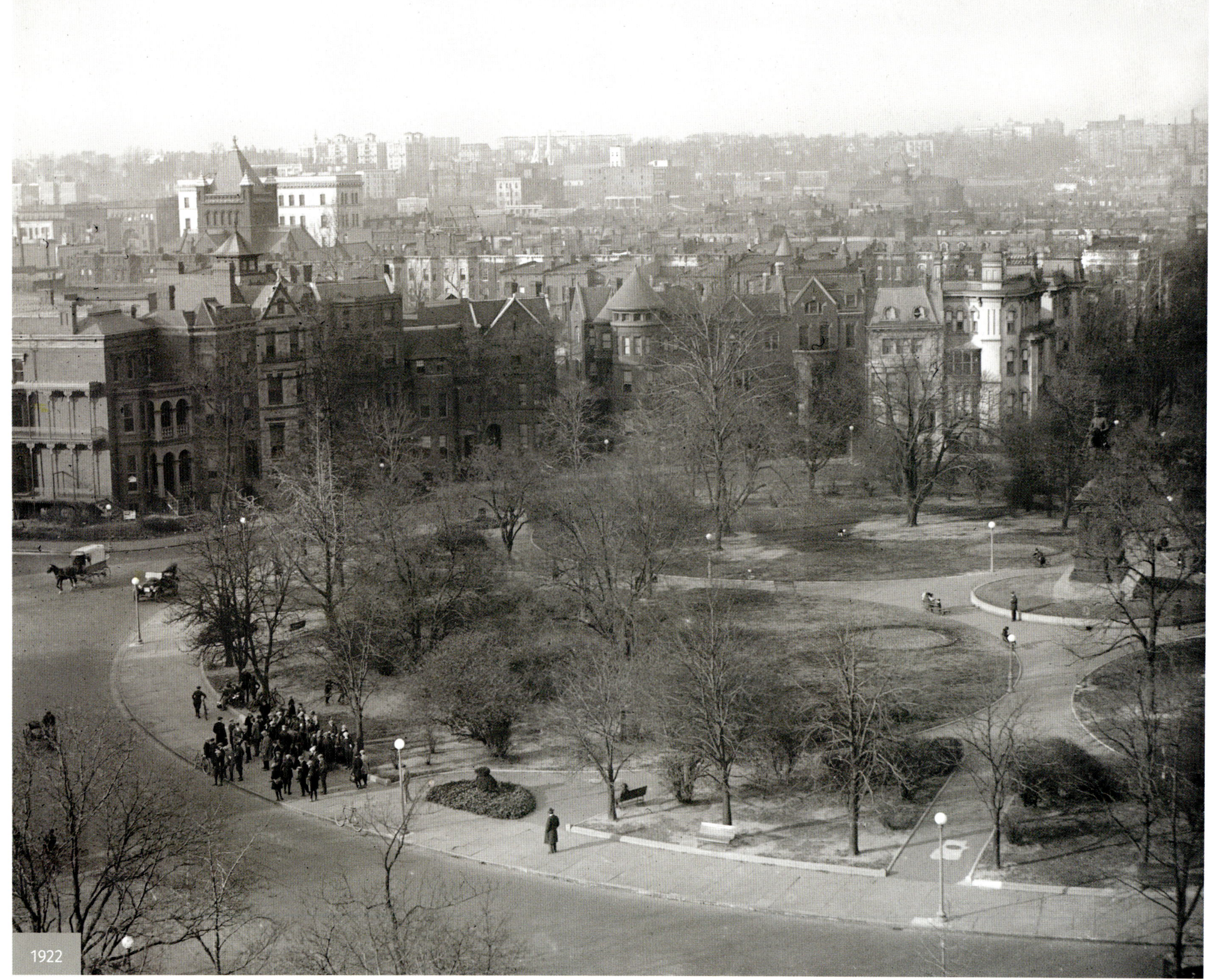
1922

LOGAN CIRCLE

D.C.s most resilient residential neighborhood

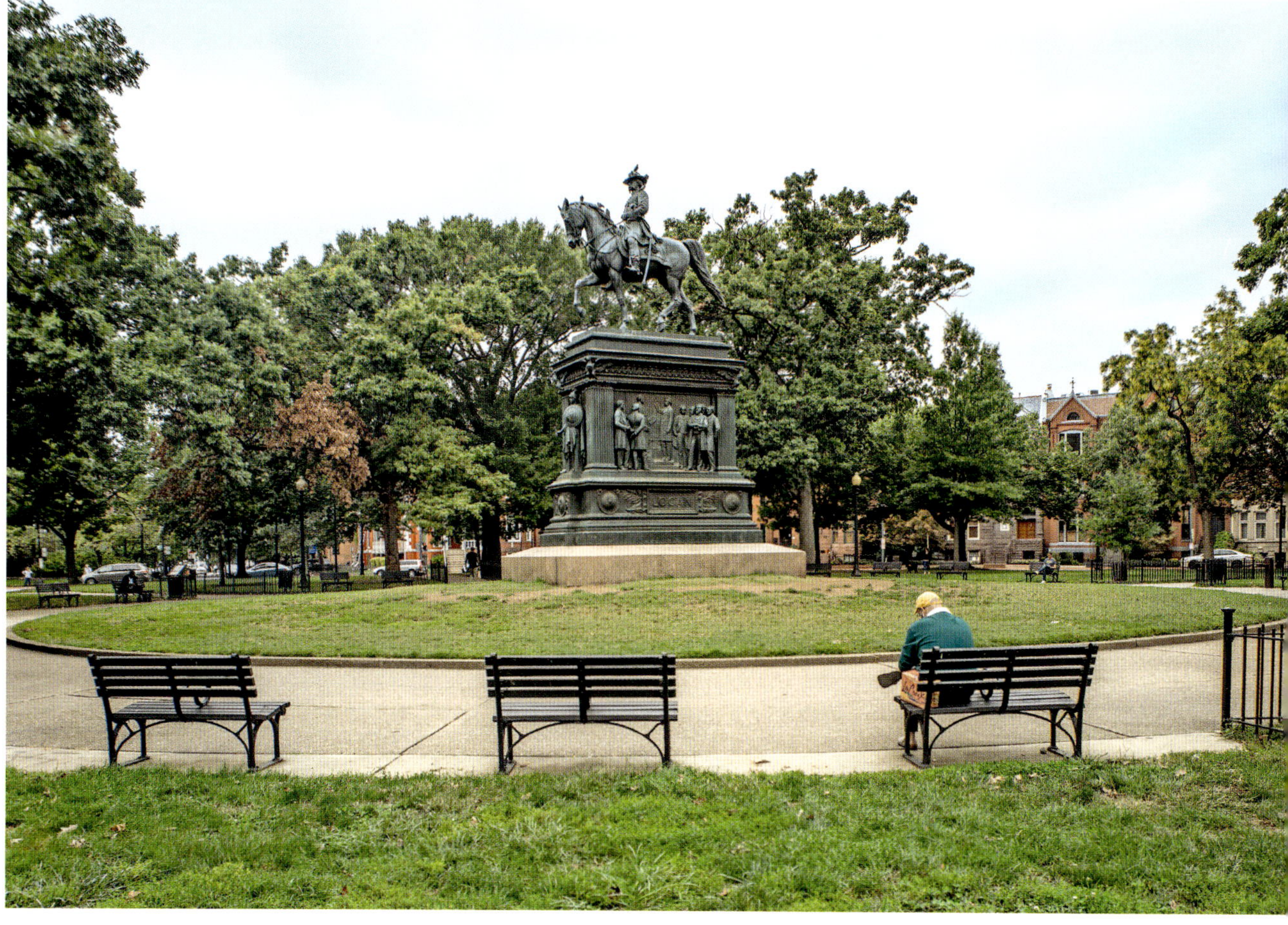

THEN: In his first plans for the District in 1790, city planner and architect Pierre Charles L'Enfant wanted Washington, D.C. to have circles that intersected vertical, horizontal, and diagonal streets. While his plan wasn't executed to his full dreams in his lifetime, Logan Circle eventually came to fruition as a reflection of this plan, although it did take some time. Once a sparsely populated field, the neighborhood that eventually became Logan Circle found greater purpose during the Civil War. As the nation's capital became an epicenter for wartime activity, more areas of the city beyond Downtown were needed for support such as medical facilities for wounded Union troops. Near what is now Logan Circle at 11th St NW and R St NW was Camp Barker, a camp that originally hosted barracks for the Union Army but eventually came to be a refuge for those escaping enslavement in the southern states. This camp eventually became Freedmen's Hospital, which has since moved and been renamed Howard University Hospital.

In the years following the Civil War, Logan Circle saw an increase in residents as more and more people moved into Washington. In the late nineteenth century, affluent families began building townhouses around the Circle, making Logan Circle a fashionable neighborhood and desirable address. Originally known as Iowa Circle, it was renamed in the 1930s after John A. Logan, who was a Union General during the Civil War, and Logan Circle began to grow with residential townhouses. These homes varied in design, but largely reflect the Richardsonian Romanesque and Victorian styles that were popular at the time. At the turn of the twentieth century, Logan Circle was a prosperous, bustling neighborhood, but this gilded era would not last forever.

NOW: Just as the Civil War did nearly a century before, World War II brought major changes to the District and its growing neighborhoods. With the United States' involvement in World War II, tens of thousands of government employees made their way to Washington all needing housing, and thus many of the glamorous houses of Logan Circle were divided into apartments. The late twentieth century saw the departure of many of D.C.'s residents as suburban regions developed, leaving neighborhoods like Logan Circle without the funding or support it had been accustomed to. The 1968 riots following the assassination of Martin Luther King, Jr. greatly affected the larger Logan Circle neighborhood as well. It seemed as though the area was going to join other out-of-date, defunct D.C. neighborhoods and receive the wrecking ball.

Alas, no wrecking ball came. In the latter half of the twentieth century, Logan Circle fell under the scope of developers and was then protected in 1972 through its inclusion on the National Register of Historic Places. Since then, the neighborhood has maintained many of its townhomes-turned-apartments and the nearby 14th Street is a popular shopping destination. Logan Circle is now one of the only circle parks in Washington to retain its residential purpose, the very aim which L'Enfant originally intended.

MUNICIPAL FISH MARKET

Always adapting, never closing: one of America's oldest fish markets

THEN: Throughout the nineteenth and into the twentieth century, Washingtonians were serviced by a vast system of markets that sold various produce and goods. One of these markets was the Municipal Fish Market, which has always had a unique specialty and continues to serve locals to this day.

Since its foundational years as the nation's capital, Washington, D.C.'s southwest waterfront has given residents access to the ocean and rivers', offerings with fishermen selling their fresh catch right from their boats. By 1805, the casual buy-and-sell of the fishermen became increasingly formal, and what we now know to be the Municipal Fish Market was born. The market continued to serve the public throughout the nineteenth century, however the early twentieth century brought with it concerns of inadequate sanitation. In 1913 an act of Congress formally recognized the Municipal Fish Market, which at this point had been in business well over a century. The congressional plan identified sanitation improvements such as more advanced refrigeration and packing facilities, all through the construction of new market structures.

The market, now formally managed by the District, continued to operate through most of the twentieth century with business as usual. The Southwest neighborhood that surrounded it (one of the oldest in the District) also continued as a self-sufficient, community-centered neighborhood. It was not until the 1950s that the market faced a new challenge: urban renewal. The Southwest Urban Renewal Project called for the demolition of the market buildings and the eviction of residents in the neighborhood that stood in the shadows of federal buildings. With no alternative space to reopen their businesses, vendors of the Municipal Fish Market refused to leave. They were able to fight off the advancements of developers before most of the brick structures, built less than fifty years prior, were torn down in the 1960s.

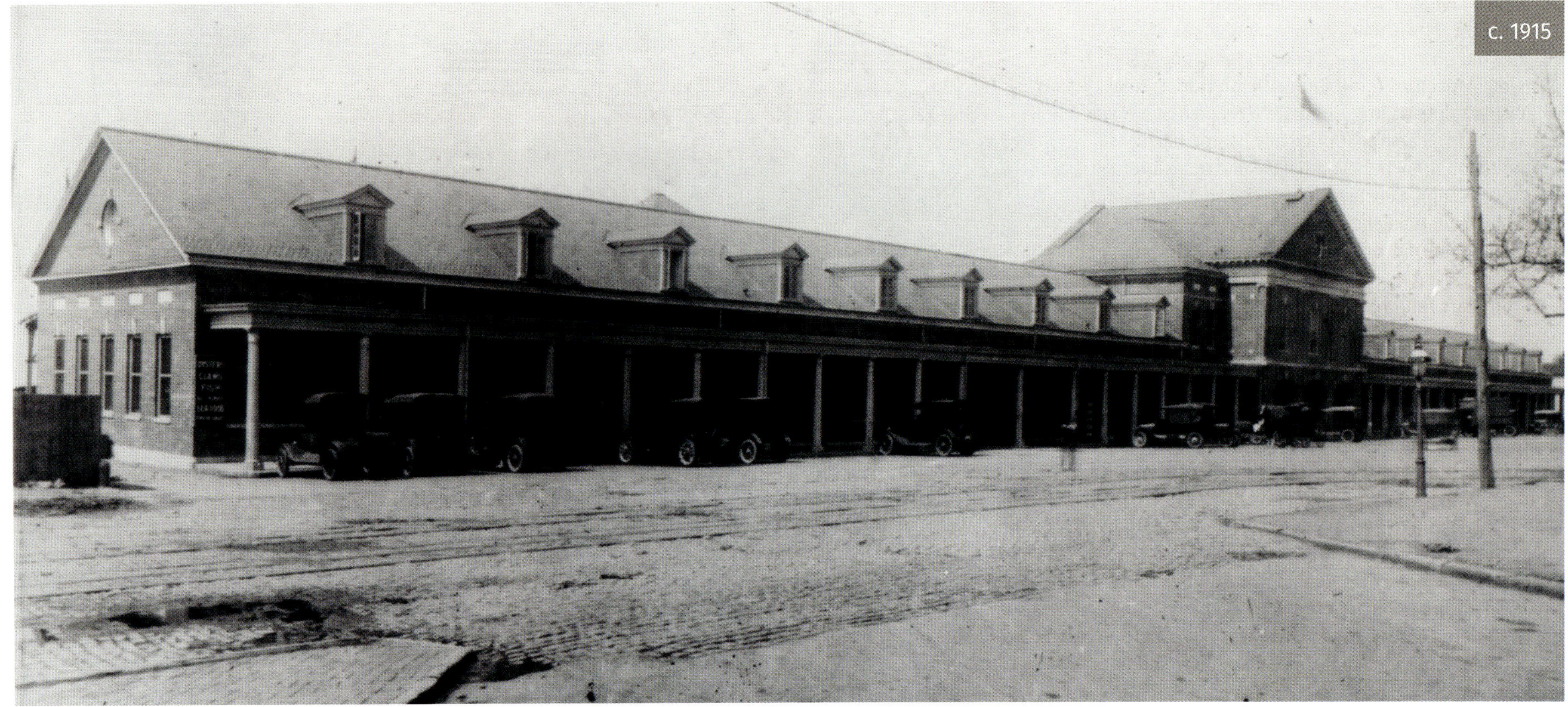

c. 1915

NOW: Since its displacement following the Southwest Urban Renewal Project, the Municipal Fish Market has adapted. The vendors occupy new floating barges around the wharf, continuing to sell their seafood specialties as the tide rises and falls. A waterfront gateway to the Southwest neighborhood, the Municipal Fish Market is considered the oldest open-air fish market in the United States.

Since the eviction of its residents in 1958, the area around the fish market has gone through many iterations. Most recently, the area now known simply as The Wharf, has become the home of new restaurants, concert and entertainment venues, and shopping spots. No matter how The Wharf has changed, the barges of the Municipal Fish Market have always remained.

RIGHT: A residential neighborhood once existed throughout Southwest Washington, D.C. Beginning in the 1950s, development projects displaced residents, many of whom were African American, to make way for renovations.

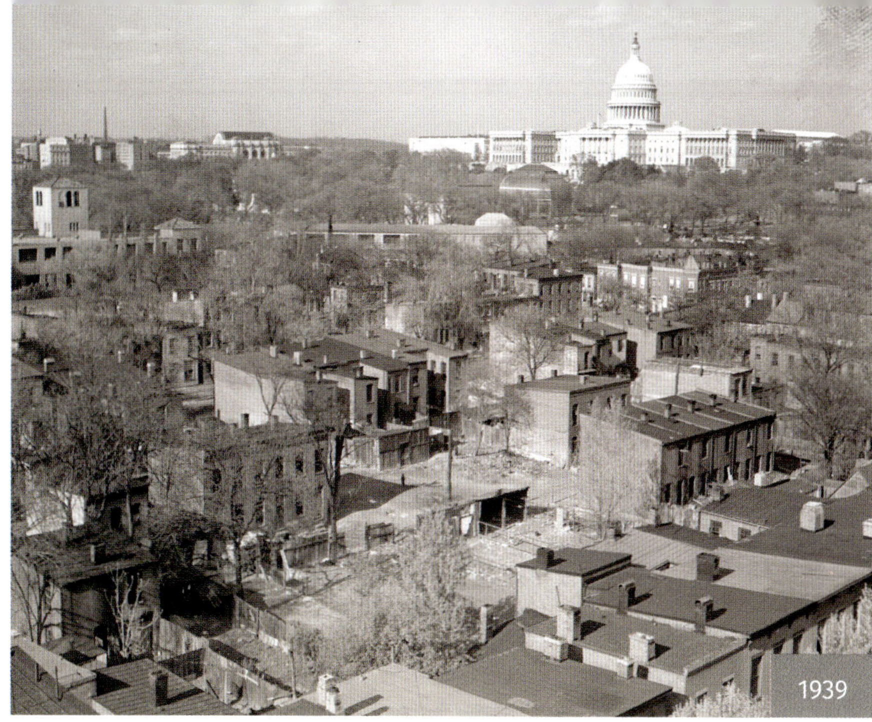

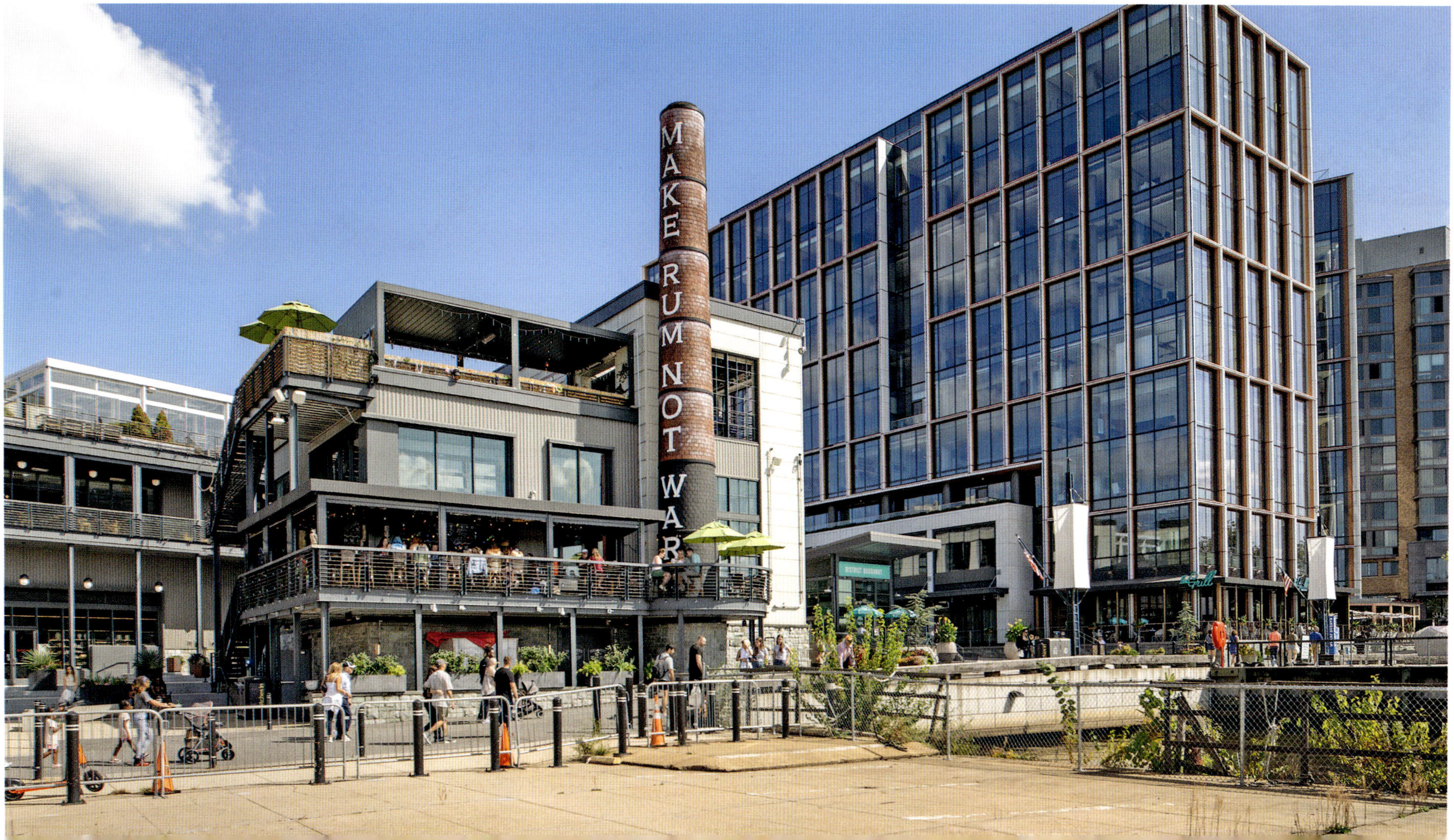

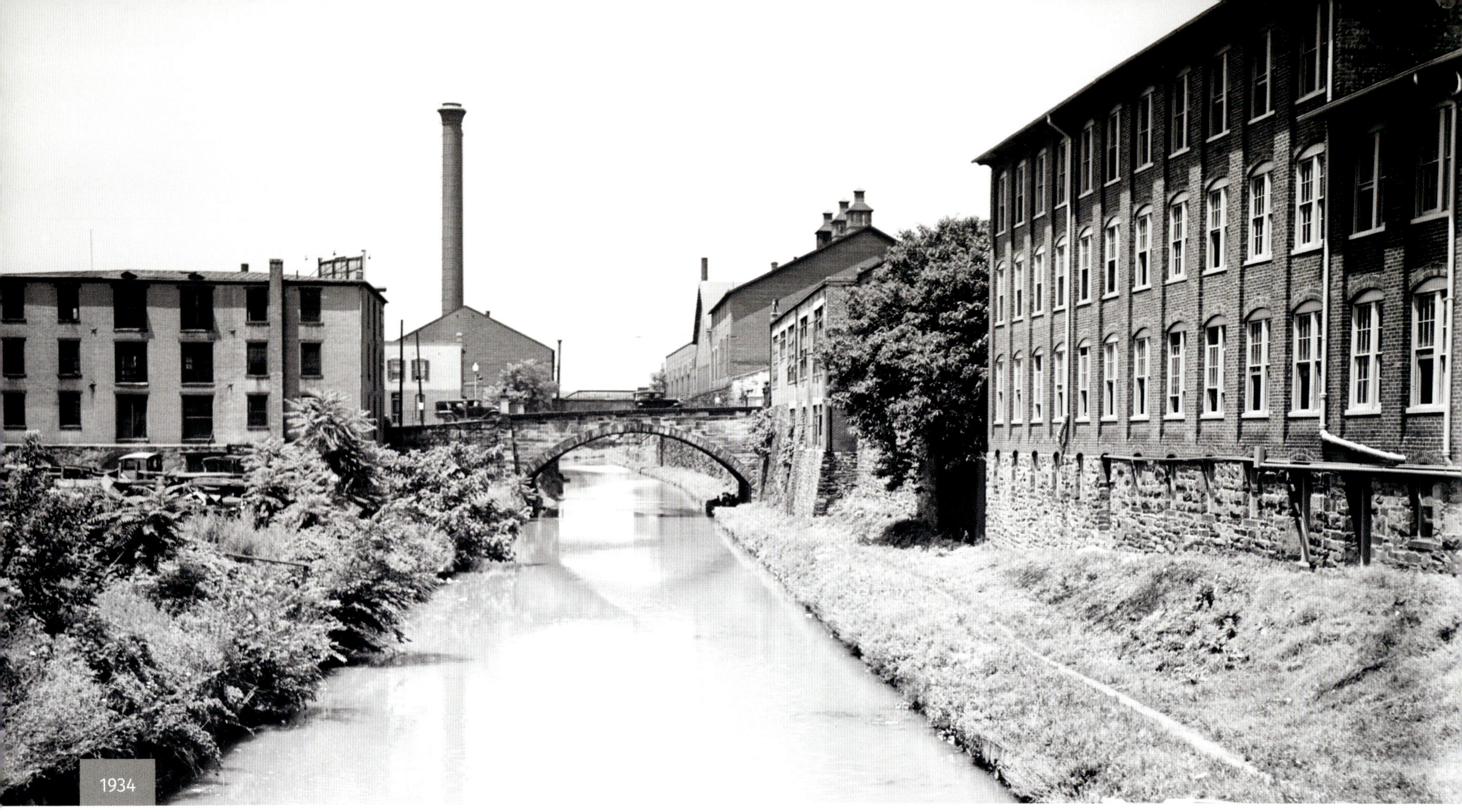
1934

C&O CANAL

A reminder of transportation before trains

THEN: While Washington always had the benefit of being surrounded by two major rivers with access to the Bay and eventual ocean, it was decided that the city should have a new canal in 1825. The district already had one canal that ran downtown, known as the Washington City Canal which connected to the Eastern Branch, now known as the Anacostia River, yet D.C. was looking to further connect this downtown canal to the natural resources of Maryland. In one of his last acts of Presidency, James Monroe signed a bill chartering this great feat of transportation: the Chesapeake and Ohio (C&O) Canal.

With the first groundbreaking of the C&O Canal in 1828, construction was officially underway. The canal was completed in sections, working its way up to Cumberland in Maryland, a town on the northern border of the state. The majority of workers on the canal were Irish immigrants, alongside some German and Native-born Americans. In the earliest years of its construction, Enslaved individuals were involved; however, this practice was later stopped. Workers were paid very little, and toiled up to fifteen hours a day, many digging the primary canal prism with rudimentary tools such as shovels and picks. These workers would travel with their families, moving the entire unit as the canal progressed.

After twenty years of construction, the completed canal made its way to Cumberland, Maryland in 1850. In Georgetown, four sandstone locks were constructed, as well as a watermill power and a large boat incline for lowering barges. The C&O Canal proved itself almost instantly, as it brought food, commercial goods, and building materials into the city. Georgetown, one of Washington's oldest and most established neighborhoods, saw increased commercial success as well as new businesses that were able to open along the accessible waterway.

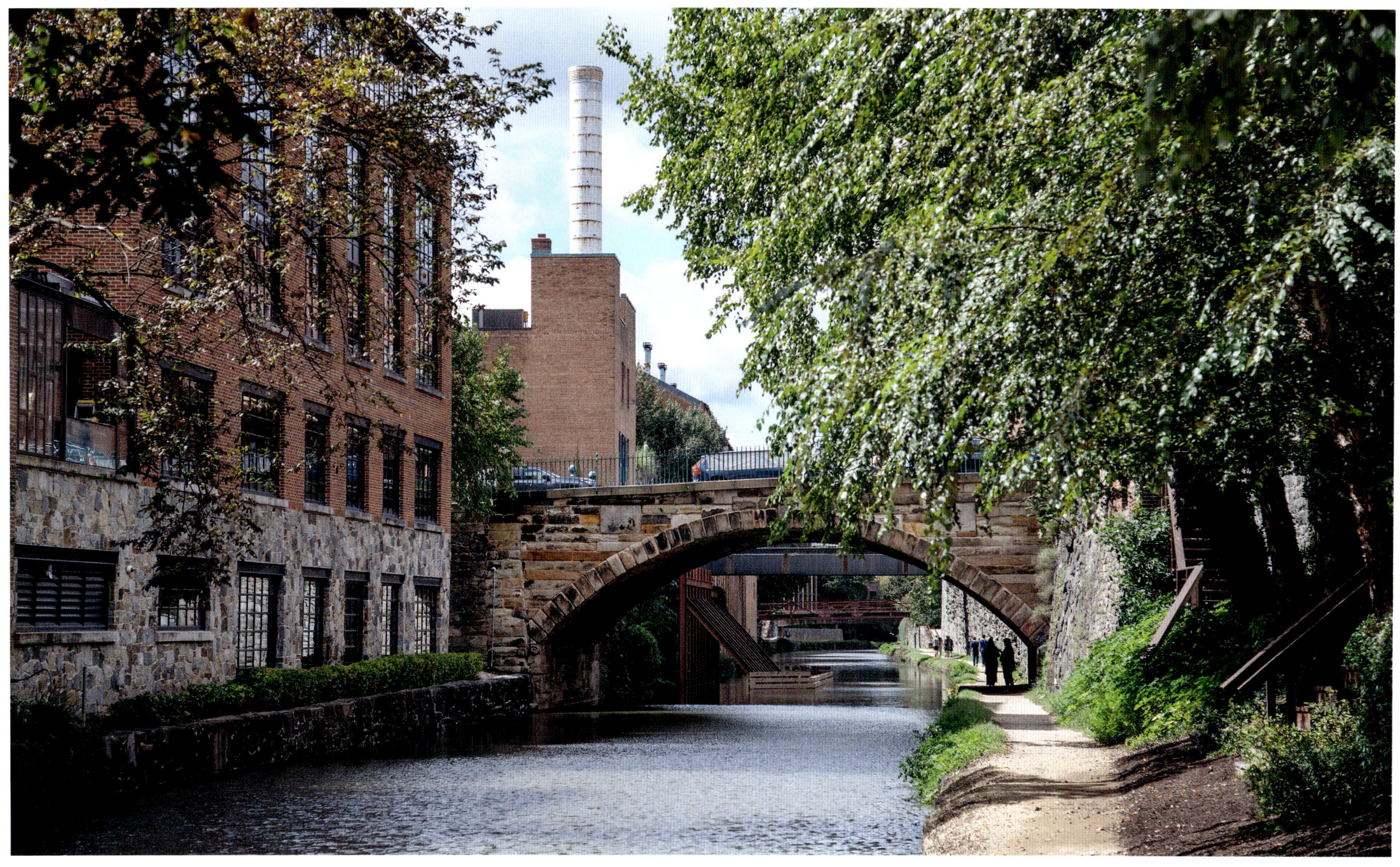

NOW: In the early twentieth century, the C&O Canal was an important point of access for many traders and locals but it could not keep up with the rise of advanced transportation technology and natural factors. In 1924, the canal experienced a flood, and with the increased popularity of train travel, its career serving Washington came to an end.

By the 1950s Washington residents were looking to replace the former waterway with a scenic highway, providing views of the Potomac River. The plan had many dissenters, including one of great influence: the Supreme Court Justice William Douglas. Justice Douglas wanted to preserve the canal, a feature of Washington he had grown up alongside, and continued to use as a nature trail for hiking. With his support and some from community preservation groups, the National Park abandoned its plan of a scenic highway, and the canal was saved. Operating for nearly 100 years, the C&O Canal today is one of the few intact surviving examples of America's canal building era. A National Historic Park since 1971, visitors can still walk alongside the historic site or take a canal boat tour today.

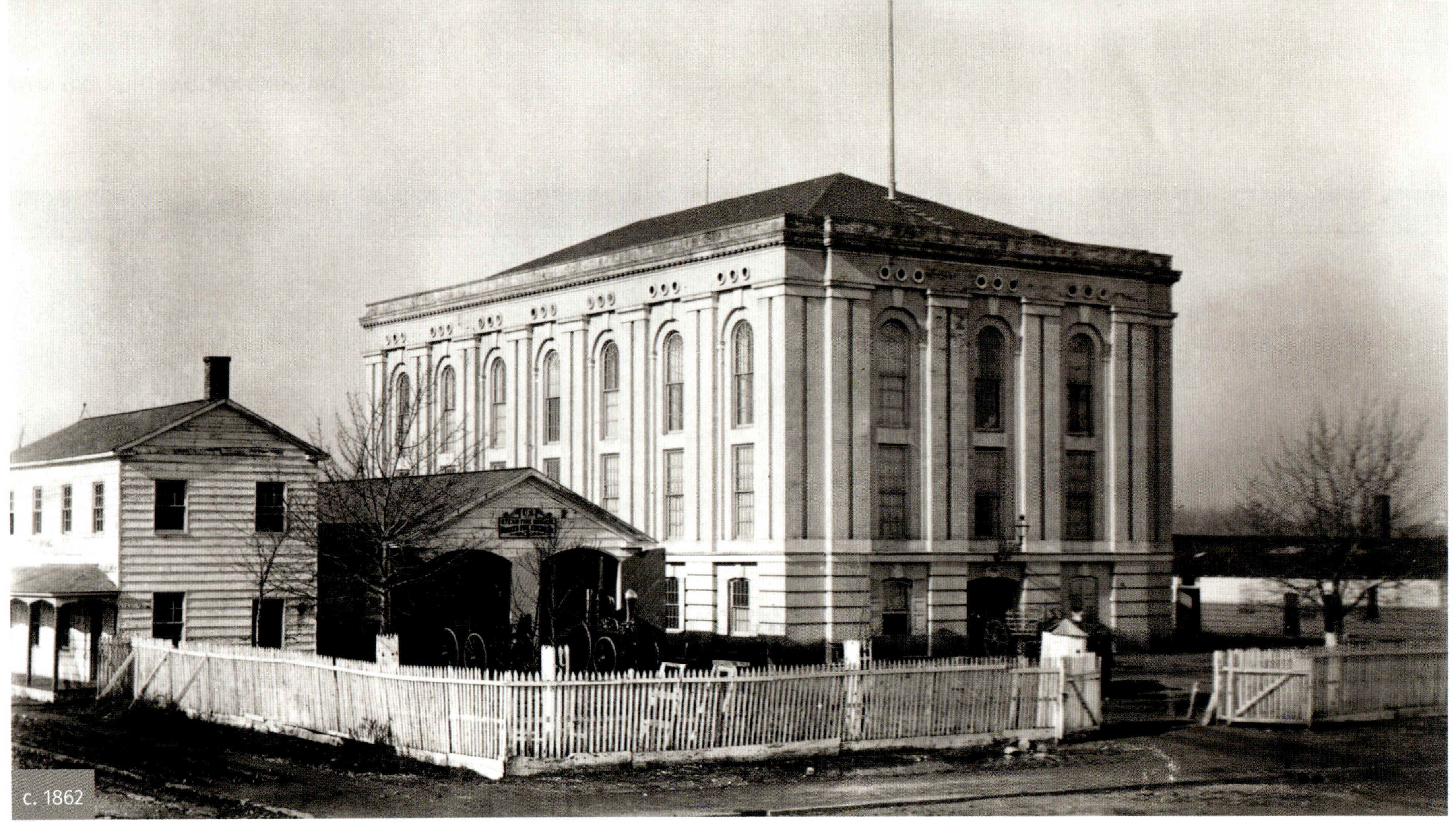
c. 1862

ARMORY SQUARE HOSPITAL

Active military hospital to internationally ranked museum

THEN: In 1856, President Franklin Pierce requested the creation of a building on the National Mall for the storage of arms and ordnances. At the intersections of B Street (Independence Ave now) and 6th St SW, a large neoclassical brick building was constructed for the purpose of holding military equipment in a central location within Washington, D.C.

The creation of this building could not have arrived at a more opportune time, as just five years later the American Civil War began. As the violence of war spread throughout the region, Washington, D.C., along with the rest of the United States, witnessed large numbers of those wounded in battle. President Abraham Lincoln saw the need for medical support and requested that Doctor Willard Bliss organize a system of hospitals around the city to support those who arrived in Washington seeking medical attention. With its convenient centralized location, the land surrounding the Armory building was utilized to include medical facilities in August 1862.

With a 1000-bed hospital complex, officer quarters, a morgue, and even a chapel, the Armory Square Hospital soon became one of the largest Civil War hospitals in the area. Due to its convenient location on the waterfront docks of the surrounding rivers, many patients and victims of war in Virginia would make their way from the battlefield to these docks and be transported to the Armory Square Hospital. Owing to its size and location, the Armory Square Hospital hosted some of the worst casualties of the Civil War battlefields, with medical professionals doing their utmost to care for the large amounts of wounded soldiers coming into the city's hospitals.

In the years during which the hospital was open and the war continued, some patients and a nurse took the time to document their first-hand accounts of the Civil War. The group wrote, edited, and printed their own newspaper called the *Armory Square Hospital Gazette* for fellow staff and patients from January 1864 to August 1865, and even documented their own reactions to the assassination of President Lincoln.

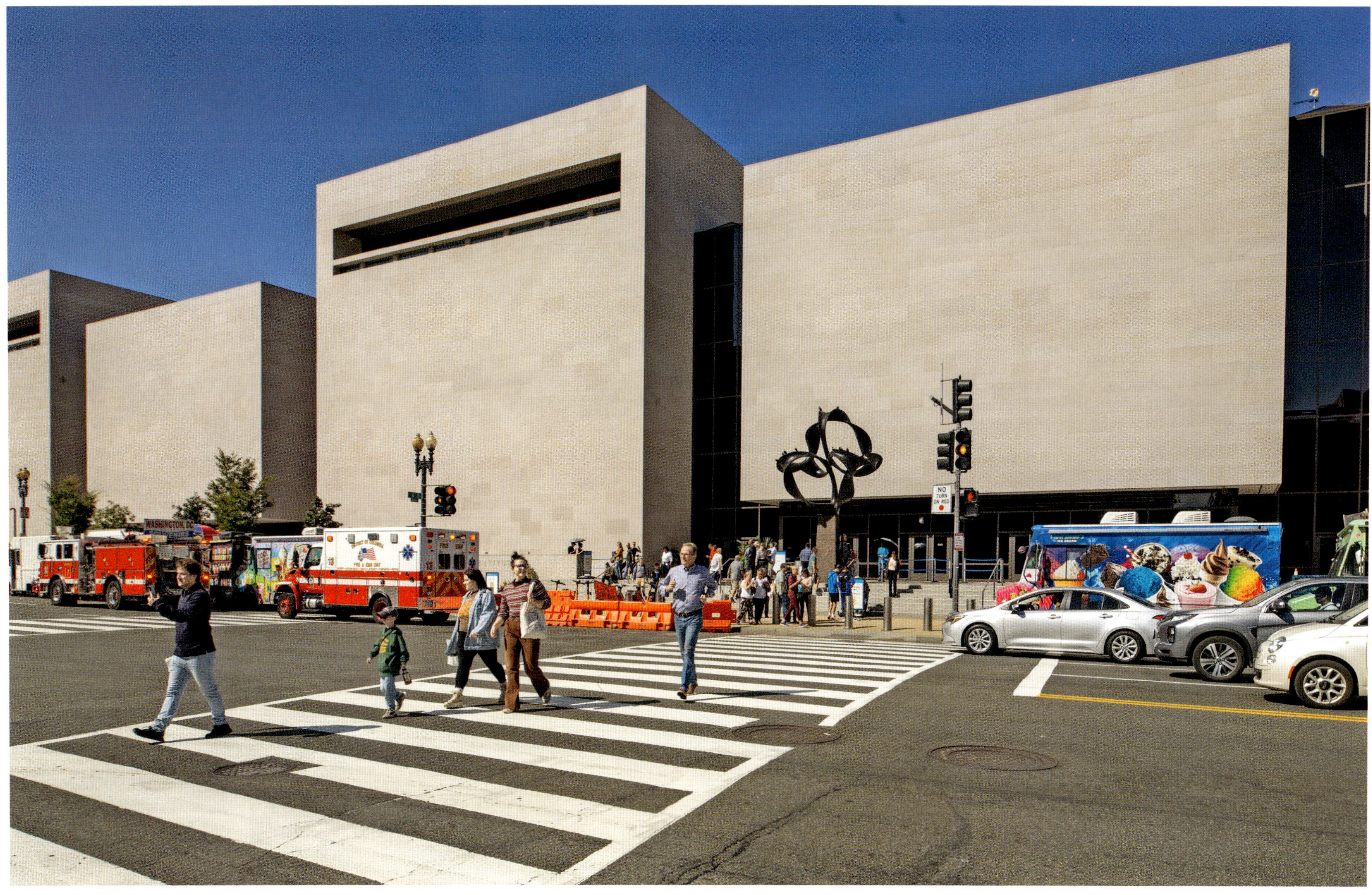

NOW: In the two years since his request to Doctor Willard Bliss, President Lincoln was responsible for the building of 187 general hospitals and around 118,000 beds for Civil War casualties. Many of these like the Armory Square Hospital were in Washington, D.C., however following the end of the Civil War, the demand for a network of hospitals in the city was no longer required and the Armory Building was returned to a storage facility. The building was later used as office space for the United States Fish Commission, before its eventual demolition in January of 1964. The lot remained empty for over a decade, until the National Air and Space Museum chose the plot for their new location on the mall, and opened in 1976. This museum holds artifacts from the first airplanes to United States spacecrafts, and is frequently ranked as one of the most visited museums in the world.

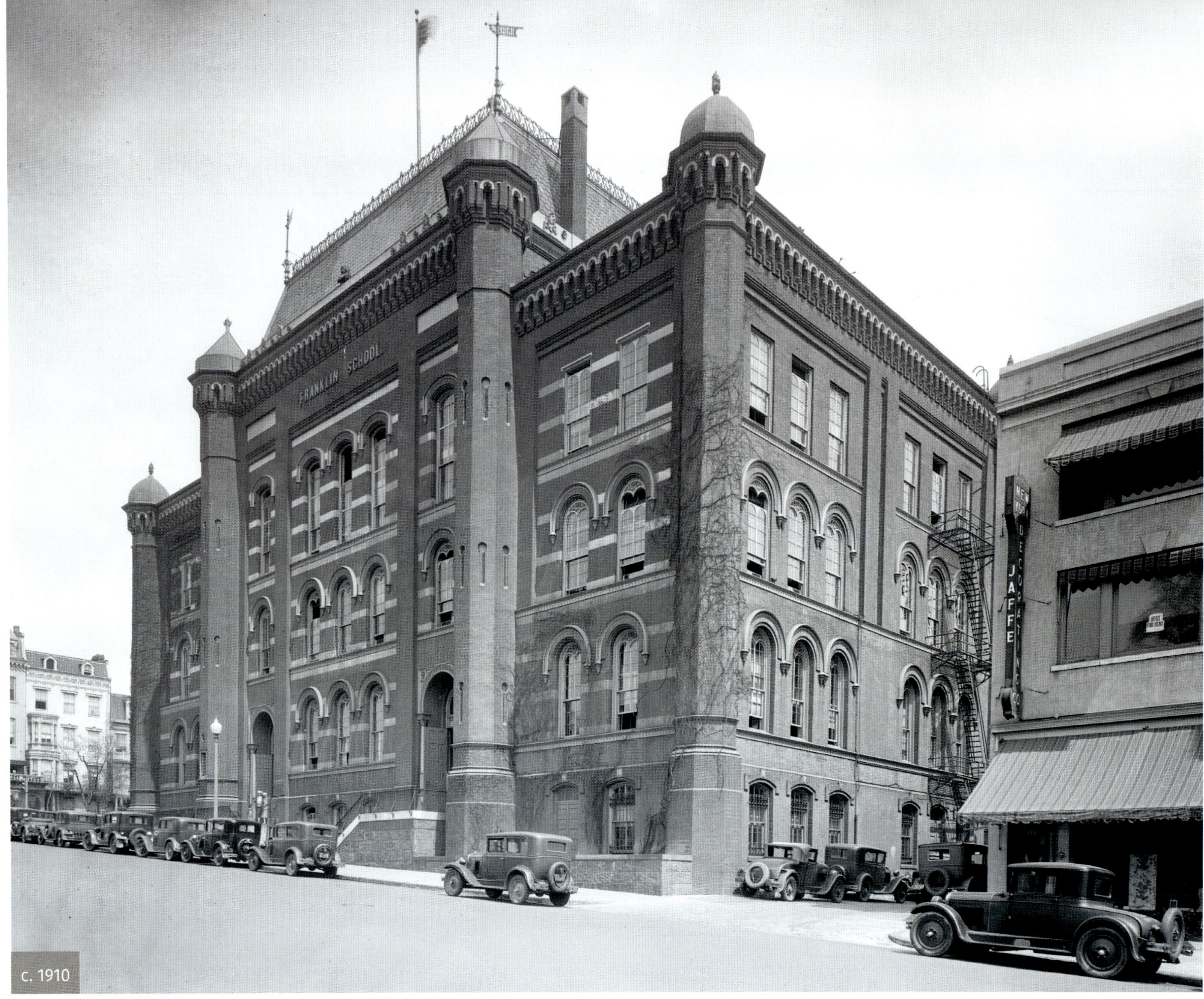

c. 1910

THE FRANKLIN SCHOOL

A blueprint for universal education in the United States

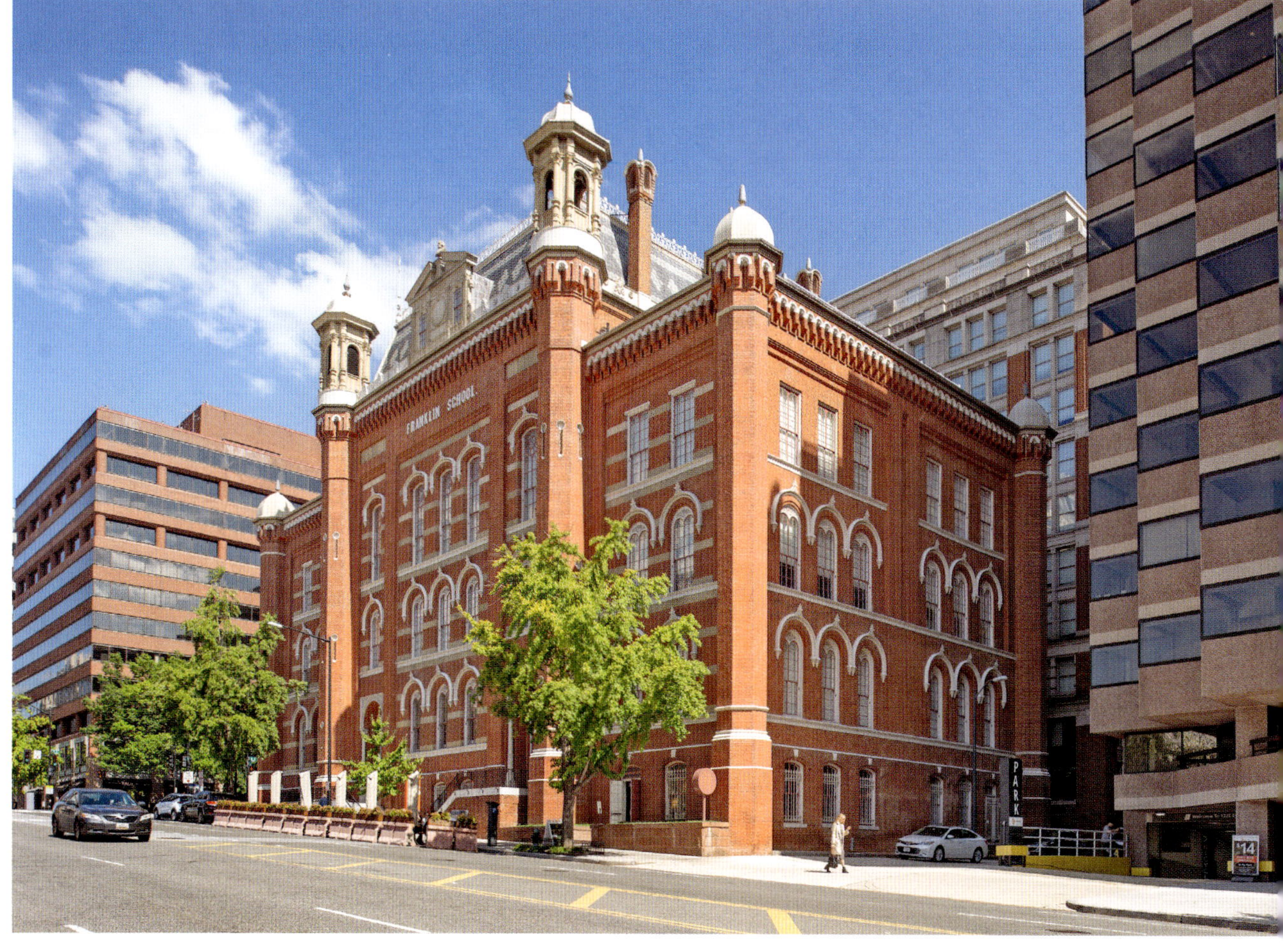

THEN: The Benjamin Franklin School was created as the flagship institution for a network of seven public schools within the city of Washington. These were created to host a system of free universal public education in Washington, D.C., the likes of which had not been seen before in the nation's capital.

Built between 1865 and 1869 on the corner of 13th St and K St NW, the Franklin School was created to push the boundaries of universal public education in the United States. The building was designed by Adolf Cluss, a German immigrant who also designed Center Market and the Patent Building in D.C. Designed in a Rundbogenstil style, or round-arched style, the exterior and interior of the public school were intentionally elaborate, pairing education with aesthetic design, as was popular in Europe in this era. The interior was spacious and included features such as a broad twin staircase and a Great Hall with original frescoes.

The proximity of the building to the White House was intended to garner city-wide attention for this new public-school initiative, and support from Congress. When it opened in the late nineteenth century the Franklin School was an instant success, showcasing to the nation the benefits of accessible public education. Many modern features of public education were first tested there including: grading and curriculum planning, vocational education, one of the nation's first high schools, and professional development and training opportunities for teachers. While the Franklin School was founded on the principle of equal educational opportunities for all Americans, in actuality this was not the case. Women and Black students were separated based on sex and race. The building saw other contemporary accomplishments and in 1880, Alexander Graham Bell tested his photophone, a precursor to wireless messaging, from the top of the building when sending a voice message to his nearby laboratory.

NOW: The arrival of the twentieth century brought changes to the city and the Franklin School saw an eventual decline in students. In 1913, the 'normal school' moved to a new facility and the rest of the building was occupied by the Board of Education which functioned primarily as administrative offices. Renamed the Franklin Administration Building in 1925, the Board of Education continued to use the facility for over forty years. In 1968, the Board of Education explored the sale of the Franklin Building to raise money for a larger administration building, although received significant backlash, deciding instead to preserve the historic property.

The building was added to the National Register of Historic Places in 1973 by the American Association of School Administrators who worked to keep historic buildings within the control of the Board of Education. After the Board of Education found new administration offices, the building hosted an adult education center until the 1990s and was later used as a homeless shelter until 2008.

In 2020, the building reopened as a museum, which currently hosts Planet Word, the only museum in the United States dedicated to language, literacy and a love of words.

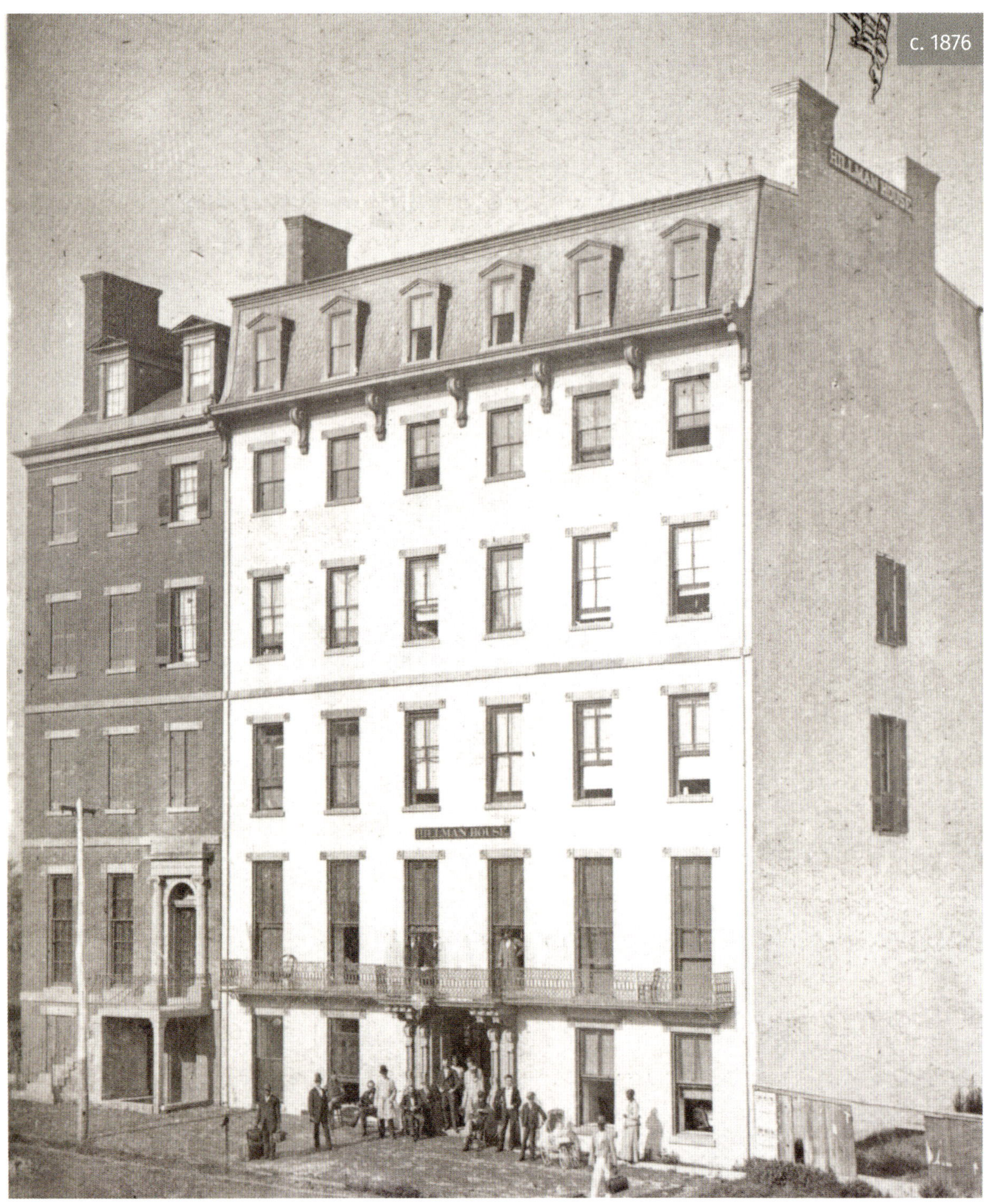

GEORGE WASHINGTON TOWNHOUSES

One president's unfinished project

THEN: George Washington left office while he was still alive, however the former president did not depart from Washington, D.C. altogether, and remained in the District as a landowner. Somewhat of a real estate tycoon, Washington owned more than 70,000 acres of land across seven different states and in 1798, the former president began scouting for property in the soon-to-be capital city. He hoped to construct two connected townhouses for his visits into the District and eventually settled on a lot on the west side of North Capitol Street, to build his new home.

George Washington himself sketched out the design of his dream property, for the review of his builder, George Blagden. Washington was adamant about the design, and obtained a second opinion from Dr. William Thornton, the man who designed the United States Capitol Building. Correspondence between Thornton and Washington continued throughout the inital planning, and despite admitting to not having much knowledge of architectural principles, Washington refused to fully compromise with the award-winning architect on his design. Construction of the buildings continued with Washington acknowledging his visits to the site in November of 1799. Washington never saw his "building in the Federal City" completed, as in December of that same year, the United States' first president passed away in his Mount Vernon estate from a suspected throat infection.

Following Washington's death and the building's completion in 1800, the townhomes took on a new Federal responsibility: housing valuable documents. In 1814, British troops made their way through Washington, igniting buildings of significance such as the White House and the Capitol. Caught in the blaze was the building known as "General Washington's house", which at the time was holding documents of significance for the House of Representatives. Not only were these important records lost, but the building of Washington's imagination was left in ruins.

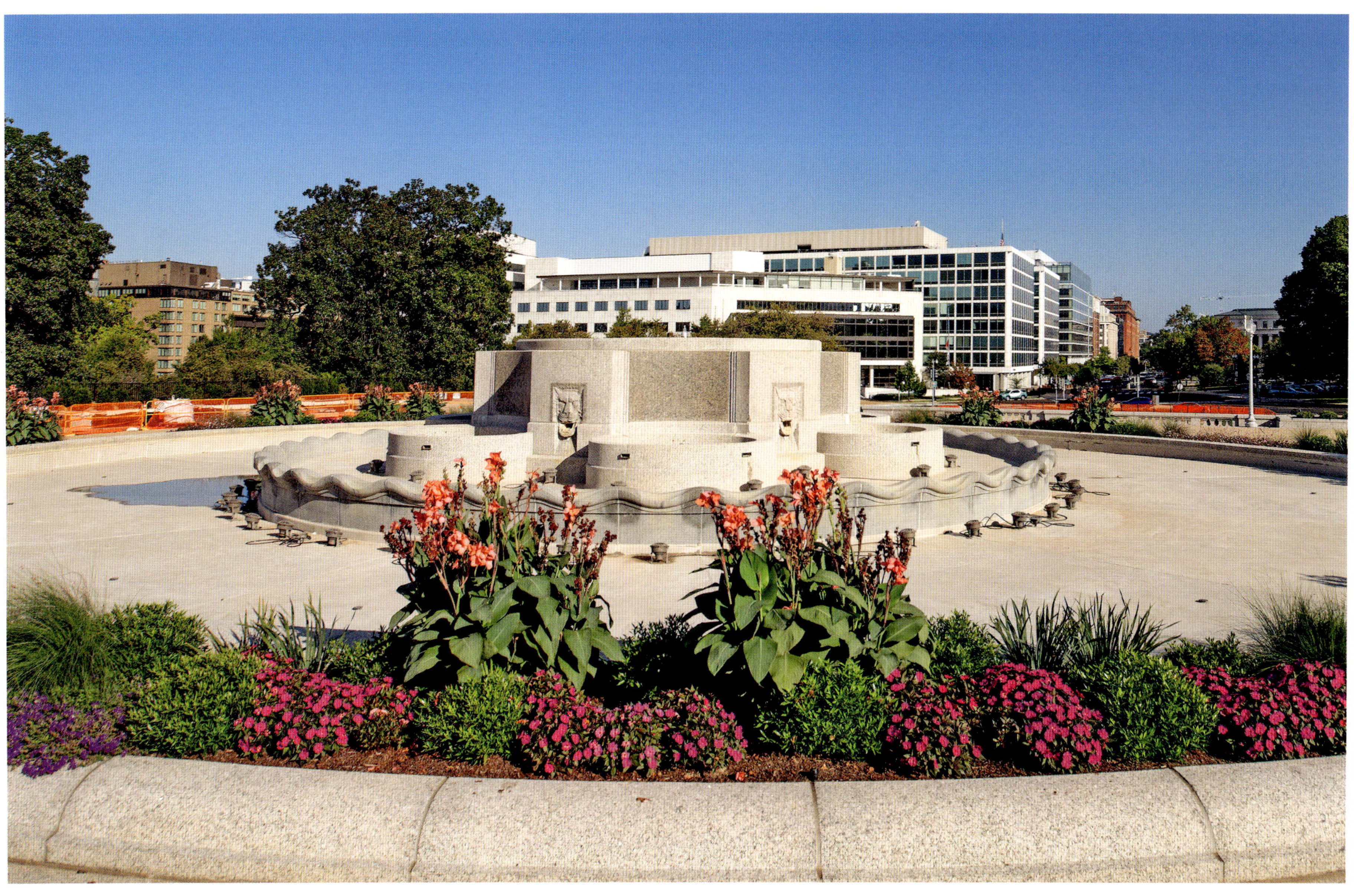

NOW: The remains of the building were purchased and the original foundation, as well as some walls, were used for the reconstruction of townhouses. Since reconstruction the building has had many lives and owners, but by the end of the nineteenth century in 1876 it was operated as a hotel called the Hillman House. In 1899 the building continued its life as a hotel and was called the Kenmore Hotel. In this iteration of the former president's dream home, the building achieved a different kind of fame when it became the center of a mysterious murder that left the city shaken and achieved national attention. In 1913, the building was purchased by the federal government and eventually razed for the creation of the Capitol Plaza, a park that connects the Capitol Building to the area around Union Station. In this park is a plaque, the sole physical reminder of the real estate aspirations of the United States' first president.

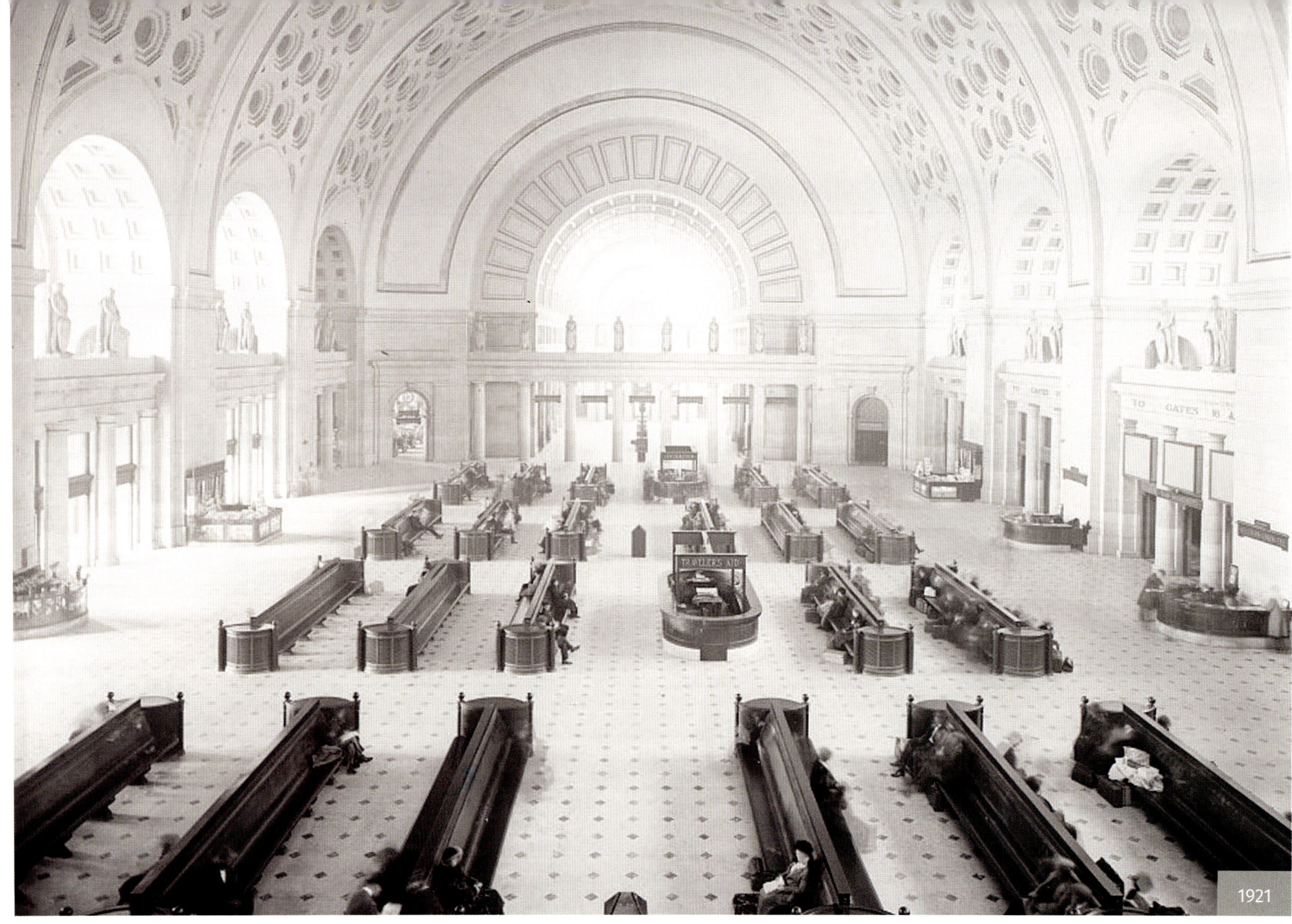

1921

UNION STATION

D.C.'s railroad solution, the world's largest railroad station born anew

THEN: Since 1853 different railroad stations had surrounded downtown Washington, servicing multiple railroad companies. In 1903, work began on architect Daniel Burnham's central station. The structure was built on the edge of Swampoodle, a former Washington neighborhood largely populated by Irish and Italian immigrants who were responsible for the building's construction. On October 27 1907, the last train left the old B&O terminal, and just a few hours later arrived as the first train in Union Station. With its inclusion of different railroad companies, Union Station was the ideal center point for all involved. The station was an immediate success, and by 1928 a train arrived or departed from the station every five minutes, with tens of thousands of passengers commuting through it. During World War II the station was the area's primary place of departure.

The station housed restaurants and stores for those waiting to transfer trains, and for locals coming to cool off during one of D.C.'s brutally hot summers. The train and station employees worked around the clock hauling luggage or managing shops to support the bustling station and patrons from all walks of life. Visitors included foreign political leaders, such as Winston Churchill and Nikita Khrushchev, as well as political actors and domestic tourists.

By the 1960s, owing to a drop in revenue from $80,000 a day to less than $30,000, decreased train arrivals and departures, and a near fatal runaway car that crashed into the station, the station no longer resembled the gateway to Washington it was intended to be.

Through the late 1960s and into the 1970s, the station was converted into the National Visitor Center for the Bicentennial of America in 1976, although on completion it was unpopular. The station's need for purpose was not its only struggle: the structure itself faced challenges. In 1977 the building was headed for major structural collapse. Union Station finally closed, although many believed it still had a future in Washington, D.C.

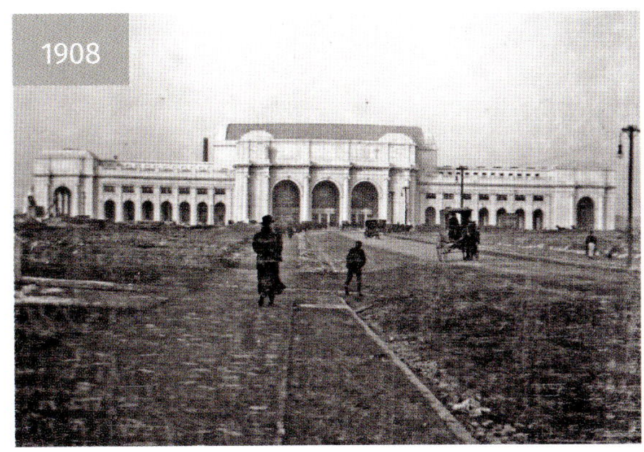

ABOVE: Designed with the classical architecture of the ancient Greeks and Romans in mind, the building was grand, with a waiting room that the Washington Monument could fit in if laid on its side. The statues were completed in Beaux-arts style by artist Louis Saint-Gaudens.

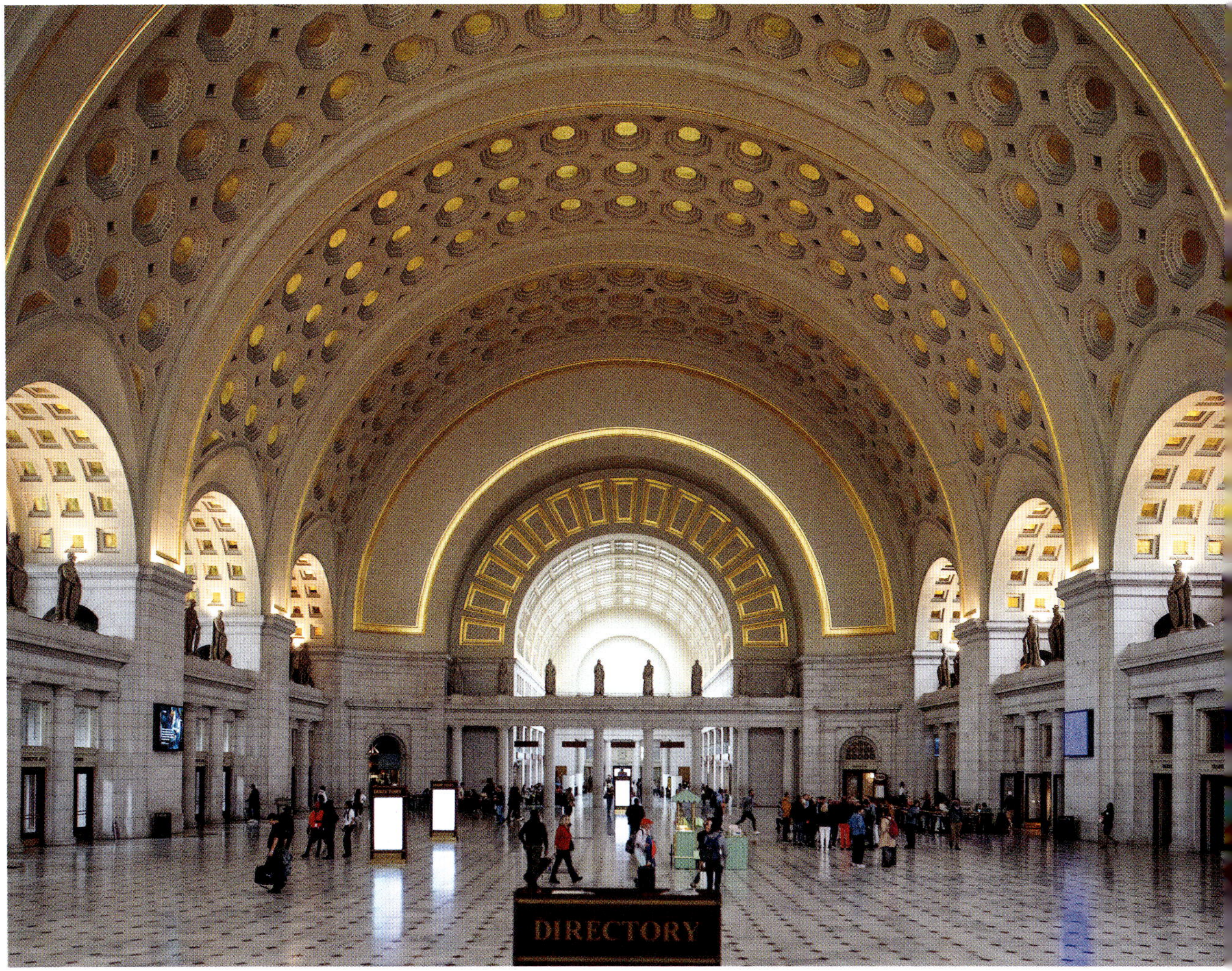

NOW: Among those who believed in Union Station's future was the United States Congress. In 1981, Congress passed the Union Station Redevelopment Act of 1981, amending the Act that established the National Visitor Center and restored the building back to its original purpose. With the support of railroad servicer Amtrak, the station reopened in 1988 with three levels of retail space, a connected bus terminal, and an Amtrak terminal that was structured behind the original concourse. Restorations of the original statues and other interior design elements were completed.

Since the station has reopened, the Union Station Plaza has greeted locals and visitors traveling to and from the nation's capital. While Union Station has faced hard times since its reopening, the resilience of Washington's grand railroad station continues to be exemplified.

RENWICK GALLERY OF ART

Forever 'Dedicated to Art'

THEN: In 1854, William Wilson Corcoran retired from his career in banking to pursue philanthropic work. He had found most of his success in 1840 when he partnered with George Riggs to form the (Corcoran and) Riggs bank, and retired in financial comfort following the bank's financing of the federal government during the Mexican-American War. Corcoran's interest in art ignited on trips to Europe in the 1840s and 1850s.

Corcoran varied from other collectors in what he acquired, as when many were focused on the European greats, he turned his attention to purchasing works by American artists. Corcoran's collection grew and he began to open his home twice a week for people to view the art. Recognizing the value of this collection, Corcoran commissioned James Renwick in 1859 to build a public space for his large collection.

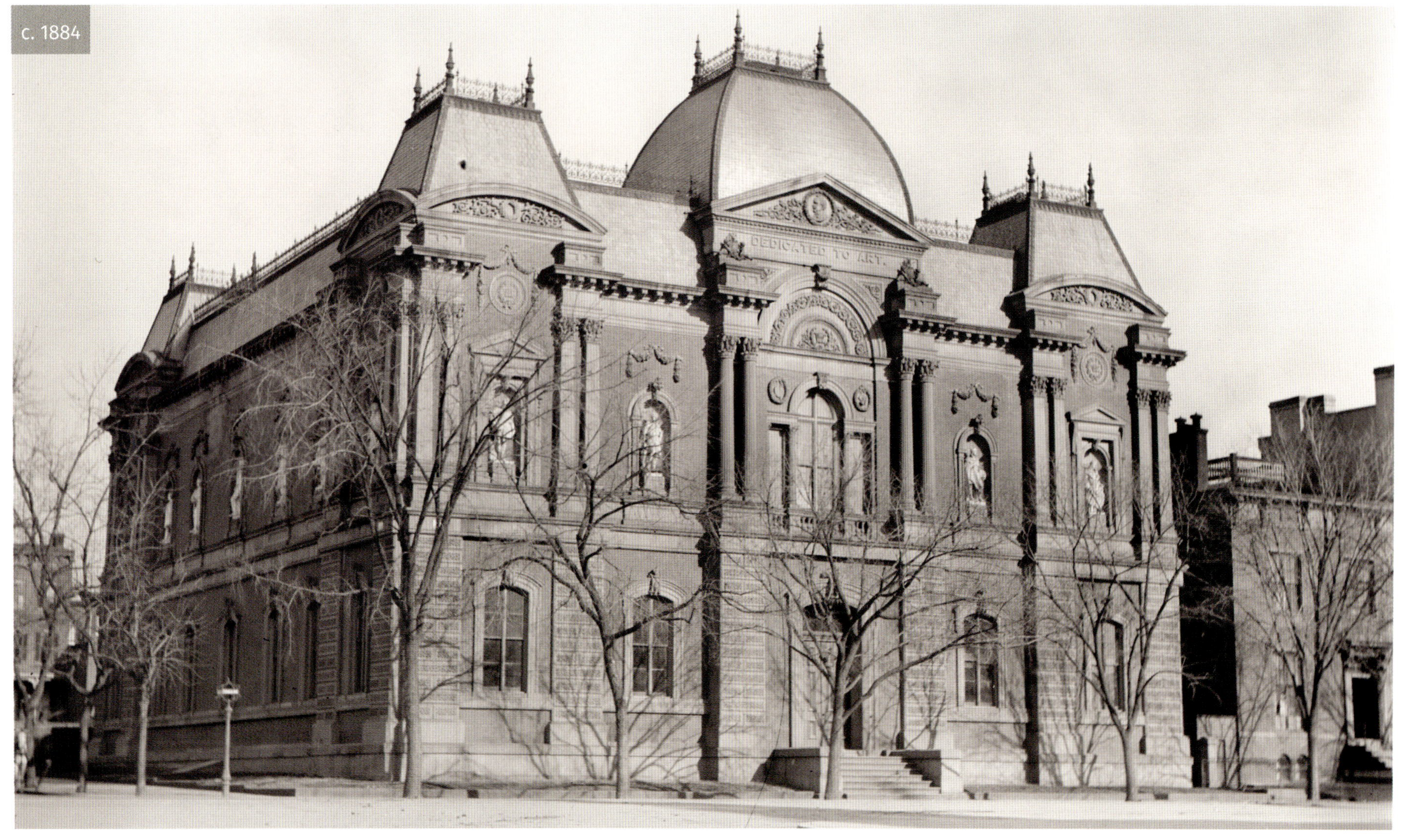

c. 1884

This plan was put on hold as the Civil War beset Washington, and the building Renwick had created was seized by the federal government when Corcoran fled to Europe. Corcoran later returned to Washington after the war ended, and his new gallery was formally opened on January 19th, 1874.

The building Corocan designed was one of the earliest examples of Second Empire architecture in the U.S.. Initially opening with an exhibit of ninety-eight paintings and sculptures, the gallery was a success, and by the end of the year had expanded to include more than 300 works. Corcoran opened his gallery free to the public twice a week and the gallery was celebrated as Washington's National Gallery of Art. Corcoran's art collection was a brilliant success and frequently growing, so twenty years later Corcoran made the decision to relocate his collection to a larger building, just blocks away on 17th Street NW.

BELOW: The First Lady Jacqueline Kennedy saw great potential in the historic buildings that surrounded Lafayette Square, from Federalist style residences to Renwick's art museum, which she called a "Victorian horror" in her communications with others. Despite her stylistic distaste for the building, she understood its significance, and worked to save the structure from demolition.

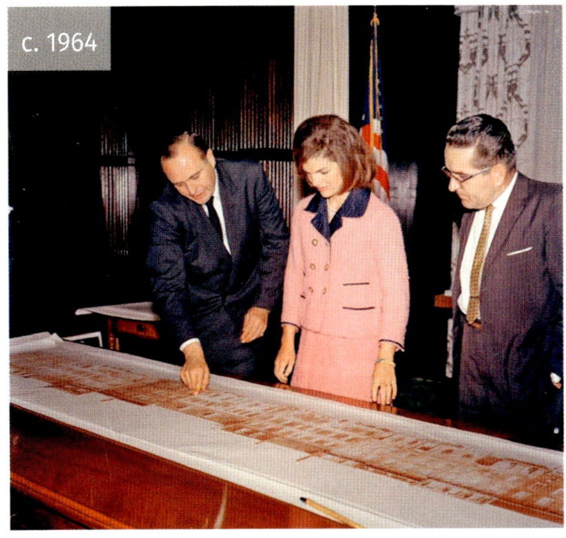

NOW: The U.S. Court of Claims took over Renwick's building, and although it was inscribed with "Dedicated to Art", the fate of the former gallery was no longer one of artistic service. In the 1950s, Congress was hoping to make space around the White House for new government office space and set its eyes upon the now dilapidated art museum designed by Renwick. It appeared as though all was lost, that is, until First Lady Jacqueline Kennedy stepped in and saved the property.

In 1965 another government organization set its sights on the Renwick building: the Smithsonian. Then secretary of the Smithsonian, S. Dillon Ripley met with President Lyndon B. Johnson and it was after this meeting that the building was once again "Dedicated to Art." In 1972, what is now the Renwick Gallery, opened as a part of the Smithsonian American Art Museum's contemporary crafts museum. It features rotating exhibits that highlight contemporary artists, and makes art accessible with free admission.

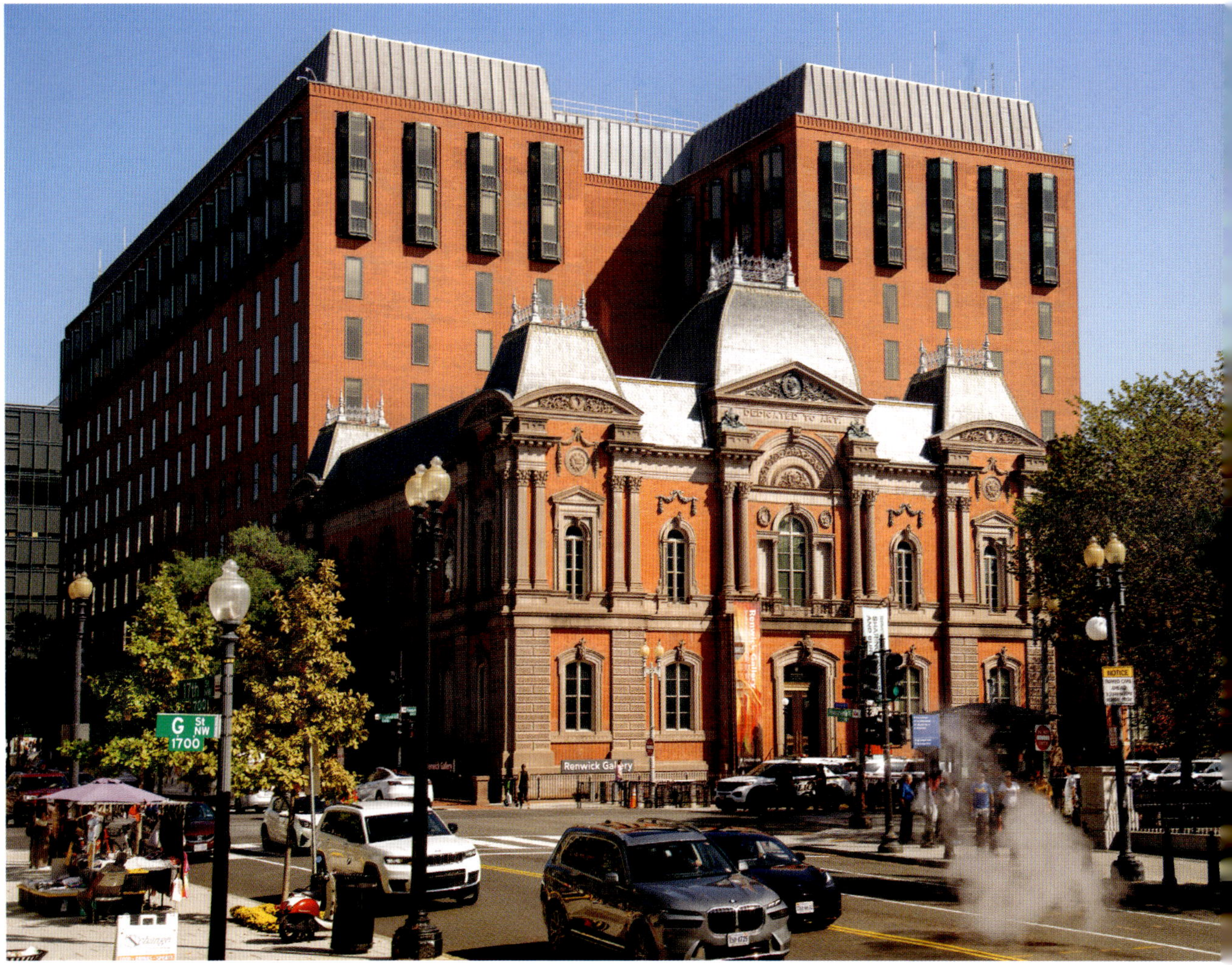

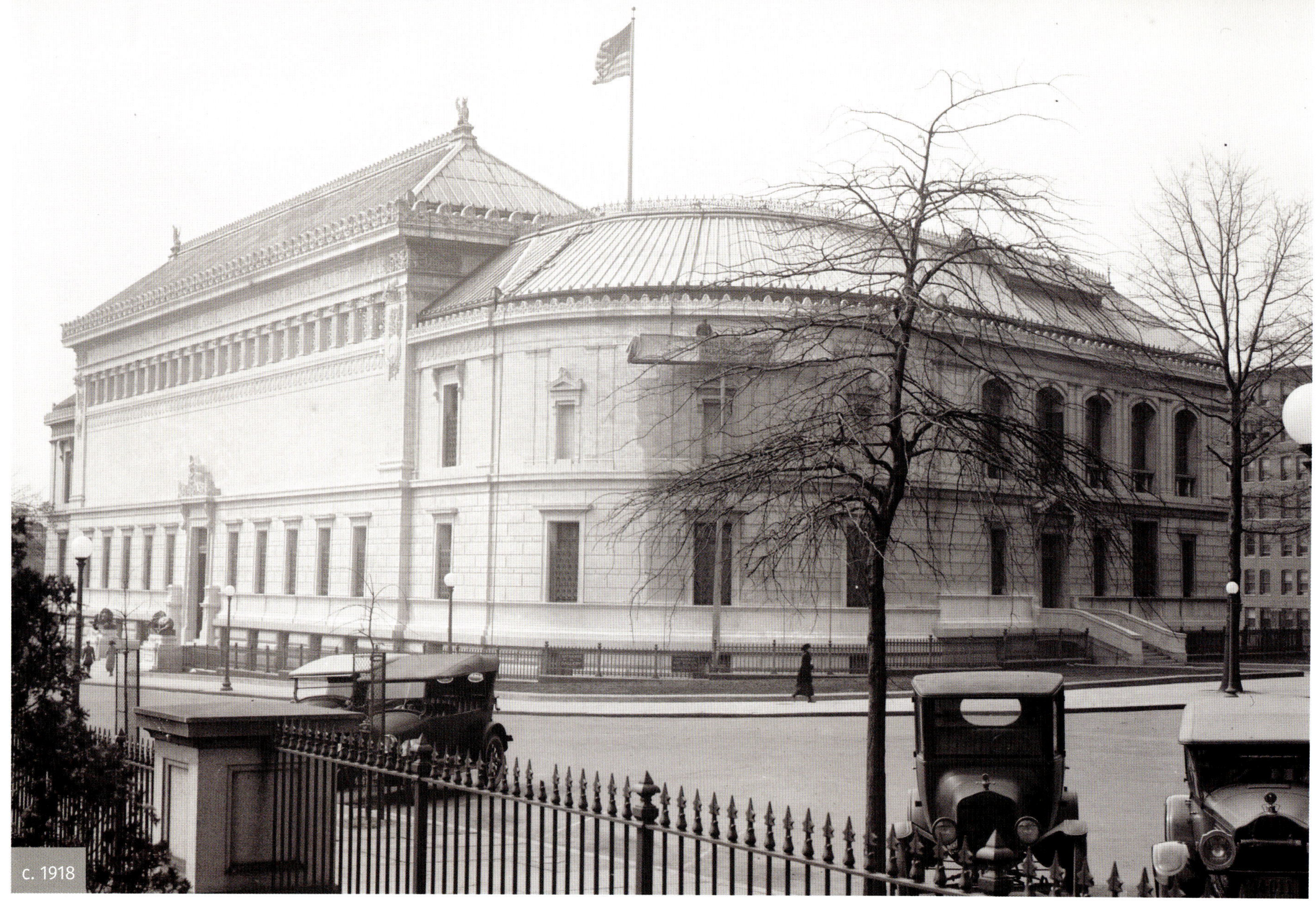
c. 1918

CORCORAN GALLERY OF ART

Accessible art for all

THEN: Washington, D.C. is well known for being the center of America's political life, where decisions for the nation are made and executed. However, Washington has also served its population in a different way, through connecting the public to art. With Corcoran's first gallery becoming such a large success, it soon needed a bigger space to hold the growing collection and large number of visitors. In 1897, a new Beaux-Arts building designed by Ernest Flagg was completed on 17th Street, blocks away from the original gallery space. This new building held the gallery, and an art school that had been developed in the first structure. Corcoran died before he could see this building completed, yet his legacy continued into the next century.

In 1926, the building and collection was expanded even further as it acquired former Senator William A. Clark's collection of European and American art. The Clark Wing was opened in 1928, and included an 18th century French period room called the Salon Doré and the large Rotunda.

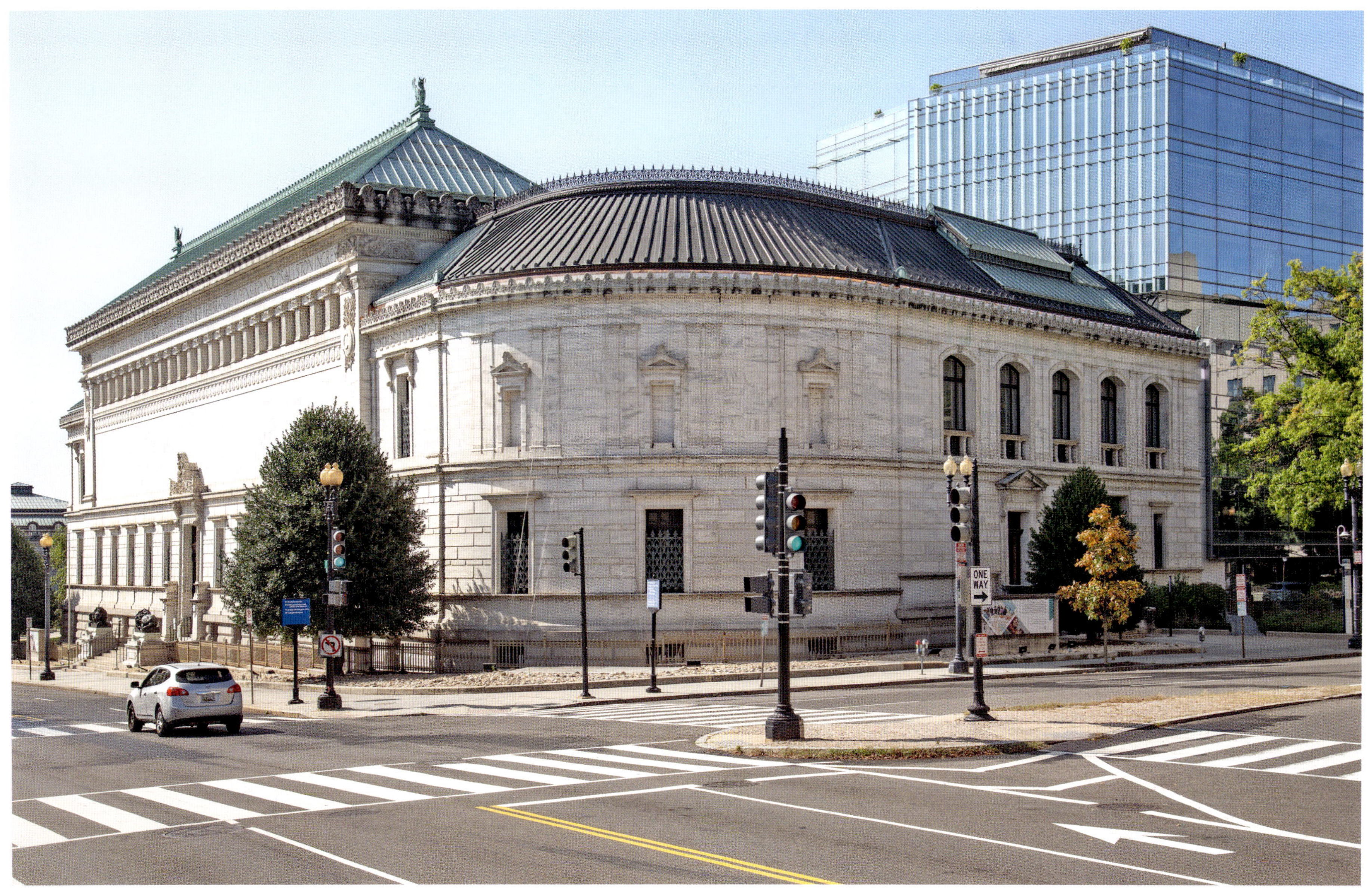

NOW: By the mid-twentieth century, the Corcoran Gallery could not keep up with the increasing competition from new, more popular museums and galleries. Some scholars believed that the museum struggled to connect with Washingtonians and serve intended social functions, from educators and school children to businesspeople and those of different social standing.

After increased leadership turnover and an unsuccessful rebrand as the Corcoran College of Art and Design, the museum and school shut its doors in 2014. The school and building were absorbed by The George Washington University, now forming part of their Columbian College of Arts and Sciences. The university is still committed to maintaining the original Corcoran mission of supporting the arts, and Corcoran's vision of accessible art can be seen across Washington today.

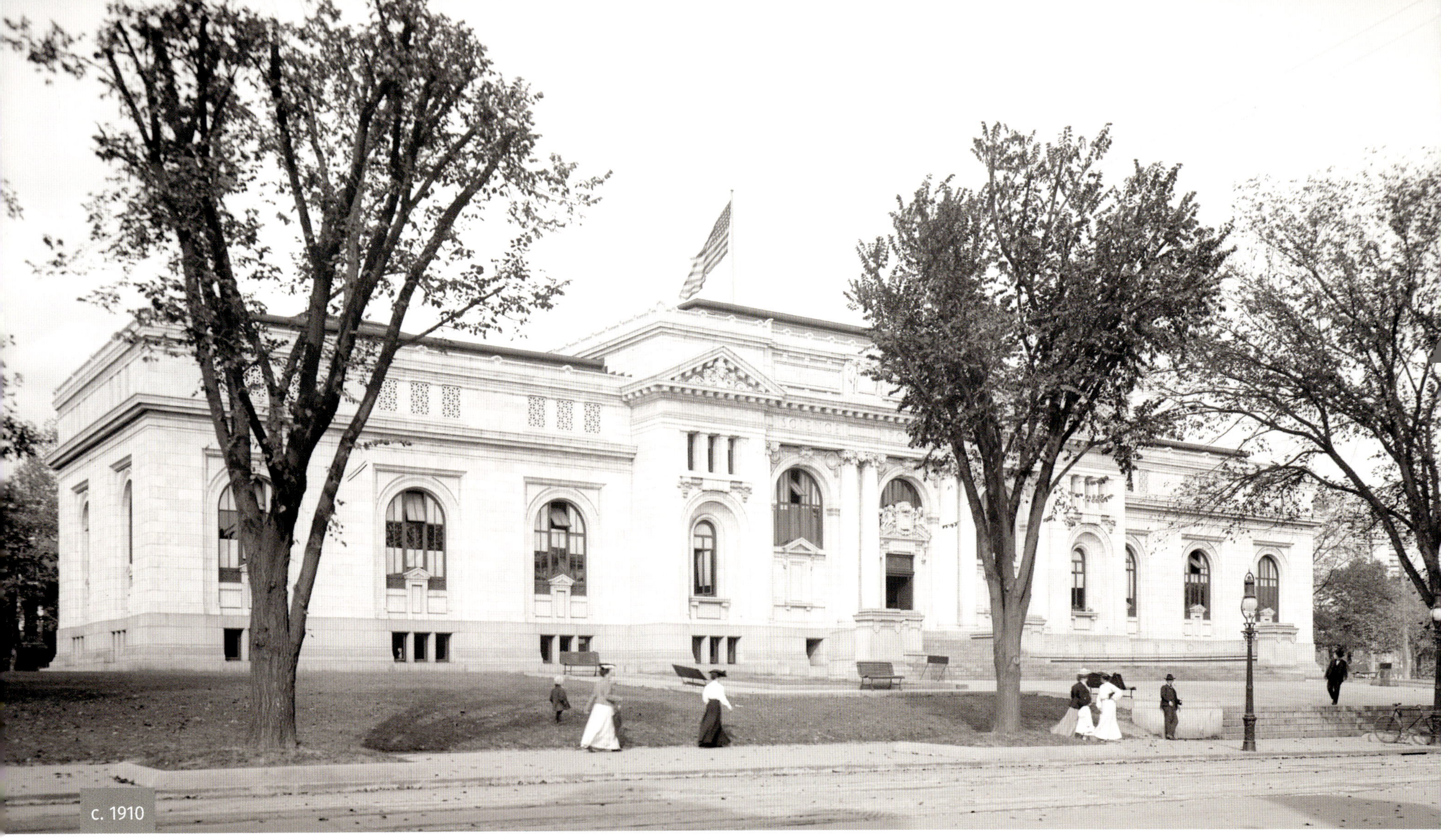
c. 1910

CARNEGIE LIBRARY OF WASHINGTON, D.C.

A library for all in a city that wasn't

THEN: In 1896, Congress signed into law a gift to Washingtonians: a public library system. Located at 1326 New York Avenue NW, the first library in D.C. was humble. Library trustees, such as Brainard Warner, knew that Washington deserved a larger library to serve the growing city, and in 1899 he got his chance to advocate for a new building. During a visit with President Theodore Roosevelt, industrialist and philanthropist Andrew Carnegie ran into the then President of Library Trustees, Brainard Warner on a chance encounter. After their conversation, Carnegie, a long supporter of libraries, agreed to donate $250,000 towards the construction of a new Washington library building.

In 1903, the Washington Public Library was open for business in its new location in the neighborhood then known as Mount Vernon Square. The construction of the Beaux-Arts building came at the time of the "City Beautiful" movement, or the McMillan Plan, where many government and municipal buildings in Washington were designed with classical European influence. Although Carnegie asked not to have the library named after him, Washingtonians have called it the Carnegie Library since its inception. It was a success with the public, and Carnegie continued to fund other sites in Washington including the Takoma Park, Mt. Pleasant and Capitol Hill libraries.

The Washington Public Library, renamed the Central Public Library when the Takoma Park location was built in 1911, introduced a new experience to Washingtonians.

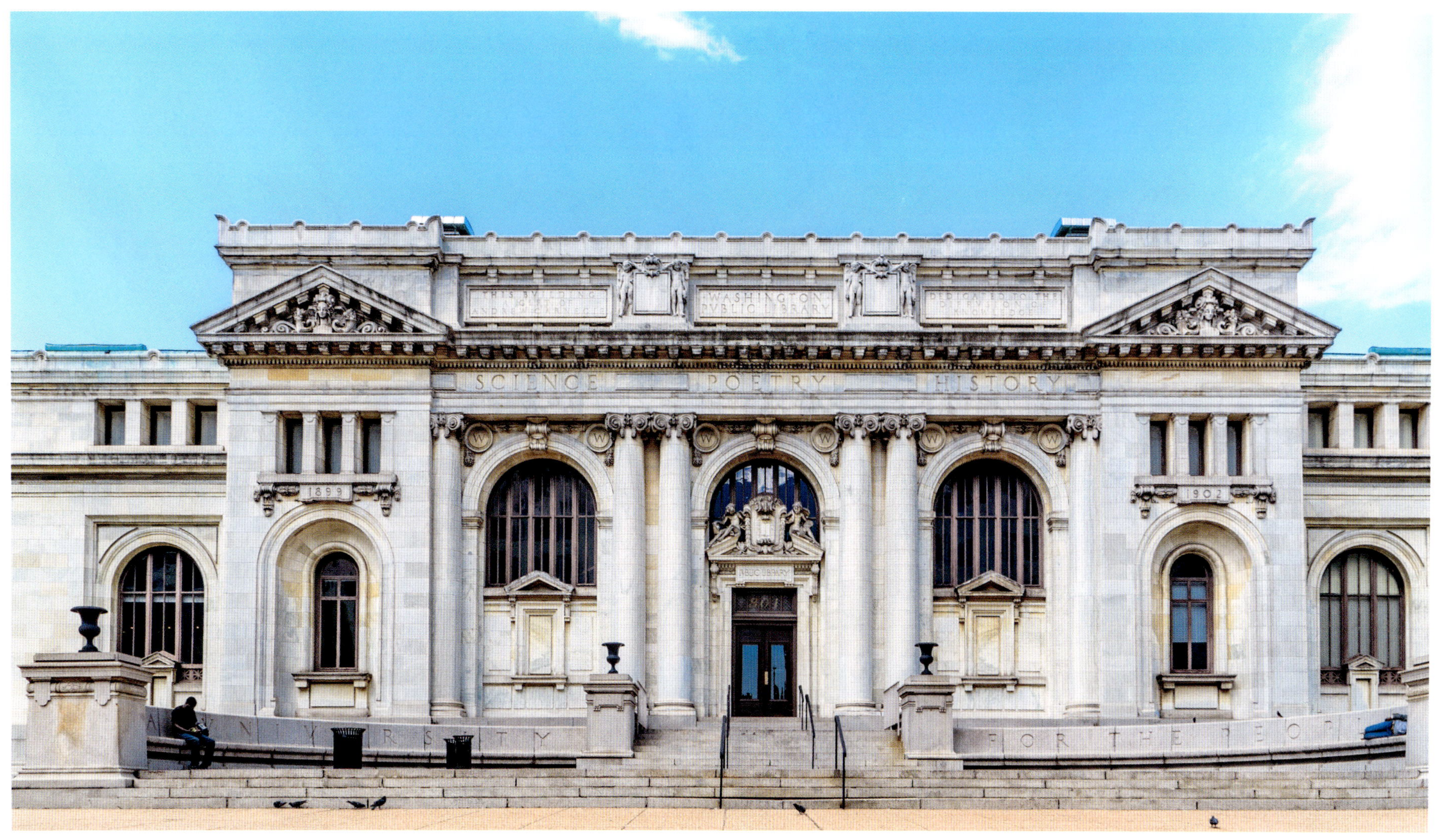

The library initially opened as a closed-stack institution, where librarians would retrieve all the books for patrons ahead of opening, but progressed to utilize the newer open shelf system for public access.

The Central library was unique for its time as it was open for all residents of Washington. In the early twentieth century, D.C. was home to an expanding middle-class of Black residents, however the city was still deeply affected by segregation. In a heavily segregated city, the D.C. Central Library would not follow precedent, and did not divide their spaces or services based on race. The library was accessible to predominantly Black neighborhoods in Washington, making it a welcome space for the Black community, when much of Washington still was not.

NOW: Due to the immediate success of the Central Library, trustees knew that it would need to expand. Library employees were unhappy with their cramped working conditions, and in 1972 the library got a new home at 9th and G Streets NW, which was later renamed the Martin Luther King Jr. Library.

The former Carnegie building sat unused for years, changing owners before it eventually housed the Historical Society of Washington, D.C. In 2011, the lease was transferred to Events D.C. who worked with the D.C. History Center (formerly the Historical Society) and Apple Inc. to restore it. The building now houses an Apple Store and the D.C. History Center, so continues to serve the Washington public, albeit in a quite different way.

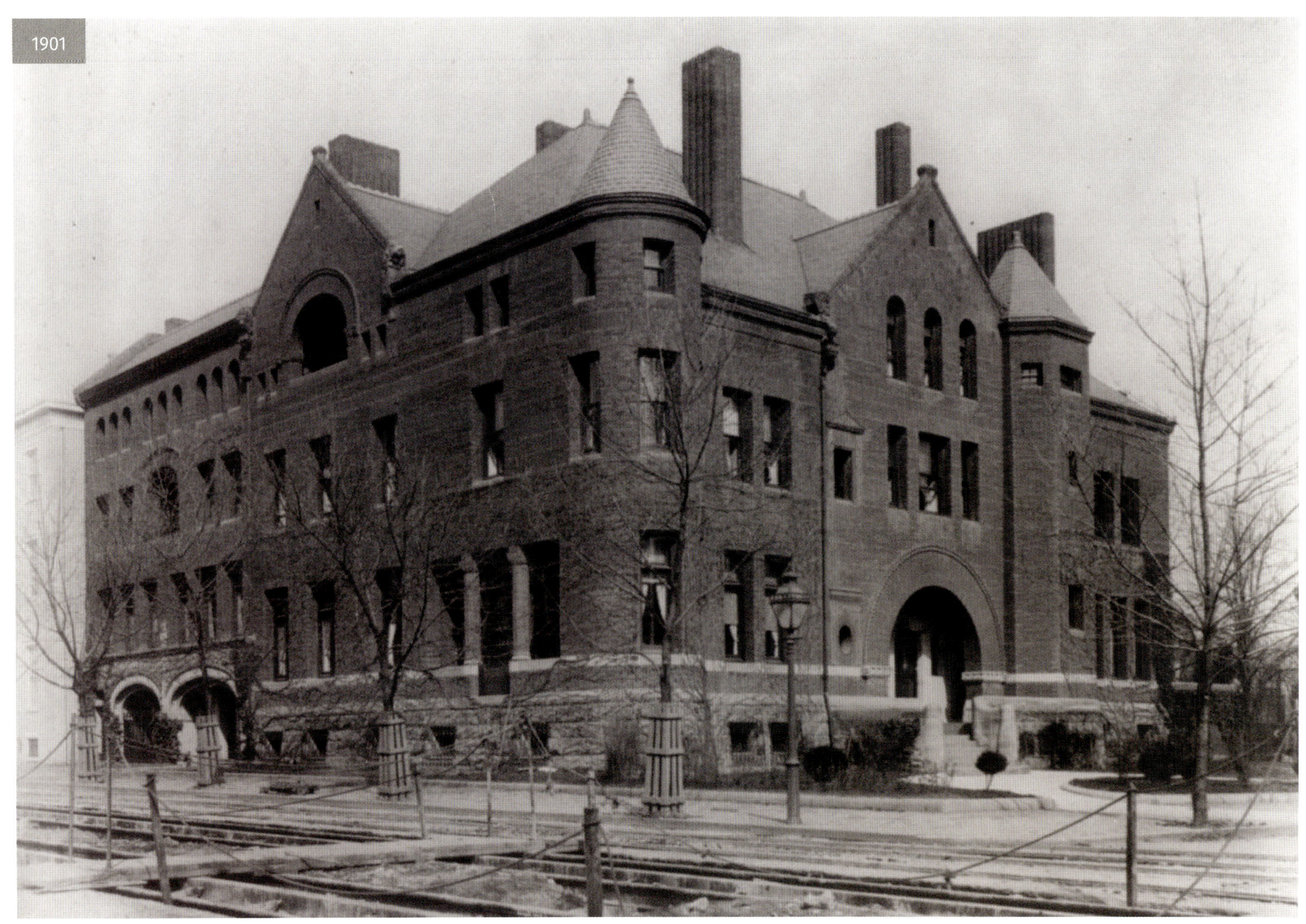
1901

HAY-ADAMS RESIDENCE

A destination for D.C.'s socialites

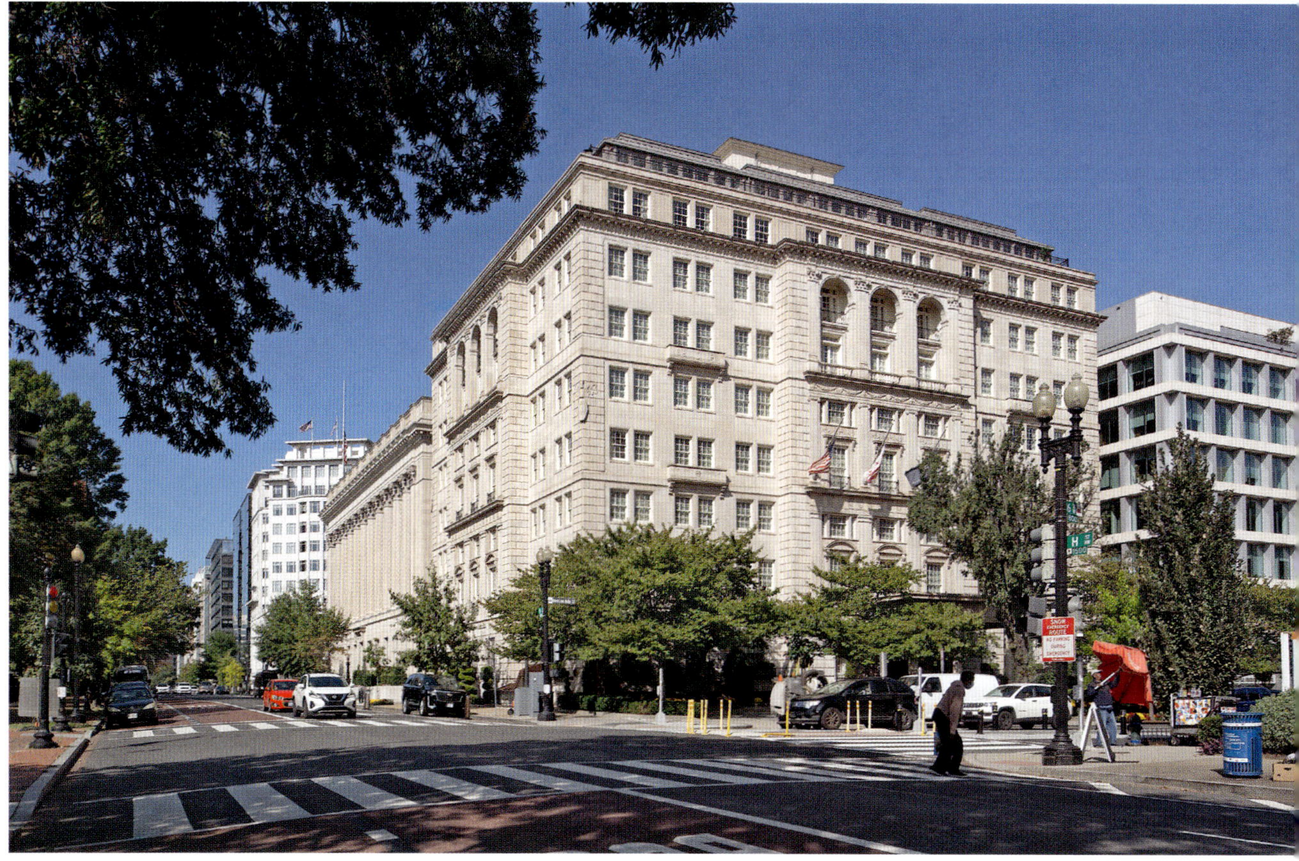

THEN: Following his time in Massachusetts, historian and Harvard professor Henry Adams and his wife Marian "Clover" Adams made their way to Washington. Adams was the descendant of two former presidents, John Adams and John Quincy Adams, and the couple became active members of Washington's social scene. As they became settled in the city, the Adamses decided to build a new home, in proximity to the White House, thus ensuring their connection to the political and social happenings of the area.

At the same time, their close friends John and Clara Hay were also looking to build a home, and purchased a plot of land on 16th and H Street right next to Adamses. The couples were notoriously close, and the four of them, along with geologist Clarence King, formed a tight-knit group. They called themselves the "Five of Hearts" and even had custom china and a letterhead made up with their self-proclaimed title. With the tight-knit nature of the Hays and Adamses, and their mutual need for a new home, they decided to commission the construction of two homes that shared a single facade.

In 1884, architect Henry Hobson Richardson designed an elaborate Romanesque building that housed two separate homes. However in 1885, just weeks before the homes were completed, Clover died. Despite speculation about the strength of their connection, Henry Adams was seemingly distraught following his wife's death and maintained his move into the recently completed home "to save what remained of life." His house was considered to be humble in its design and did not reflect an elaborate taste whereas the Hays' home was notably more formal, serving its intended purpose of entertainment. The couple hosted vibrant discussions of all topics; from art and literature to science and politics. The guests who participated ranged in background, and included famous artist Augustus Saint-Gaudens, novelist Mark Twain, and even former President Theodore Roosevelt.

NOW: The Hays and Henry Adams enjoyed their joint home until all three had passed in the early twentieth century. Alice Wadsworth, daughter of the Hays, inherited her parents' home and purchased Henry Adams's residence following his death in 1918. She leased the home to the Brazilian Embassy, however the two buildings were eventually purchased by a Washington developer and razed. In its place, an Italian Renaissance style hotel was constructed in 1928, which repurposed some design aspects from the Hay-Adams home such as its wood paneling. The hotel has hosted many notable guests throughout history such as Amelia Earhart, Sinclair Lewis, and the Obamas. Called the Hay-Adams Hotel today, the building maintains the glitzy and welcoming spirit the four friends intended with their joint home.

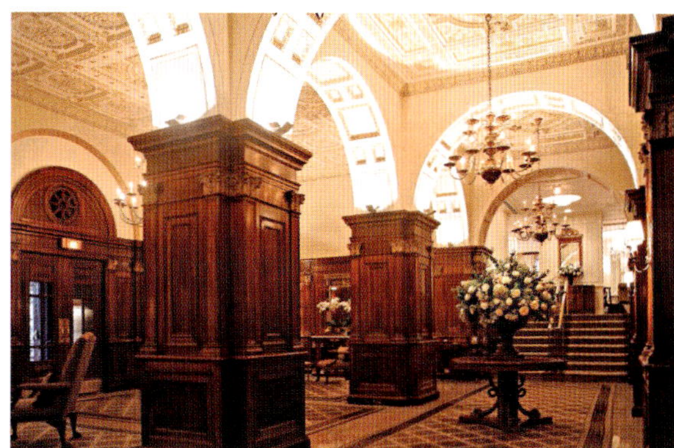

ABOVE: While Clover did not get to enjoy the joint residence in its totality during her lifetime, some guests of the Hay-Adams Hotel claim to sense her spirit on the haunted site of what would have been her home.

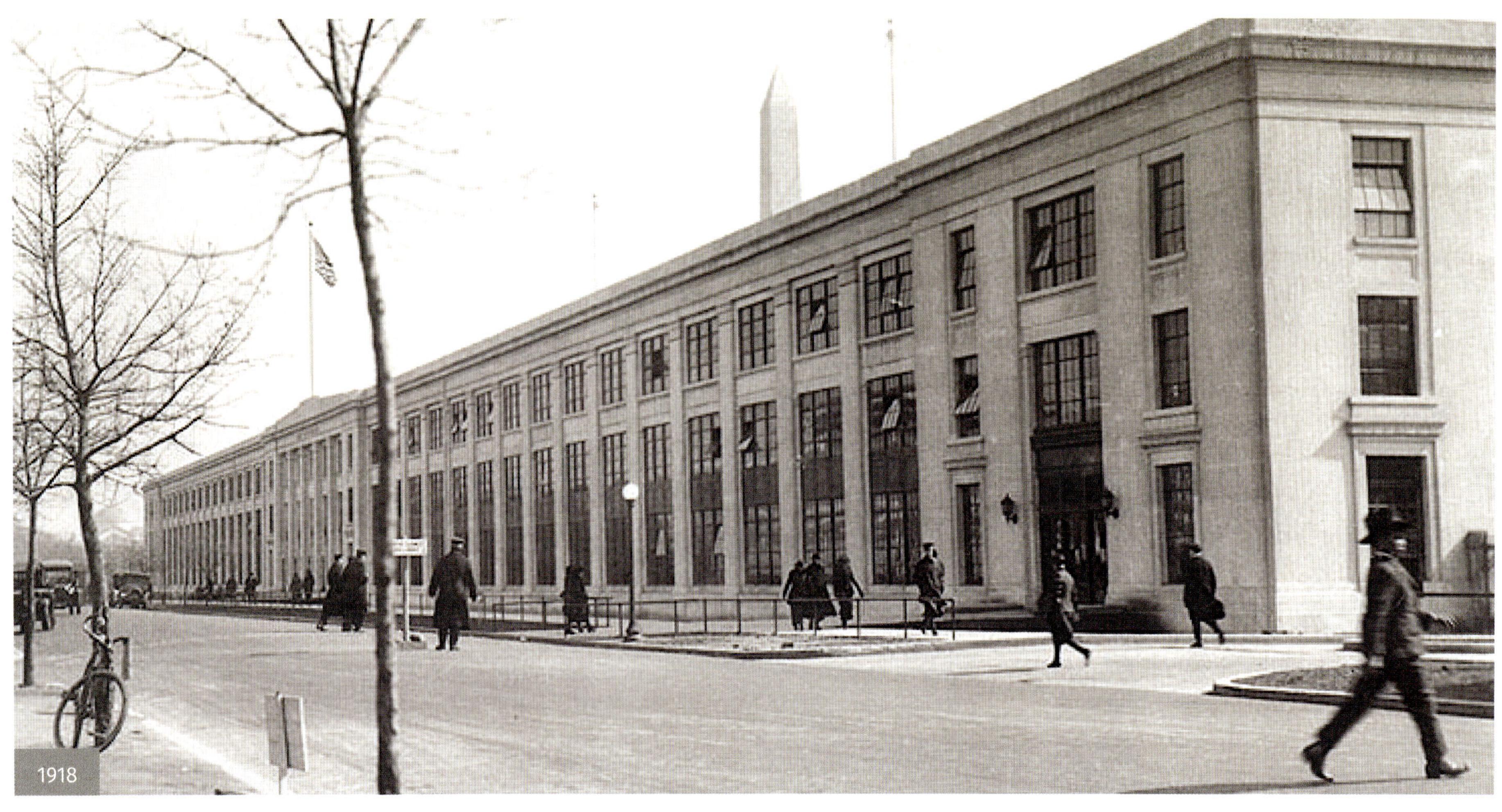
1918

MAIN NAVY AND MUNITIONS BUILDING

A military command center which overstayed its welcome

THEN: Throughout the twentieth century, the United States participated in several military endeavors, including two World Wars. These conflicts directly affected the Washington landscape and population. Throughout the late nineteenth century, the nation's military command struggled to find a permanent residence as its branches grew and the demands of the military changed. In 1918, along Constitution Avenue stretching from 17th St and 21 St NW, the Main Navy and Munitions Buildings were constructed. These were two different buildings, each hosting several different wings that were connected by a covered bridge. The buildings' office space was only occupied for a few months before World War I ended, however at that point 14,000 navy, army, and civilian personnel worked inside its concrete structure. The navy's high command held their offices here, including the Secretary of the Navy and the Chief of Naval Operations.

When the war ended, the question arose whether these buildings were permanent or temporary. In 1923, the former Assistant Secretary of the Navy who had advocated for the buildings, Franklin Delano Roosevelt, believed they took away from the beauty of the National Mall. Alternately, the navy, previously having offices spread throughout the city, was finally working from a cohesive command center. The future of these "tempos," as they were called for their original non-permanent nature, became

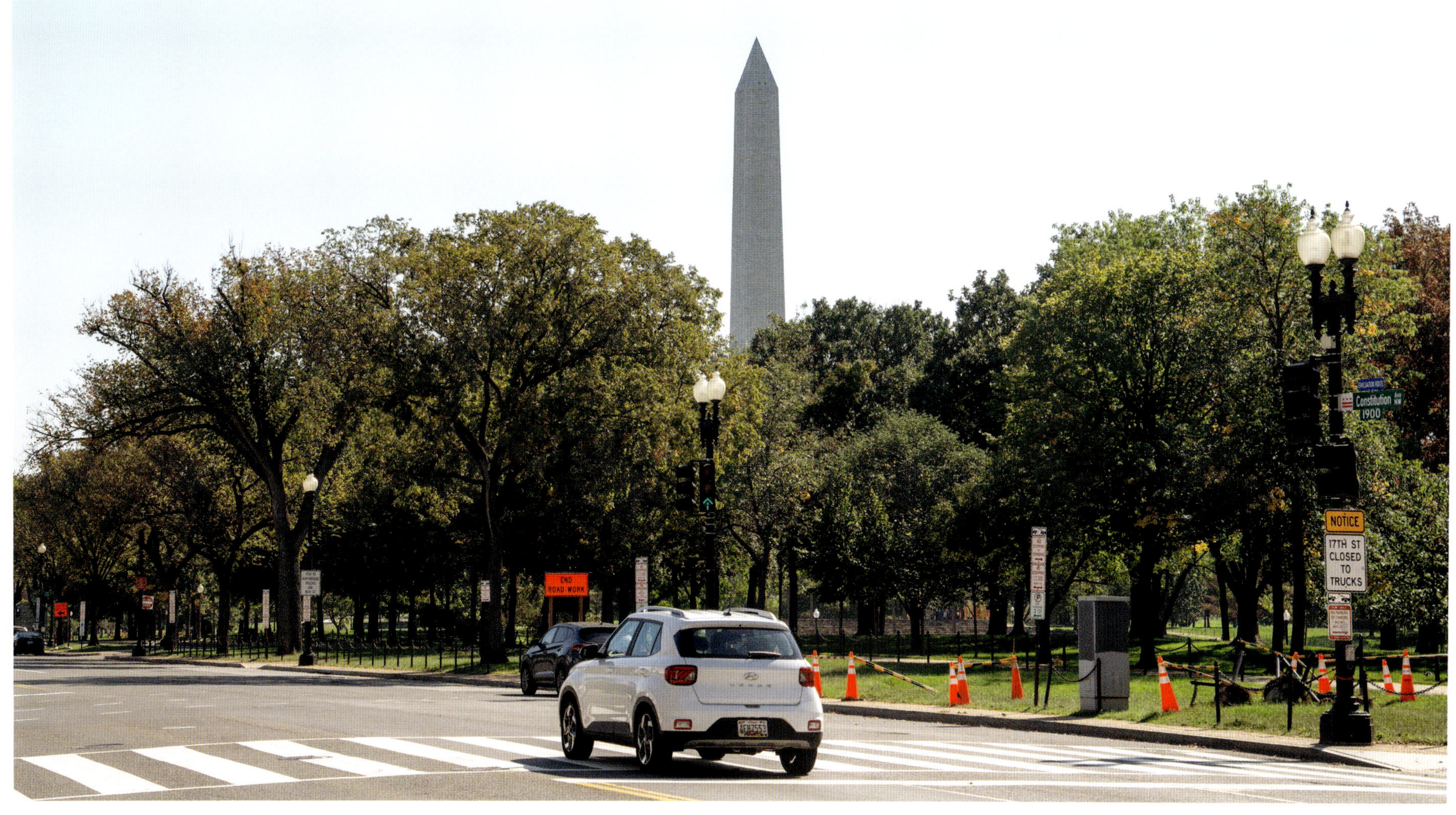

even more unclear with the beginning of World War II. Along with the Main Navy and Munitions buildings from 1918, a new collection of tempos was added to support the war effort. These structures cut through the National Mall on the grounds surrounding the Washington Monument and the buildings were swiftly filled by new government personnel.

During World War II, another temporary building for military command was created, however this one became a mainstay for the military and the surrounding area: the Pentagon. With construction complete in 1943, the Pentagon was created to provide additional office space for military personnel during World War II, however, in the years following the war many of those who worked in the tempos on the mall were moved to the Pentagon, in what eventually became the Department of Defense.

NOW: With the two World Wars in Washington's past, the future of the tempos on the Mall was once again brought into question. The tempos constructed during World War II, which divided the National Mall, were razed in the early 1960s and the park land that connects the Lincoln Memorial to the Washington Monument was finally restored. The Main Navy and Munitions Buildings, although threatened for the entirety of their existence, were not torn down until President Nixon ordered their destruction in 1970. In place of these buildings, and what was once a bustling center of military activity sits the peaceful Constitution Gardens, added for the United States' Bicentennial.

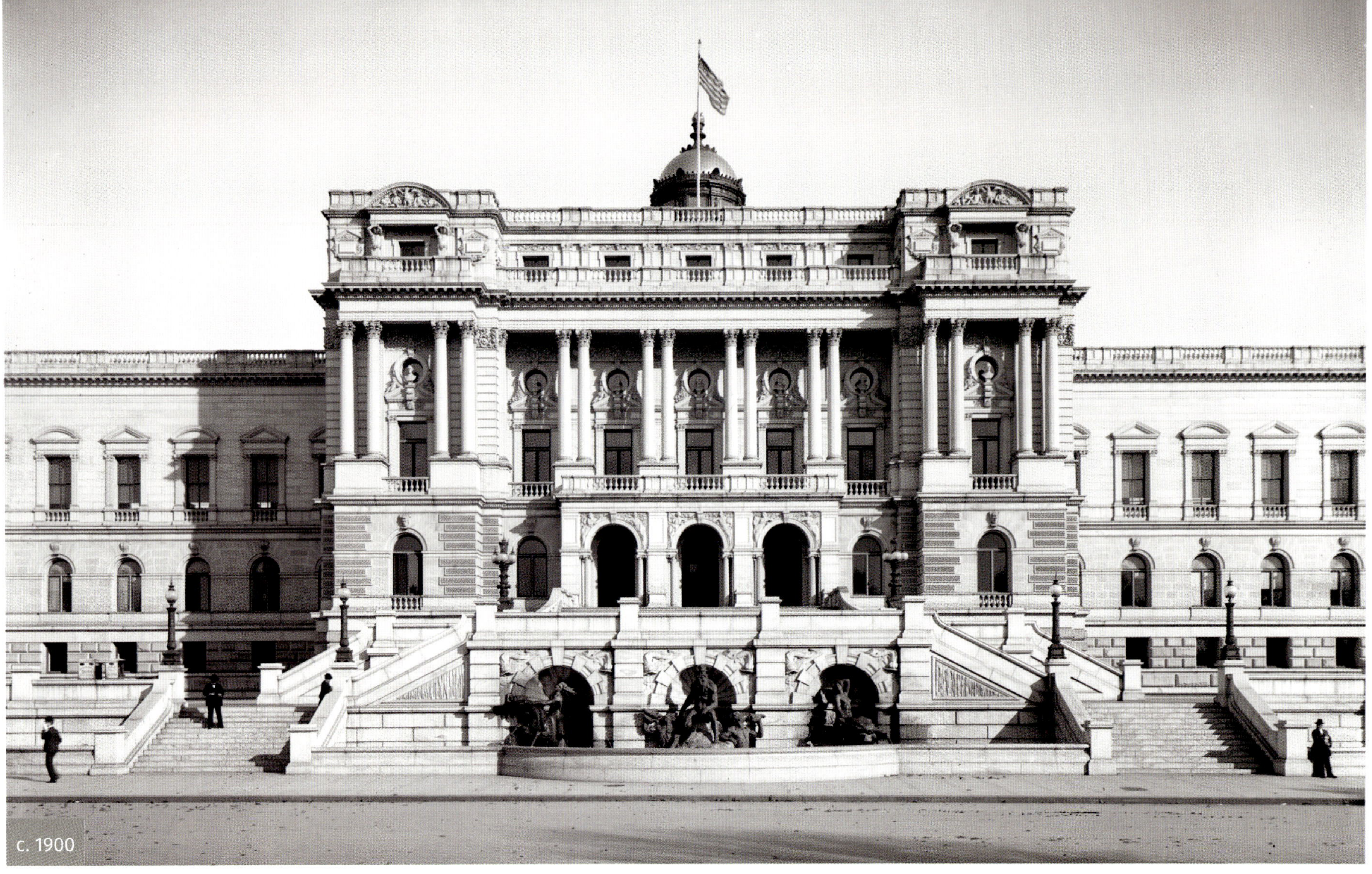
c. 1900

THE LIBRARY OF CONGRESS

A library for all of America

THEN: In the year 1800, Washington received its official title as the capital city of the United States, and the home of the "new national government." As they established themselves in the federal city, Congress requested $5,000 in funds to be used for Congressional books. This was the start of the Library of Congress.

The Library of Congress, having a primarily legislative purpose in its earliest years, was originally housed in the U.S. Capitol building for easy congressional access. Unfortunately, the collection of 3,000 books met an early demise in 1814, when British soldiers invaded Washington and set the new capital ablaze, taking the library's contents with it. Instead of rebuilding their collection book by book, the Library received a generous offer from a man in retirement. Former President Thomas Jefferson. Jefferson offered to sell his personal collection of over 6,000 books to the library for $23,950, and in 1815 Congress agreed. His collection was extensive with works that focused on history, the arts, science, economics, and more. These volumes also varied in their language, with books in German, Spanish, French, and Russian. Jefferson's donation not only doubled the library that had been lost but also introduced an expansive world view to the Congressional collection.

Although a new international perspective was injected to the Library with Jefferson's collection, it was not until after the Civil War that it was incorporated into the staff's collecting policies. Throughout the mid-nineteenth century, many members of Congress believed that the library should be limited to national participation,

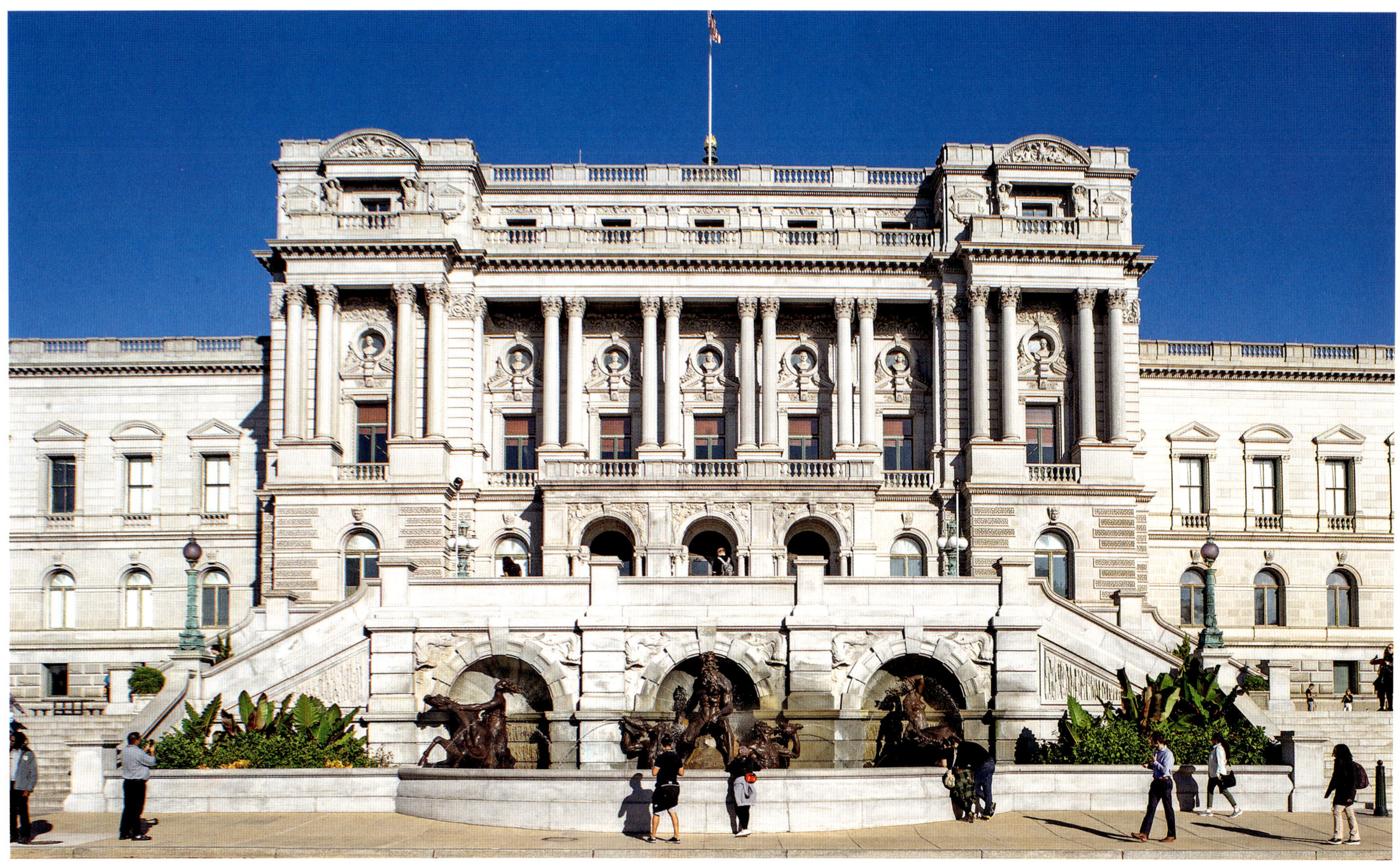

primarily collecting American materials that would be useful to the U.S. Congress. This perspective changed with the Librarian of Congress' Ainsworth Rand Spofford administration of 1864-1897. Spofford advocated for the library to increase its collection of international works and centralized U.S. copyright activities to the library, expanding the collection from books to include artifacts such as copyrighted musical compositions, photographs, and maps. Using Jefferson's rhetoric, Spofford pushed for Congress to see its previously small collection as one of national significance.

Spofford's term also saw the construction of the Library of Congress Building, now the Thomas Jefferson Building, as the new home for the rapidly growing collection, as pictured here. Built in 1897 in a Beaux-Arts style by several architects in its eleven-year construction, the Library's new home was close to Congress for legislative needs, and also served as the American public's national library.

Continued...

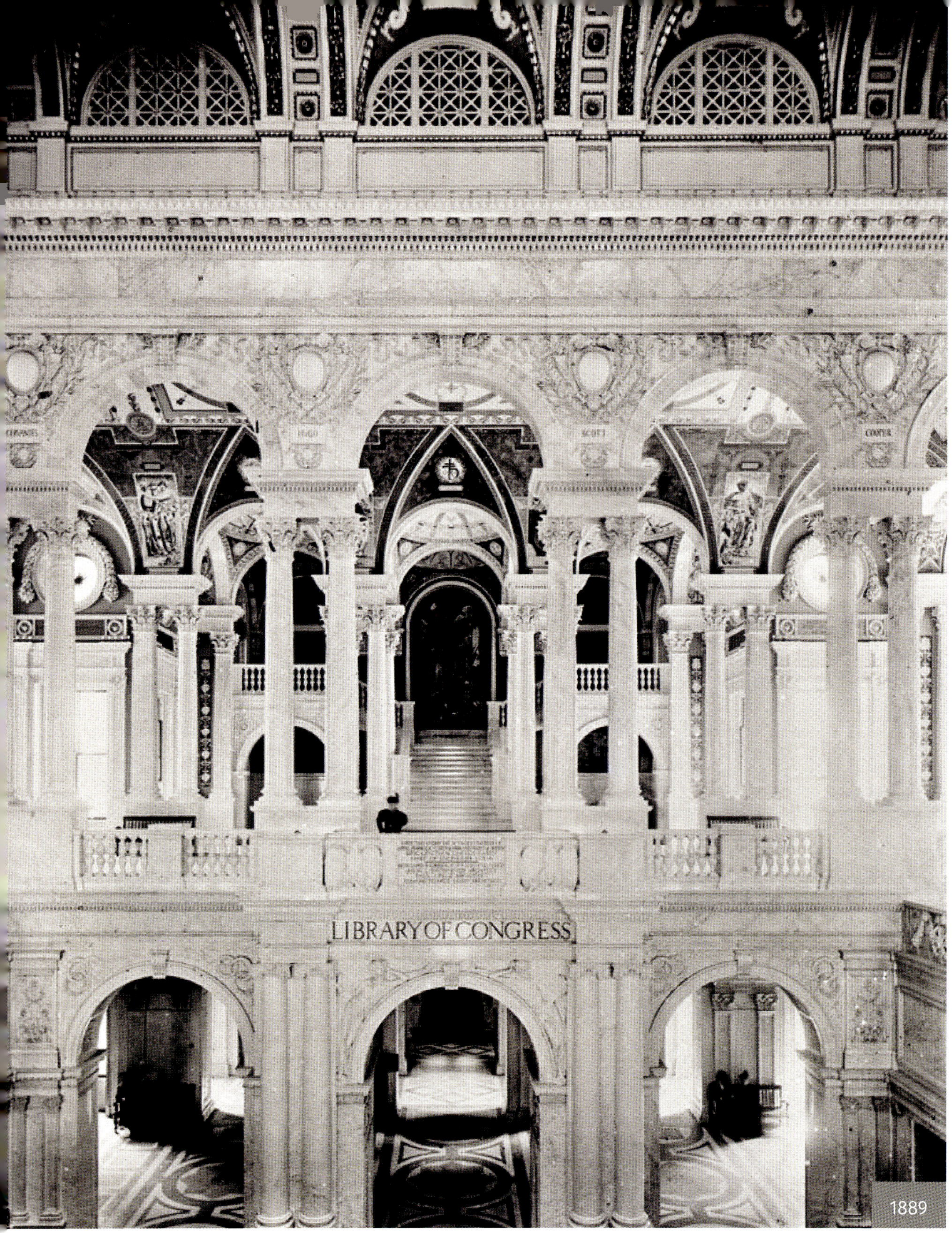

THE LIBRARY OF CONGRESS

A library for all of America

THEN: Other Librarians of Congress, such as Herbert Putnam who served from 1899-1939, continued to expand the library's international collection, actively reaching out and using the library's funds to purchase foreign works. As the library's collection grew, so did its physical space in Washington; the building now known as the John Adams Building opened to the public in 1939. World War II added a sense of urgency and significance to preserving the library's artifacts of international significance as Librarians of Congress saw the importance of these documents supporting visiting researchers. One of the library's largest periods of expansion, both nationally and internationally, was throughout the 1950s to the 1970s as global networks increased with technological advancements.

BELOW: The Main Reading Room, with its circular reference desk and corresponding researcher tables, is a long standing fixture at the Library of Congress.

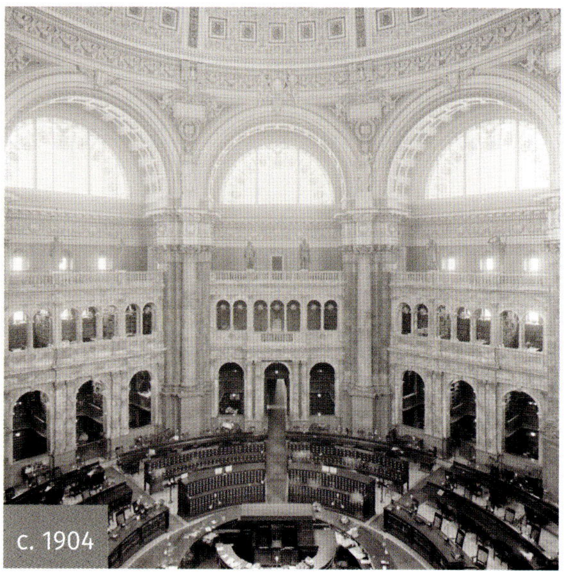

NOW: In 1980, the Library of Congress added a third building to Capitol Hill, the James Madison Memorial Building. The library now boasts over 164 million items in its collection, spanning multiple centuries, formats of expression, languages and various subjects. Recognized as the largest library in the world, the Library of Congress still serves its original purpose of supporting the United States Congress but has also developed a new role throughout its expansive history – as the national library for the United States. Today visitors can tour its museum and gallery spaces, and those doing research can procure a free library card and grab a chair in their Main Reading Room.

RIGHT: The Great Hall is stately and grand in its design, representing works from almost fifty American painters and sculptors. A showcase of American achievement, the Great Hall also ties these achievements with references to ancient classical thought leaders and styles.

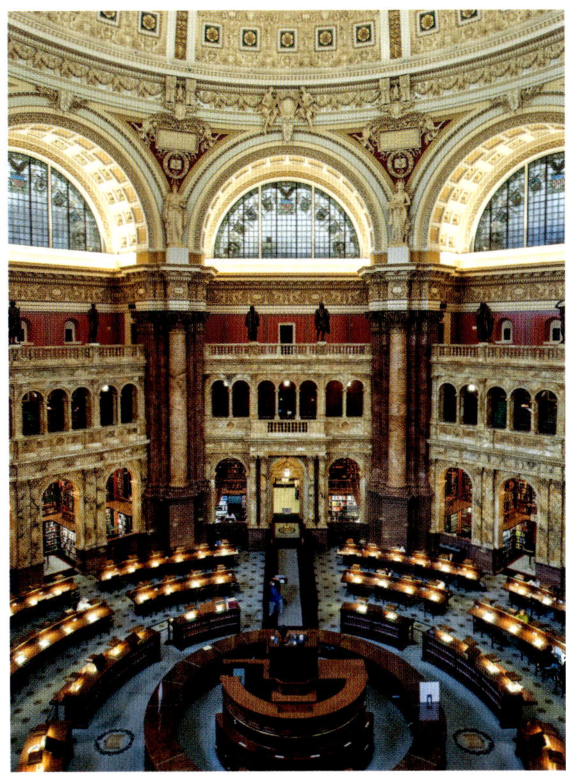

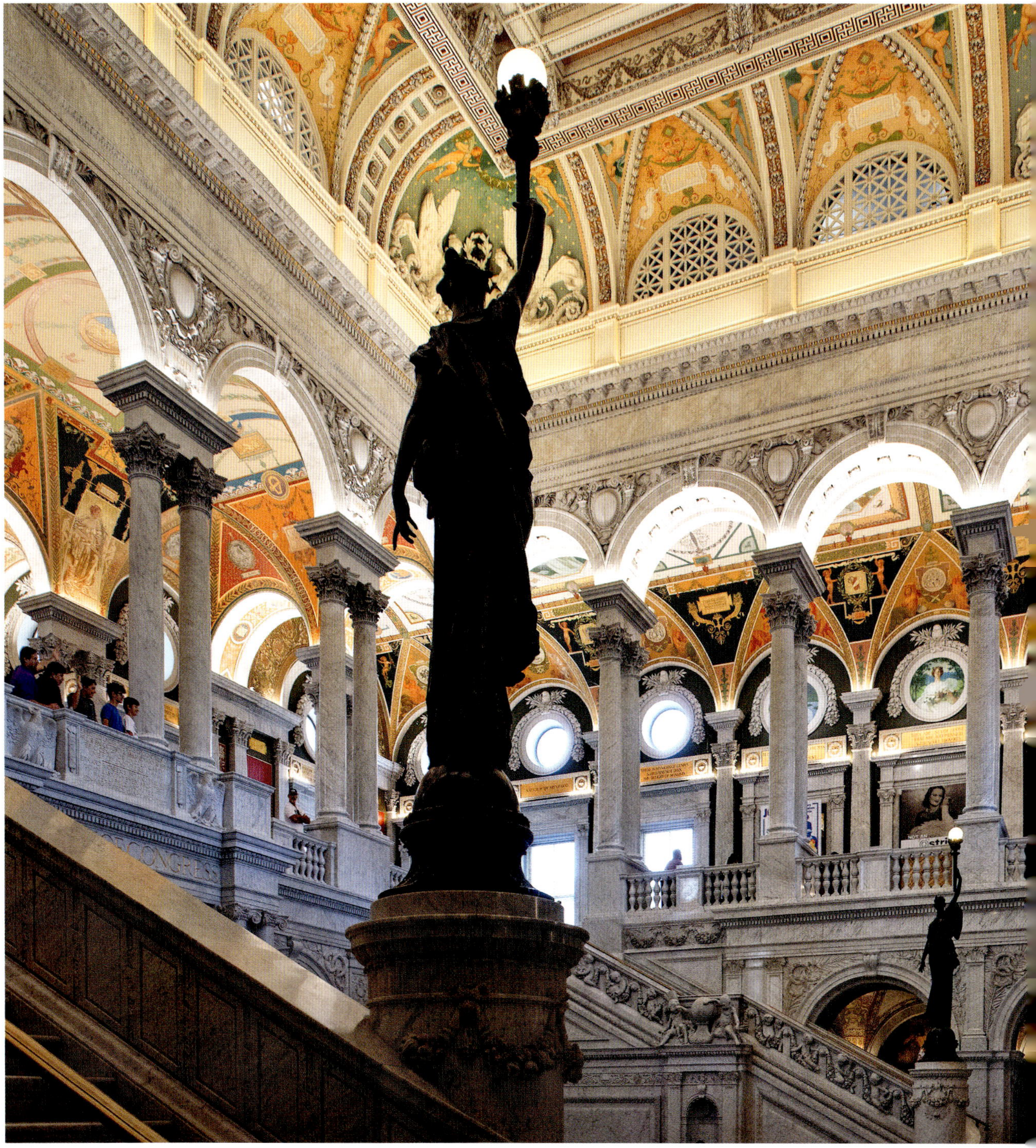

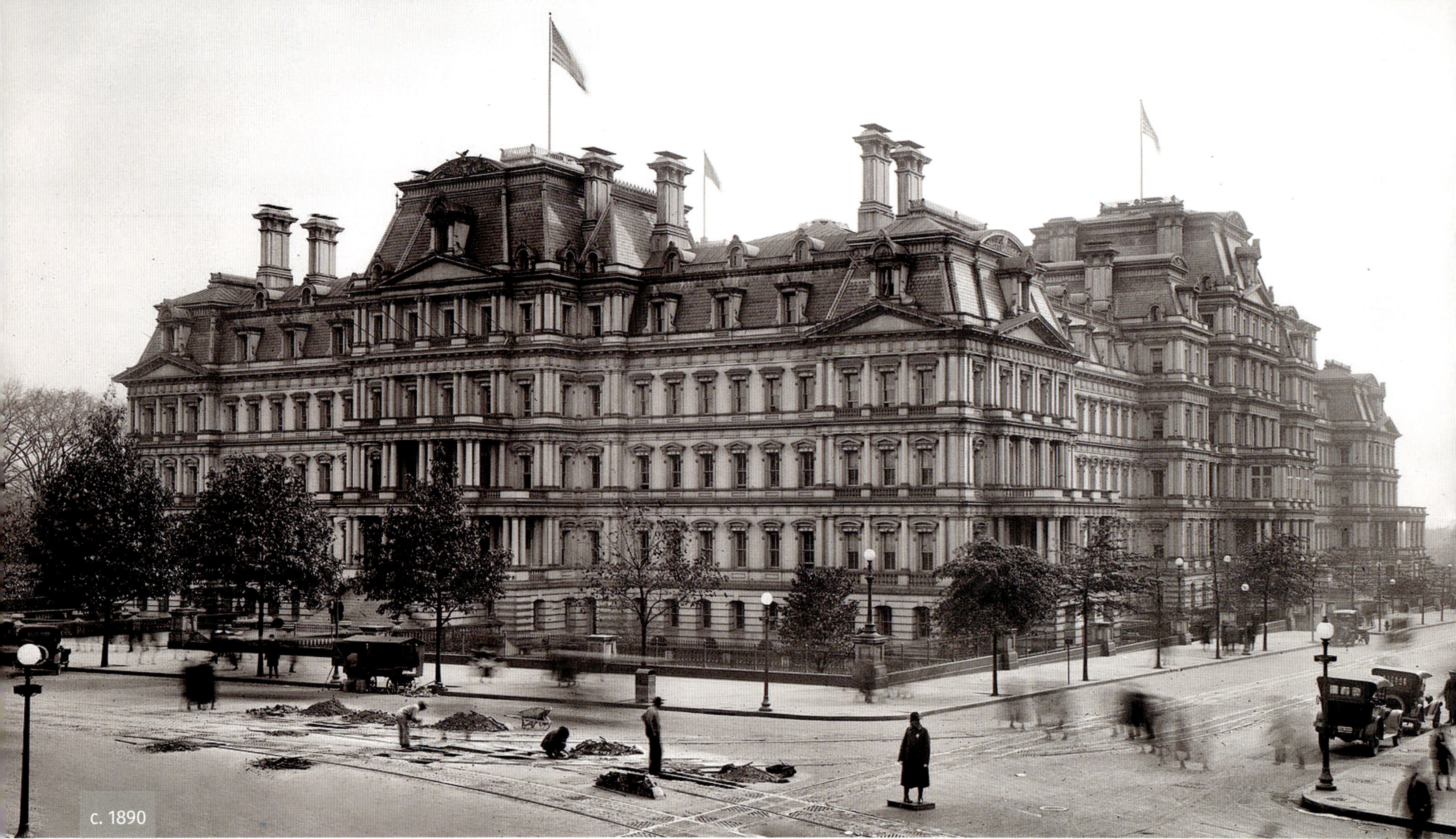
c. 1890

STATE, WAR AND NAVY BUILDING

"The greatest monstrosity in America"

THEN: In 1870, the Department of State was in desperate need of a new office building. For three years prior, the department had been working out of the Washington City Orphan Asylum Building however due to high rent and lack of space for the growing staff, a commission of six members was appointed by Congress to find the department a new home. The group decided that the new government office should be near Lafayette or Scott Square and settled on a plot of land for the new building just west of the Executive Mansion. They faced only one problem: there were already active government offices there. The Old War Building and the Old Navy Building occupied this land, although these two offices were also facing issues of overcrowding. Secretary of State Albert Fish proposed an idea; one building that was not just for the Department of State, but for the War and Navy Departments as well.

Construction on the new building, designed by Alfred B. Mullet, began in 1871. The erection of this French Renaissance style building was unique in that it was constructed wing by wing which allowed the Old War and Old Navy Buildings to stay in use during construction. Its elaborate structure took seventeen years to build, with the Department of State occupying their section in 1875, to the relief of federal employees. The War and Navy Departments moved into the building in 1879, and each department finally had their own part of the large structure. By 1888 and around $10 million later, the new building was fully occupied.

By the early twentieth century the Department of State once again found themselves with not enough space. In 1918, the Navy Department building moved out and the bureaus of the Department of State were reunited in the grand building

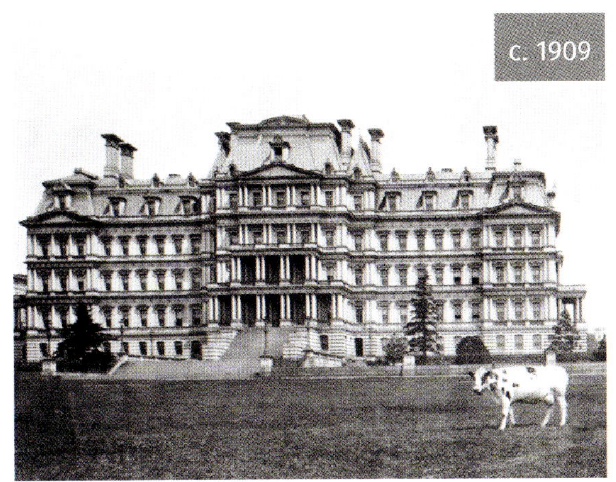

ABOVE: The State, War, and Navy Building would sometimes attract visitors that were less diplomatic in nature, including President William Howard Taft's beloved cow, Pauline Wayne.

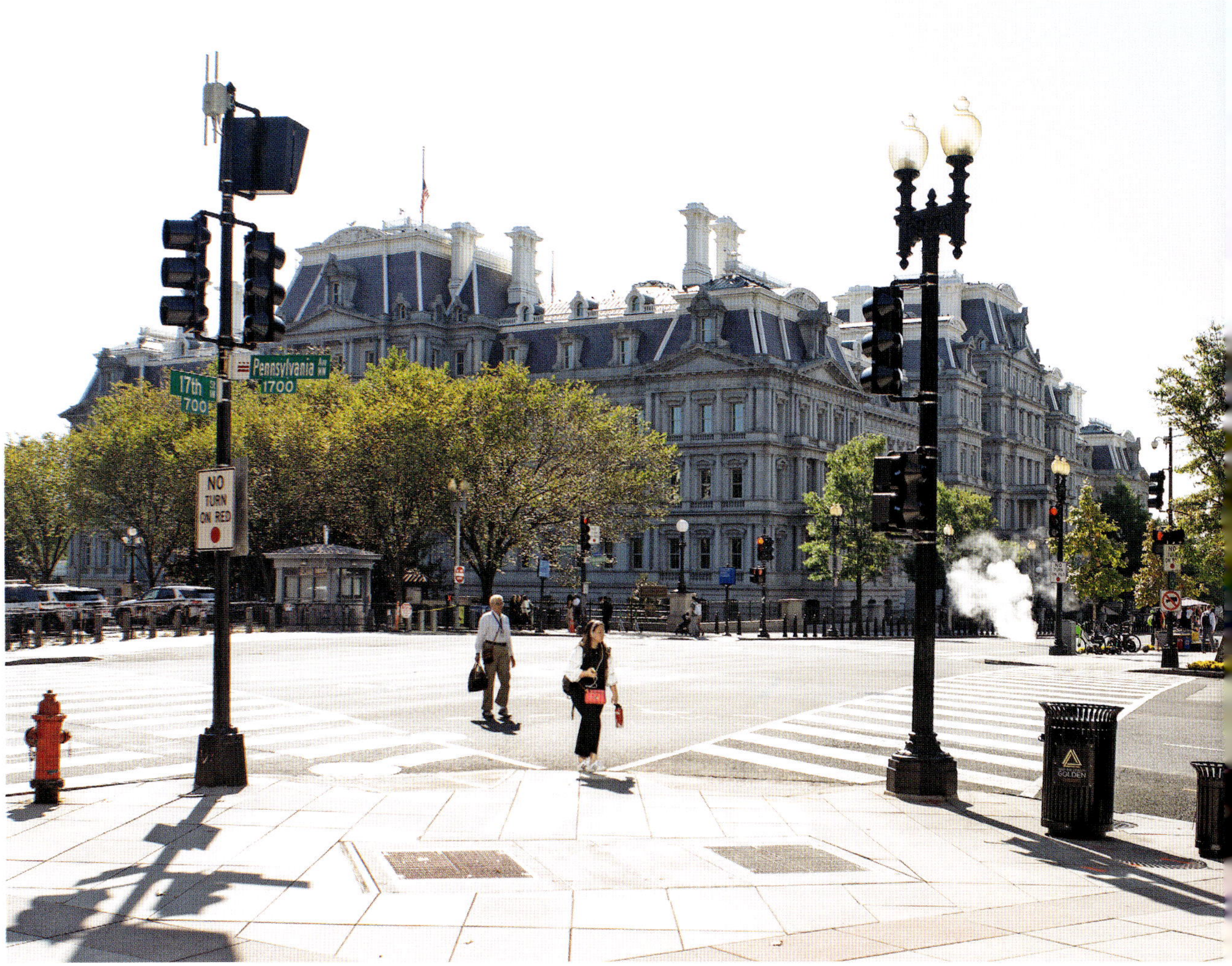

again. The Department of State's time in the building ended formally in 1947, as the demand of World War II increased their original staff from fifty-five to over 7,000 employees. The War Department faced similar issues and moved into the Munitions Building on Constitution Ave in 1938.

The large rectangular building, six stories high and with two interior courts, had been built in the elaborate French Renaissance style which was now an unwelcome reminder of past architectural preferences that were no longer popular. By the mid-twentieth century the building with its purple-gray Virginia granite walls and slate mansard roof was destined for demolition.

NOW: Many came to the defense of the building, including President Truman, who affectionately called it "the greatest monstrosity in America." This public opposition paired with the huge cost of tearing the building down prevented its destruction. In 1949 the building was turned over to the Executive Office of the President and renamed the Executive Office Building. It is now called the Dwight D. Eisenhower Executive Office Building, and continues to house various executive agencies, including the Office of the Vice President and the National Security Council.

THE WHITE HOUSE

The President's Home, and one for the People's Protests

THEN: In Pierre Charles L'Enfant's 1790 plan for Washington, he detailed wide avenues, a lush green space, and the location of important federal buildings. One of these buildings is the most recognizable in Washington: The White House. L'Enfant designed the District in good time, as there was still a decade before Washington would officially become the capital city in 1800. However, Washington wanted to be ready for its new government and leadership, and began construction on the Executive Mansion only a year after L'Enfant announced his plan in 1792.

Despite his oversight of the project, President George Washington would never live in the mansion himself, as it was completed in 1800. Designed by James Hoban, an Irish-American architect, the building had a neo-classical design similar to many other seen in the early plans for D.C. Eager to live in the Executive Estate, President John Adams and his wife moved into the unfinished building in 1800. The President's House finally had its first resident and federal work in Washington could now begin in earnest.

The work of the executive came to a screeching halt in 1814. America was deep in conflict with the British during the War of 1812, and the British invaded the young capital city, attempting to burn all buildings of significance; including the President's House. President James Madison and his wife Dolley were residents at the time and were forced to flee the building, but not before saving some of America's most precious heirlooms, such as a framed portrait of George Wasington rescued by

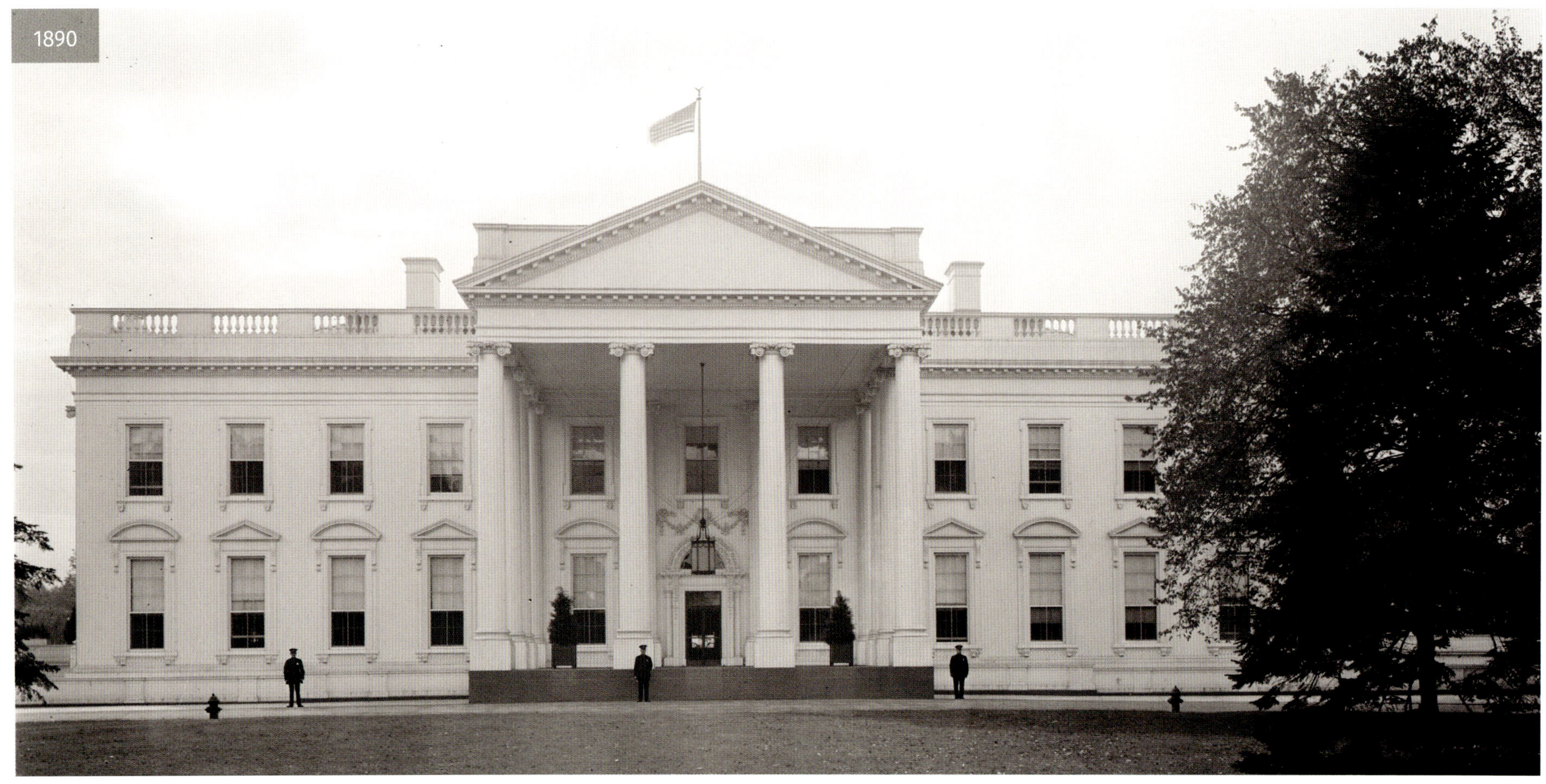
1890

Dolley on her way out. Architect James Hoban was once again tasked with the reconstruction of the President's House, which saw its next presidential residence of James Monroe in 1817.

As one of the oldest federal buildings in Washington, the White House required frequent maintenance and updates. During President Theodore Roosevelt's time in office, he moved the President's offices from the second floor to the Residence, where the President now lives, and constructed the West Wing, where White House staffers work. It was also during Roosevelt's presidency that the building garnered its current name, "The White House."

NOW: Since its inception, the White House has been the site of political activism attempting to earn the attention of the President. For much of its life, the White House has been open to the public, who were invited to attend inaugural celebrations and greeted by the President. Today, the site continues to host visitors attempting to catch a glimpse of the President as well as foreign dignitaries on state visits. On any given day, visitors may see staffers walking to their offices, reporters using the Executive Mansion as a backdrop for their stories, and eighth graders learning about one of the most contentious and famed branches of the United States government.

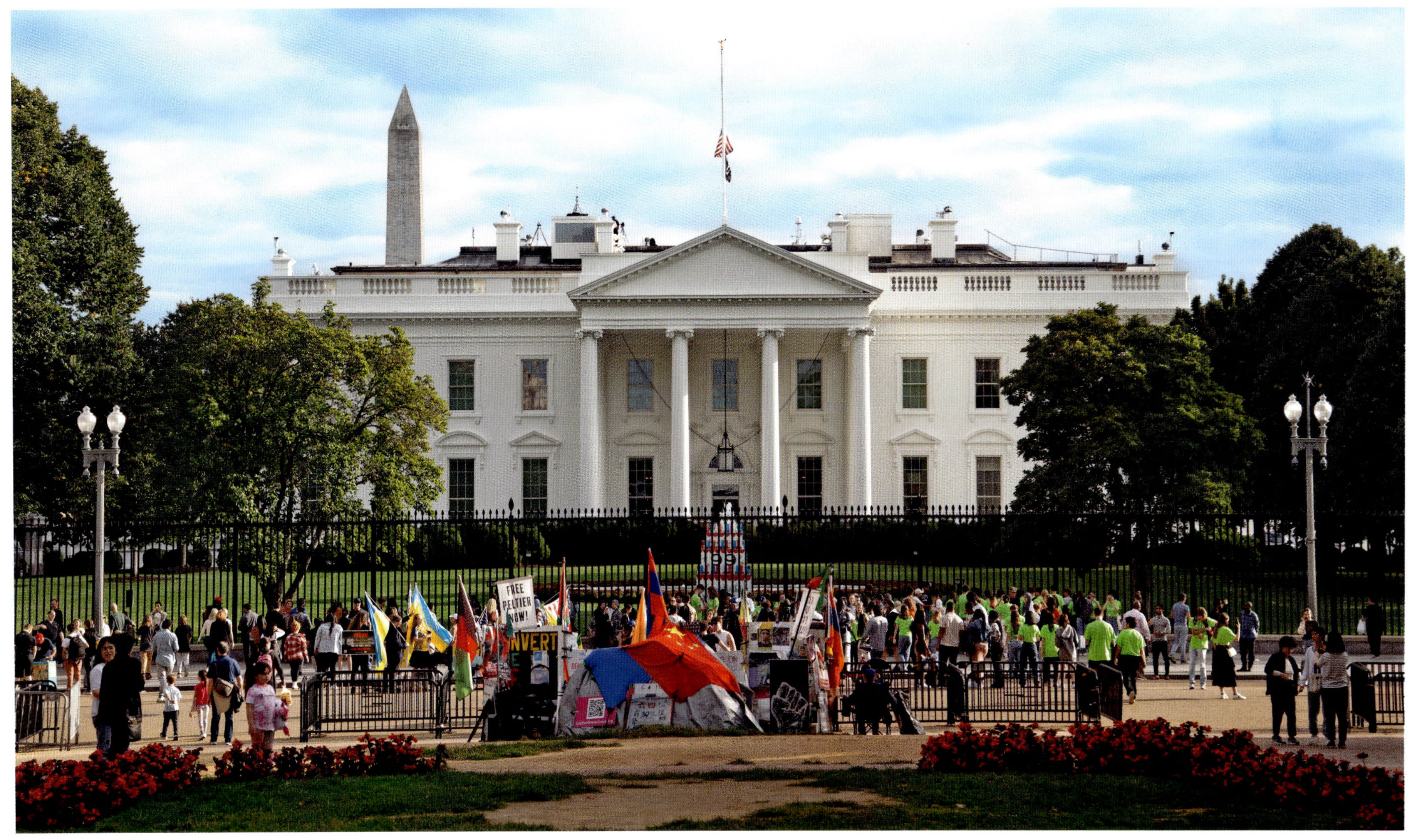

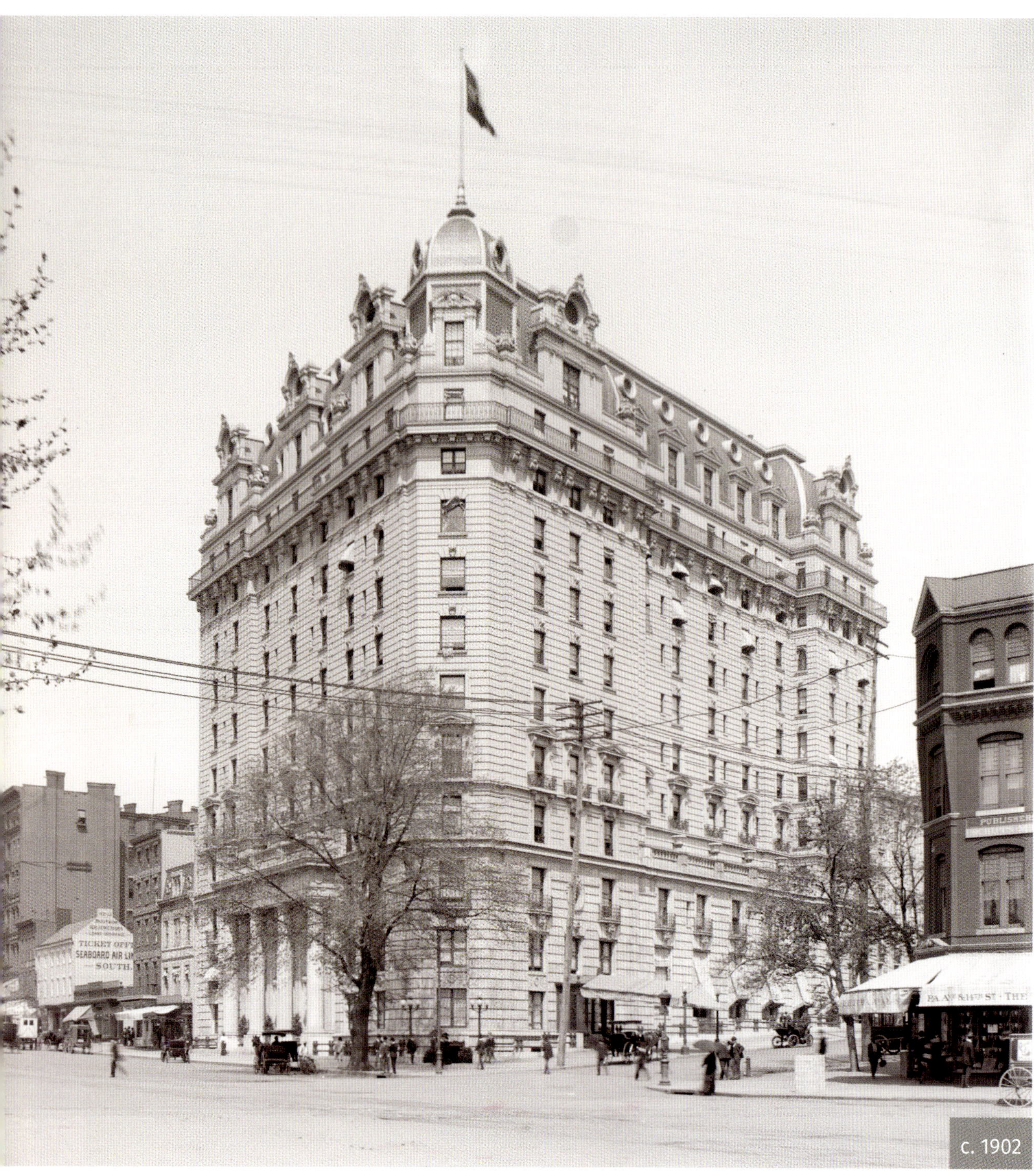

c. 1902

THE WILLARD HOTEL

Home of the great presidents, both old and new

THEN: In 1816 six wooden houses were constructed and eventually connected, acting as the first hotel to occupy the block. Management of the hotel passed through various parties before 1847, when Henry Willard came to Washington to run the hotel for the building's original owner, Joseph Tayloe. Upon his arrival, the hotel manager was greeted by a recently refurbished building, with many modern improvements. The business which came to be known as Willard's City Hotel was an instant success under his management. This was due both to his business acumen, and its location in proximity to downtown Washington and the White House.

The hotel began hosting guests of national prestige as early as the 1850s. The hotel's first presidential patron was Franklin Pierce, who made his home there in 1853 and in 1861 President elect Abraham Lincoln also took a room at the hotel, prior to his inauguration. During his presidency, Ulysses S. Grant would often enjoy a cigar and brandy in the lobby of the Willard, where he was frequently interrupted by those who wanted to discuss or influence political matters. Due to these interactions some credit Grant with coining the term lobbyist and these political actors became frequent visitors to the Willard.

In 1901 the old Willard was partially torn down and replaced in three sections, over a period of time. While the Willard City Hotel had experienced early success with political figures, as time continued additions to the property had made the structure inconsistent and inflexible, and nearby competition rose in popularity. The original section of the structure was replaced with a thirteen-story Beaux Arts structure and the new building drew back lost business. The Willard continued to serve figures of all backgrounds including world class artists and authors, such as hotel regular Mark Twain.

NOW: During World War II the Willard served up to three thousand meals a day, attempting to support a city facing an extreme housing shortage and a booming population. In this time, the hotel left the hands of the Willard family, after one hundred years of management and ownership. The business continued to be involved in Washington's most important moments and was the site at which Martin Luther King Jr. made his final edits to his famous "I Have a Dream Speech" at Lincoln Memorial.

In 1968 the Willard faced challenges once again. The 1968 riots changed the landscape of the city and helped realize plans introduced by the former President John F. Kennedy to revitalize Pennsylvania Avenue earlier in the decade. The Willard Hotel officially closed in August 1968. It was nominated for demolition in order to make way for a new National Square. These plans for demolishing the famous hotel were replaced with ones for preservation throughout the 1970s. In 1986, with support from descendants from the Willard family, the hotel reopened. Celebrating its bicentennial just ten years after the United States did, the Willard Hotel continues to operate on its original block.

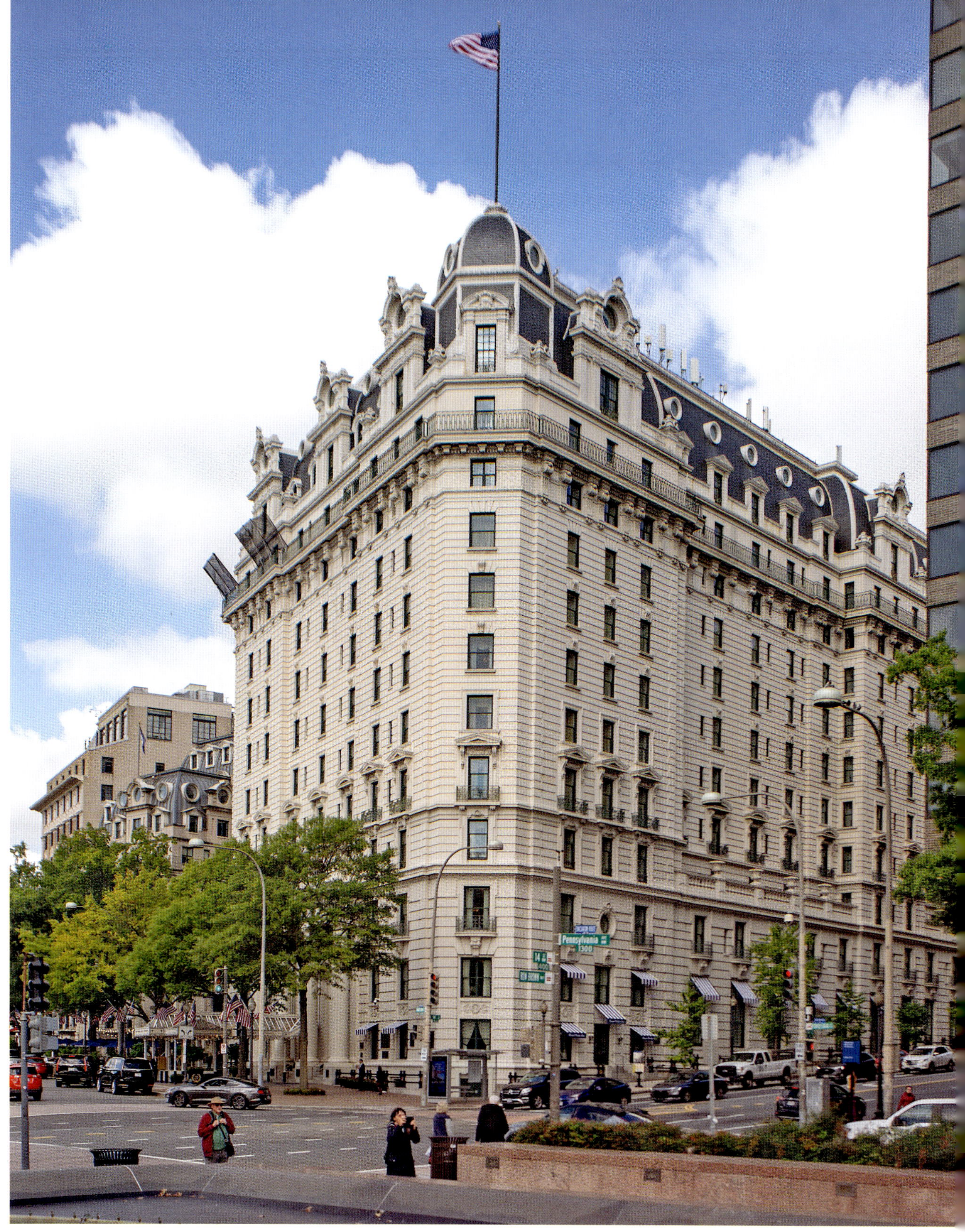

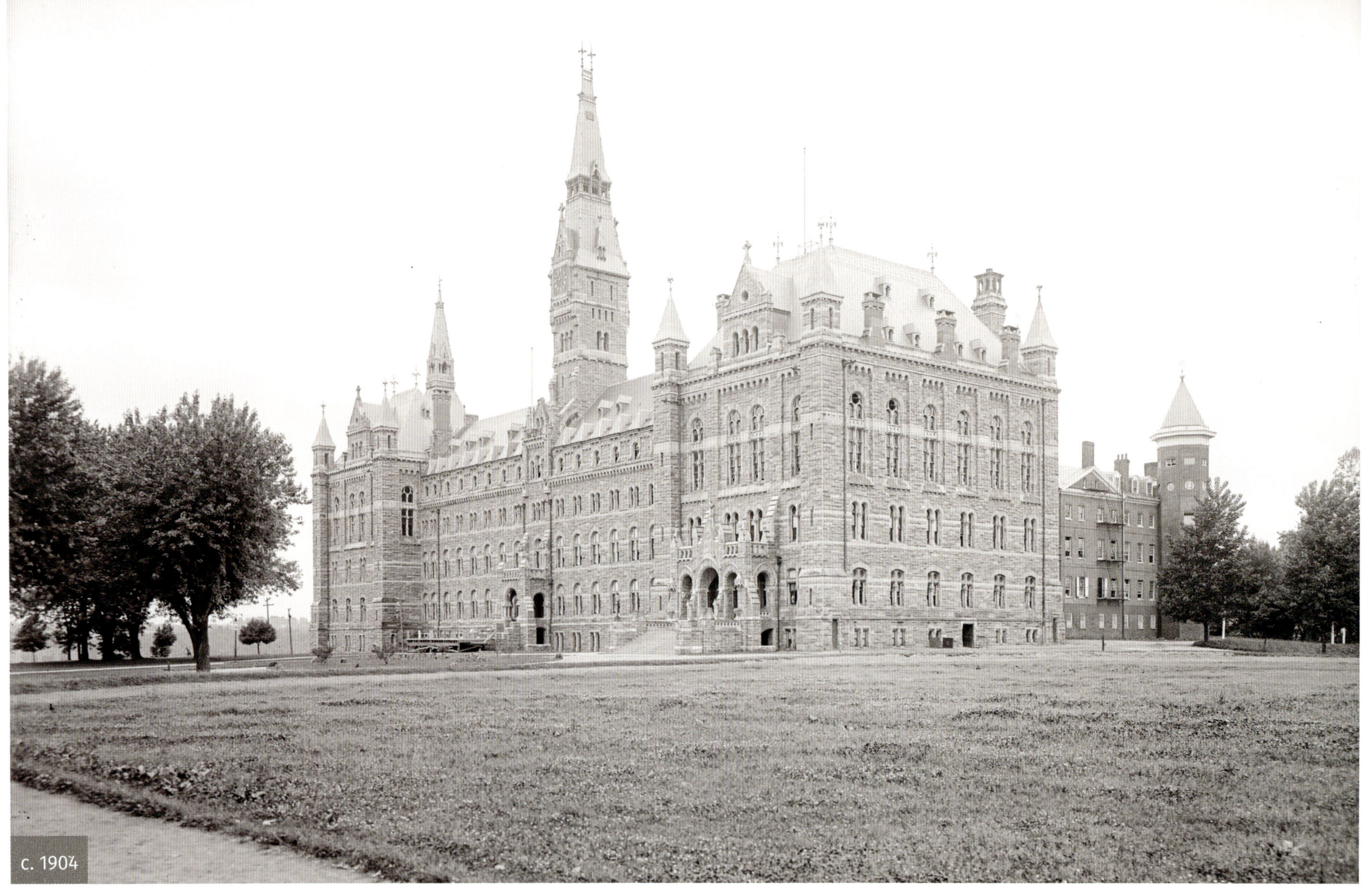

c. 1904

GEORGETOWN UNIVERSITY

Washington's oldest university

THEN: Georgetown College was founded in 1789 by John Carroll, on a hilltop in Georgetown, which was then a part of Maryland. Since Europeans had first arrived in America, there had been educational institutions founded along the East Coast, so John Carroll's university vision was not an unusual one. What set Georgetown apart was the lack of guaranteed funding which came along with its creation. Carroll had no guaranteed church or state support, and there was no endowment to support the new college. Carroll hoped that the appeal of the university would draw people to it who might make contributions and eliminate the need for tuition. Thus began the oldest Catholic and Jesuit institution of higher learning in the United States.

Classes began at the new Georgetown College in 1792 in a small Georgian-style building known as Old South which boasted a sweeping view of the nearby Potomac River. The first intake to the student body was forty students, however the campus remained small. In the early nineteenth century, the site had expanded to a few small, unassuming buildings. This did not prevent the success of the university and by the mid-nineteenth century, the college had over 300 attendees.

The Civil War had a large effect on Georgetown, as the student body dropped from 313 to only seventeen students, nearly forcing Georgetown to shut its doors. According to Georgetown's own records, 141 students and alumni entered the war on either the

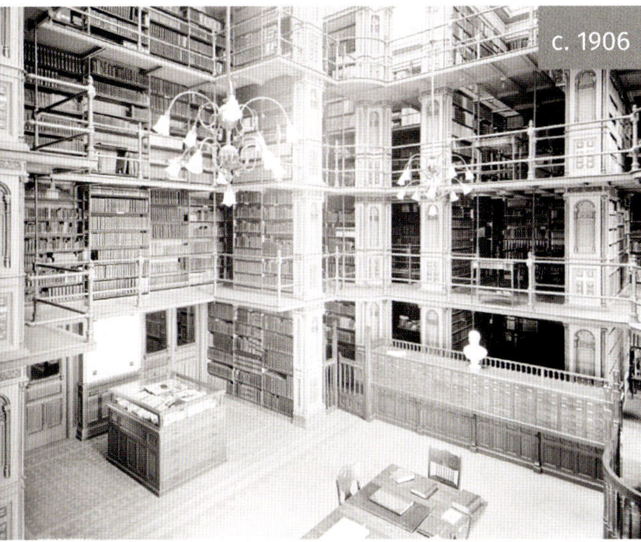

ABOVE: Once the primary library to serve Georgetown students, the Riggs Memorial Library housed historic texts in it's elaborate interior. The library is now primarily used as an event space.

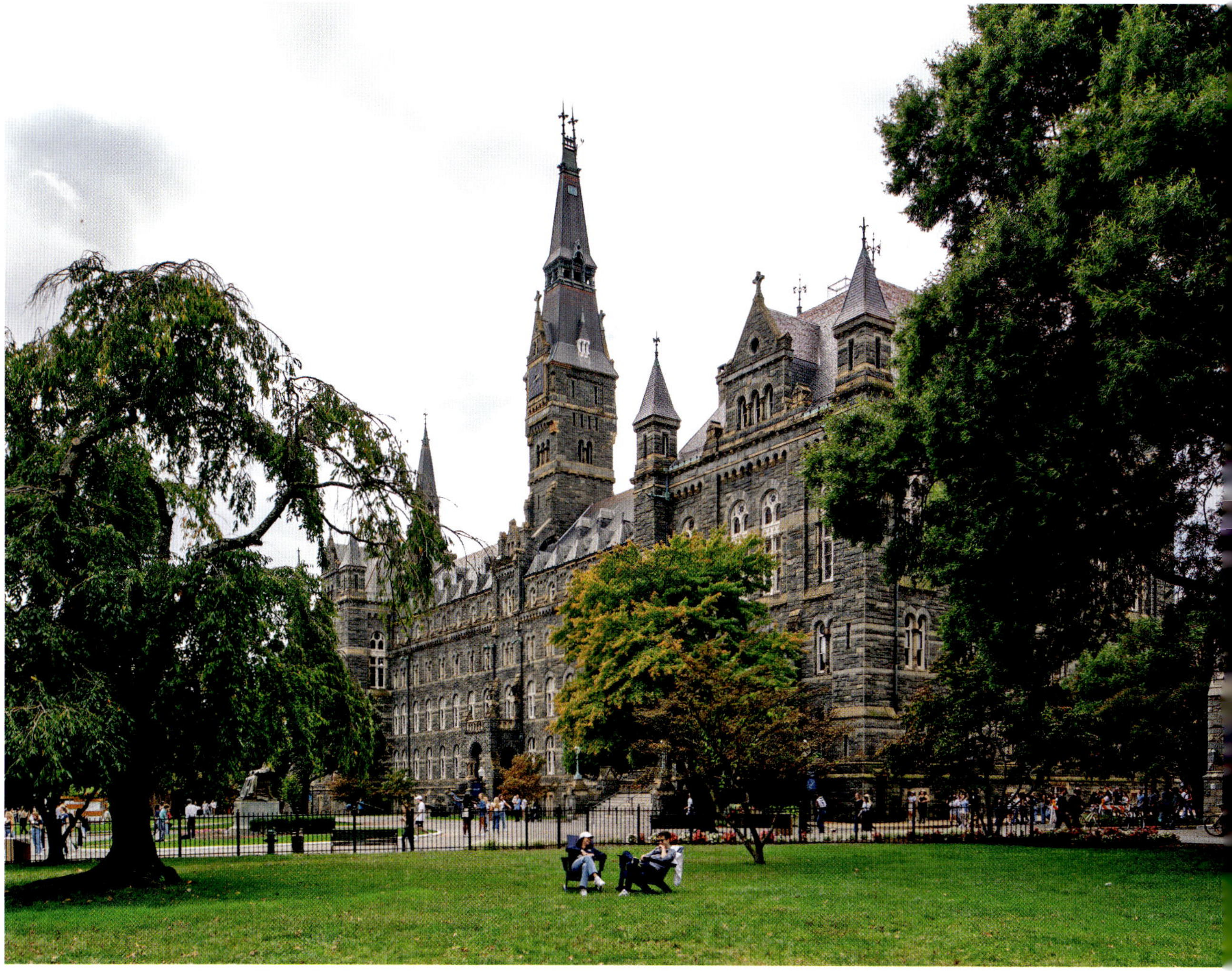

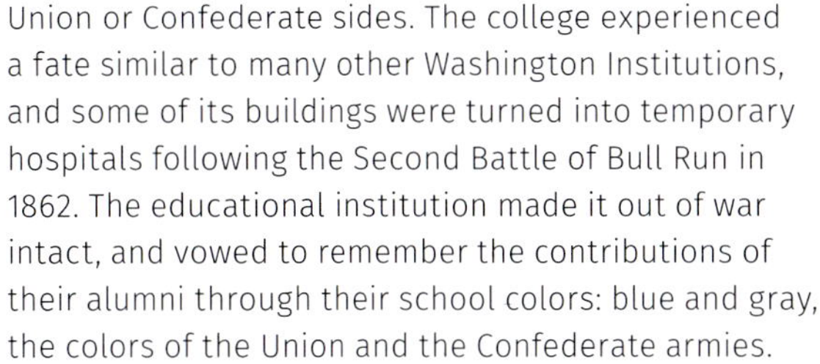

Union or Confederate sides. The college experienced a fate similar to many other Washington Institutions, and some of its buildings were turned into temporary hospitals following the Second Battle of Bull Run in 1862. The educational institution made it out of war intact, and vowed to remember the contributions of their alumni through their school colors: blue and gray, the colors of the Union and the Confederate armies.

Georgetown saw significant growth in the post-Civil War years, especially under the leadership of Patrick F. Healy, who was president of the university from 1873 to 1882. Healy's appointment as president held additional significance: he was later revealed to be the first Black president of a major American university and was the first Black person in America to earn their PhD. While Healy respected Georgetown's humble beginnings, he saw great potential for the University and pushed for the construction of a large Flemish Romanesque-style building. Healy also refocused the institution's curriculum, centering it on history and the natural sciences.

NOW: Throughout the twentieth century, Georgetown University, which offered a robust medical, law, and – by the 1930s – graduate school, continued to grow with the times. In 1969, the university began accepting women and the first Black tenured professor began teaching in 1976. Not only a member of America's select few Ivy League schools group, it is also the oldest university in Washington, D.C.

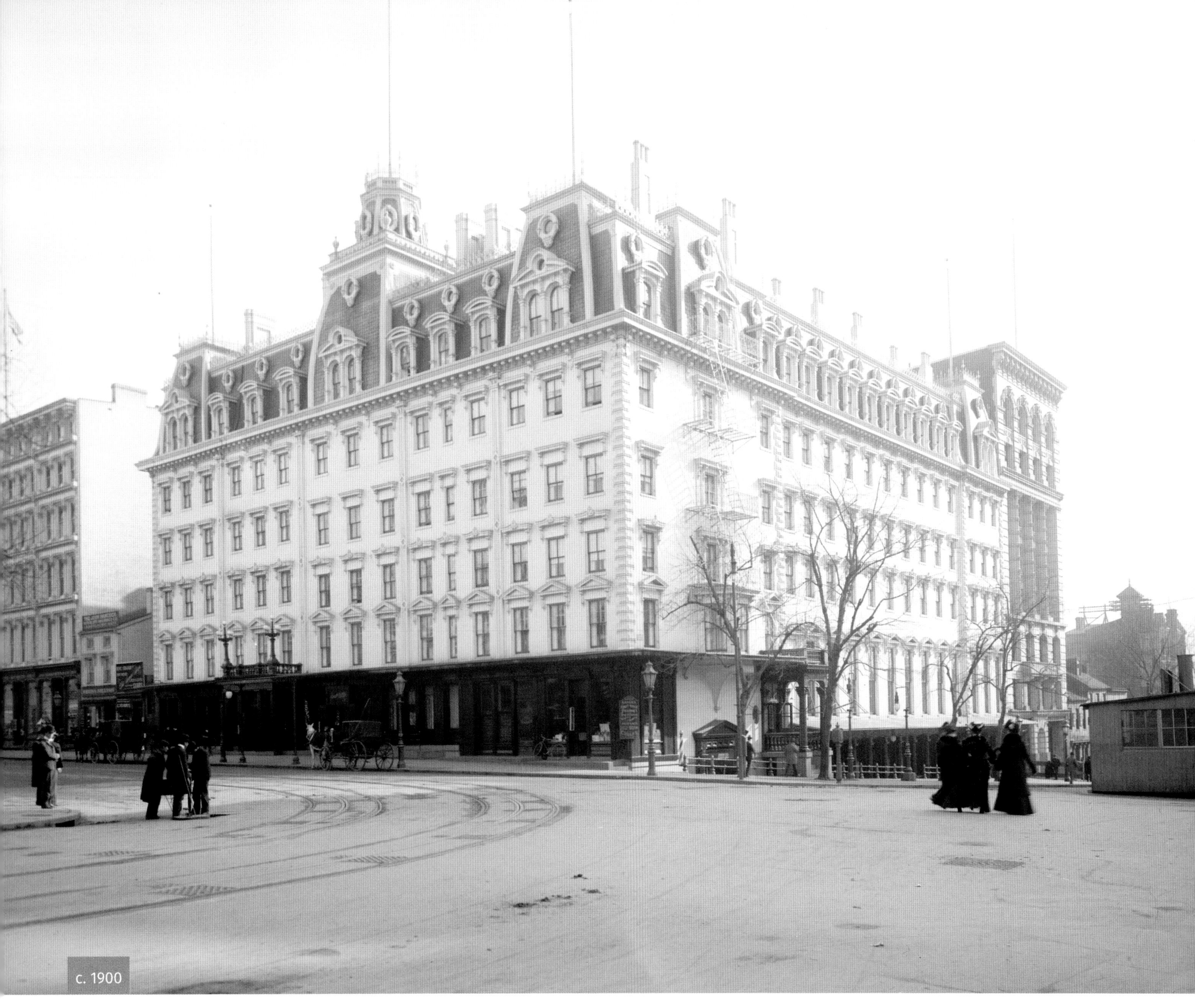
c. 1900

THE EBBITT HOUSE

One of Washington's most popular bars, almost lost to history

THEN: Since the mid-nineteenth century, the Old Ebbitt Grill has been open to visitors and locals alike. Founded by William E. Ebbitt and opening in 1856 as the Ebbitt House, the business originally functioned as a boarding house and dining spot. The first iteration of the Ebbitt House was along 14th Street, in what would eventually become the Northwest quadrant of the District. Its close proximity to the White House and downtown proved important, however the grill also welcomed guests from another hospitality landmark in Washington: the Willard Hotel.

Caleb Willard eventually purchased the Ebbitt House to expand his hospitality empire. In 1872, Willard razed the building and turned what was once a boarding house into a glamorous six-story hotel. The most distinctive feature of the new Ebbitt House was its dining room, which was two stories high, with white marble floors and large glass chandeliers that earned it the title of "the Crystal Room." By the late nineteenth century, Willard had turned this once humble business into one of Washington's most popular destinations. Guests included memorable figures in American history such as high-ranking military official William Tecumseh Sherman and presidents Ulysses S. Grant and Theodore Roosevelt. President William McKinley and his wife even lived at the Ebbitt throughout the duration of his congressional career.

The twentieth century brought continuous obstacles for the grill, despite its beautiful appearance. The building was razed and rebuilt in the early twentieth century, and then struggled to maintain itself throughout Prohibition. In 1926 the building was demolished to make way for the National Press Club building and finally rebuilt on F Street NW. The 1970s brought a further challenge and it seemed that one of Washington's oldest continuously operated saloons had met its final fate when the business was met with charges of tax fraud.

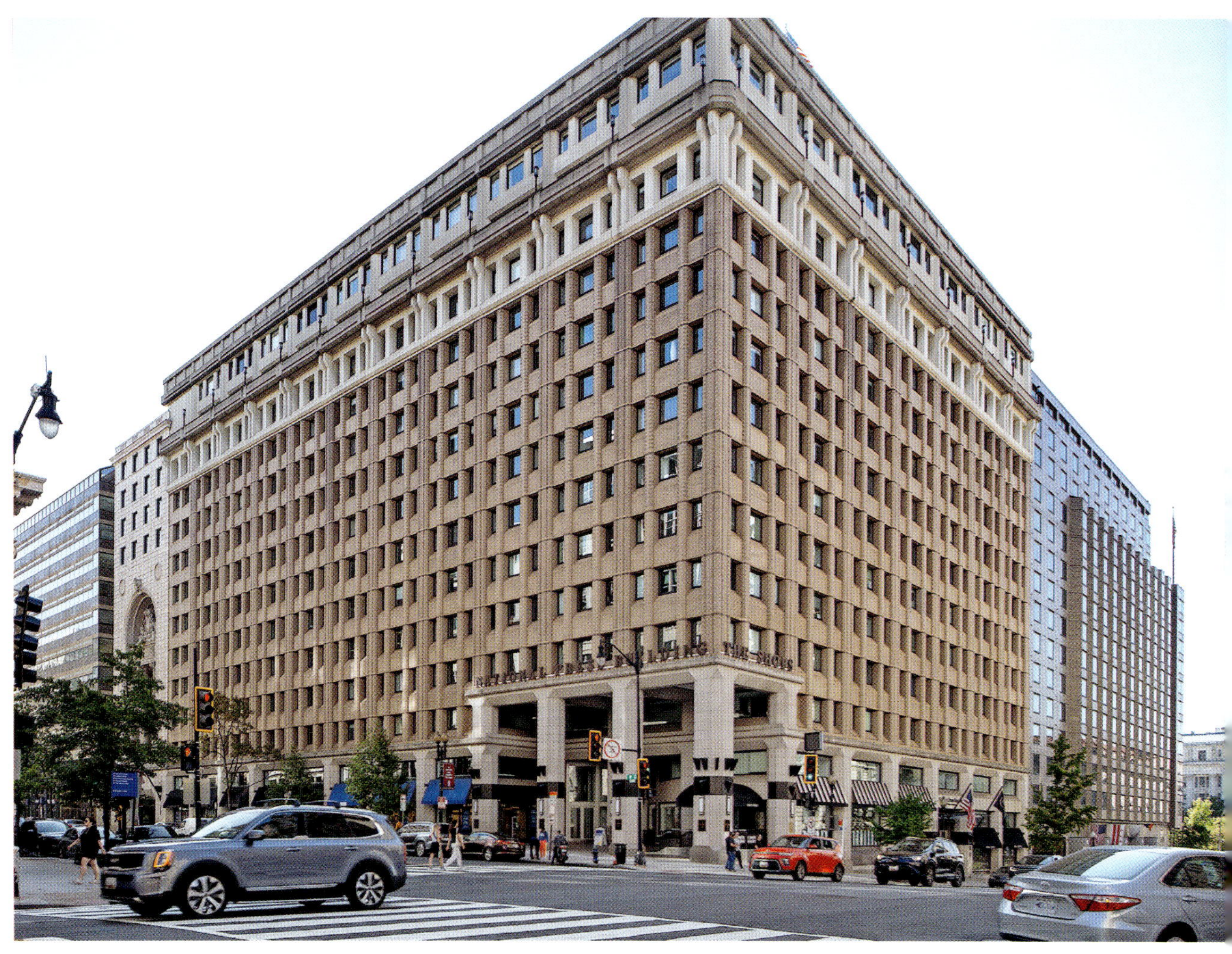

Though it seemed all hope was lost, the owners of another popular Washington destination, Clydes, saved the restaurant. In 1970 they had entered the failed establishment looking to buy its historic beer steins, and left with the entire restaurant. Finally, it seemed that the Ebbitt was saved once and for all; but not after being demolished and relocated for a fourth time.

NOW: After its demolition in 1983, the Old Ebbitt Grill reopened along 15th Street in a Beaux-Arts style building, still in a location with proximity to the White House and those working downtown. It was designed to emulate the F Street location with a turn of the century style, with taxidermy animals, credited to the hunting of President Theodore Roosevelt, displayed on the walls, and wooden bears allegedly imported by Alexander Hamilton. Although the grill's current location is relatively new, the Old Ebbitt Grill has retained artifacts that showcase its longstanding history in the nation's capital.

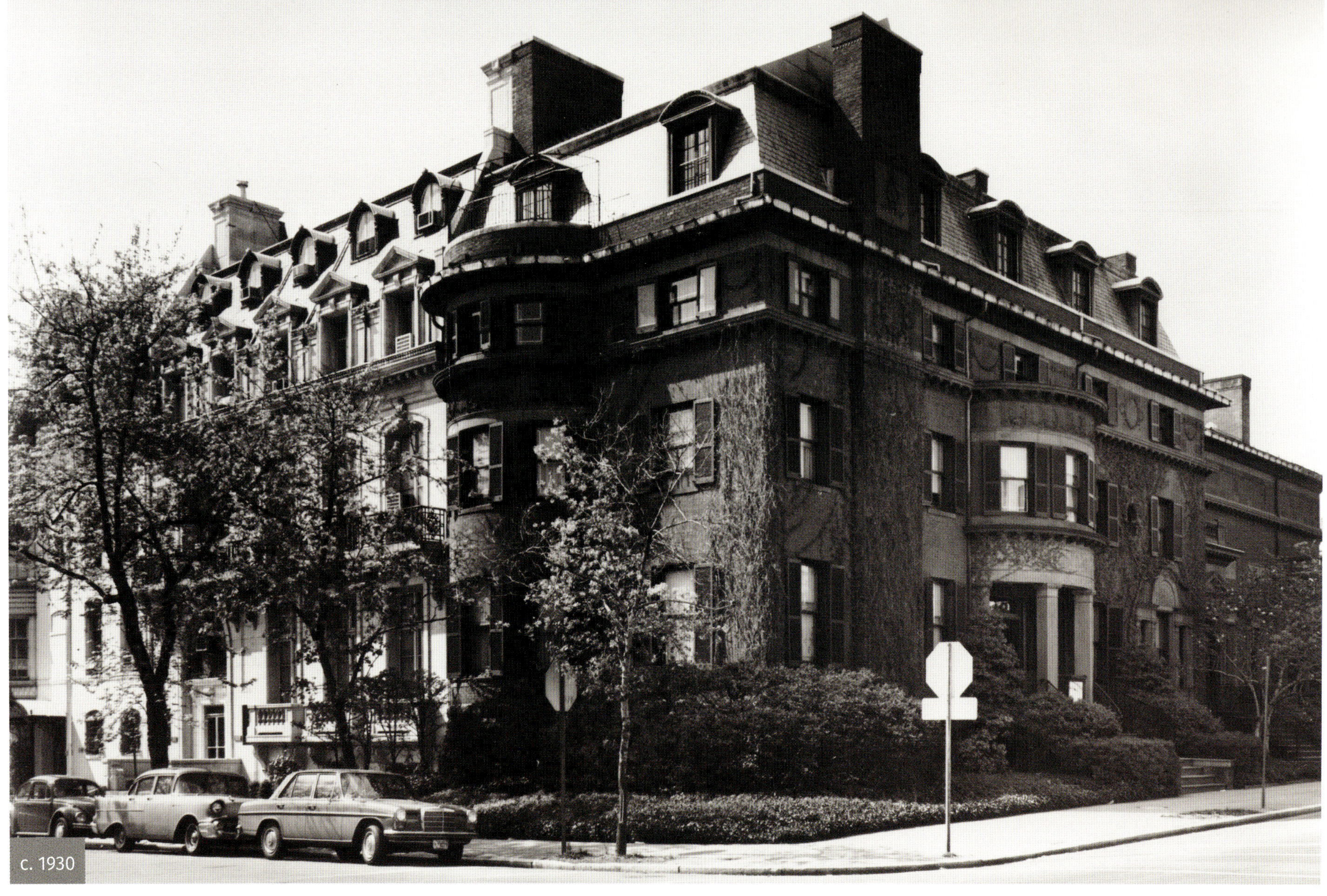
c. 1930

DUNCAN PHILLIPS HOUSE

America's first museum of modern art

THEN: In 1896, Major Duncan Phillips, a Civil War veteran who made his fortune in glass manufacturing, and his wife Eliza Laughlin Phillips decided their family needed a change of scenery from the harsh Pennsylvanian winters. That year, with their two sons James and Duncan, the close-knit family moved to the federal city. Almost as soon as they arrived, the family began building their home in an up-and-coming neighborhood known as Dupont Circle. In 1897, architects Hornblower and Marshall constructed a three-story Georgian Revival town made of red brick and sandstone for them in Dupont Circle, in keeping with the growing landscape of mansions in the area.

The two boys were close and the older of the two, James, put off attending college for two years so they could attend Yale together. It was here that Duncan pursued his interest in art. Duncan junior found inspiration for his studies in Europe, and at the new Corcoran Gallery in Washington, D.C., and the MET in New York. In 1916, with the support of his brother, the two Phillips sons convinced their parents to set aside $10,000 annually for the collection of contemporary American painting.

In 1917 tragedy struck the family, not once, but twice. Major Duncan Phillips died suddenly due to a heart condition, and the following year James died from the flu.

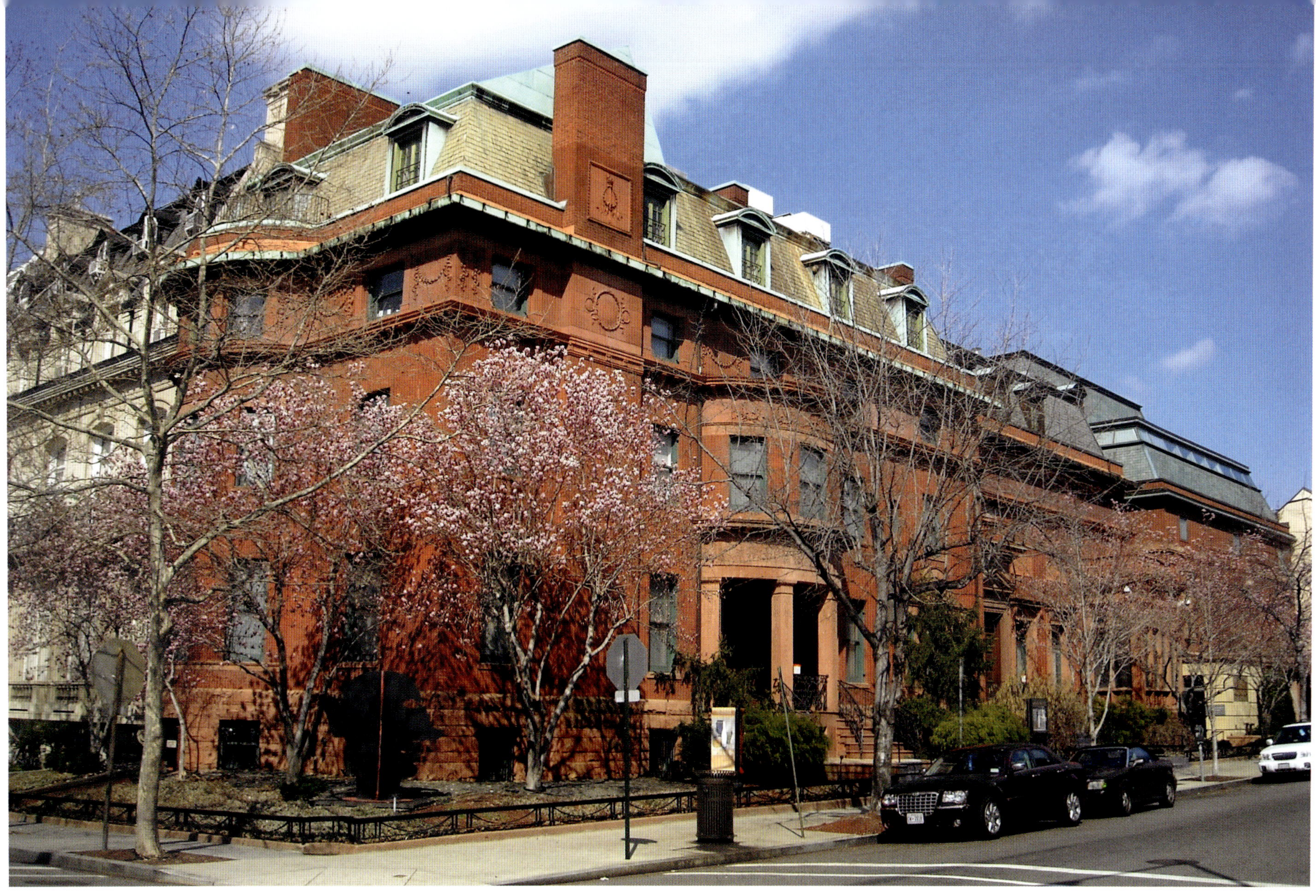

Devastated by the loss of his father and brother, Duncan wanted to pay tribute to them. The dedication of a statue felt too solemn and so he founded the Phillips Memorial Art Gallery in their familial home in Dupont Circle. In his new gallery, which opened in 1921 to the public, Duncan presented D.C. with a museum that showcased modern artists and old masters on equal terms. The gallery opened to a disappointing low attendance and Duncan resolved that if he could get his hands on one truly famous painting, it would attract the visitorship he had intended. Duncan set off for France to pursue the one piece he wanted most for the collection: Renoir's *Dejeuner des Canotiers* (Luncheon of the Boating Party). After a trip to Paris with his wife Marjorie Acker, the painting was sent on its way to Washington, D.C. Once it arrived, Renoir's work served its purpose, and Washingtonians finally gave the Phillips Memorial Art Gallery the attention Duncan always believed it deserved.

NOW: Thrilled with the positive attention from the public, Duncan moved out of the Mansion and dedicated the whole building to his collection. The museum grew to include a school for artists and a chamber music series, expanding the type of art which was shown at the Phillips Collection – as it was renamed in 1961. Duncan avoided a board of trustees and instead made all decisions with the consultation of his wife.

Since Duncan's passing in 1966, the Phillips Collection has remained open. Two wings have since been added, yet the feeling of home that Phillip's intended for his art collection is maintained.

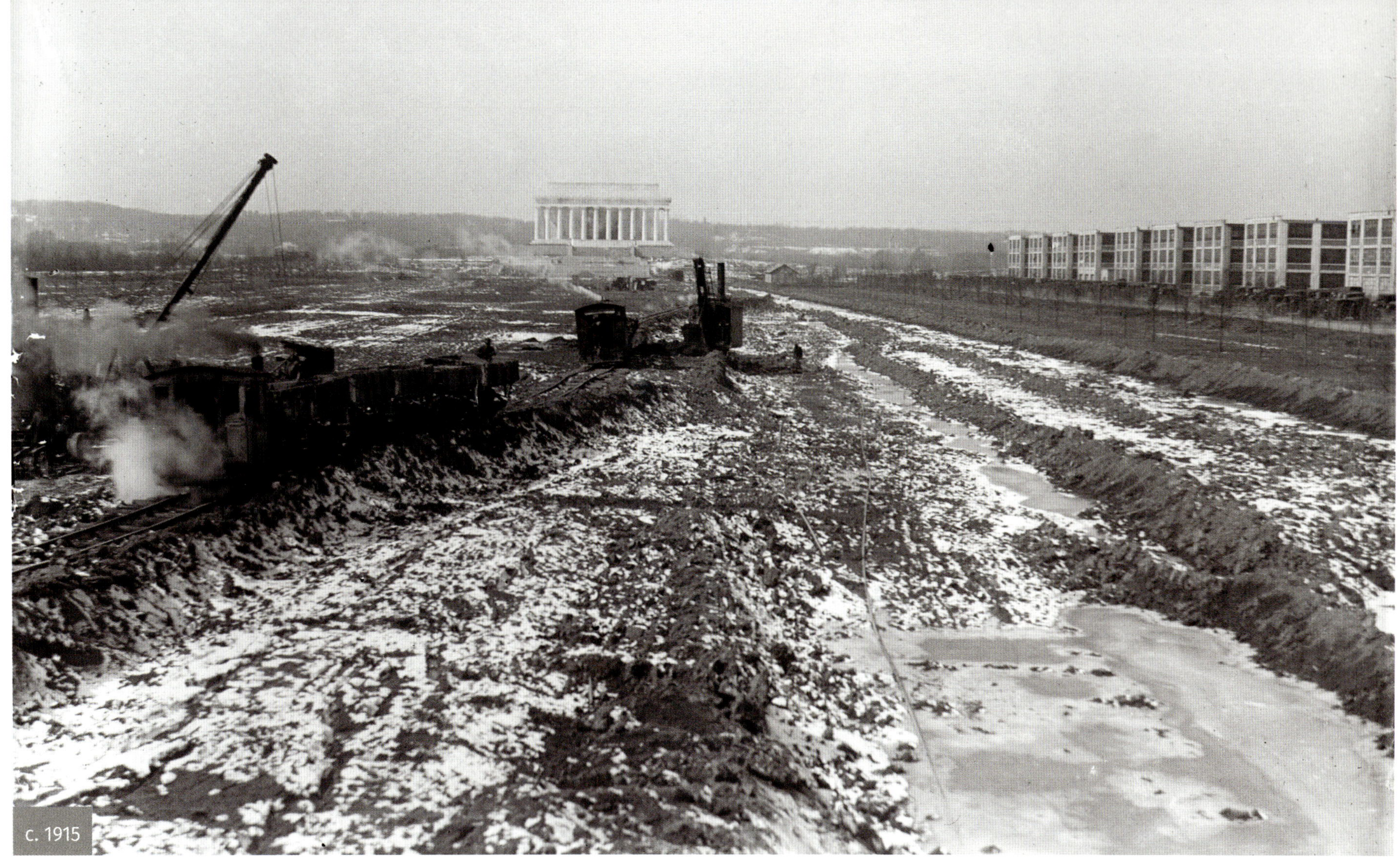
c. 1915

THE LINCOLN REFLECTING POOL

A monumental change bears witness to history

THEN: In the late nineteenth century, Washington, D.C. was not the capital city that many had envisioned. Almost one hundred years later architect and planner L'Enfant's vision of a grand city had not been achieved, with federal buildings of different architectural styles scattered throughout D.C. With growing criticism of the federal city and competing expectations for a new design, the Senate Park Commission was formed in 1901 to bring Washington consistency. Drawing inspiration from L'Enfant's original vision of European influence, city planner Glenn Brown intended to bring in classical European designs including a large water feature.

Along with the official plan in 1902, the Senate Park Commission, also known as the McMillan Plan, detailed two large pools on the western end of the National Mall. While some of this new city plan was started upon, other parts such as the planned pools were ultimately delayed due to World War I. During the war, Washington saw an increase in temporary structures along the National Mall, such as the Main Navy and Munitions buildings used for wartime offices. After the war these buildings remained and interfered with the original two-pool plan for the National Mall's large water feature. As a result the Reflecting Pool was reduced to one large rectangular pool by the time construction began.

The Lincoln Memorial, which would eventually sit at the western end of the Reflecting Pool, had already been built so the team knew they would face a similar challenge when construction began: D.C.'s marshland environment. With banks of the Potomac River nearby, the area that would be the pool had to be excavated appropriately in order to hold the large structure.

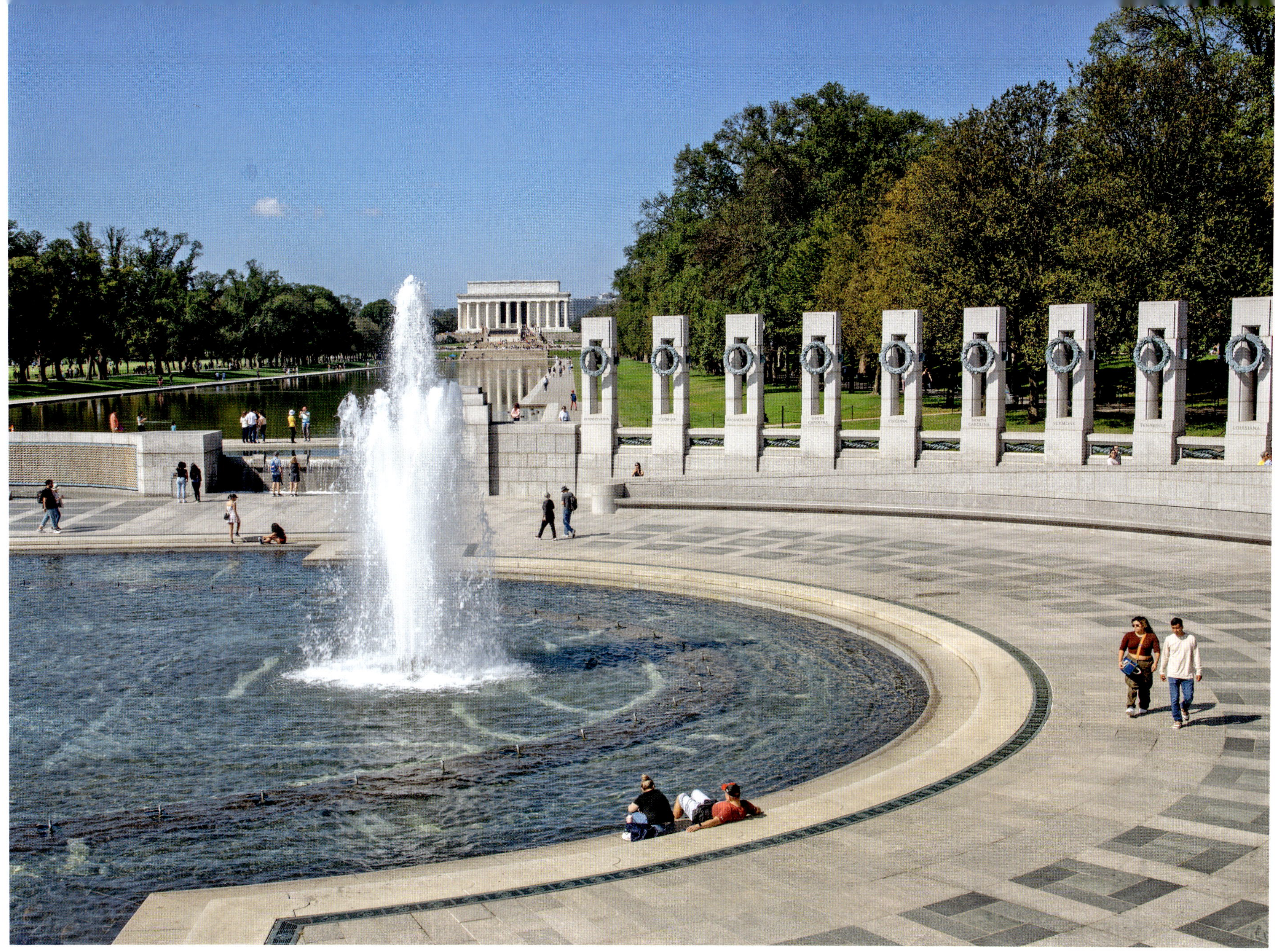

NOW: Between 1922 and 1923, the Reflecting Pool was finally completed. Made of cinder and asphalt, the pool is 2,029 feet long and thirty inches deep at its deepest point, holding 6,750,000 gallons of water. The monument was a roaring success and was not only in line with the ideals set out by the original city planner over one hundred years prior, but also instantly popular with current residents. In 1922 during the time of its construction, a frozen over Reflecting Pool served as an ice-skating rink where Washingtonians could enjoy a winter's day.

The Reflecting Pool has also seen some of America's greatest moments and demonstrations. In 1963 more than 200,000 people gathered around the Reflecting Pool at the end of the March on Washington for Jobs and Freedom to see a last-minute speaker: Martin Luther King, Jr. The famous civil rights activist deviated from his original speech, which had been allotted four minutes, to deliver some of America's most influential rhetoric in his "I Have a Dream" speech. Depending on where a visitor stands today, the Reflecting Pool displays the reflection of monuments dedicated to two American leaders: the Washington Monument and the Lincoln Memorial.

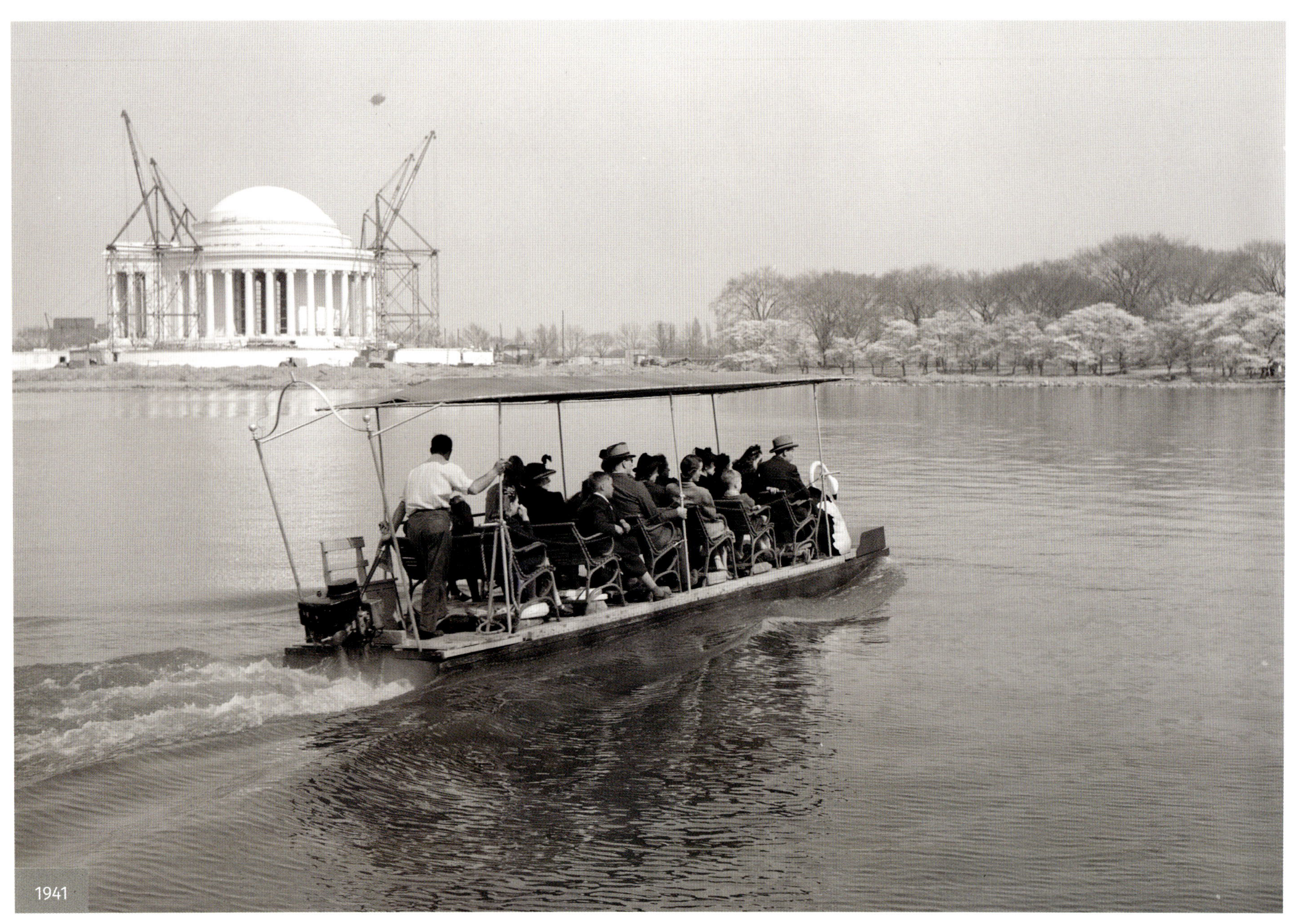
1941

TIDAL BASIN

A monumental swimming hole for the masses

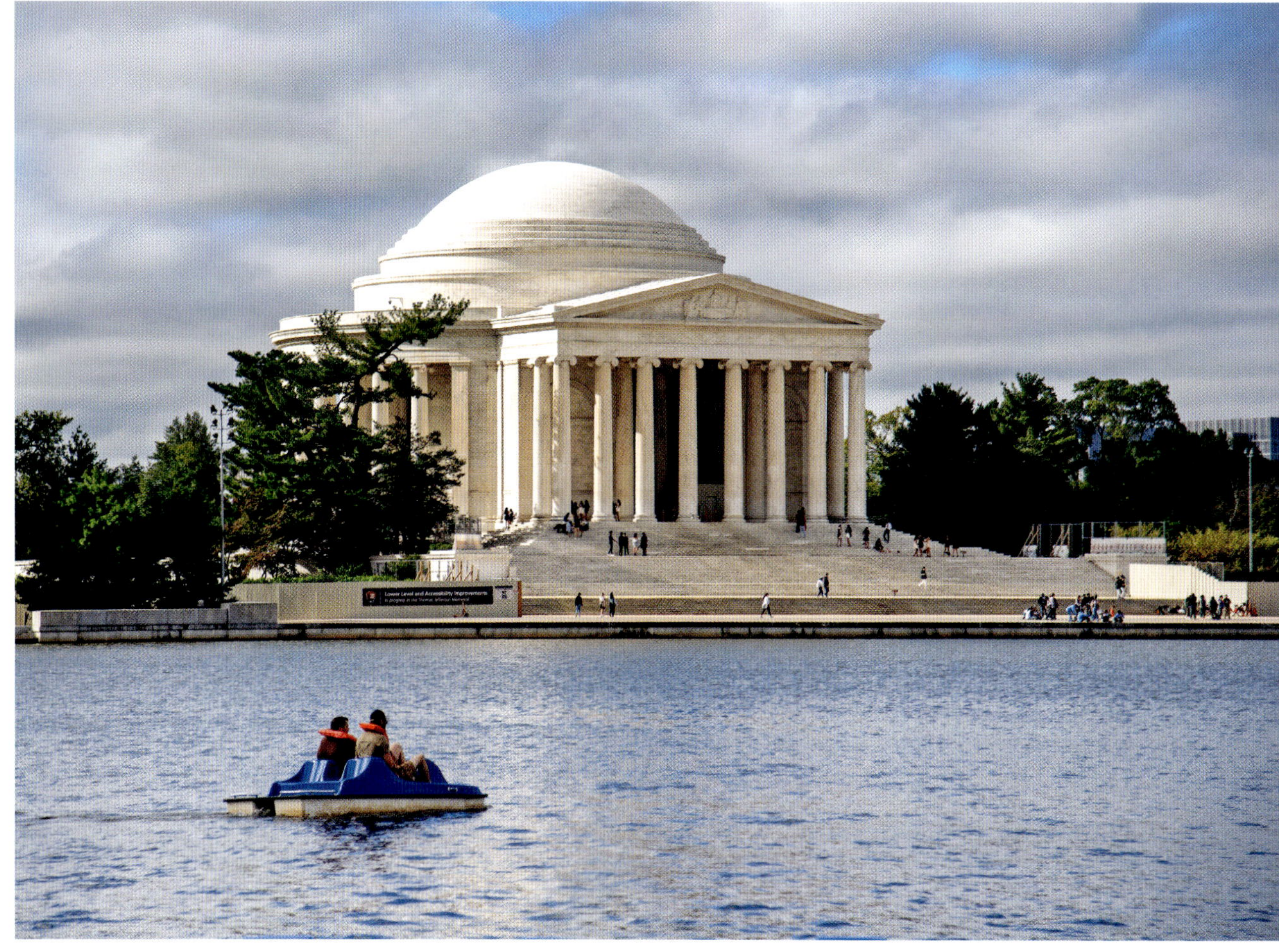

THEN: Located in West Potomac Park, the Tidal Basin was originally created to prevent damaging floods in Washington. In 1881, the District had experienced an overflow from surrounding rivers that was so devastating the southern part of the city was only reachable by boat. To counteract a future natural disaster, the Tidal Basin was created with gates that helped balance the water levels, based on the level of the tide. The bridge and seawall supporting it were designed by the engineering firm Alexander and Repass. One of the partners of the firm, Archie Alexander, was a Black man who overcame many challenges in order to achieve great success. Archie and his partner hired both Black and white laborers for their projects, including the work on the Tidal Basin, a practice that was unheard of for its time.

The Tidal Basin, a necessary water feature, was surrounded by filled-in land that Washingtonians wanted for their own use. Some suggested a monumental park dedicated to the Founding Fathers and President Grover Cleveland even suggested a truck garden for growing vegetables. Yet as Washingtonian's faced rising temperatures in the summer months and the Tidal Basin became a great destination to cool off, it was settled that the surrounding land would become beaches for visitors.

Opening in 1918 to white male patrons only, the Tidal Basin encountered immediate success as a location to swim. Eventually white women were allowed to swim and join on the beaches, as were Black patrons, however they had their own "separate but equal" facilities. In 1920, the swimming spot saw 20,000 visitors in a single ten-hour period, and having reached such a capacity it became clear that the facilities needed expansion.

In the early twentieth century, Congress approved and funded the creation of a large beach on the southeast side of the basin, although this new beach was only accessible to white patrons. Black leadership questioned this decision and in 1924 Congress appropriated funds to construct a new beach for Black Washingtonians around the Tidal Basin.

NOW: The dream of a second beach was never realized. Various reasons were cited, however it was clear that some southern senators had shut down the project. In addition to rising health concerns about the water and backlash regarding expansion of the beaches into nearby park land, Congress relented and decided to close down the beaches for everyone, instead of desegregating them.

The 107 acres of the Tidal Basin today is no longer surrounded by beaches or eager swimmers. Instead it is overlooked by some of Washington's most famous monuments, including the Jefferson Memorial which was constructed in 1943. Other nearby monuments include the Martin Luther King, Jr. Memorial and the site of the first cherry tree planting in 1912. Now surrounded by several cherry trees, Washingtonians and tourists alike flood the Tidal Basin each summer not for the beaches, but to see the pink blossoms reflected in the Basin's waters.

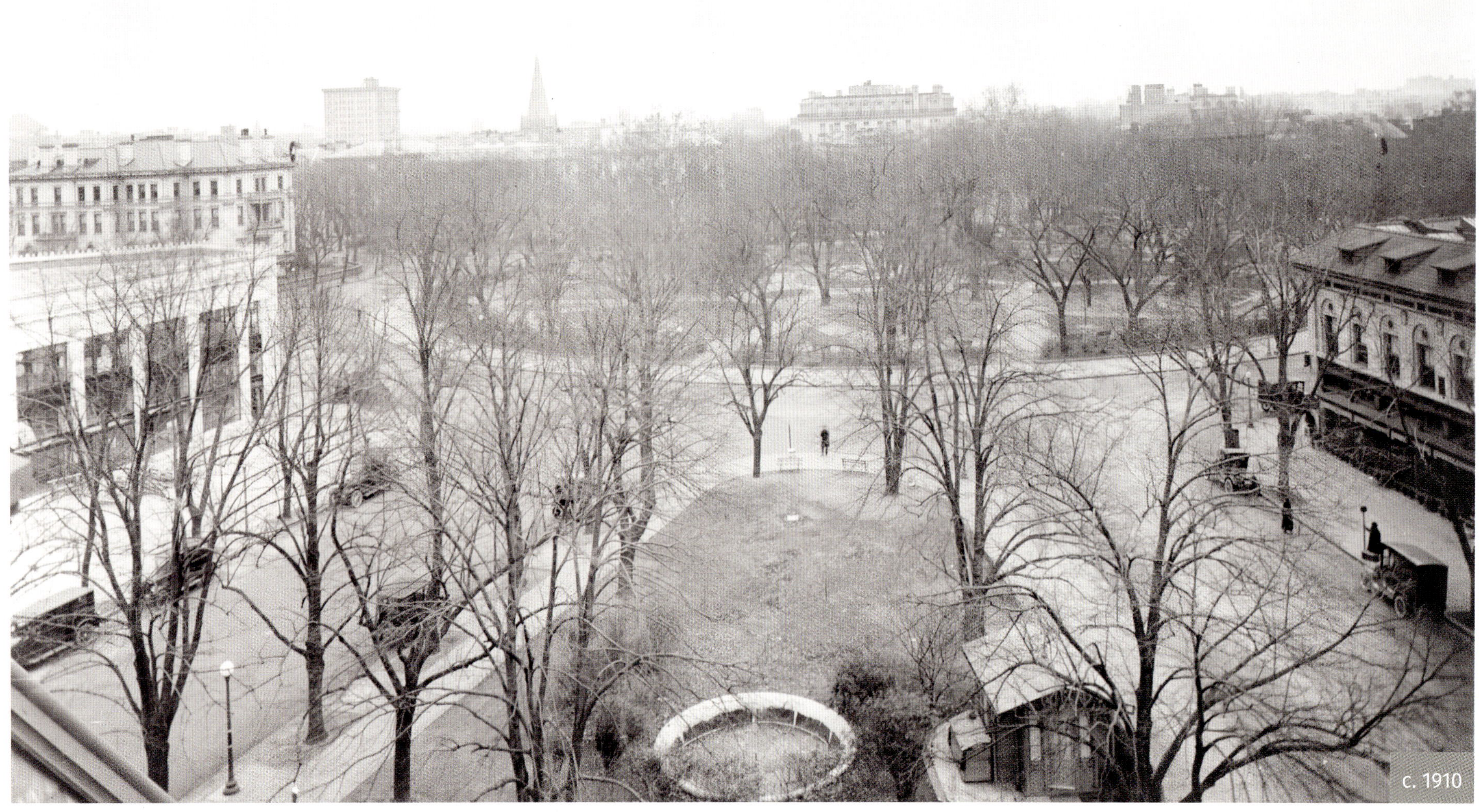

c. 1910

DUPONT CIRCLE

An amalgamation of the lives of Washingtonians

THEN: In the original plan for Washington, D.C., a series of green circular spaces at the intersection of diagonal avenues had been outlined. At the intersection of the Massachusetts, Connecticut, and New Hampshire Avenues in Northwest Washington sits one of these circles, known as Dupont Circle. Since its inception, Dupont Circle was a desirable rural area, located with the throughline of Connecticut Avenue connecting the green space to the White House, making downtown easy to access.

In the 1870s, Alexander Shepherd, head of the Board of Public Works, expanded improvements from beyond downtown and into previously undeveloped neighborhoods. Shepherd's plans paved the connecting street Connecticut Avenue for ease of transportation and improved the landscape around then Pacific Circle. Those privy to his vision for the fledgling neighborhood bought tracts of land well below their future market value and went on to build their estates there. One of these buyers was Senator William Stewart from Nevada who built his large home on the northern section of the circle in 1873.

Pacific Circle, which was renamed Dupont Circle after Samuel F. Dupont, a Civil War Naval Admiral, became a new center point for Washingtonian life. A bridge was constructed along Dupont's P Street, connecting Washington to the existing Georgetown neighborhood via a a horse drawn trolley. Another trolley system along Connecticut Avenue made Dupont Circle a hub of transportation and a turning point for many commuters in the city. By the turn of the nineteenth century, Dupont's architecture reflected decades of changing design tastes, and tourists came just to see the expansive mansions.

Included among the eclectic mansions were row houses, which were homes to teachers, craftspeople and laborers. Prior to the Civil War there was a large, free Black community in the area, with their activism continuing as Dupont Circle became an important site of abolitionist work and educational reform.

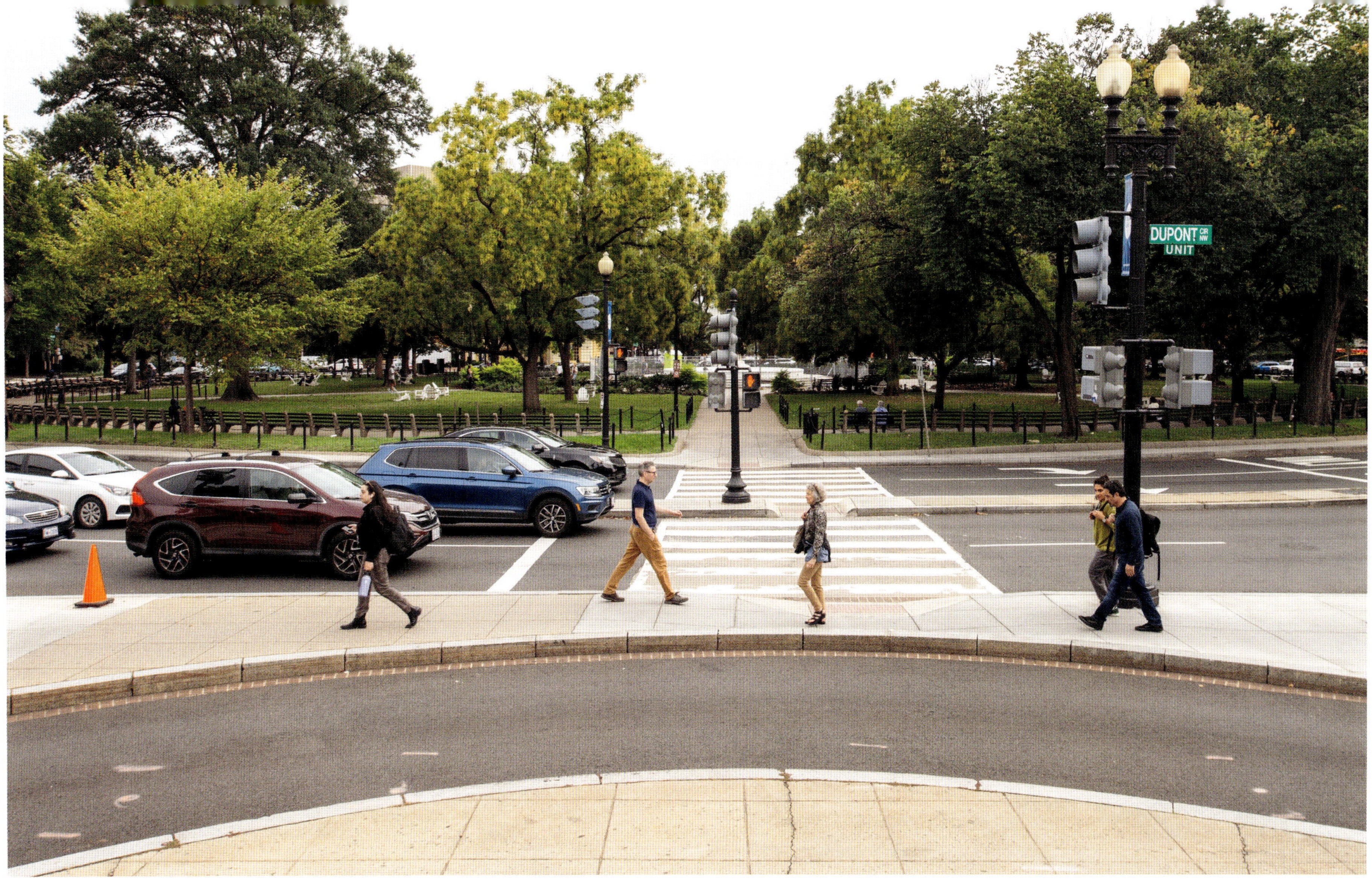

NOW: Dupont Circle began to change throughout the twentieth century. The statue of the Naval Admiral was taken down and replaced with the white stone foundation that sits there today. It was designed by Henry Bacon and Daniel Chester French, the pair who designed the Lincoln Memorial. There was also a push to make the Circle a popular shopping destination, and it became an area for automobile salerooms.

Changes in Washington's population affected permanent change to the circle. Once a tourist destination, the mansions were turned into apartment buildings and others demolished for office space. The only surviving building from when the green space was called Pacific Circle is the Blaine Mansion built in 1882, which sits on the corner of 20th St and P St.

In the latter half of the twentieth century, a younger generation brought new life into the neighborhood. In the 1970s, Dupont Circle was considered a welcoming space for the city's LGBTQIA+ community and saw Washington's first openly gay business that was not a bar. The neighborhood still boasts reminders of history through its architecture, and is constantly evolving.

RIGHT: A Gay Pride Day was started in 1975 in the heart of Dupont Circle with the event continuing annually to this day. Today it is known as Capital Pride, and draws tens of thousands of visitors to Dupont Circle every June.

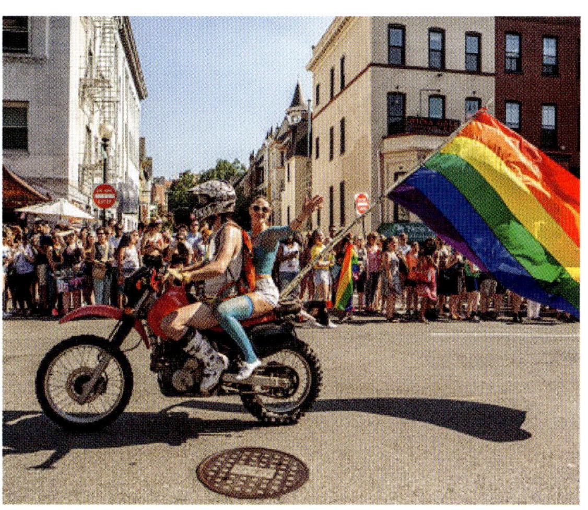

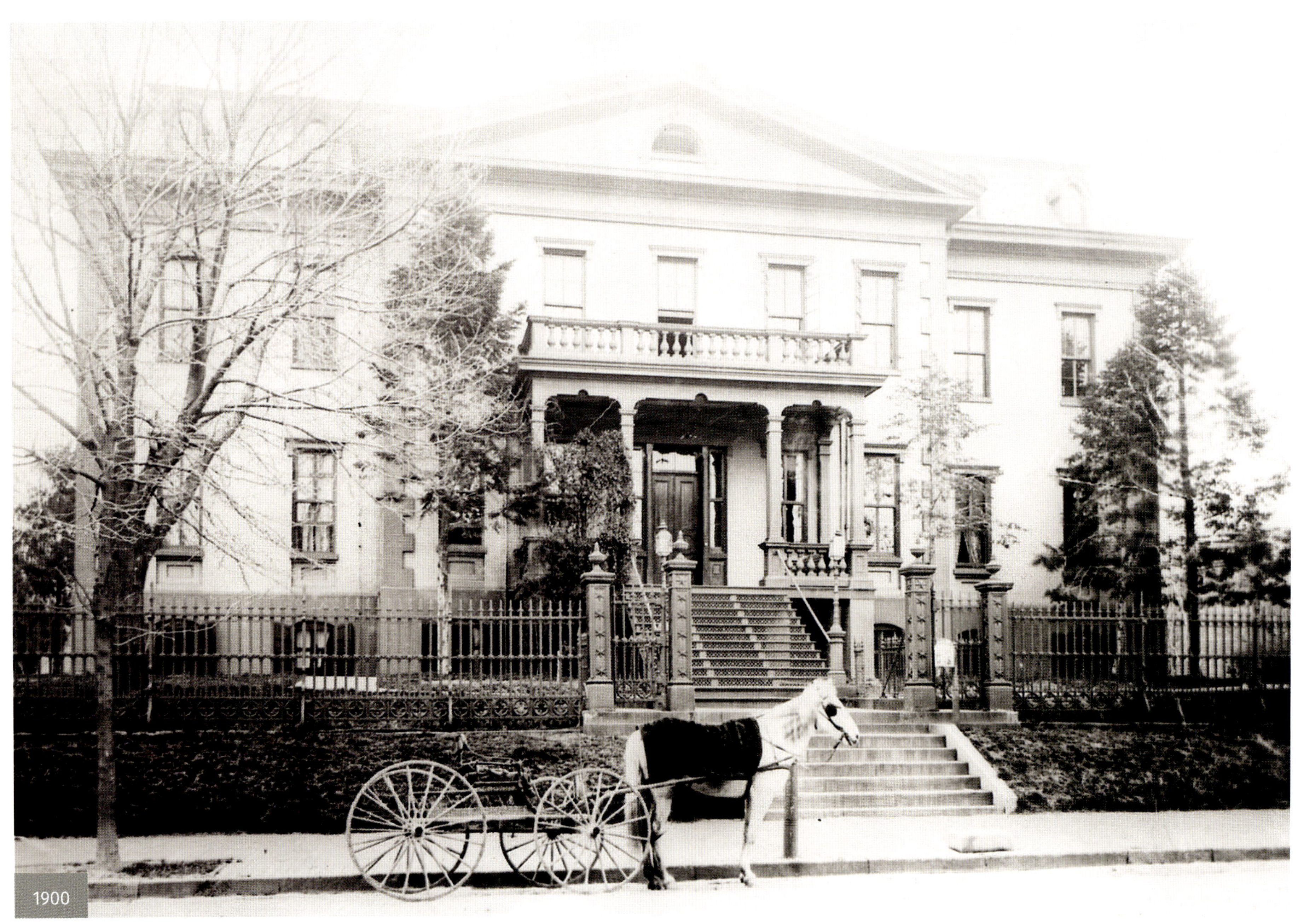
1900

NAVAL HOSPITAL

Washington's first naval hospital

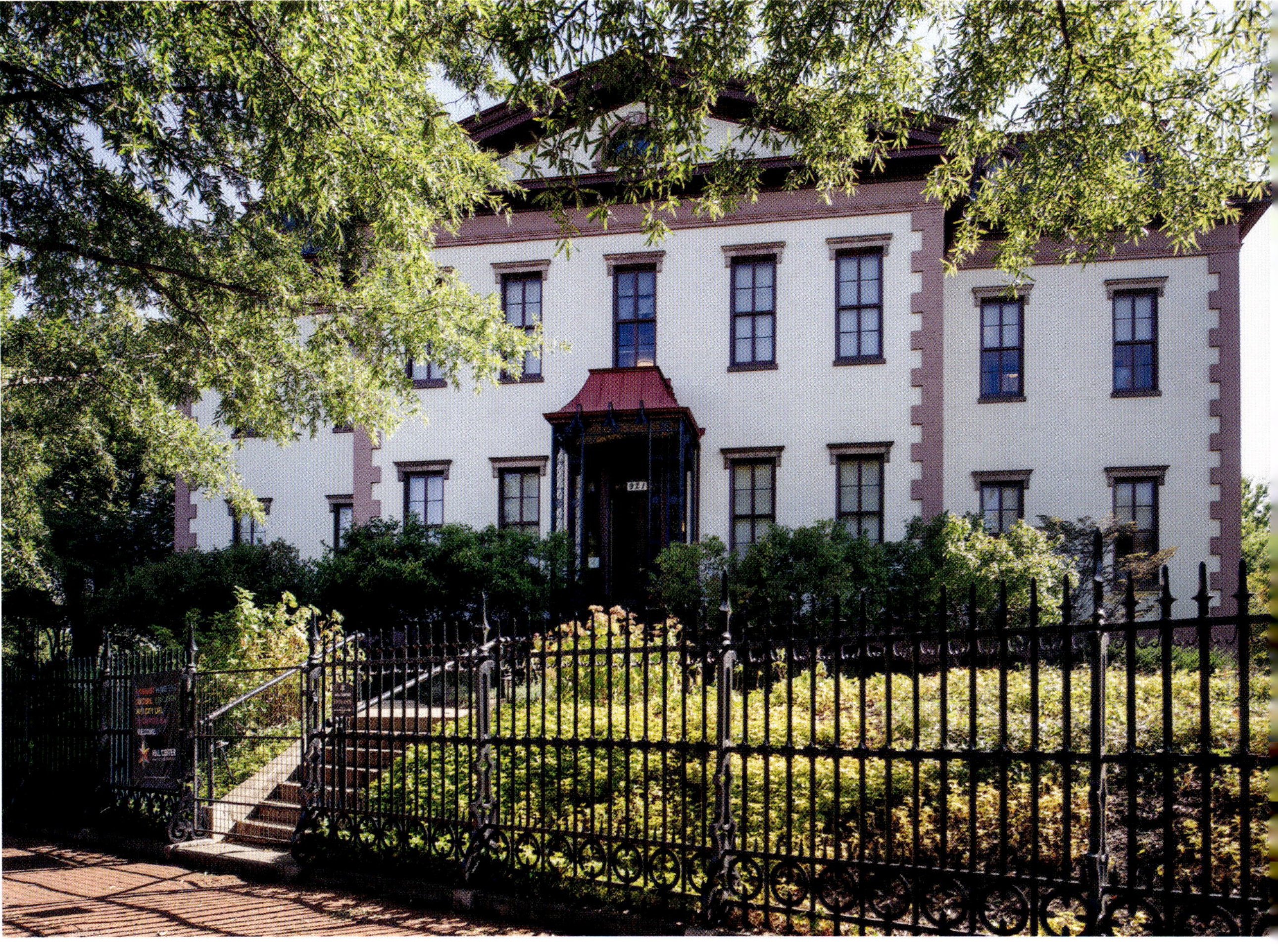

THEN: In the mid-nineteenth century, Washington, and America as a whole, was faced with a military presence. The Civil War, which divided the country in half, left Washington on the side of the Union with President Abraham Lincoln. In close enough proximity to the South, there was always the imminent threat of invasion. Lincoln knew the important role the capital city would play in the Civil War, especially as battles commenced closer and closer to the city. Washington, which was then not the bustling metropolis it is today, was also in need of some infrastructural support, so President Lincoln built Union hospitals all across the District.

One of these hospitals was Washington, D.C.'s first naval hospital, constructed just steps away from the Capitol Building. In 1864 President Lincoln commissioned the construction of this square brick building at 8th Street and E Street SE. The building included important modern amenities, including running water and gas lighting. With its state-of-the-art accommodations, the hospital was ready to serve the needs of the Civil War.

The hospital's first patient did not arrive until a year after the war had ended. In 1866, Benjamin Drummond was admitted to the hospital for an injury he received at a Confederate jail three years earlier. While he was eventually discharged two years later, the hospital, commissioned by President Lincoln at a high point of fighting during the Civil War, proved to have other purposes. It continued to serve the needs of the sick and wounded from the navy until 1906, when the hospital was moved into a new facility.

NOW: The former hospital continued to serve its medical purpose during the first half of the twentieth century. It was a Hospital Corps Training School for a few years before becoming an emergency hospital for veterans of the Civil and Spanish-American wars. From 1922-1963 it was the Temporary Home for Union Ex-Soldiers, Sailors, and Marines and provided lodging for veterans making pension claims in Washington.

The Old Naval Hospital met a fate similar to many Washington sites. The building changed hands several times through various social service organizations, before reaching a point where it was mostly vacant and faced demolition. Fortunately for the dilapidated building, a local group of neighbors valued the historical structure and wanted to see it restored to its former glory. The group worked to have the building preserved and find a long-term occupant to avoid constant turnover. Since their campaign in 2002, the building has been repaired, and is now occupied by the Hill Center, an organization that provides arts, education, and cultural programs. The building, which once served Washingtonians out of military necessity, now serves Washingtonians in a new cultural manner.

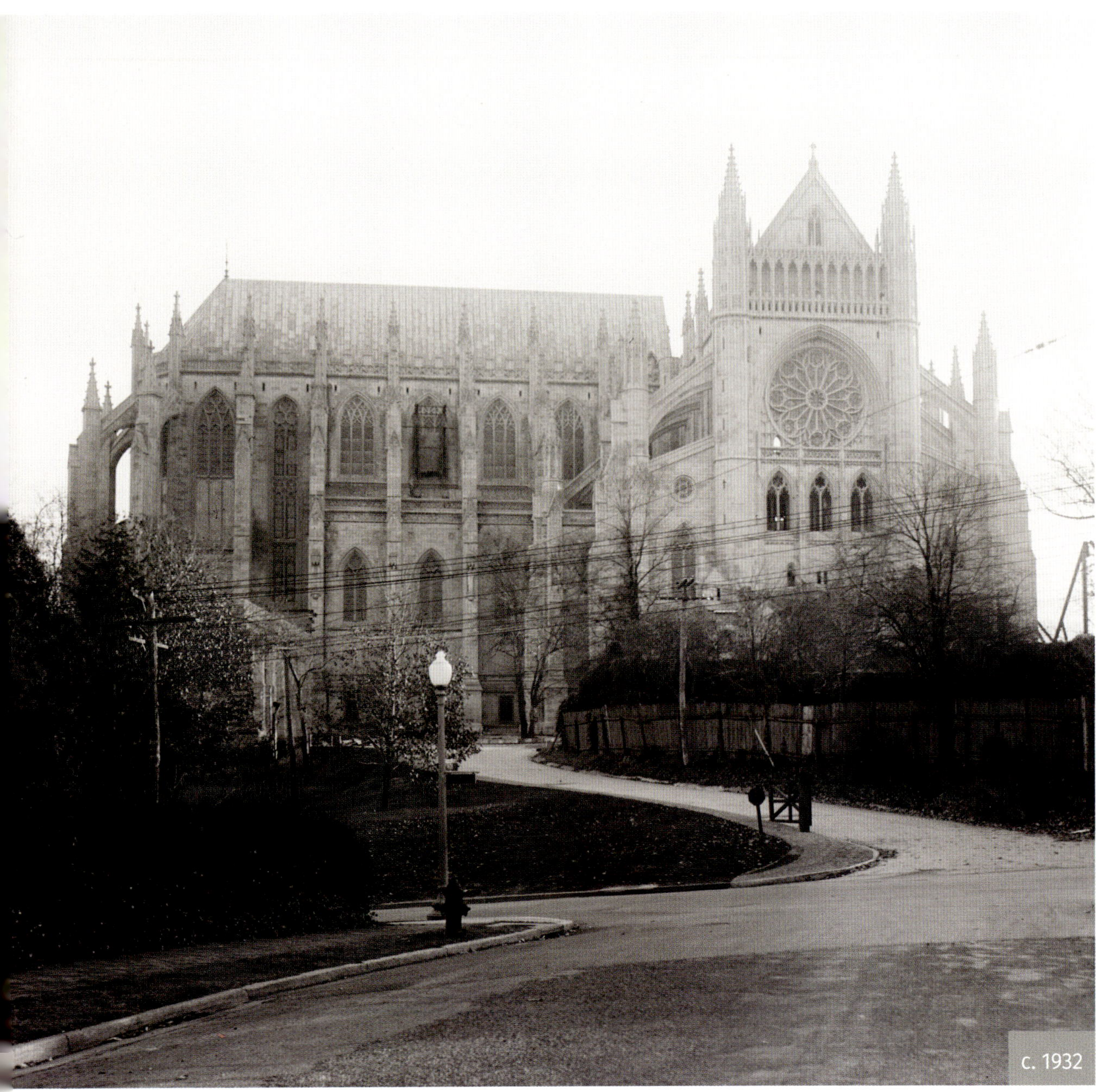
c. 1932

THE NATIONAL CATHEDRAL

A national church, two hundred years in the making

THEN: Washington's original plans had outlined a "great church for national purposes" that was to be nondenominational and centered downtown, yet none had materialized. Thus, in 1893, Congress decided that Washington would finally get its national church, and chartered a cathedral.

In 1907 construction began on the great structure, with President Theodore Roosevelt laying the foundational stone. The plan was for a large cathedral designed in the English Neo-Gothic style, with medieval structural features such as flying buttresses and load-bearing masonry walls. The design had been inspired by late fourteenth century English Gothic style; however, included alongside these historic design features were modern construction elements, bringing the cathedral into the twentieth century.

As the nation's capital, Washington experienced hardships brought on by the twentieth century with great intensity. This included two World Wars, economic depression, and periods of great social change, brought on by civil rights movements. Construction continued on the cathedral throughout these events, but at a much slower pace than originally intended. Individual sections of the building and its grounds were completed throughout the twentieth century, yet the cathedral was not officially finished until 1990, eighty-three years after construction had begun. President George H.W. Bush laid the final stone on top of the cathedral's towers, the fifteenth successive president since the one who laid the first.

Due to its gradual construction, different areas of the cathedral opened at different times. The Bethlehem Chapel opened in 1912 for services, with various presidents hosting national events here, and Martin Luther King, Jr. preached his final Sunday service in the chapel in 1968. The fifty-nine acres around the cathedral were also intentionally designed by Frederick Law Olmstead, Jr., and constructed from 1907-1927. Miles away from downtown Washington, Olmstead wanted this area to be a natural refuge from the crowded and busy D.C. experience in the city's center. The exterior includes curated gardens, park-like open spaces, and a preserved native woodland.

NOW: Officially named the Cathedral of Saint Peter and Saint Paul, the structure is the sixth largest cathedral in the world and is made of entirely solid masonry with no steel supports for the building. Its medieval design elements include 112 gargoyles and 215 stained glass windows, which are interspersed with some notable American features. Situated among the medieval gargoyles on one of the northwest towers is a sculpture, or a "grotesque", of Darth Vader, the infamous antagonist from the *Star Wars* franchise.

Although the original church was intended to be non-denominational, the National Cathedral regularly hosts Episcopalian services. Several presidential funerals have been held here, including for Dwight D. Eisenhower, Ronald Reagan, and Gerald Ford. President Woodrow Wilson was interred here, alongside other famous Americans such as Helen Keller. Located away from downtown, the National Cathedral sits away from the commercial activity of D.C., providing an opportunity for faith, and natural contemplation for everyday Washingtonians.

BELOW LEFT: Alongside beautiful colored windows depicting religious and natural scenes is a stained-glass window depicting outer-space and honoring America's participation in the Space Race. It even holds a piece of lunar rock.

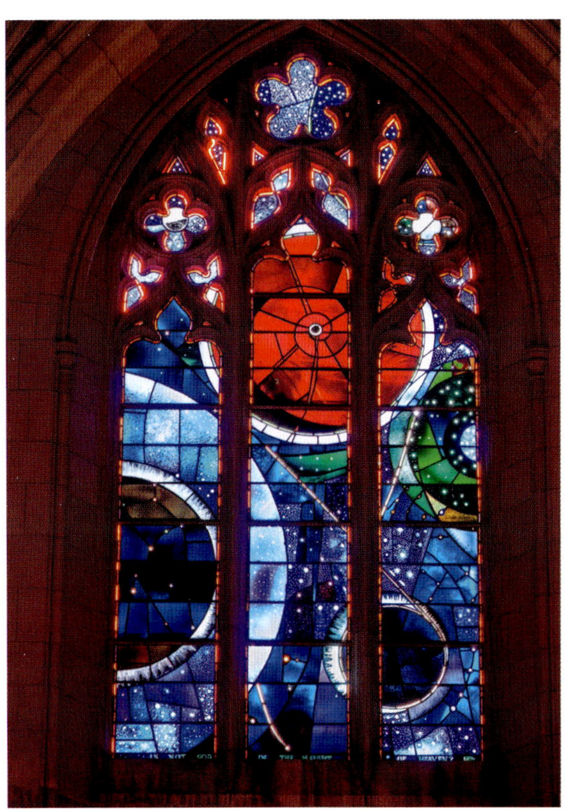

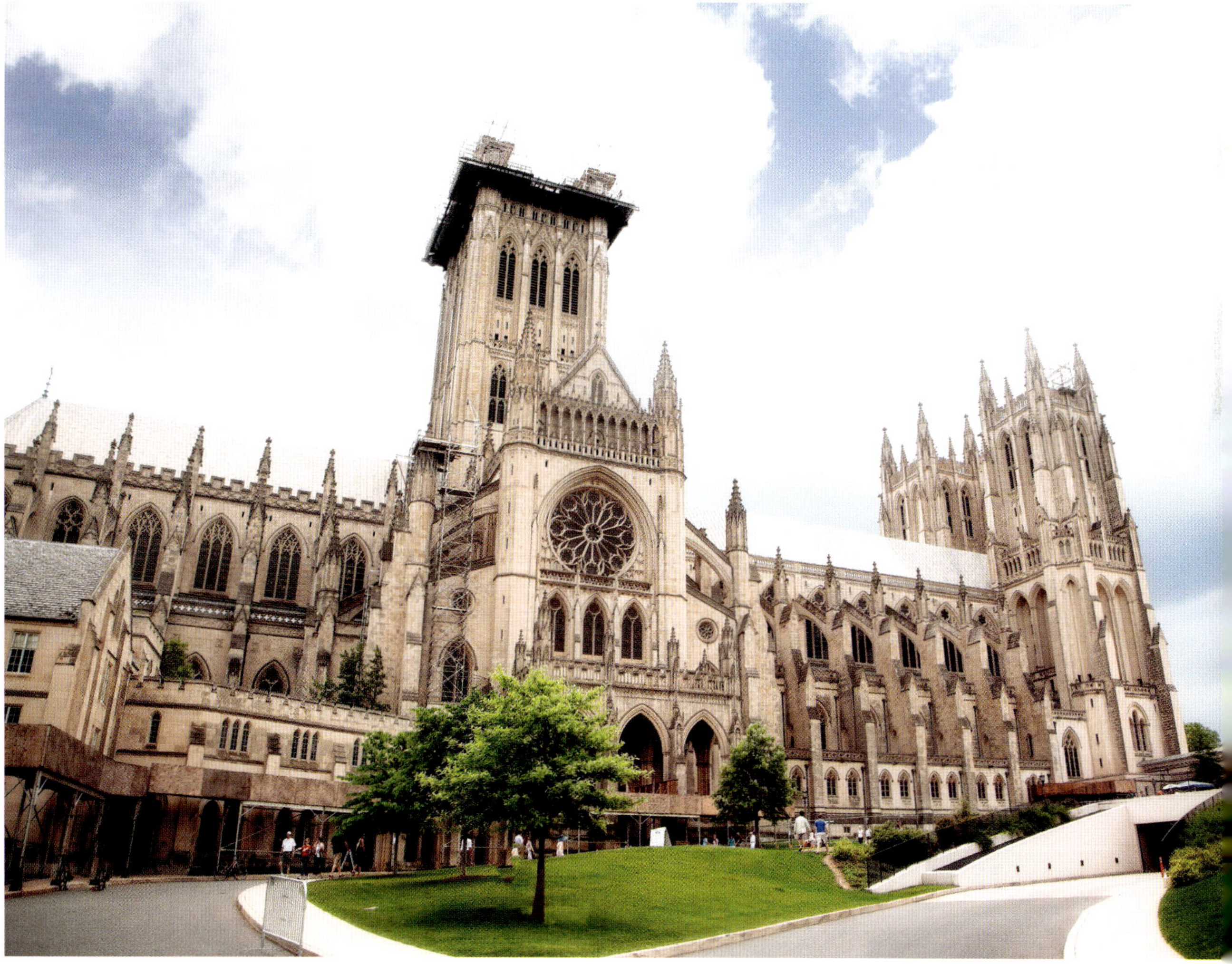

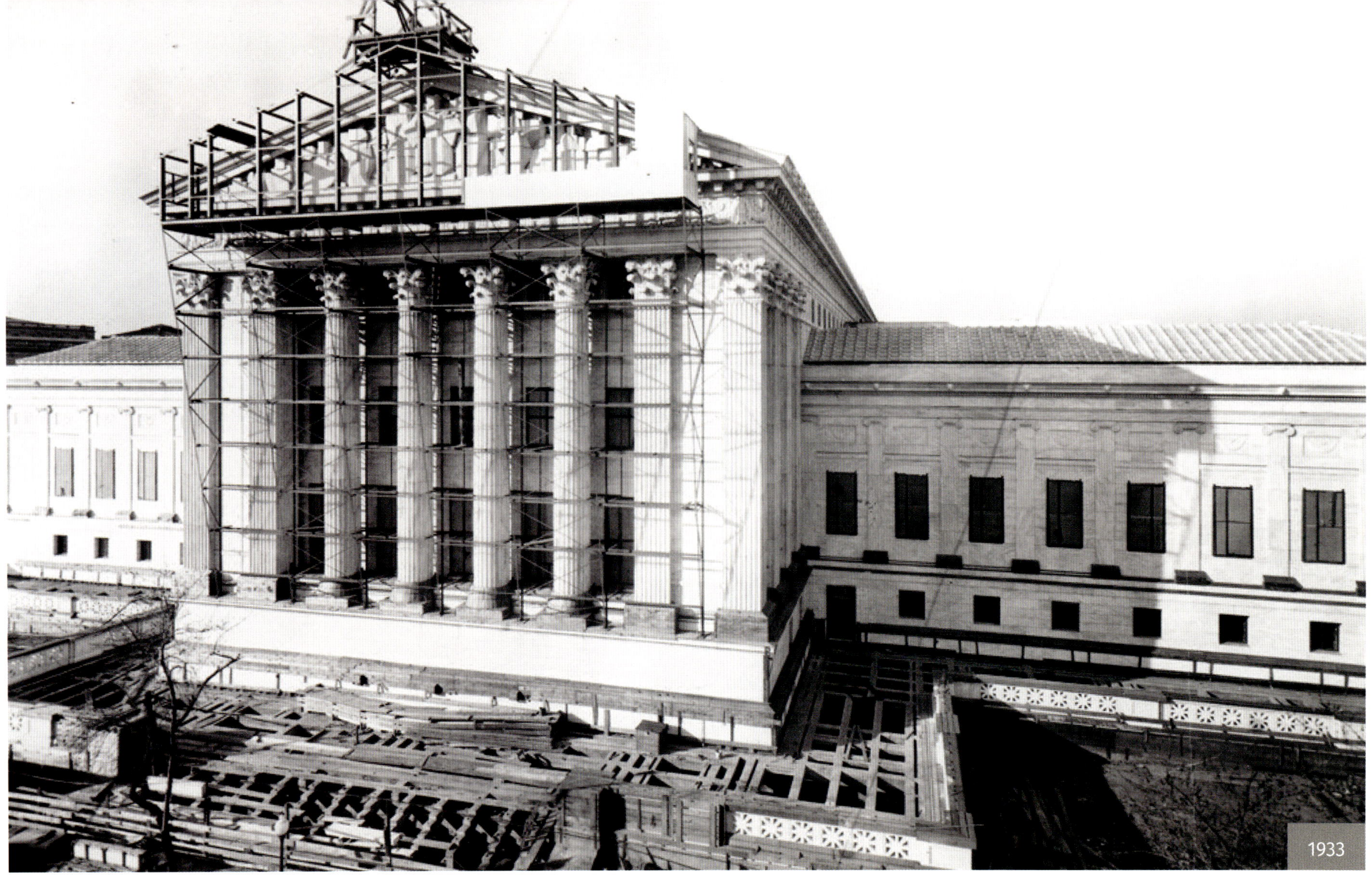

THE SUPREME COURT BUILDING

Washington's last government branch building

THEN: In America's earliest years as a nation, throughout the Revolutionary War and in the years following, there was uncertainty about how America's governance was to be structured. When the British eventually left New York there was an expectation that George Washington was to crown himself king, and rule the country as a monarch. However, this did not happen; George Washington became President of the United States and the leader of the Executive Branch, which allowed scope for two other branches to share the remaining power, representing and protecting the people. These came to be known as the Legislative Branch and the Judicial Branch. However, it was not until 146 years after its initial foundation that the Supreme Court of the United States received its own building.

Before the United States government made its way to Washington, it briefly convened in New York City where the Supreme Court had its start. The Court moved to Philadelphia next, as the government did, before landing in Washington in 1800 during its first year as the capital city. Upon their arrival, however, the Supreme Court had no formal meeting place. It was not until architect Benjamin Henry Latrobe made additions to the Capitol Building that the Supreme Court had a place to convene and rule on the laws of the new country.

Space in the Capitol Building was cramped, especially as it was shared between two branches of the United States government. Following the destruction of the Capitol in 1814 after the British invasion, Congress and the Supreme Court were forced to find

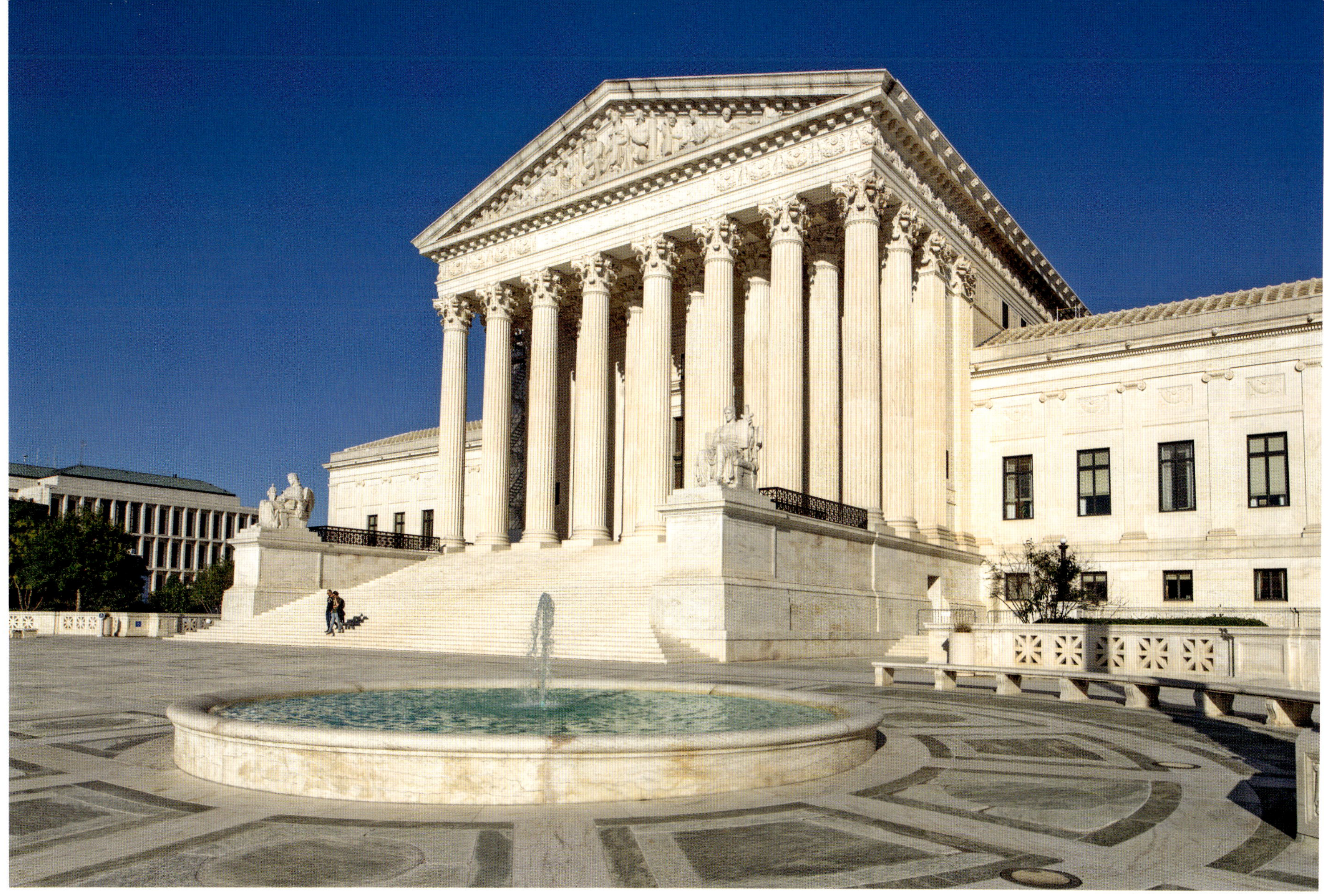

temporary offices to support the government. Once the Capitol was reconstructed, it became clear more space was needed, and fast. Congress was growing as U.S. land holdings increased, and committee meeting spaces, congressional chambers, and the Supreme Court were being regularly moved around to accommodate residences in the Capitol Building.

One believer in a physical separation of powers was William Howard Taft. In 1921, the former president was appointed to the bench, and served as the 10th Chief Justice of the United States. Holding this appointment was one of Taft's greatest honors, greater even than being President, and he left not only a judicial legacy, but his mark on the city of Washington as well. In 1929, Taft had had enough of running out of rooms and he advocated for the Supreme Court to have its own building, one that truly represented the strength of the Judicial Branch.

NOW: While Taft died before the building was completed, the Supreme Court Building maintains his legacy. Designed by architect Cass Gilbert on the site of the Old Capitol Prison, the Supreme Court Building was designed in a neoclassical style that was popular at the time. Opening in 1935, the Chief Justice and the associate Supreme Court justices finally had a work space of their own, after 146 years of sharing.

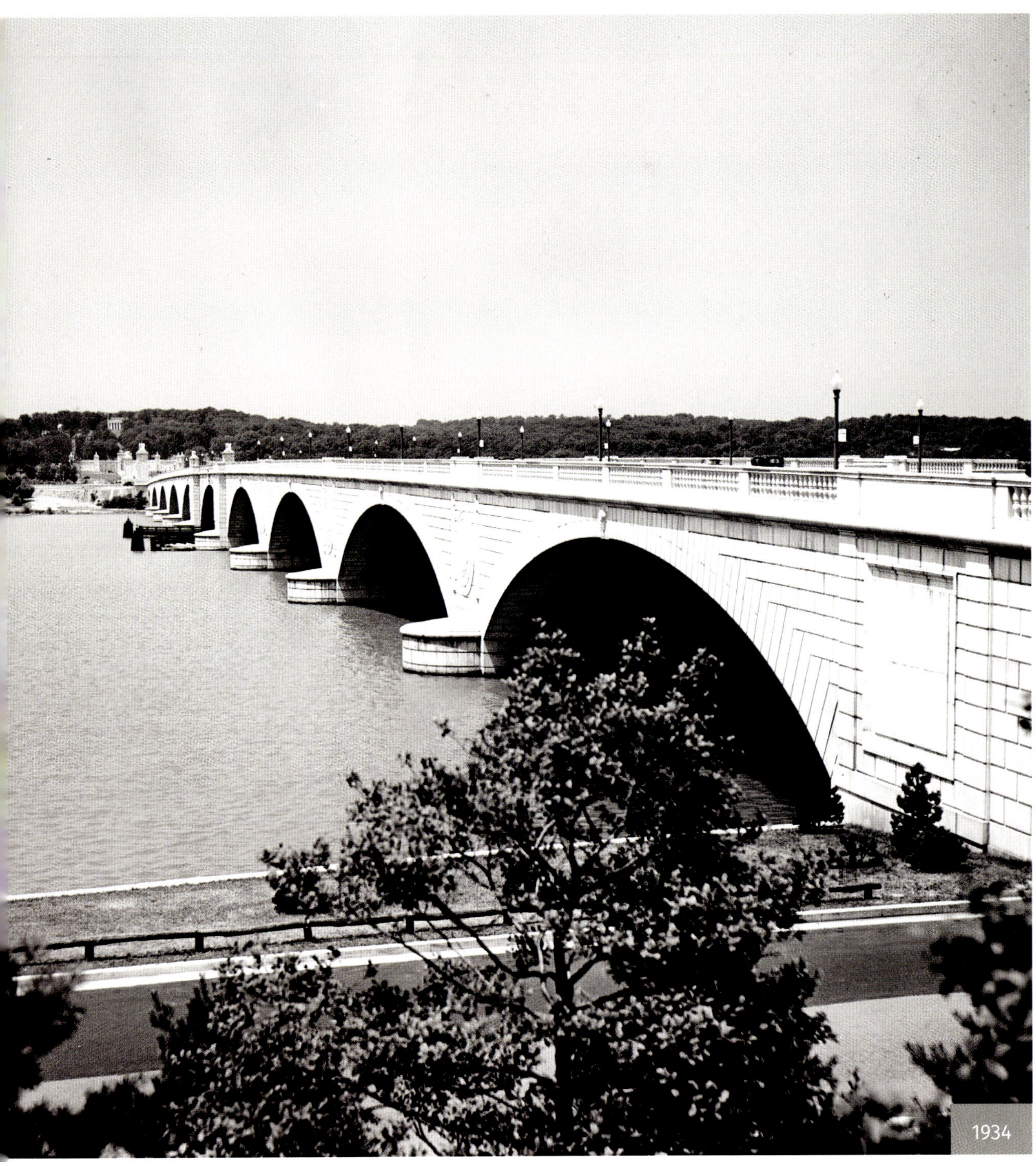
1934

ARLINGTON MEMORIAL BRIDGE

Connecting Lincoln to Lee, and Arlington to Washington, D.C.

THEN: There are many locations in Washington from which to view the capital city: from the top of the Washington Monument to travelling past U Street Northwest into Columbia Heights which brings visitors to colorful townhouses and a residential view of downtown. Arguably, however, there is one view which beats them all, and is best viewed from the ground by crossing the Memorial Bridge.

In 1926, Washington was at an important point of infrastructural renovations. The McMillan Plan was instituted at the turn of the century to update some of Washington's most historic buildings with a uniform design. The plan also proposed improvements to an idea that had been in the works for many years already: a bridge that crossed the Potomac River and linked Washington to Arlington, Virginia.

This bridge was an important route into Washington from the growing city of Arlington and had a symbolic significance as well. The bridge would connect the new memorial honoring President Lincoln with what was once the home of Confederate Civil War General Robert E. Lee. Directly across the water from the Lincoln Memorial was Arlington House, Lee's Virginia home, which was situated on a hill overlooking the new Arlington National Cemetery, also connecting the Presidential Memorial with soldiers who had been laid to rest. This decision was intentional and was conceived to show the rekindled connection between a divided America, north and south, in the years following the Civil War.

Construction on the neoclassical-style bridge began in 1926 organized by the firm McKim, Mead, and White who were the bridge's primary architects. The bridge was envisioned to extend the monumental structures of Washington across the water, with memorials along the bridge. On the northeastern end of the bridge near the Lincoln Memorial were two large gilded bronze statues titled *The Arts of War*. These matched another

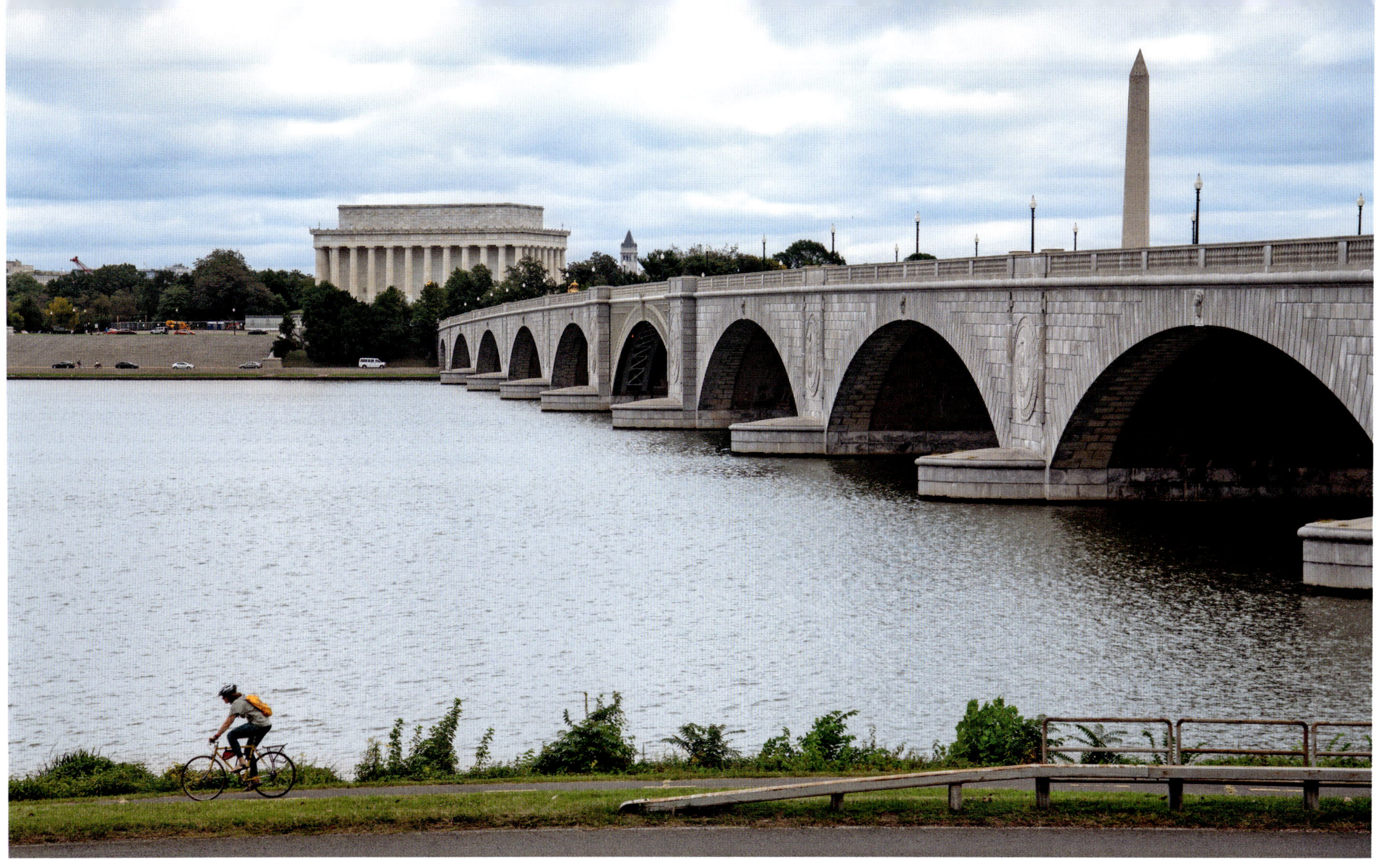

pair of statues at the entrance of the nearby Rock Creek Parkway titled *The Arts of Peace*. The statues had been commissioned in 1928, but were donated by the Government of Italy following American support during World War II. The bridge eventually housed seven memorials, with the first placed in 1961 and the most recent addition in 2001. The bridge is technically a drawbridge, although it has not been opened since 1961.

NOW: Memorial bridge officially opened for traffic in 1932 with a dedication ceremony led by then President Herbert Hoover. Since its opening, the bridge has remained an important connection between Washington, D.C. and the growing suburb of Arlington, Virginia. Importantly this bridge allows ease of access from the nation's capital to Arlington National Cemetery. Commonly depicted in media portraying Washington, D.C., the Arlington Memorial Bridge shows one of Washington's most recognizable views. Visitors entering the city at night from Arlington via the bridge can see the Lincoln Memorial, the Washington Monument, and the Capitol Building lined up in a row.

LEFT AND ABOVE: The view on the left of the Memorial bridge faces Arlington House, Robert E. Lee's residence in Arlington, VA while the view above shows the back of the Lincoln Memorial within the boundaries of Washington, D.C. The two viewpoints juxtapose the history of the city, the Civil War and Arlington's increasing development beyond the Arlington National Cemetery and its own historic past.

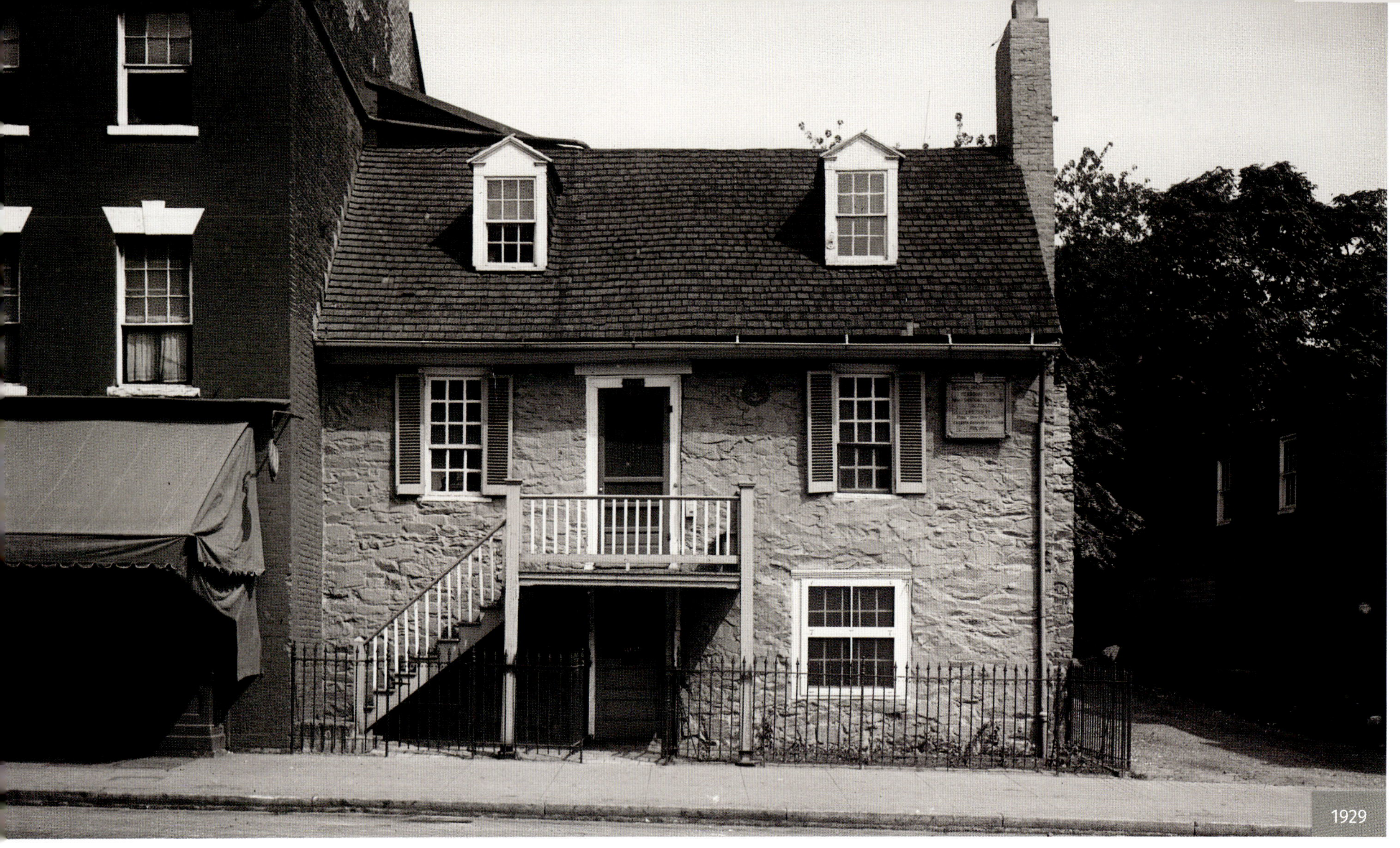
1929

OLD STONE HOUSE

The presidential headquarters that never were

THEN: In the eighteenth-century, Bridge Street in Georgetown, which is today referred to as M Street, developed up the way from the Potomac river. The street hosted new residences for businessmen looking to make their mark in the growing port town. One such home was Lot Three. Although its first recorded purchase was in 1752, the small stone structure is not believed to have been added until 1764. The original shape of the house remains unclear, however the local blue fieldstone was most likely quarried just two miles away, and the labor that went into its construction is still evident, with saw marks visible on ceiling beams.

The small stone structure served its intended purpose well, in a time that lacked many modern luxuries. The ceilings were intentionally built low to conserve heat in colder months, while the stone walls were thick and the floor comprised of dirt to protect the Layman family who lived there from the changing seasons of D.C. Despite its primarily utilitarian design, the house was sold to a member of Washington's growing upper-middle class, Cassandra Chew.

Renovating the home with a new kitchen and additional floors, Cassandra rented it out as a source of income around the 1770s, before it was given to her daughter. The Chews were slave owners, and there is some evidence to suggest that additional buildings on the lot were structures for Enslaved people to live in. The commercial development of the town relied on the labor of Enslaved individuals prior to Emancipation, as Georgetown's Black population made up about a third of the total.

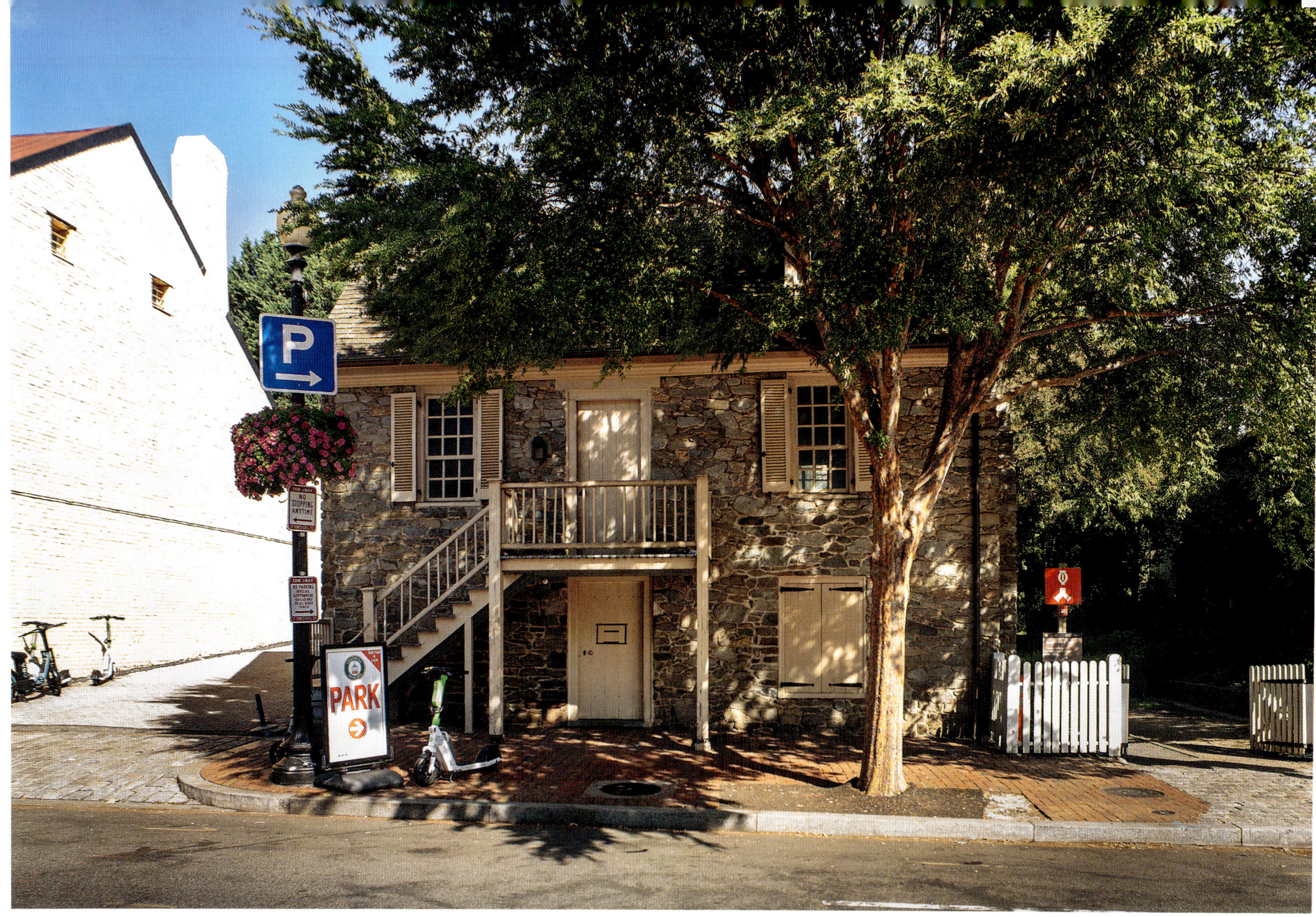

The Old Stone House changed hands several times, with the property housing different businesses such as a paint shop and boarding house, and at one point, earned fame for being the site of General George Washington's headquarters during the Revolutionary War. This legend was discovered to be a fabrication, developed through the building's passage of hands which began in the 1890s under the ownership of James and Morgan Goddard. General George Washington had been known to visit a nearby tavern, John Suter's Tavern. Suter's son, John Jr. was involved with the Chew family during the late eighteenth century, connecting the tavern and General Washington to the Old Stone House. Suter's Tavern remained a popular destination before a change of ownership caused it to fall into disrepair, making the property seem an unlikely place that the First President would have visited.

NOW: An archaeological dig at the Old Stone House site proved that while it had been used for whiskey production, printing, painting and even baking, it had never been a tavern and therefore was not the site of accounts of General Washington's visit. Despite the story proven as myth, the Old Stone House remains an important part of Washington's history. It is Washington's only remaining example of a pre-revolutionary house and stands out among the elegant homes of Georgetown's neighborhood. Currently owned by the federal government and acting as a museum, the small structure is a reminder of the many changes that parts of Washington have experienced since its conception.

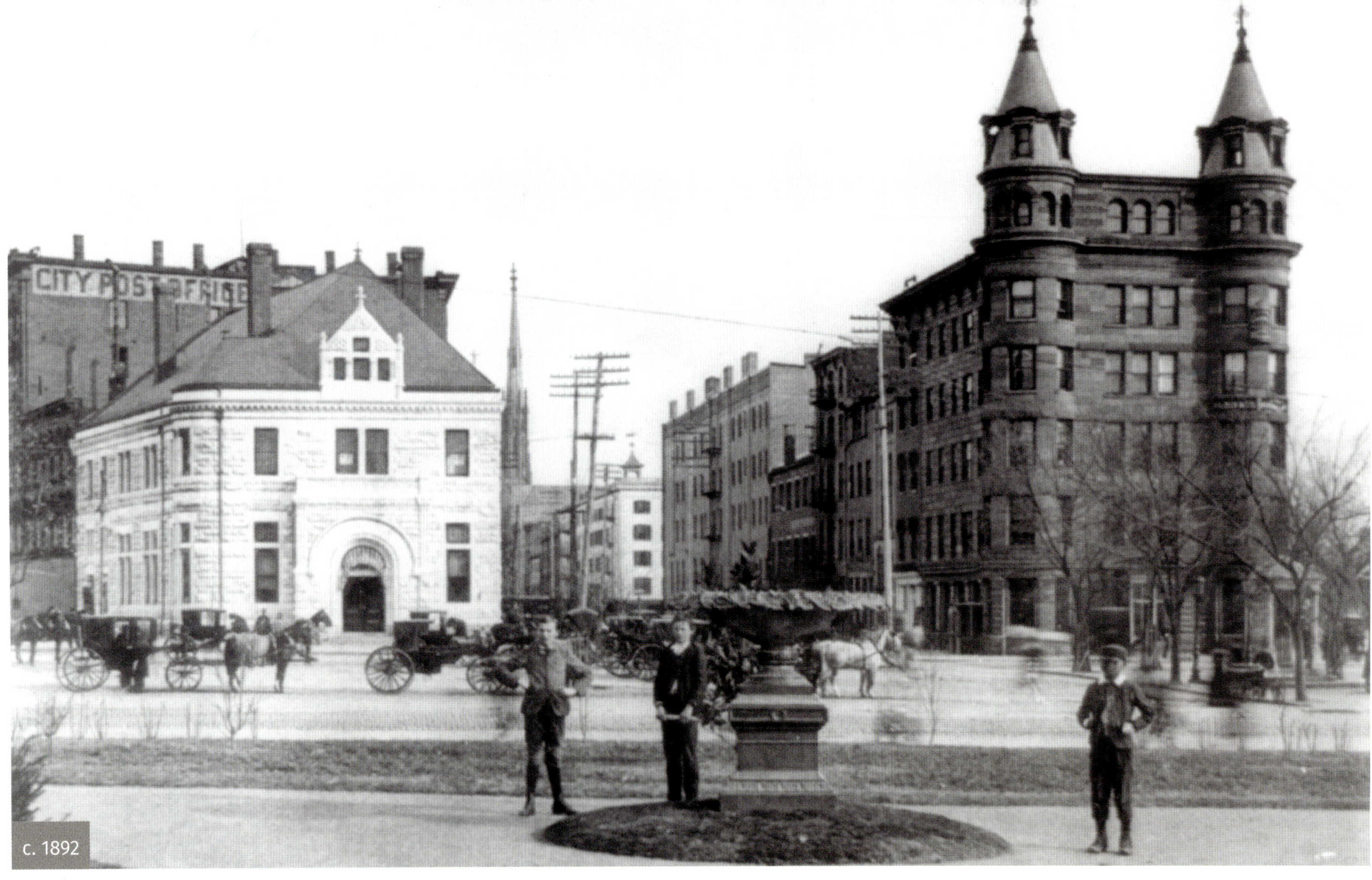

c. 1892

NATIONAL BANK OF WASHINGTON

A reminder of Washington's financial boom

THEN: When Washington, D.C. was determined to be the new capital with the Residence Act of 1790, there were only three banks in the territorial United States. The Bank of Columbia in Georgetown was one of the first, and its members were primarily large landowners whose finances supported the land expansion of the city. Despite this early success, Washington needed a central bank as downtown began to develop into the city center, and so The Bank of Washington, originally opened in Southeast D.C. in 1809, moved into Northwest Washington in 1829.

Sharing offices with the nearby National Hotel, the Bank of Washington purchased the current site of Indiana Avenue, 7th Street and C Street NW as its final home, bringing with it a central financial system in Washington. Originally a gable-roofed brick building, the structure was destroyed and replaced with the marble and granite structure in 1889, a rare example of Romanesque Revival Style that still stands today.

The proximity of this institution was not lost on the federal government, who took full advantage of loans offered by the bank to fund their activities. These three banks, including the Bank of Washington, enjoyed the increased population following the Civil War, however this success was short lived. The Civil War also brought a loss of business, as the federal government began distancing itself from local banks. While the Bank of Washington was largely involved in city government, it no longer had the influence it previously enjoyed in supporting the developing city.

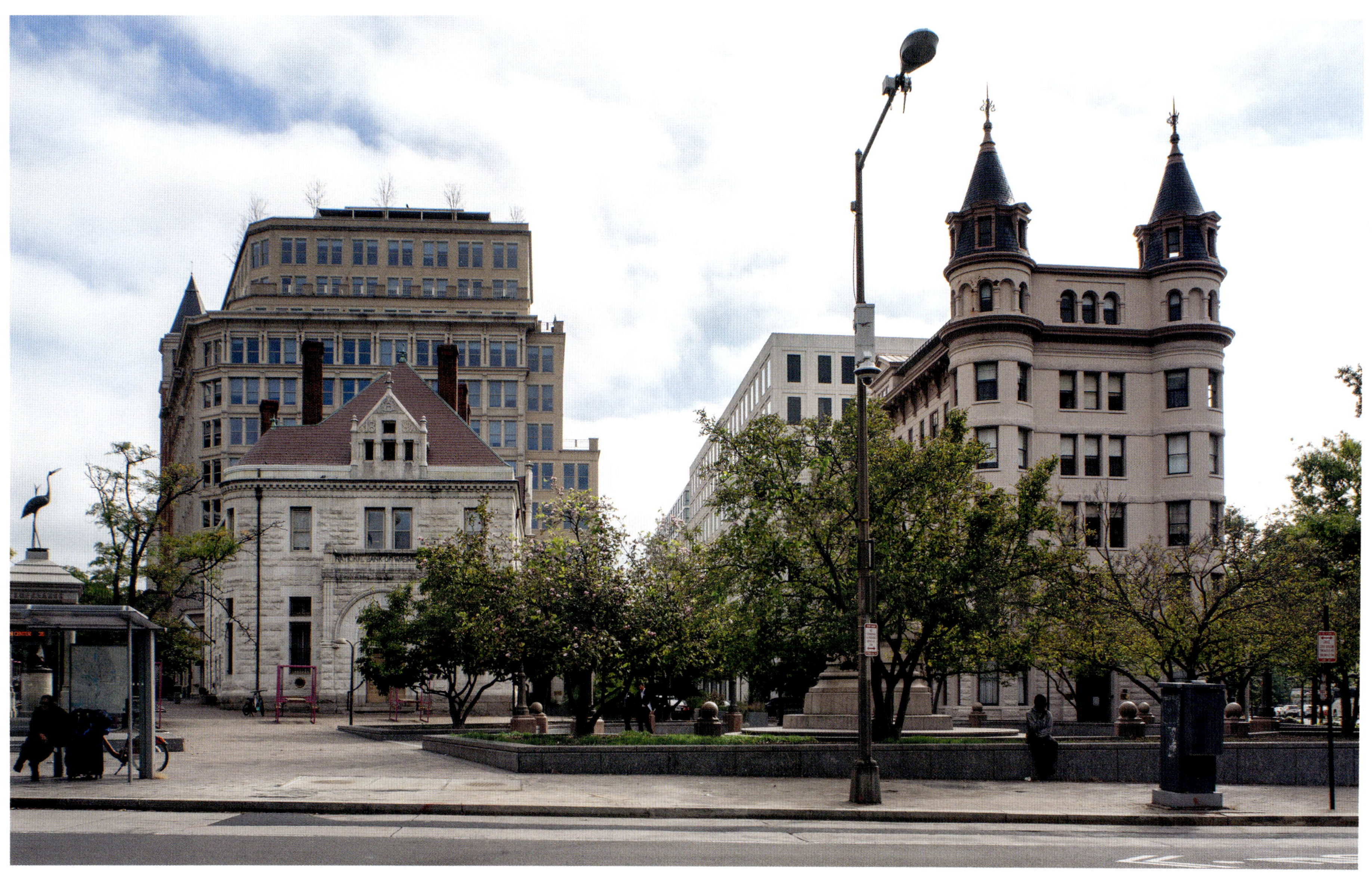

NOW: The Bank of Washington continued as one of the longest surviving banks in Washington, although its participation in Washingtonian life was not always deemed positive. As one of the most historic financial institutions in the city, the Bank of Washington played a role in the bankruptcy of the first major Black banking institution, the Freedman's Savings and Trust Company. Chartered by a government act that was signed by President Lincoln in 1865, the Freedman's Savings and Trust Company offered a place for recently emancipated individuals to begin their financial futures. Due to the Economic Panic of 1873 and other financial pressures, the Freedman Savings and Trust Company was forced to close and, unable to pay back its depositors, perpetuated social and financial strain on Black communities in Washington who had only one other bank to turn to. This was not the first or last bank to close in Washington, and was added to a collective of such businesses known as the "bank graveyard."

TUNNICLIFF'S TAVERN

A saloon in Washington, before it was Washington, D.C.

THEN: While many restaurants in Washington boast the title of "longest operating saloon in Washington" or "Washington's oldest bar," few can truly claim to be one of Washington's first. In 1796, William Tunnicliff opened the Eastern Branch Hotel, near Pennsylvania Avenue on the east side of town. At the time, Washington, D.C. had only six hotels making Tunnicliff's an easy choice for those coming to the new capital city. Tunnicliff offered everything a visitor could need: housing, a meal, and even a clean shirt. The tavern was also the site of the Washington Dancing Assembly's first ball in 1796.

By the time Congress had made its way to Washington in 1800, it became clear Tunnicliff's Eastern Branch Hotel was too far away to serve the needs of the new

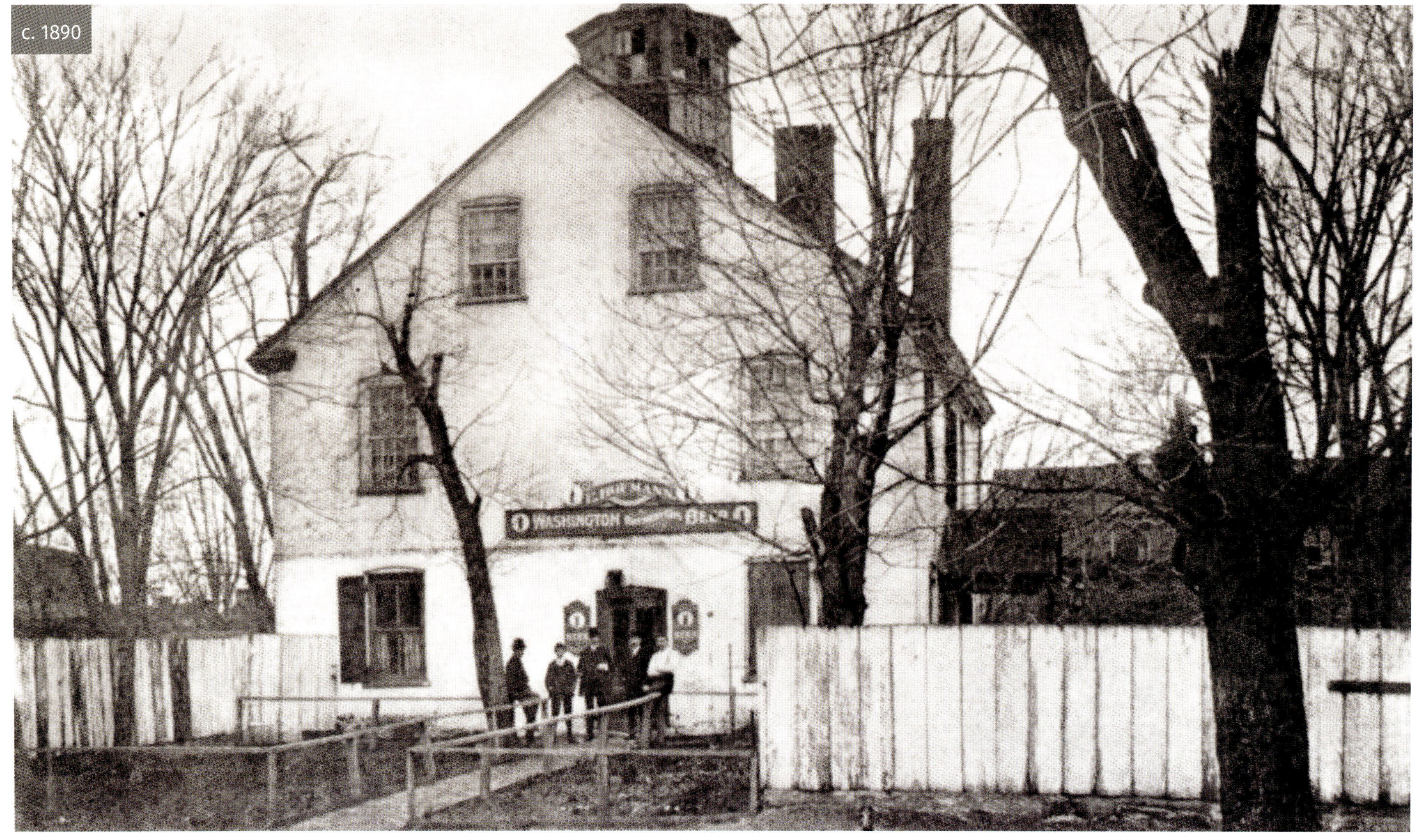

c. 1890

government. Additionally, the shifting of the Post Road through Washington moved traffic away from the once popular tavern spot and so, William Tunnicliff made a change.

In 1799, Tunnicliff announced the opening of his new Washington City Hotel, often referred to as 'Tunnicliff's'. The building stood on First Street and A Street in what would be the Northeast quadrant of an expanding D.C. This brought Tunnicliff's hotel not merely close to the Capitol, but right next to it. It was obvious that making the move closer to the seat of Congress was a smart move, with President John Adams noting that he enjoyed his stay at Tunnicliff's in a letter to wife Abigail in 1800.

Following the death of his wife in 1804, Tunnicliff sold his hotel and the building continued to change hands throughout its years. Most notably, it was included in the Old Brick Capitol, later a Civil War prison, and the eventual site of the Supreme Court Building.

NOW: In 1821, Tunnicliff's became the family home of master shipbuilder Captain William Easby, who needed a home in proximity to the growing naval yard in Southeast Washington. Following his death in 1854, the Easby family remained in the house until the 1880s when they sold the house. The building then served many purposes as a restaurant and a salon, a boarding house, and an auto garage. The building was ultimately razed in 1931 to make way for a gas station, a purpose which it continues to fulfill today.

While the original site is now a gas station, a nearby institution has continued the legacy of one of the first taverns in Washington. Opening in the Capitol Hill neighborhood of Eastern Market in the 1980s, the new Tunnicliff's Tavern has become a popular watering hole for those who live on the hill. Northwest Washington boasts several of the city's most popular culinary destinations, but Tunnicliff's Tavern in Southeast Washington honors the brief, yet important, legacy of the original tavern in its name and function.

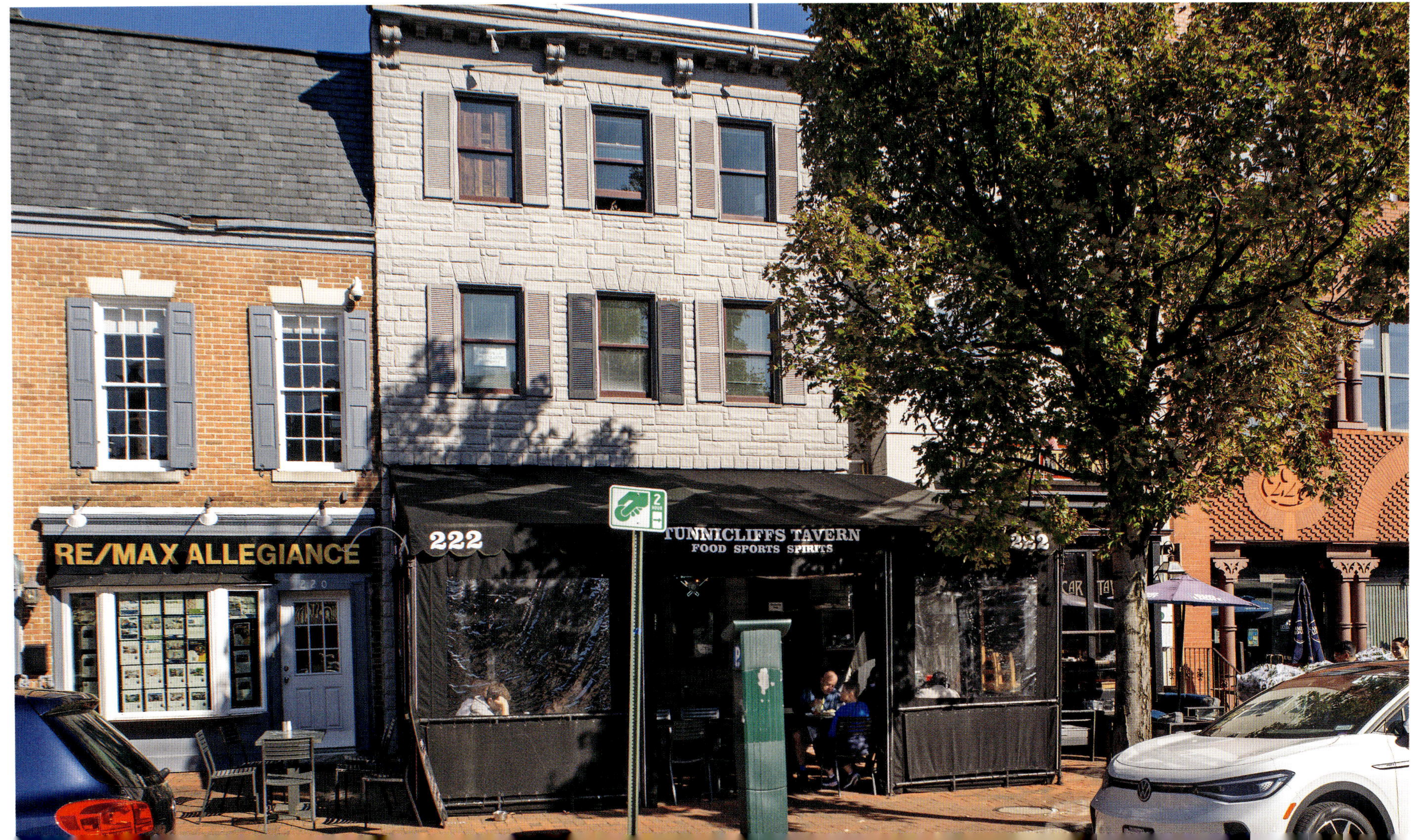

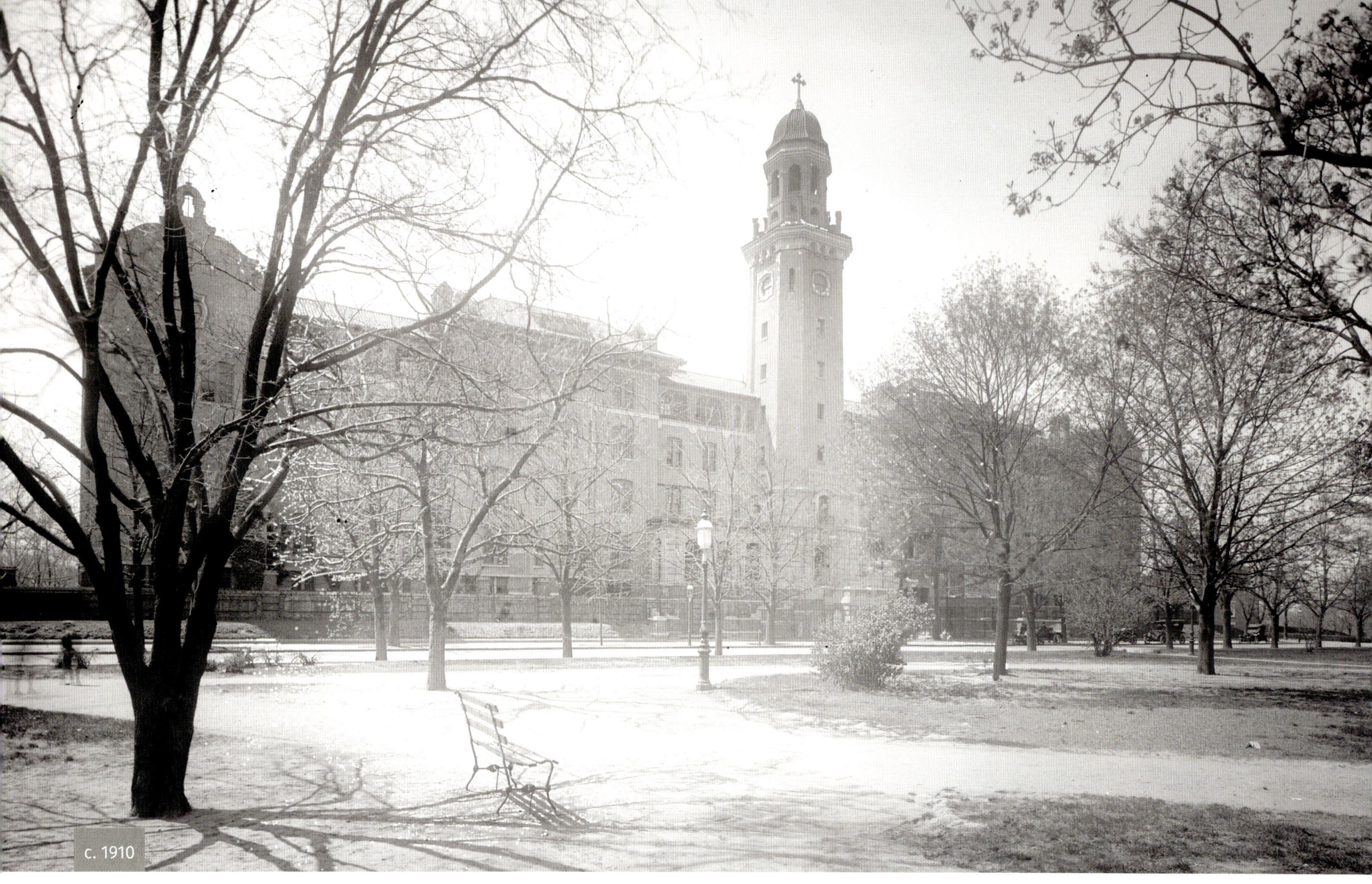
c. 1910

PROVIDENCE HOSPITAL

One of the longest running hospitals in Washington

THEN: Due to its location between the North and South, Washington, D.C. was in close proximity to many battles, and therefore needed adequate hospitals. President Abraham Lincoln understood the importance of Washington's need to provide adequate medical support to wounded soldiers, and commissioned dozens of hospitals throughout the Civil War. One of the ninety-two new hospitals was Providence Hospital.

Opening merely six weeks after the start of the Civil War at the corner of 2nd and D Street SE, Providence Hospital served a unique purpose. While many medical institutions were used for strictly wartime support, few were used to support Washingtonian civilians. The United States military had confiscated only other civilian hospital at the time, leaving only Providence Hospital, which was run by the Sisters of Charity, to serve the public of Washington. The sisters could not ignore the need for

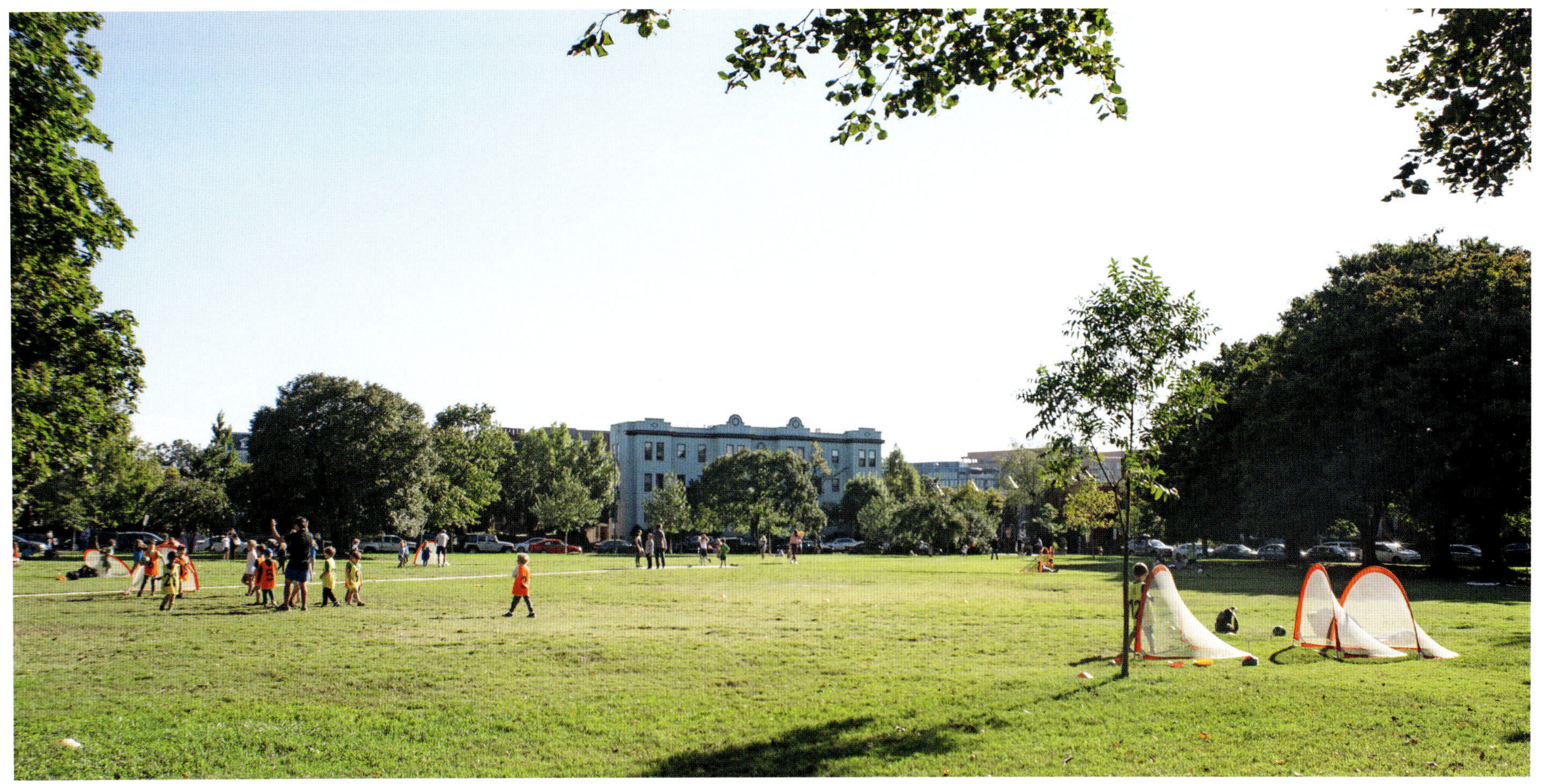

medical care that the war brought about, so Providence Hospital served both civilians and wounded Civil War soldiers.

Their inclusion of both civilian and military patients proved to be important, as the hospital expanded outside its large building, and tents were erected outside to create the space needed to treat incoming patients. The area around the hospital and the nearby neighborhood of Capitol Hill became known as "Bloody Hill" as soldiers were treated in these medical facilities; brick and mortar or makeshift. Those treated at the hospital hailed from both the North and the South's militia, echoing a commitment to unbiased humanity that the Sisters of Charity upheld in a war torn America.

In 1864, Providence Hospital received congressional funding to renovate the medical space and in 1872, these renovations revealed a Second Empire-style building which gave the hospital a traditional look. The new building held 250 beds, making it the largest hospital in D.C. at the time. With the war now over, the hospital once again focused on its intended purpose, of serving Washington civilians.

NOW: Throughout its time as the longest running hospital in Washington, Providence Hospital has made many advancements within the medical field. The hospital had the first medical amphitheater in the U.S. in 1882, and distinguished itself as a teaching hospital. Some of those educated at the hospital were nurses from the Sisters of Charity, who were trained and treated wounded soldiers in the Spanish-American War and World War I.

The hospital was renovated to accommodate its increasing number of patients at the beginning of the twentieth century, yet by World War II the spike in residents proved to be encompassing for Providence Hospital's current location, and the hospital was relocated to the Northeast neighborhood of Brookland in 1949. The old building changed owners several times before being torn down in 1965. After much debate, in 1978 the former site was turned into a Folger park, which still exists today.

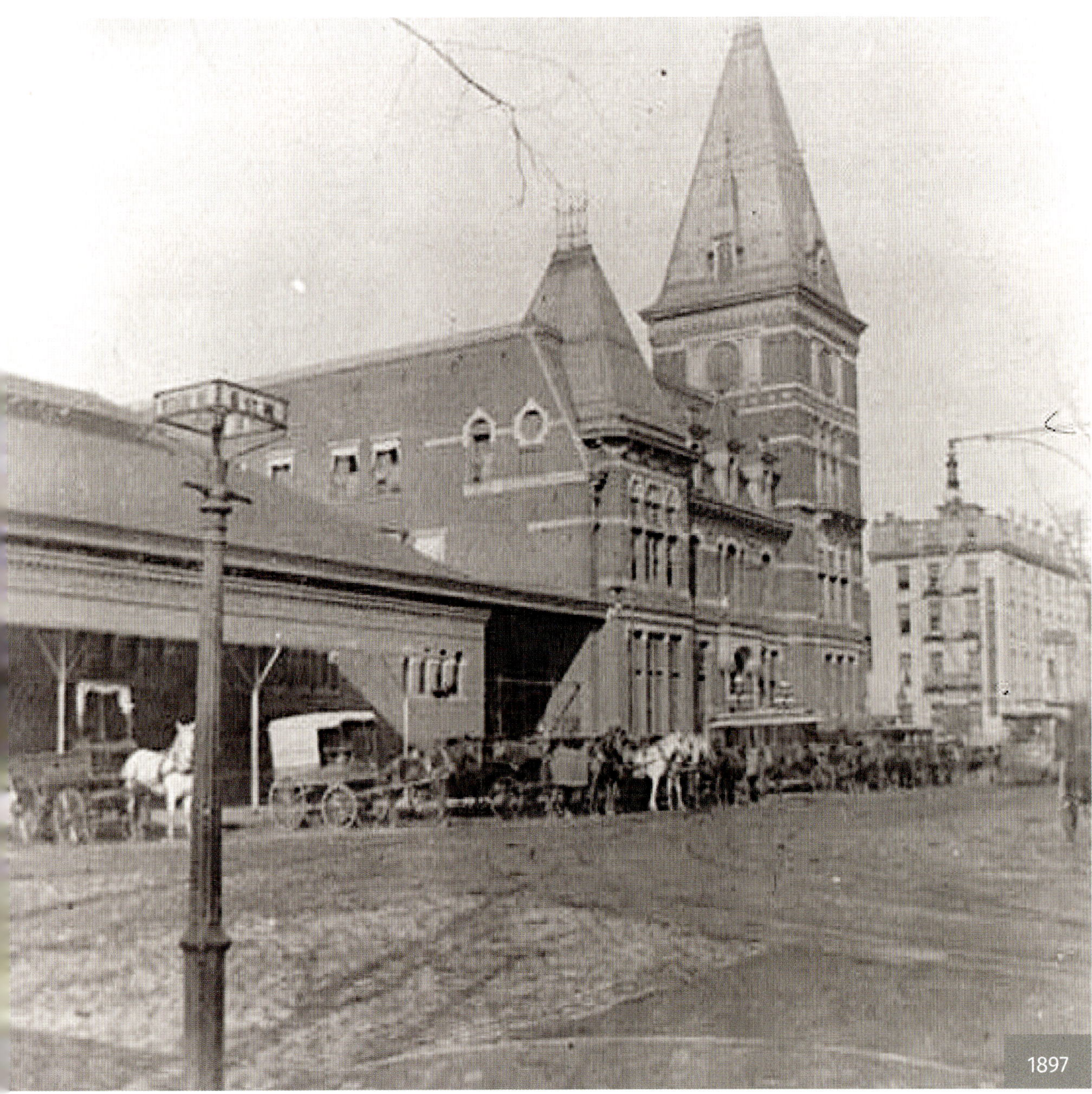
1897

BALTIMORE AND POTOMAC RAILROAD STATION

Revolutionary transportation or constant disturbance

THEN: In the nineteenth century, the Baltimore and Potomac Railroad Company and the Pennsylvania Railroad Company made their way to Washington, itching for their empires to enter the federal city. Congress made the final decision to allow the B&O Railroad Company to build their tracks and corresponding passenger depot in the District.

The location of the depot, was originally at Virginia Avenue between 6th and 7th Streets, but the building was eventually moved to Constitution Avenue and 6th Street NW. This downtown location was intentional as new arrivals would be greeted by a bustling downtown D.C. The Washington Canal also ran along Constitution Avenue and was essentially an open sewer surrounded by overgrown vacant lots, so placement of the passenger depot aimed to bring new life into downtown.

Since its proposal, the Baltimore and Ohio railroad and passenger depot was met with disapproval. While these improvements to the city were important steps towards a more technologically advanced D.C., some argued that the railroad tracks cutting through what would be the National Mall were disruptive to the natural landscape of Washington. This argument had carried little weight at the time, as the National Mall area was essentially an overgrown pasture for animals as a result of the Civil War.

Construction finished on the depot in 1874 and initially stunned the public with its elaborate Gothic design. A rich example of Victorian ornamentalism, there were; three towers, including a clockless clock tower; red brick with black mortar; decorative ironwork and painted roof crests that were blue and gold. The building was an improvement to downtown, however the tracks greatly disrupted what would eventually be the National Mall.

Railcars stayed parked on the green space, pollution increased dramatically, and downtown was covered in a layer of soot and smoke. Those who ventured too close to the prominent tracks were injured by speeding trains and one great tragedy, the assassination of President James Garfield, occurred in a station waiting room in 1881. Many who had noted that the Baltimore and Potomac Railroad Company had brought new technology to Washington, began to ask at what cost.

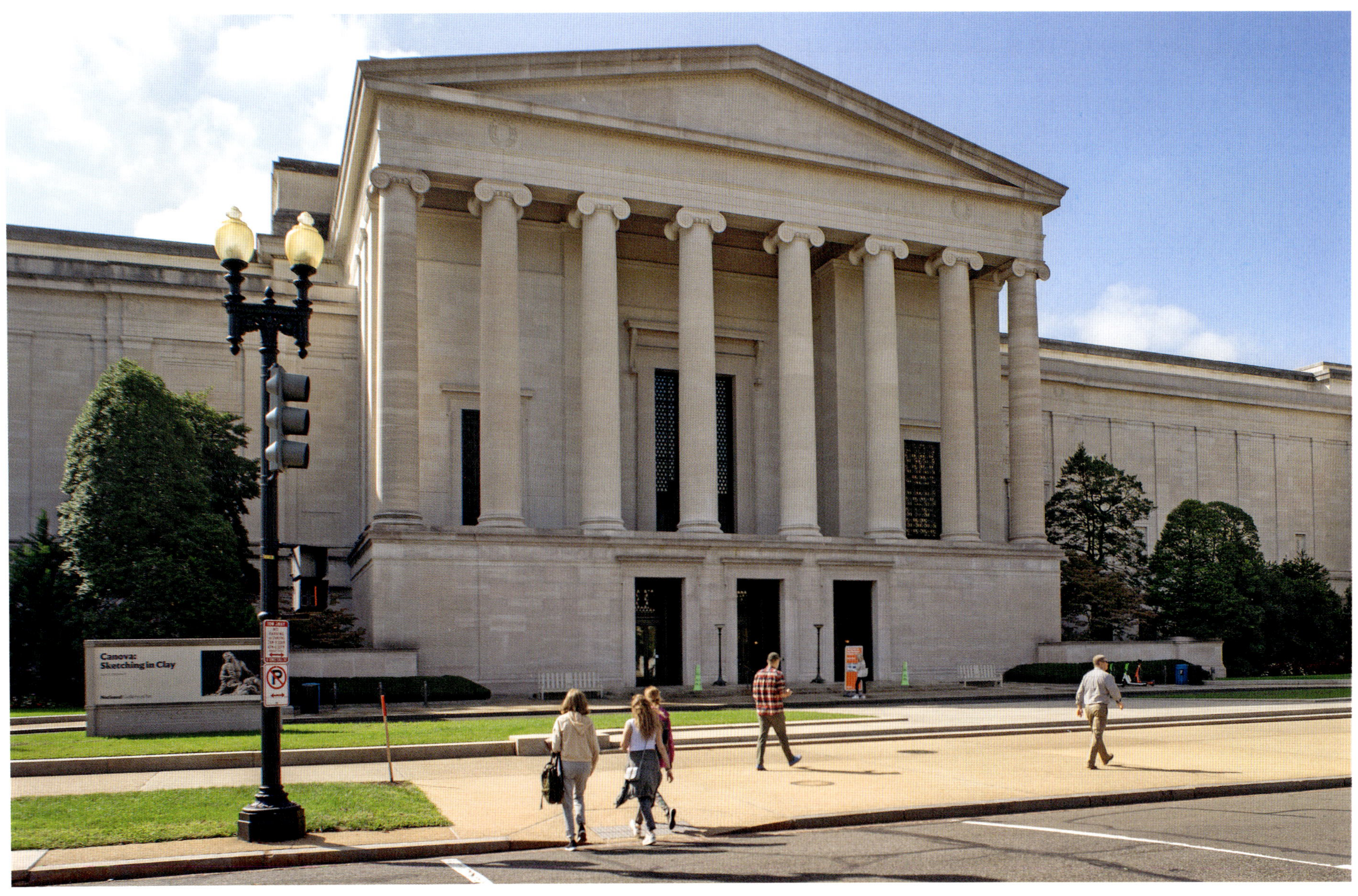

NOW: By the late 1890s the elaborate station was rapidly becoming too small for the personnel who used it, and Washingtonians remained unhappy with the hazardous tracks and railcars. In the early twentieth century The City Beautiful Movement was underway in the District, and the Baltimore and Potomac Railroad Company Depot became a target of infrastructural change.

With different depots around the city for multiple railroad companies, the City Beautiful Movement proposed the destruction of this depot for one collective rail station: Union Station. To the relief of the protesting public who were excited to have their green space back, the depot was demolished and the tracks removed from the Mall. The last traces vanished as in 1941 when the National Gallery of Art was constructed on the site of the railroad station.

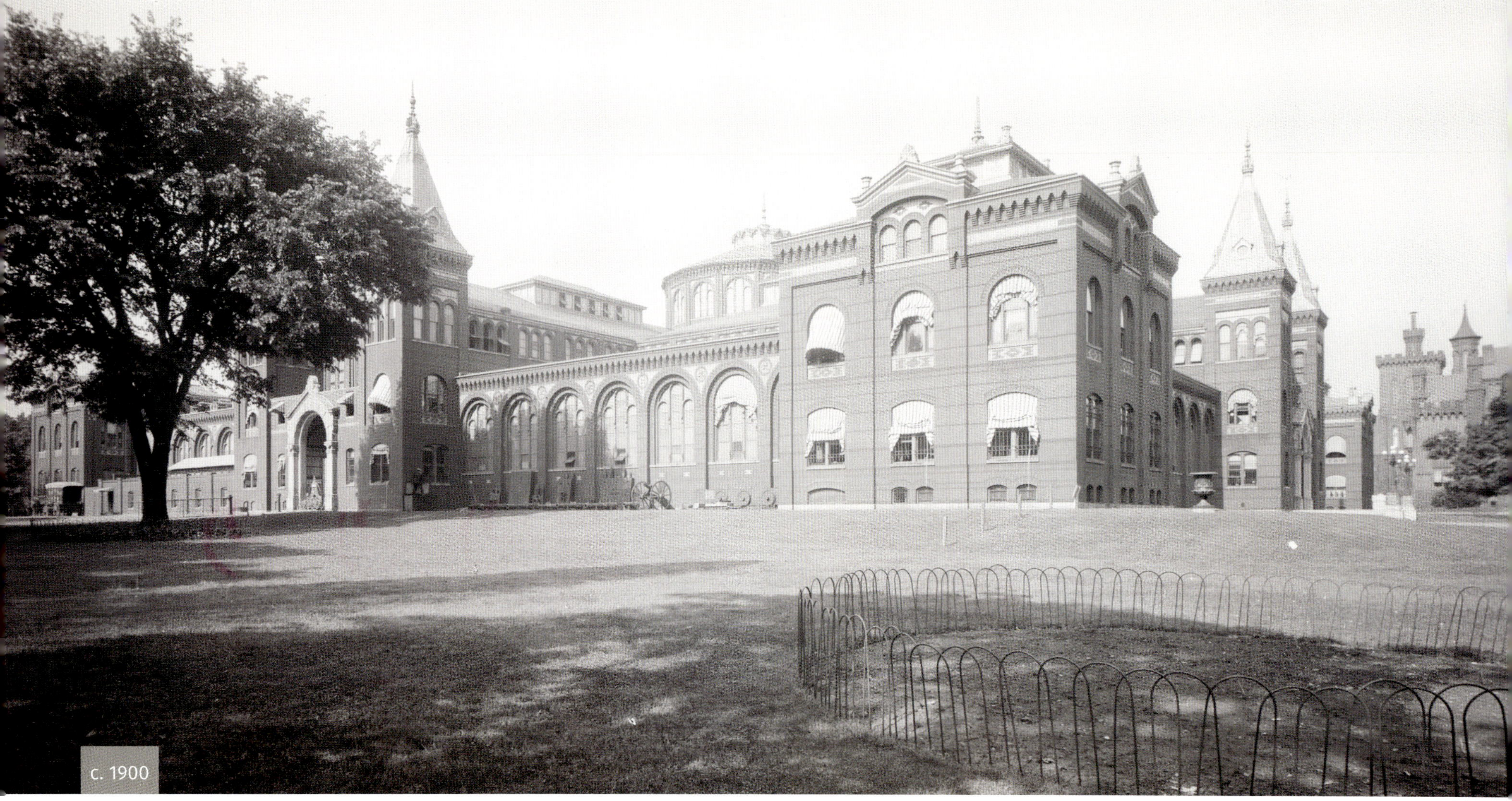

c. 1900

OLD NATIONAL MUSEUM

Washington wants a World's Fair

THEN: Designed by popular Washington architects Adolf Cluss and Paul Schulze in 1879, the new Smithsonian museum was built directly next to the Smithsonian Castle in 1881. The building was a resolution intended to house objects from the U.S. first World's Fair on the 150 year anniversary of the Declaration of Independence, which had been a success in Philadelphia. Despite its proximity to a building that had been a D.C. landmark for more than thirty years, the National Museum became a site of interest in its own right. The building was constructed to be one floor, with a large cross path and large central rotunda. Covered by an iron roof, the space included nearly 1,000 windows, allowing it to be almost entirely lit by natural light. The architects built this structure with European World's Fairs in mind. However, these

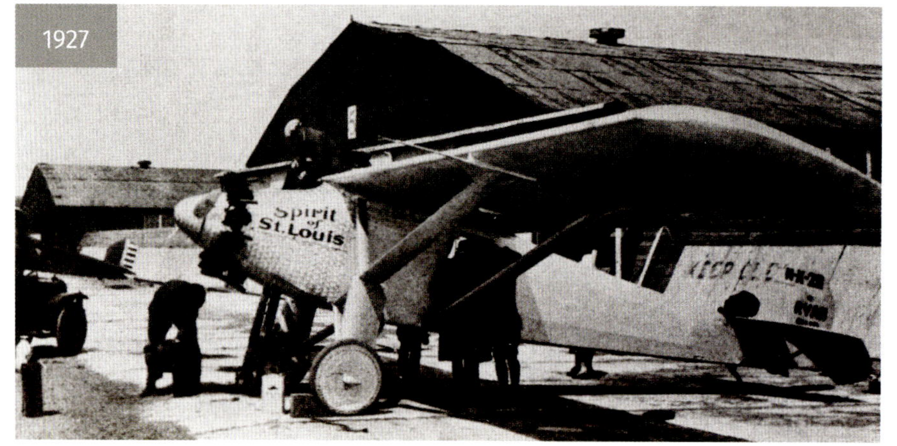

1927

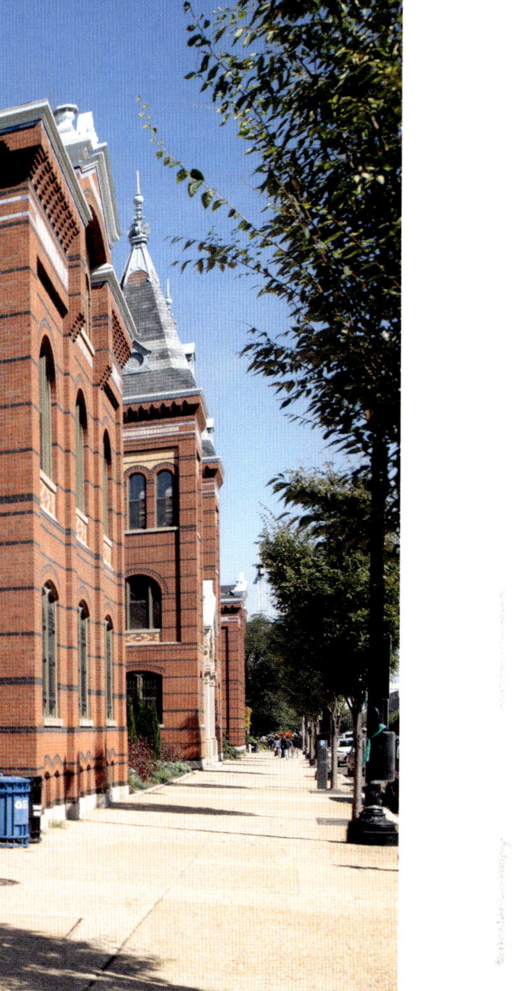

expositions were largely temporary, except for some notable displays such as the Eiffel Tower in Paris and the Crystal Palace that once resided in London. European inspiration was paired with an American desire to create a permanent exhibition space in the nation's capital.

The building's collection included artifacts from the Centennial Exposition, including Betsy Ross's Star-Spangled Banner and the dresses of many of the First Ladies. Eventually, as the collection developed, the museum faced a recurring problem: space. In 1910 the Smithsonian expanded again, and the National Museum of Natural History was built across the mall, hosting the nation's growing ecological and zoological collection.

LEFT: Before it was moved to the National Air and Space Museum, the Arts and Industries Building held the Spirit of St. Louis, the first plane to reach airborne status.

NOW: The National Museum, renamed the Arts and Industries Building following the opening of the National Museum of Natural History, continued to hold some of America's greatest treasures. In 1974 the building became a designated historical landmark and underwent renovations for the next century celebration, the United States' Bicentennial. The museum went on to host different experimental exhibitions and installations, living up to its original purpose of displaying cultural moments and technological advancements for the public. The building underwent major renovations in 2009 and reopened in 2021 with the *Futures* exhibition, a showcase of upcoming and important advancements in America's society and infrastructure.

The space today serves as an impressive example of exhibition-space design, and a reminder that what is shown throughout the plethora of Smithsonian buildings belongs to the American people. While the Arts and Industries Building never hosted a World's Fair, the intention with which it was constructed makes it one of the best surviving examples of World's Fair architecture in the nation.

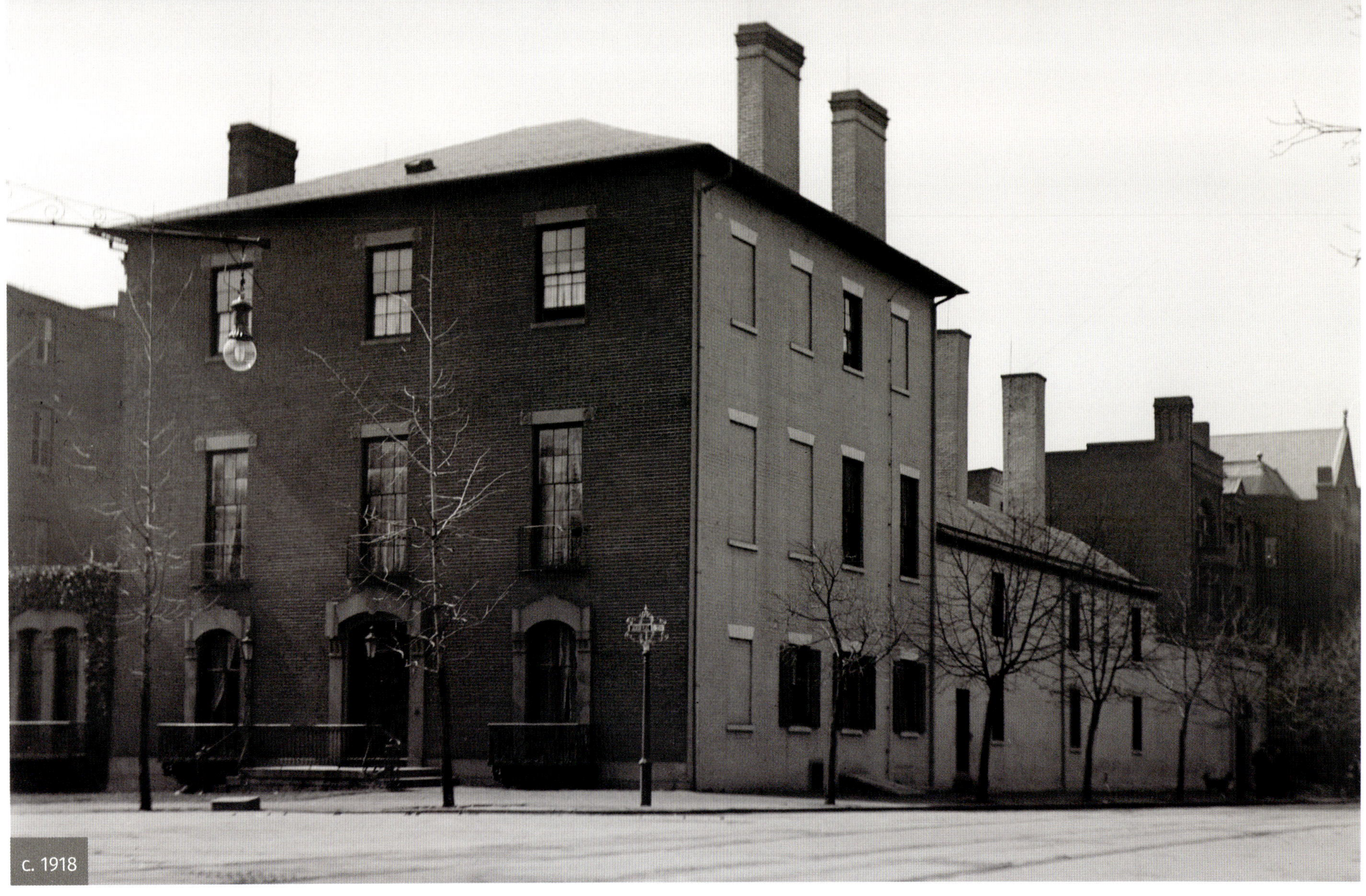
c. 1918

DECATUR HOUSE

A residence for Washington changemakers

THEN: In 1816, two new residents to Washington were Commodore Stephen Decatur, Jr. and his wife Susan. Gaining financial and social recognition from his military successes during the war of 1812, the Commodore wanted to capitalize on their accomplishments. To grant ease of access to Washington's most important figures, the couple decided to build their house just steps away from the White House.

Constructed between 1818-1819, the Decatur House was the first private residence in the White House neighborhood. The square three-story Federal style building was designed by famed Washington architect Benjamin Henry Latrobe, who had also designed some of the features on the White House. The house was constructed with entertaining in mind, and the Commodore became an important figure in Washington society in the early twentieth century, known for his military capabilities and his lavish home, which became synonymous with extravagant parties and social gatherings.

A mere fourteen months after they had moved into their stately home however, Commodore Decatur lost his life in a duel against Commodore James Barron. Susan was forced to sell much of their furniture and move into a smaller house in Georgetown. She did not sell the Decatur House; instead renting it to some of America's earliest political figures. This residence became the unofficial home of Secretaries of State, including Henry Clay and Martin Van Buren. In 1829, an Enslaved

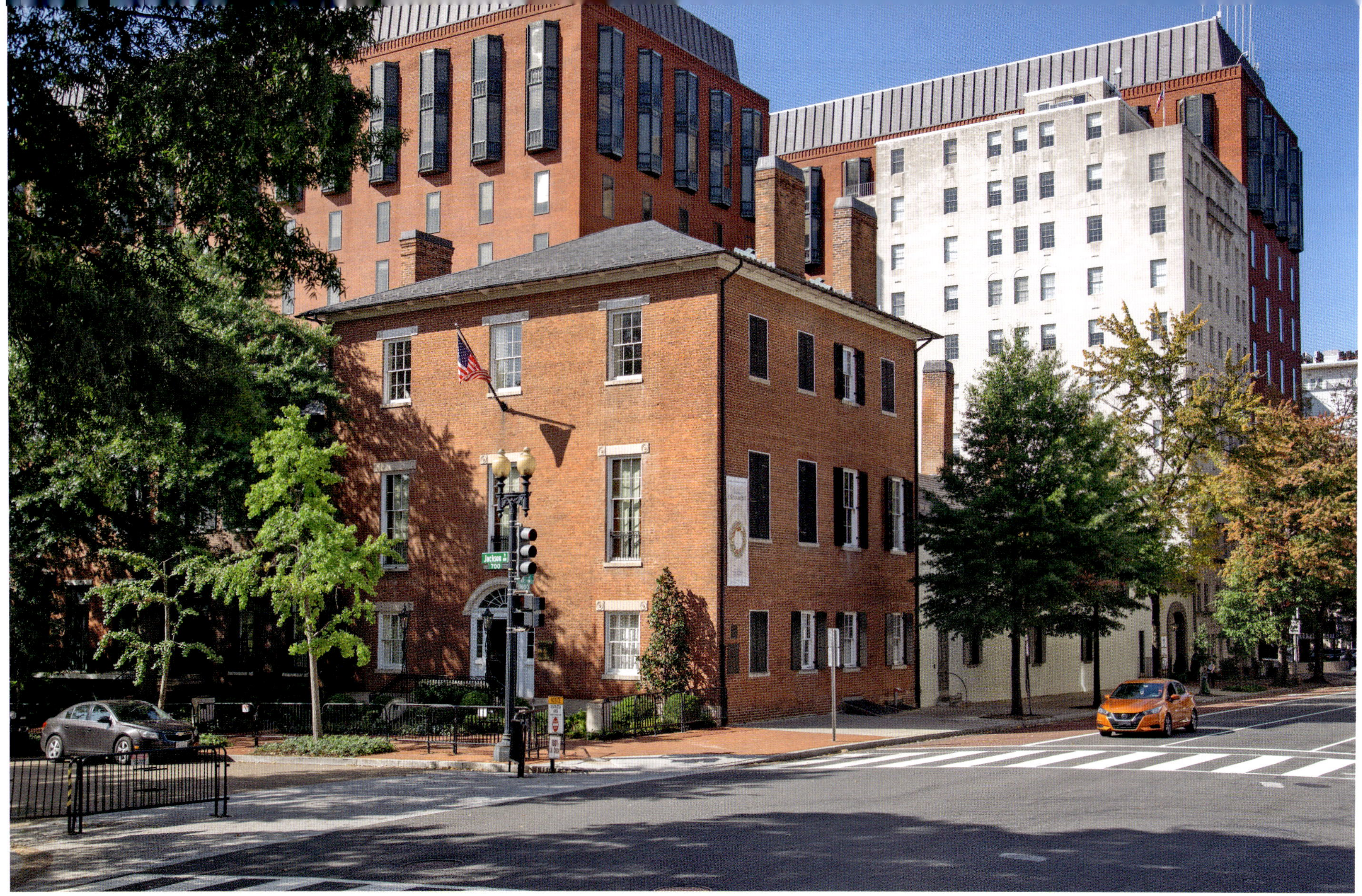

woman named Charlotte Dupuy, who was working in Decatur House, sued her owner Henry Clay for the right to her freedom. The trial was lengthy, and ultimately resulted with Dupuy not being granted her freedom in any legal setting. While she was eventually freed by Clay, Charlotte's advocacy for her own freedom was considered radical for the time.

Many Enslaved individuals lived in the house and in 1821-1822 a two-story addition was added specifically for these residents. When the house was purchased in 1836 by local hotelier John Gadsby to be his private residence, he moved many Enslaved individuals from his hotels over to the new family home. The two-story addition to the Decatur House remains today, and is a rare example of urban housing for Enslaved persons that existed throughout Washington.

NOW: After the Gadsby family relinquished involvement with the property, the Army used it at Civil War headquarters for their Subsistence Department. The Beale family later purchased the home, raising it to the Victorian standard with fashionable decorations and gas chandeliers. The house stayed in Beale family's ownership for over eighty years, before Marie Beale gave it to the National Trust for Historic Preservation in 1956.

The area around the White House changed dramatically and larger buildings crept into the formerly residential neighborhood meaning historic neighborhood structures were slated for demolition. First Lady Jacqueline Kennedy intervened, saving the house in 1962.

Today the site is a museum dedicated to all those who had lived in the house, representing both residents who came to Washington to make a name for themselves, and those who fought for their freedoms there.

VAN NESS MANSION

A home fit for an heiress

THEN: The Residence Act of 1790 changed the trajectory of the District and new president George Washington was excited by the possibility of developing the farmland into a thriving metropolis. To avoid seizing land from those who relied upon it, George Washington purchased from several landowners in the area, until the area officially belonged to the government. He continued this campaign until he reached David Burnes, a man who owned a 700 acre plantation. When David Burnes was asked to sell, he refused, stubbornly defying America's military hero and president. "The most obstinate man" George Washington had ever met, Burnes sold off his land acre by acre, earning a large sum of money that would eventually be inherited by his daughter: Marcia Van Ness.

In 1801, Marcia met a young Congressman from New York named John Peter Van Ness and soon after, the couple were married. The pair initially lived in the Burnes's family cottage, before moving to a house on Pennsylvania Avenue and 12th Street, where they were active participants in Washington life. In 1816, the Van Nesses moved their small family into a new estate on the Burnes's original land. With her familial cottage still standing nearby, Marcia and John built what was considered "the finest house in America."

Created by Benjamin Henry Latrobe, the architect of the Capitol, the home was full of extravagance. It had beautiful interior decorations and a large portico for welcoming distinguished guests, as well as modern luxuries for the time; such as

1860

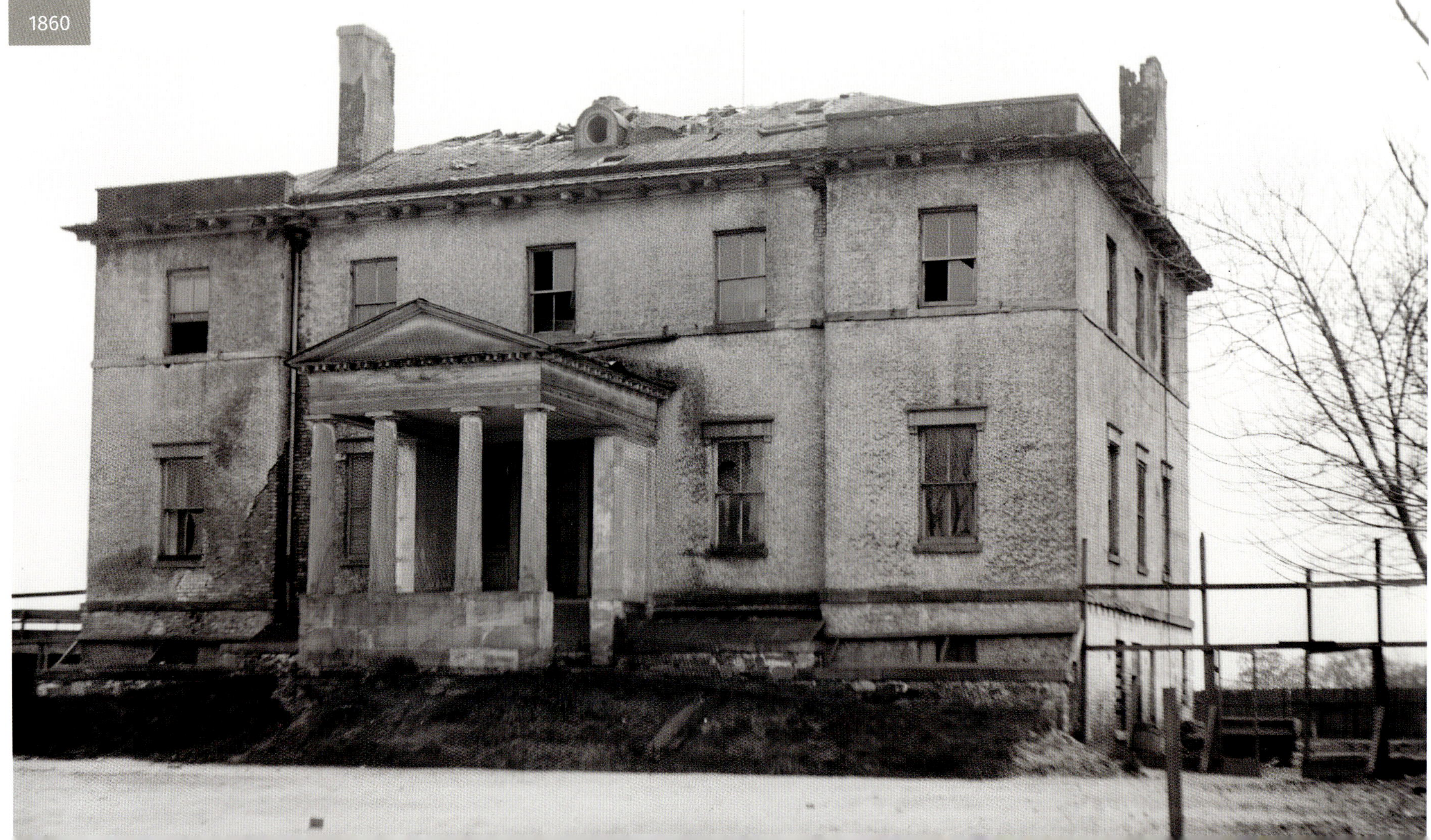

running hot and cold water. The Van Nesses began entertaining Washington's elite, including close family friends and their neighbors: President James Madison and his wife Dolley. Marcia's inheritance and stately home earned her the unofficial title as "the heiress of Washington."

In 1818, Marcia and John lost their daughter and granddaughter to illness, and Marcia dismissed her interest in Washington life. Most notably, she was absent from the festivities that welcomed Gilbert du Motier, Marquis de Lafayette's stateside visit in 1824, although Marcia did host him and his wife at the Van Ness Mansion for a private dinner. John remained involved in all aspects of the District, and in 1830, he was elected mayor of the city, and reelected in 1832. Tragically this was the year that Marcia passed. Her funeral literally stopped Congress, which had adjourned to pay their respects to the Washington heiress — the first time the house had ever stopped their business for the sake of a woman.

NOW: The Van Ness Mansion, once glamorous, fell into disrepair. David Burnes's original wooden cottage was demolished in the 1890s, and the Van Ness Mansion was torn down in 1907. In its place on 17th Street, across from the White House, stands the Pan American Union Building, which houses the Organization of American States. Reminders of this early Washingtonian family remain: the Van Ness House Stables stand nearby, honoring the successes of a family who committed whole-heartedly to supporting Washington in its early stages.

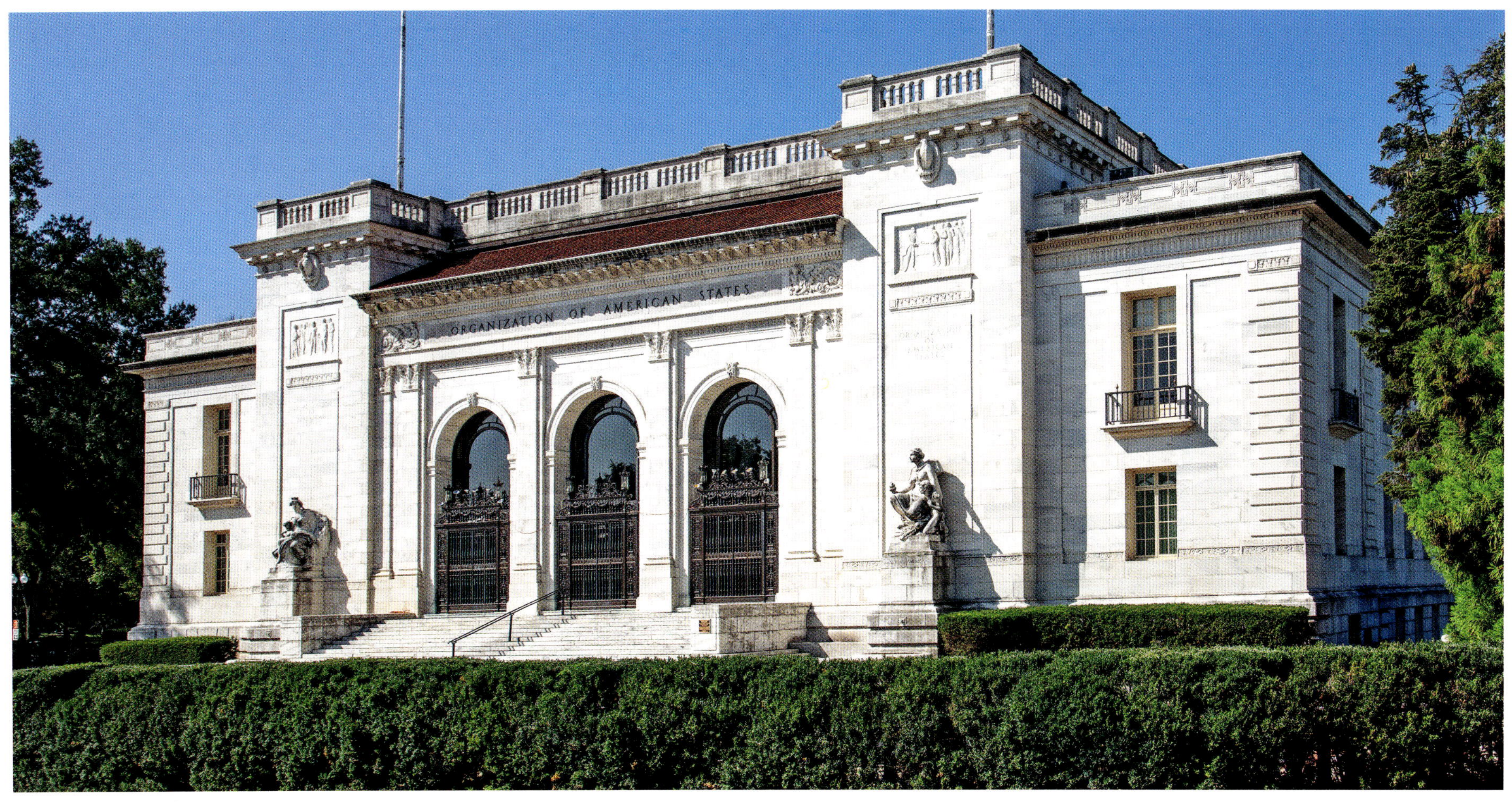

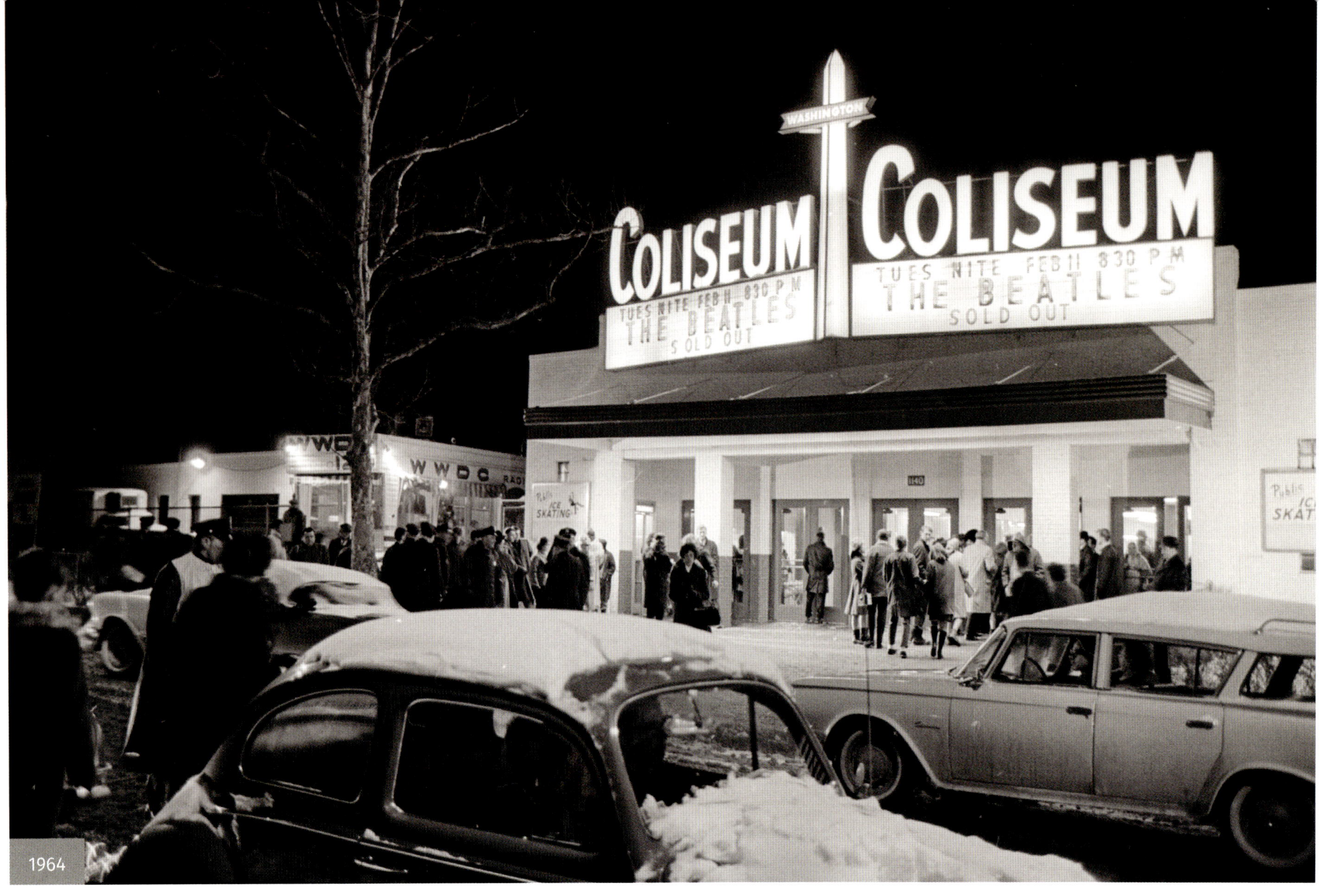

1964

ULINE ARENA

More than just an ice plant

THEN: In 1931, Netherlands-born Migiel Uihlein was a successful businessman in Ohio, the owner of several ice plants and patents related to the ice making industry. By 1931 however Uihlein, whose name was eventually changed to Michael Uline, needed a change of scenery. He made his way to the nation's capital bringing along with him his ice-making expertise. On what is now known as the 1100 block of 3rd Street NE, Uline built his ice plant, venturing into the ice-making business yet keeping his eyes set on other possibilities and a venture into the world of sports.

Washington lacked an arena that facilitated large sporting events so Uline, alongside other Washington businessmen Frederick H. Bucholtz and James Colliflower, built a $300,000 sports center that offered everything from boxing to ice hockey to basketball. Built in 1941 by architect Joseph Harry Lapish, the barrel shaped structure could hold a capacity of around 8,000 people. The same year it was built, Uline was granted a hockey franchise by the American Hockey League, in which the Washington Lions eventually played and also purchased a Basketball Association of America franchise, where famous coach Red Auerbach went on to lead the former Washington

Capitols. Uline was not precious in what he chose to offer. Known to "turn a white elephant into a concrete piggy bank," Uline invited the IceCapades to perform, hosted rodeos attended by Roy Rogers, and even attempted to turn the facility into a beer garden during World War II.

Despite his financial success, Uline faced controversy for his segregation policies. While he claimed that each promoter was allowed to determine their own attendance policy, he was the primary promoter for many events. Black community members boycotted some of Uline's events, claiming he would allow Black participants entry only when he could make money off them, and did not offer them the same privileges as the white attendees. Uline was eventually forced to change this policy when he received ongoing pressure from boxing organizations and civil rights groups.

The Uline Arena fell under new ownership when Harry Lynn purchased it in 1959. With this change, a musical act like no other made their debut in America. The ice factory turned sporting arena was now turned concert venue and on stage, performing their first concert in America, was a new group from Europe called The Beatles.

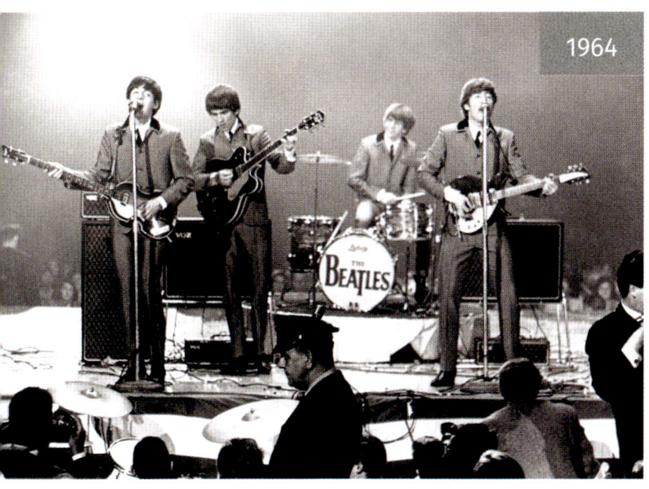

ABOVE: On February 11 1964, the building now known as the Washington Coliseum was full as 8,092 guests piled inside to witness The Beatles perform for the first time in America.

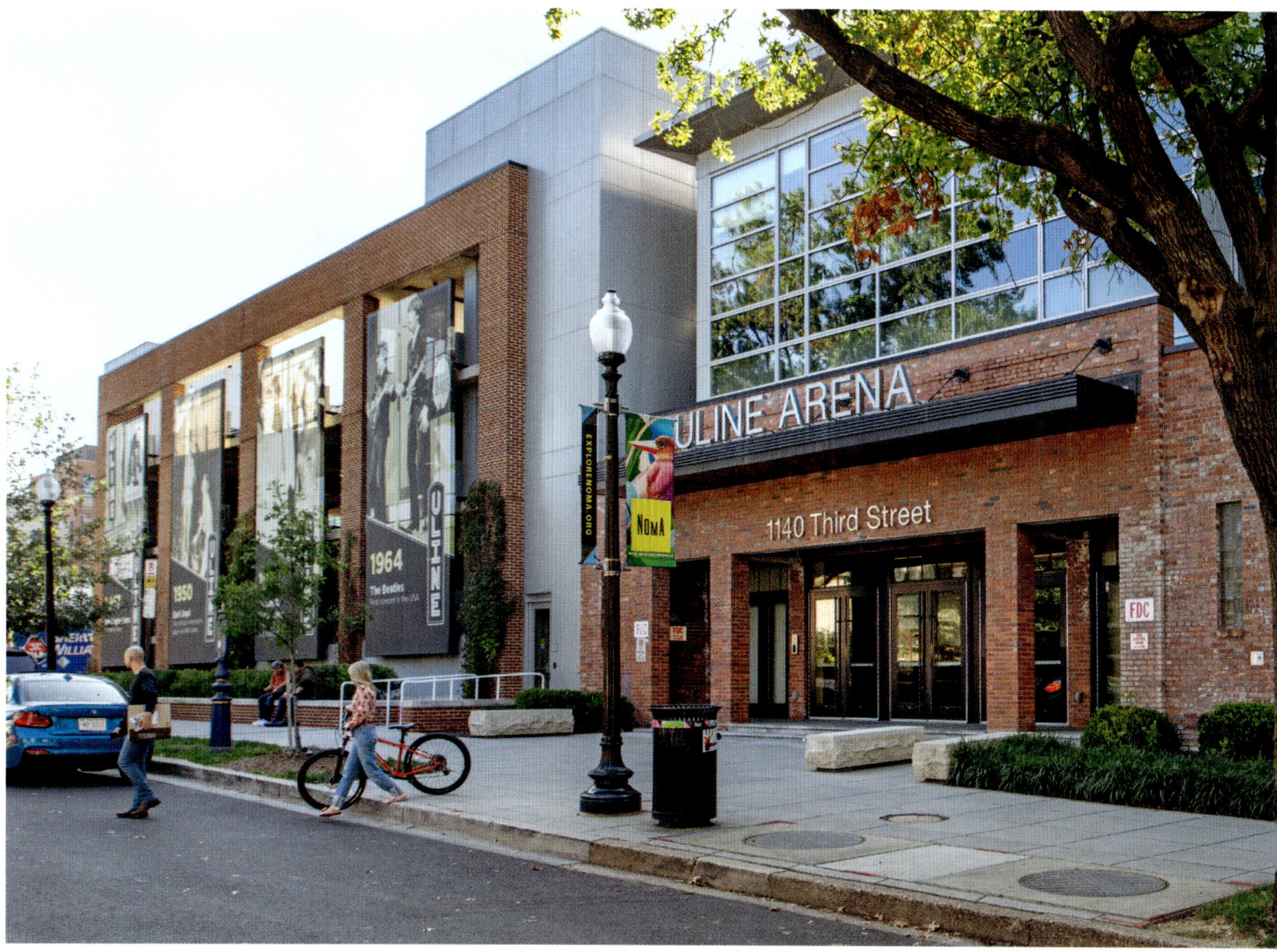

NOW: The Washington Coliseum continued as a concert venue until the late 1960s. This status changed when a loud noise at a Temptations concert caused panic and violence to break out, leading to the injury of five concertgoers. Many concerts afterwards were canceled at the Coliseum, and the following year nearby neighborhoods like H Street Northeast suffered during the 1968 riots following the death of Martin Luther King Jr. In the 1970s, the opening of the Capital Center in Maryland attracted potential fans to the rapidly populating suburbs and the Coliseum couldn't compete, forcing it to close its doors in 1985.

Since its closure, the area around the building has changed dramatically. What was once known as the North of Massachusetts Avenue neighborhood is now called NoMA, and townhouses are now shadowed by large apartment buildings. The arena has also changed, acting as a parking garage before finally landing as a retail and office space.

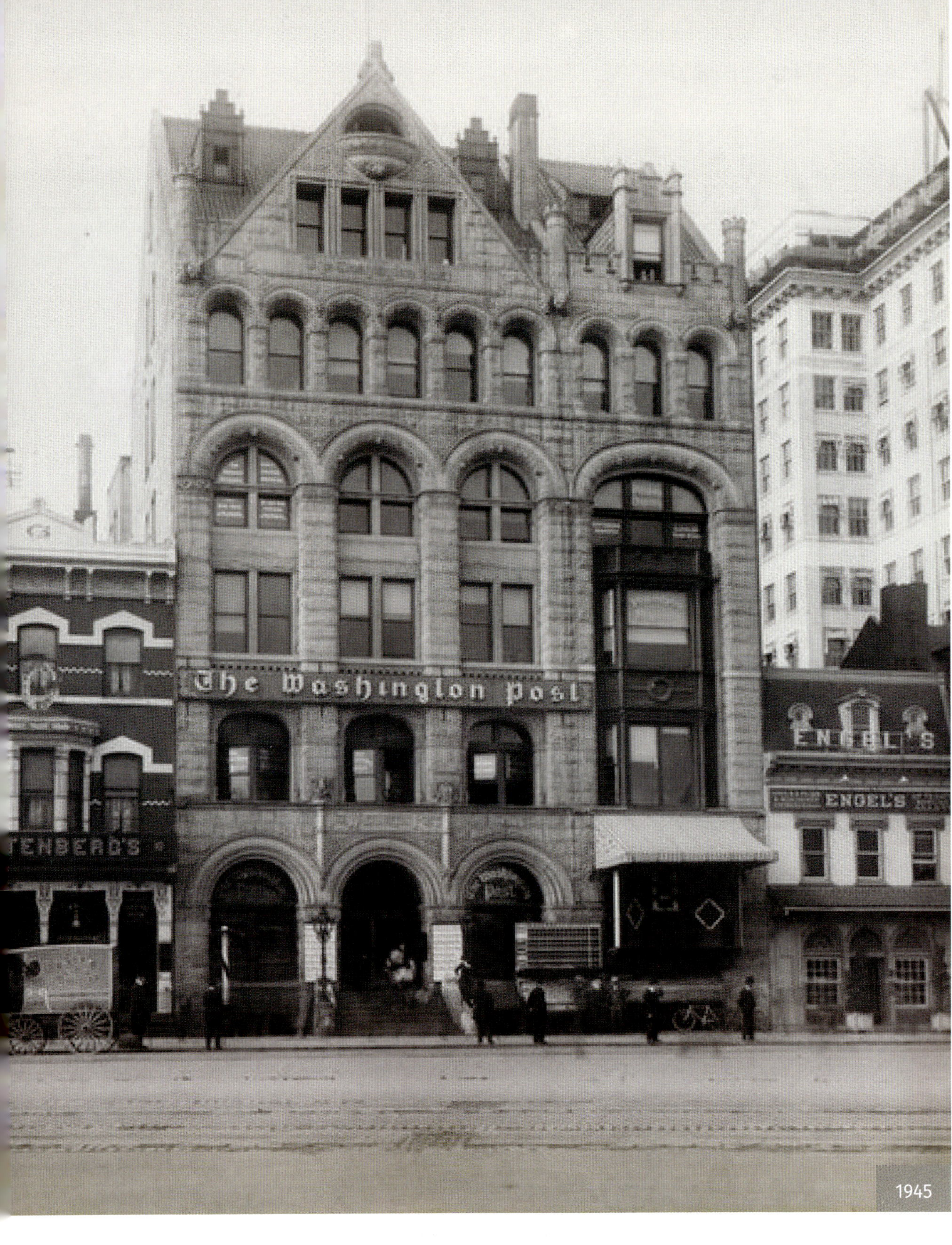

1945

THE WASHINGTON POST

A local newspaper makes it big

THEN: Increased newspaper activity in Washington started during the Civil War, when a Western Union Telegraph Company opened an office right on the corner of what is now 14th Street and Pennsylvania Avenue NW. With privileged access to incoming communication about the war, different newspaper companies opened offices around the communication office. From *The New York Times* to *The Boston Advertiser* and *The Baltimore Sun*, the press were eager to report on incoming intel, creating an area known as Newspaper Row.

There was one newspaper that was late to the press junket, and therefore did not secure a spot on the iconic street, *The Washington Post*. Founded in 1877 by Stilson Hutchins, *The Washington Post* offices were opened on a spot in nearby rum row, a stretch of taverns and saloons. Further away from the connection to Western Union, *The Washington Post* had an advantage in their large Gothic building being flanked by two taverns. In need of relaxation after a long day on the Hill, Congressmen would come to Pennsylvania Avenue to drink, and talk openly to its reporters.

The Washington Post grew in popularity throughout the late nineteenth century, with early contributing writers including Joseph Pulitzer and lesser known author Theodore Roosevelt, who wrote westerns for the publication, without his byline. As the company grew, it needed more space, and moved into the building on 1335 E Street NW in 1893. Ownership of the paper changed several times, bringing success at times, and at others great instability. In 1933, the newspaper switched its political alliance, which brought decreased circulation so low that the owners were forced to sell the company at auction.

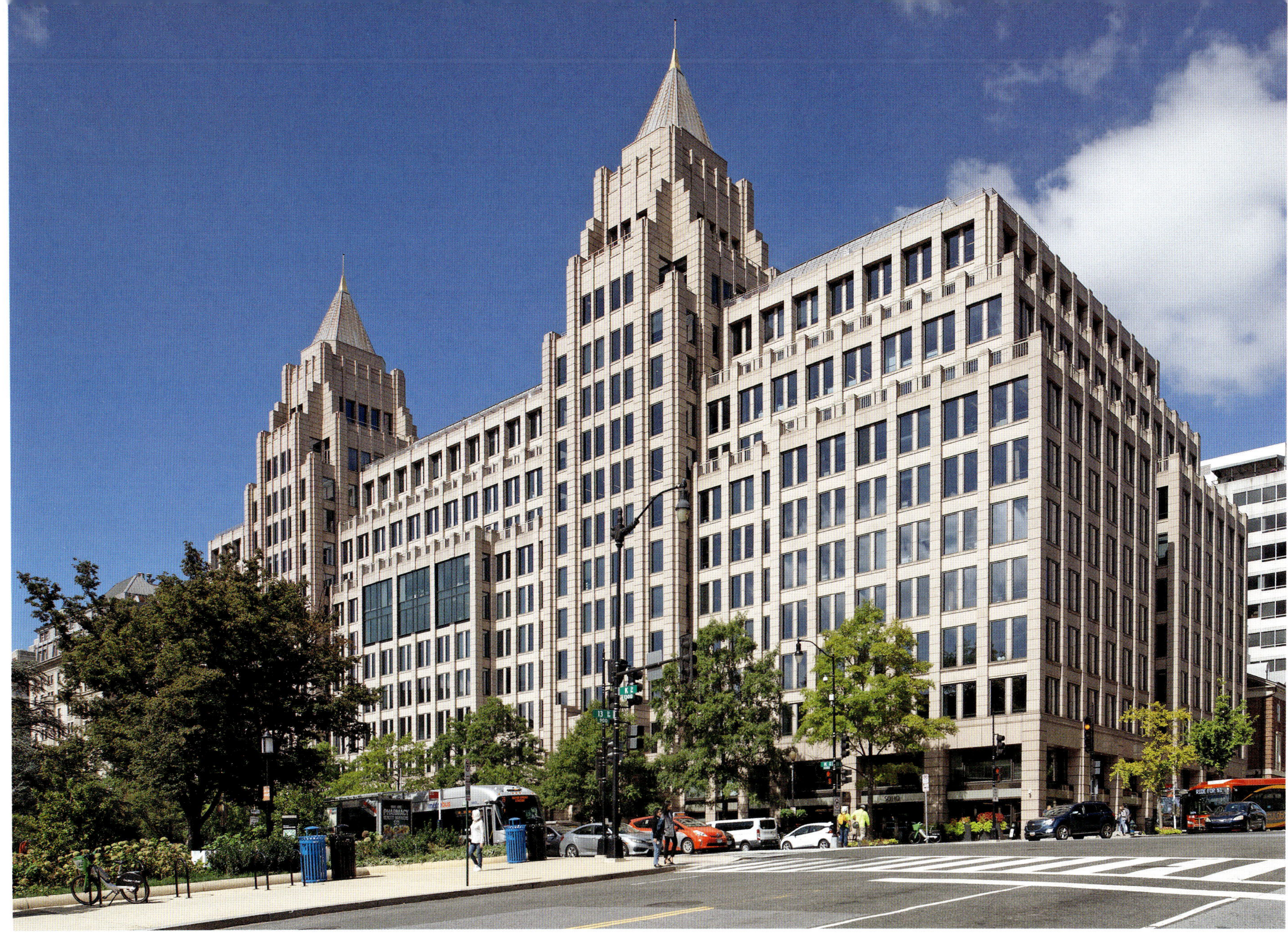

NOW: The new owner, Eugene Meyer, believed that the news industry had a duty to serve the public. Meyers' belief guided much of *The Washington Post* through the second half of the twentieth century, allowing the newspaper to reclaim its space as a legitimate news source. In 1950, the company moved into a new building at 1515 L Street with modern equipment and technology.

Katherine Graham, Eugene's daughter, became president of *The Washington Post* following the death of her husband, and the first twentieth-century female publisher of a major American newspaper. Under her leadership *The Washington Post* achieved great notoriety, when two investigative reporters published a story about a break-in at the Watergate Hotel. It revealed that President Nixon had spied on opposing political leadership during his campaign for reelection, and ultimately led to his resignation.

In 2013, the owner of Amazon Inc. Jeff Bezos purchased *The Washington Post*. Two years later, the newspaper moved to a larger building once belonging to IBM on K Street NW. From humble beginnings as an alienated newspaper company on the city's Rum Row to discovering hard truths leading to a presidential resignation, *The Washington Post* and its readership have certainly come a long way.

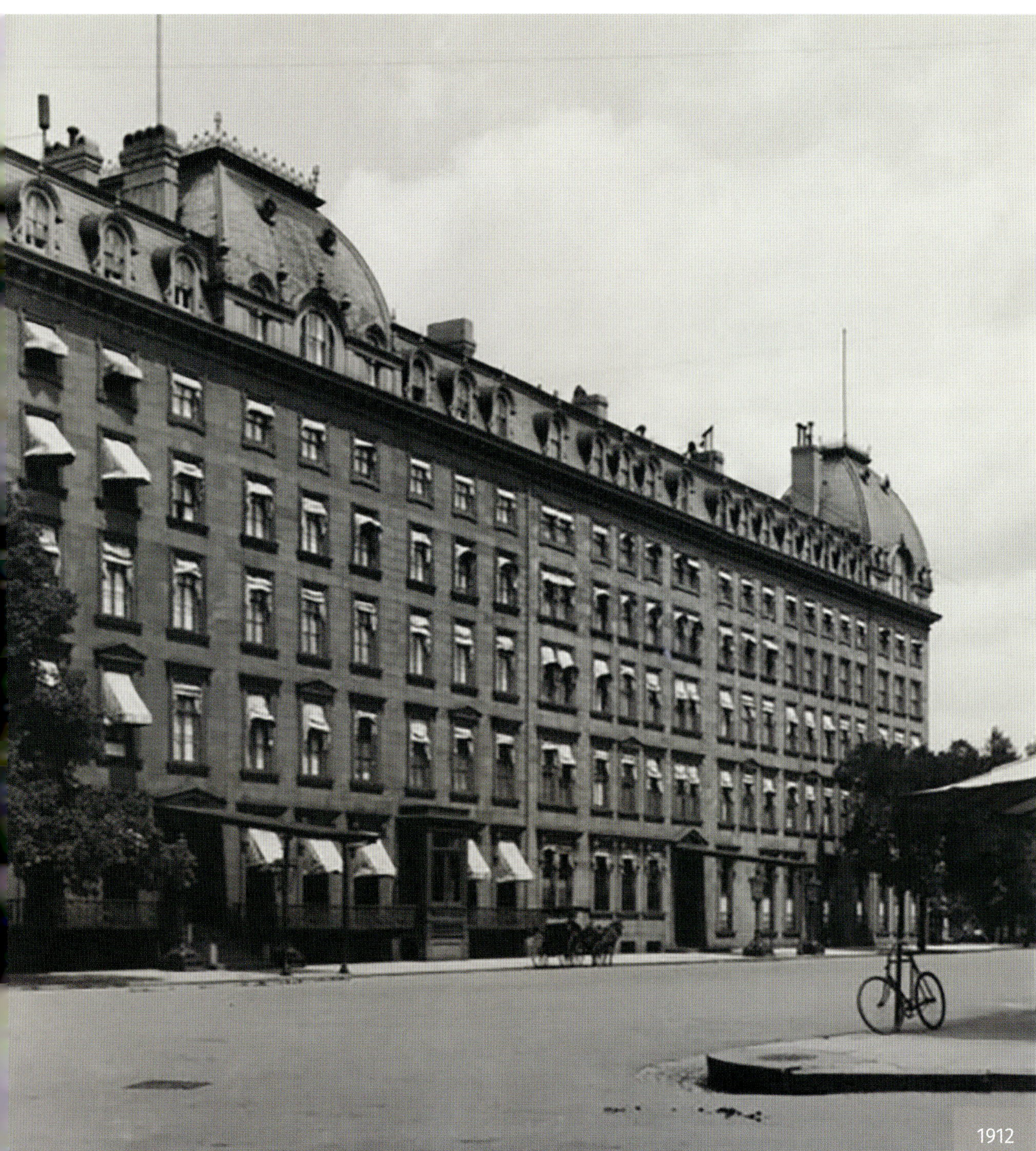
1912

THE ARLINGTON HOTEL

Competing to be the best in Washington

THEN: In the late nineteenth century, the area surrounding the White House was expanding. While the streets around Lafayette Square had grown to include various residences, the greater neighborhood of the White House north of the square was becoming a fashionable place to live.

William Corcoran, who had accumulated great wealth from entering the banking business alongside esteemed Washington banker George Riggs, was now retired and itching to increase his real estate ownership and expand his landholdings. After acquiring a block of mansions on Vermont Avenue near I Street in 1869, Corcoran replaced these homes with a large hotel structure, a building he called Arlington House. Corcoran had relied heavily upon the work of James Renwick in the past, but for this building he hired E.G. Lind, who constructed the building in a Second-Empire style, using stately red brick.

From its inception, the Arlington was a hotel that appealed to the Washington elite, proclaiming a difficult-to-find exclusivity. Vermont Avenue was one of the first streets in the District to be paved, and therefore brought a level of comfort for those staying at the hotel. The Arlington's visitors were some of America's most influential figures. While some presidents and politicians stayed at the nearby Willard, the Arlington House welcomed guests such as Andrew Carnegie, J. P. Morgan, leaders of foreign countries, and hosted an inaugural event for then President-Elect Benjamin Henry Harrison. During its time, the Arlington was a place of grandeur, appealing to those of great wealth and influence in the growing nation.

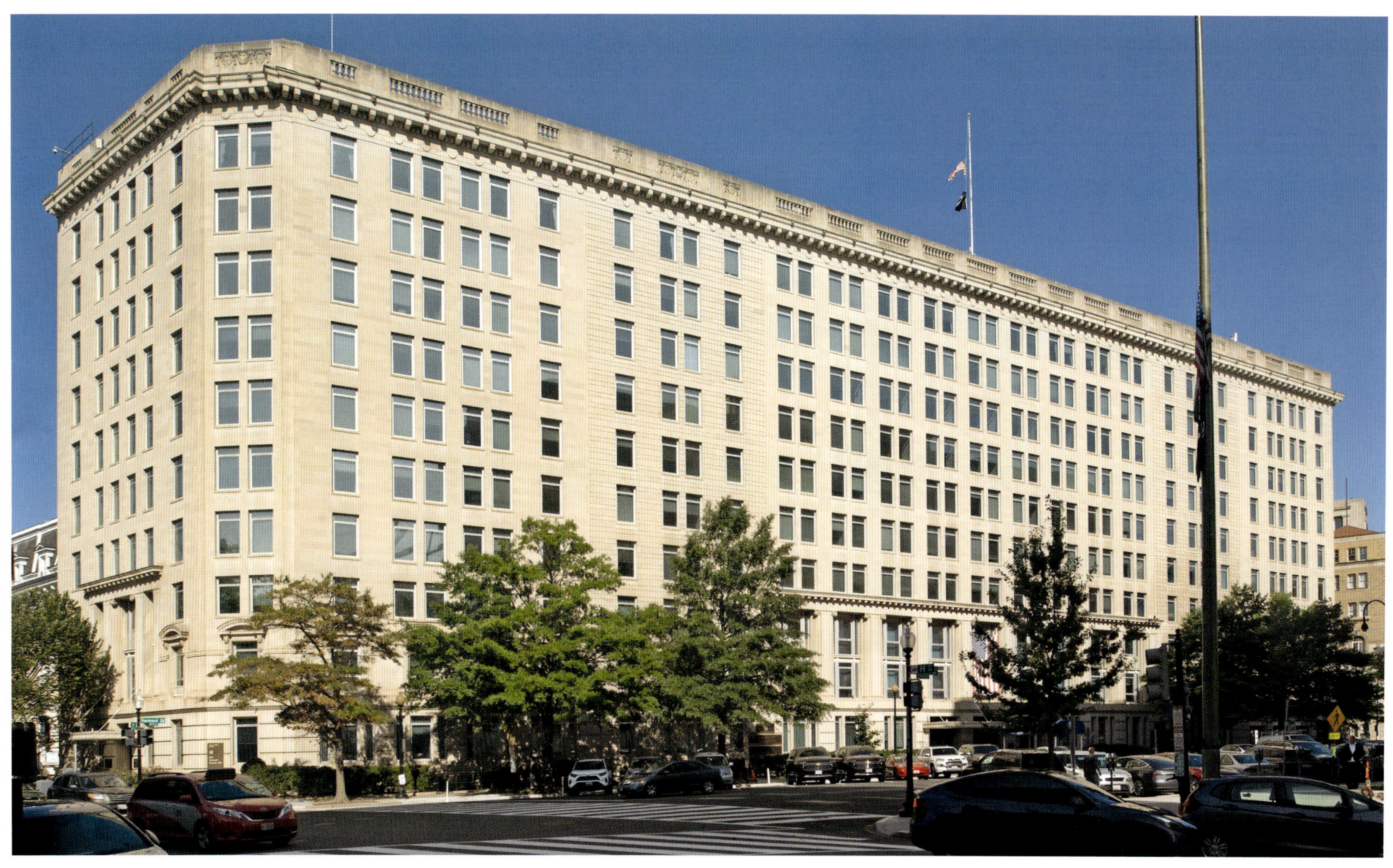

NOW: In 1911, it was decided that the Arlington Hotel would be replaced with a new building. This decision came as other hotels in the region were making improvements to their design and offerings, to draw in new clientele. The red brick of the Arlington had long since fallen out of fashion, and a neoclassical design was the new trend in D.C. Many esteemed Washingtonians supported the construction of a new Arlington Hotel, and helped to fund its elaborate design. The new building was set to include the largest hotel ballroom ever constructed in the United States, a swimming pool, and other enthralling amenities.

Despite the Arlington's support, the construction faced issues as early as 1912, such as unreliable financing and tensions between its architects. Issues persisted, and what was once one of Washington's grandest hotels was left in disarray.

It was not until the federal government became involved that the plot of land saw life again. World War I saw an increased need for office space, and the government constructed an office building on the site in 1917. The structure of the Arlington, once the highlight of Washington's social scene, is now the Department of Veterans' Affairs.

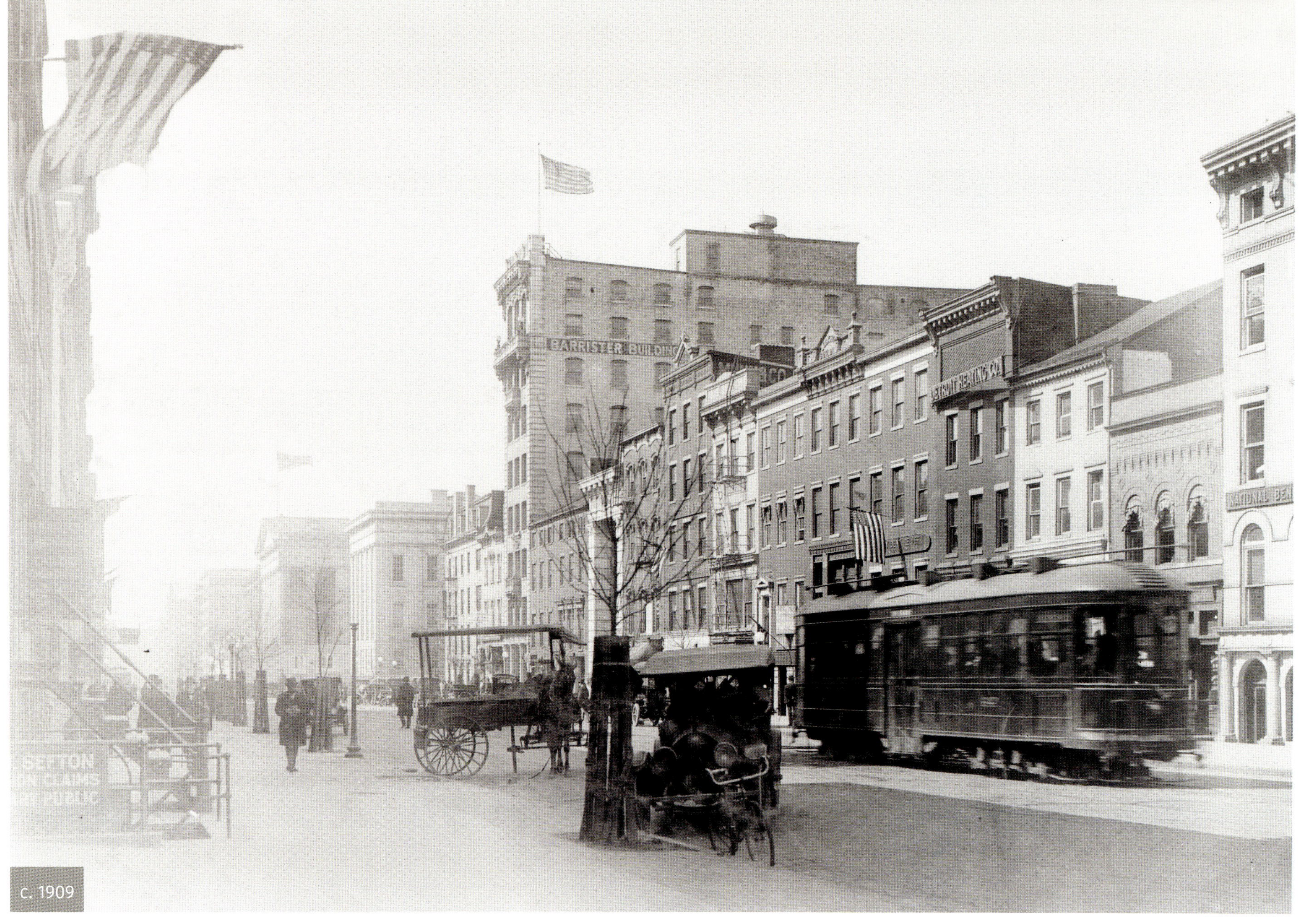

c. 1909

F STREET AND COMMERCIAL SHOPPING CENTER

From shopping center to sports hub

THEN: Many reasons bring Washingtonians to the Downtown neighborhood today. A bustling area full of offices, museums, galleries, and retail stores, whether visiting for work or pleasure, there is always something to see or do Downtown. At the turn of the twentieth century, Downtown served a very similar purpose, and specifically F Street and 7th Street NW were known to be the commercial hubs of the city. With the large Old Patent Office at its center, the area that is considered Downtown offers a unique side by side of the various architectural styles of Washington's construction, giving visitors a peek into the changes the city experienced. From the neoclassical design of the large Patent Office to smaller townhouses that held small businesses, and Romanesque revival architecture in some of the commercial buildings, this area highlights how the federal government and the residents of Washington, D.C. coexist.

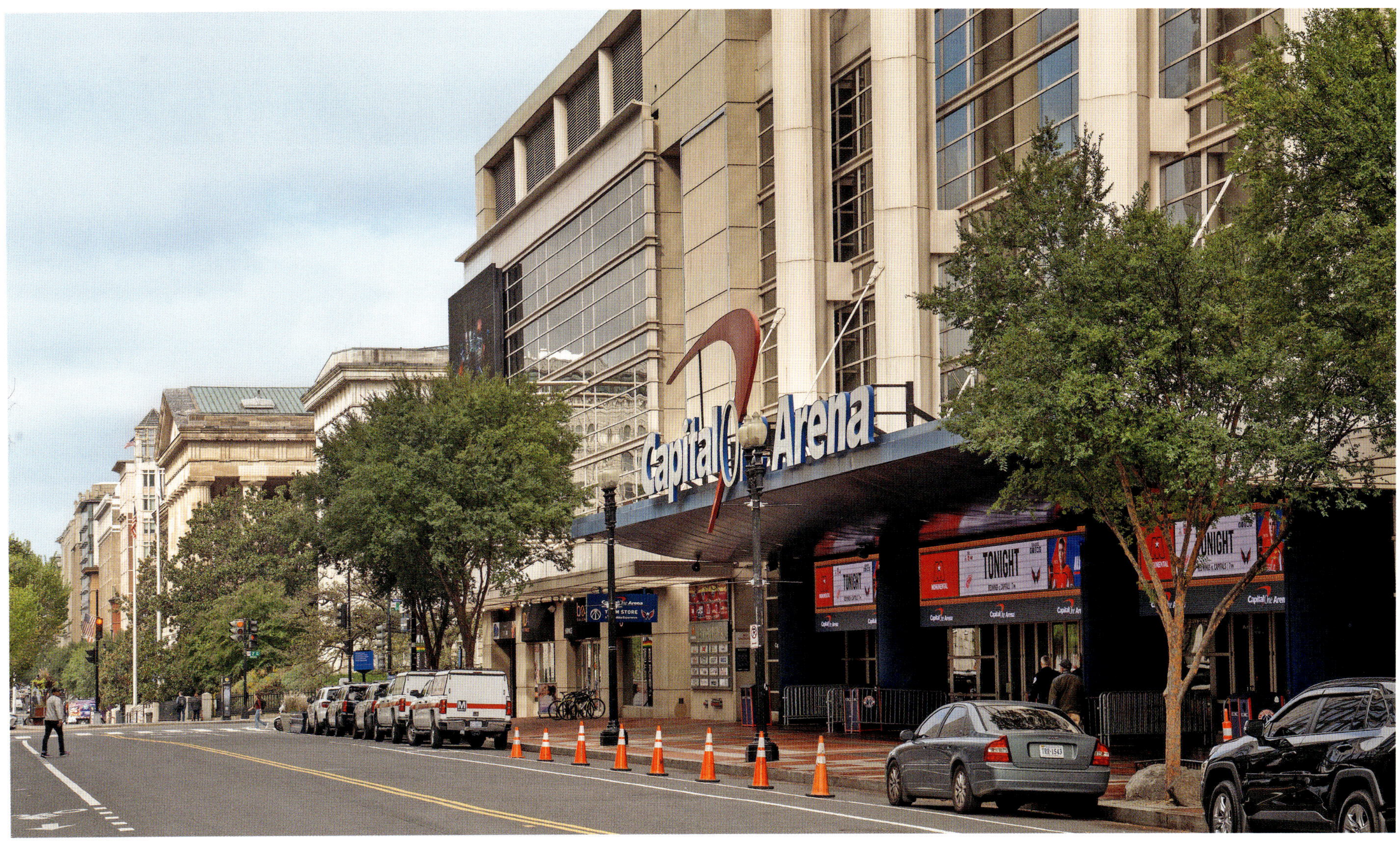

It was specifically the intersection of 7th and F Street that boasted the growing commercial undertakings of Washington, and rapidly distinguished itself as the city's commercial hub. As early as 1838 there were reports stating that the area had a variety of offerings from grocers to other merchants, and stage lines which ran directly through the city. The construction of the Patent Office led to many lawyers moving into the area, and one of the city's earliest office buildings, the Corcoran Building, was constructed at F and 15th Street. In the late twentieth century, the area around downtown was largely untouched, and the popularity of the shopping streets had been abandoned.

NOW: The view of this street includes the Capital One Arena, where the city's hockey and basketball teams – the Washington Capitals and the Washington Wizards respectively – play. The arena also hosts large concerts and other events. While Washingtonians used to come to this street for shopping, the arena has now brought a new source of joy for Washingtonians and visitors alike.

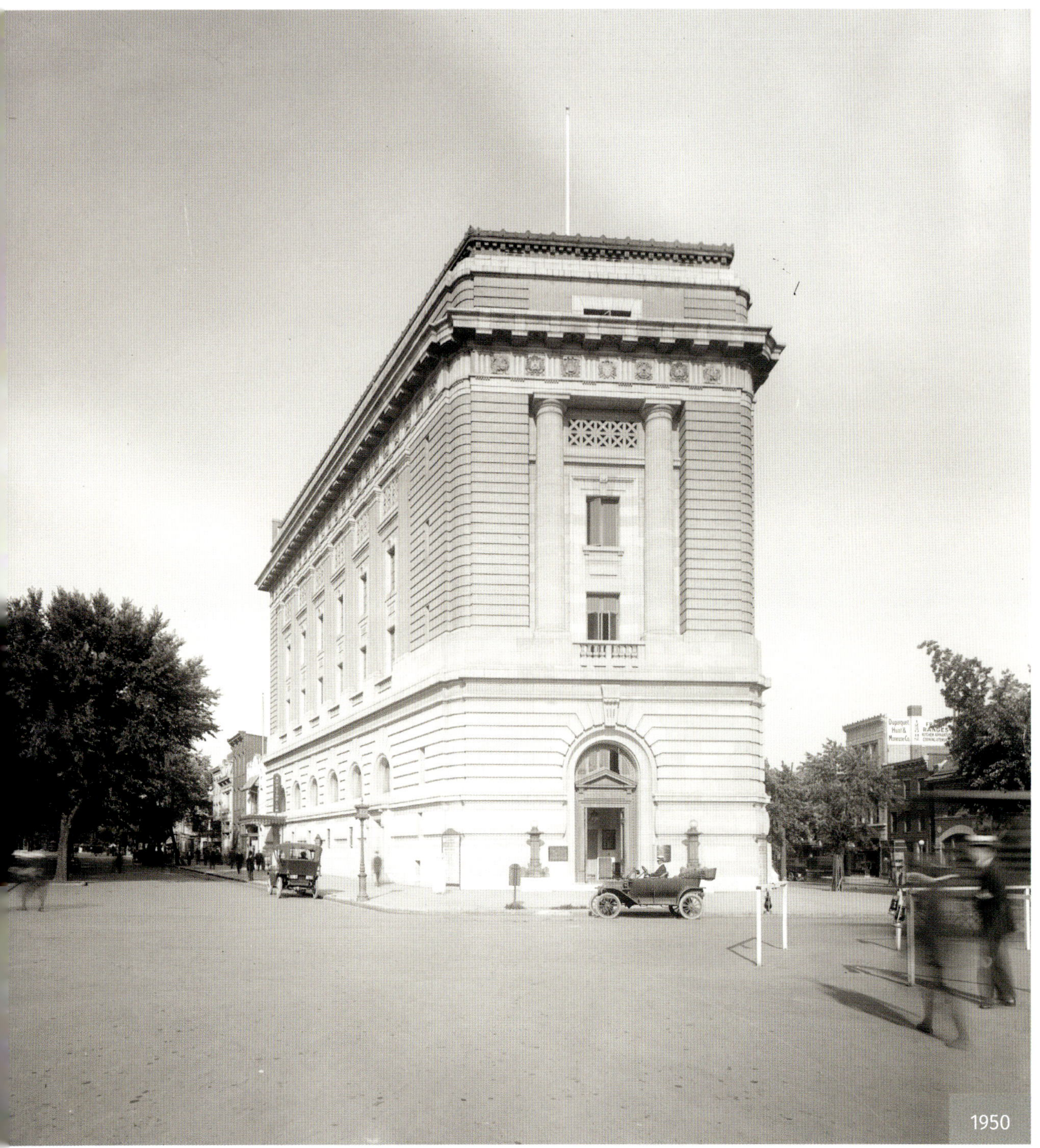

THE MASONIC TEMPLE

Fraternal temple to a space dedicated to women's success

THEN: The first lodge in Washington was assembled in 1789, when a group of Georgetown residents formed Lodge Nine, which met in the former Suter's Tavern. Freemasonry persisted within Washington, as Freemason James Hoban, who had been selected to design the White House, moved to the District. For the construction of the Executive Mansion he recruited fifty men: skilled laborers from around the United States and abroad. Out of the fifty men who worked to build the White House, twenty were known Freemasons. Work on the White House was demanding, and the group of twenty men often found themselves unable to make their way to Georgetown, to join the Lodge Nine meetings. Instead, they made their own lodge, meeting informally in 1793 and later becoming Lodge One.

Modeled on a medieval guild system, with beliefs rooted in Enlightenment era philosophy, the Freemasons of Washington were growing and needed a larger Grand Lodge to fulfill their structure. First identified in 1811, the Grand Lodge in D.C. was at various locations throughout its lifetime and in 1870 moved to the corner of 9th and F Streets NW, into a building that is still standing today. By the 1890s however, with dozens of smaller lodges throughout the city, they needed an even larger venue.

On a cluster of land once known as Seven Oaks, the Freemasons built their temple. The piece of land was unique in shape, as it was at the intersection of what is now New York Avenue, 13th St NW, and H Street NW. The trapezoidal plot lent itself to a unique building, and architects Wood, Donn, and Deming built their uniquely shaped masterpiece on this spot. Following a popular trend at the turn of the twentieth century, the building was designed in the classic Renaissance Revival style, and featured a large auditorium space with elaborate decorations in the interior.

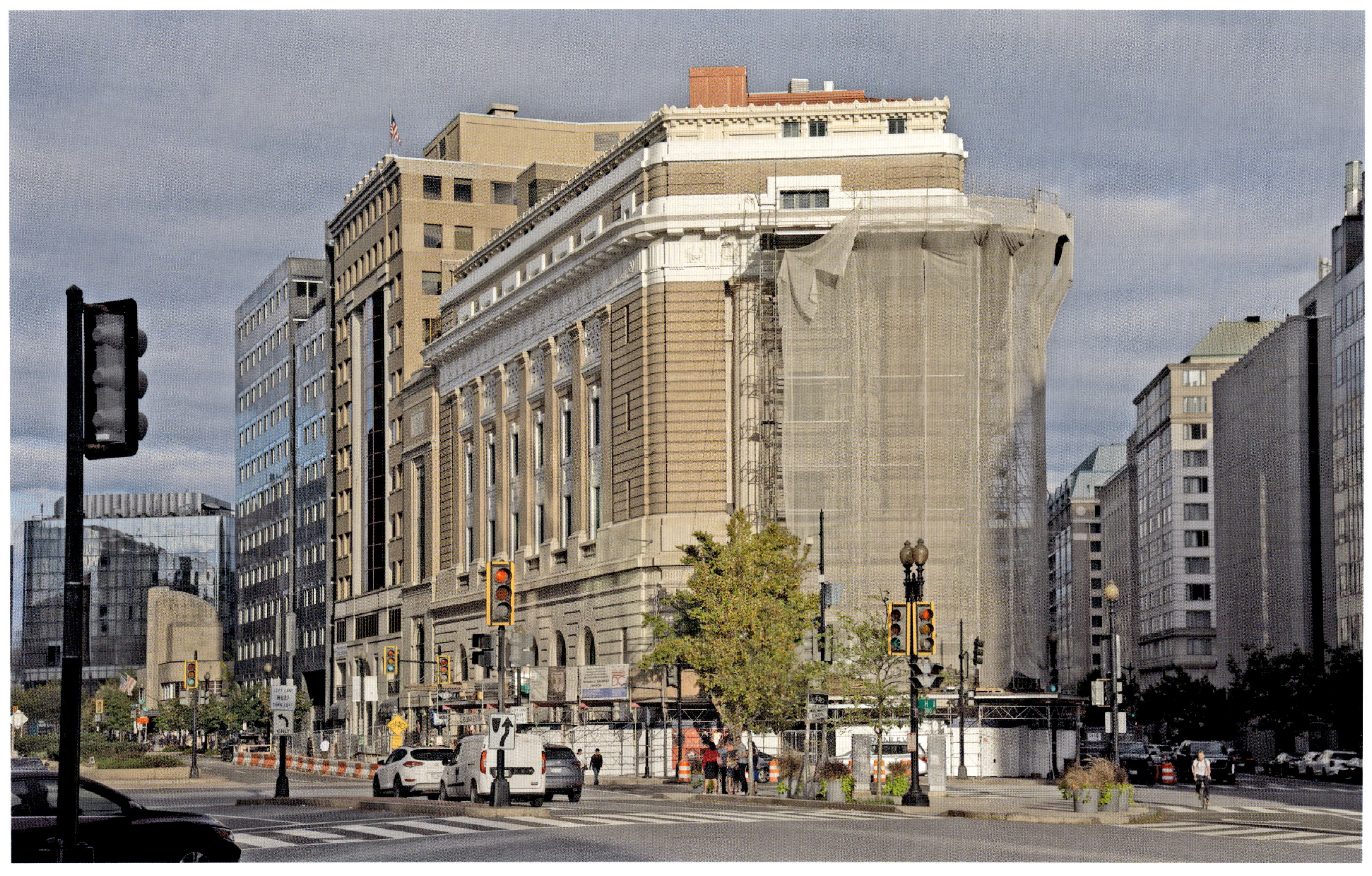

NOW: The Freemasons occupied the temple from 1908, and while they utilized their new gathering space themselves, they also saw it as an opportunity for income. Throughout the early twentieth century, the group rented out the auditorium for early motion picture shorts, office leases, and to various shops. By 1941 the first floor was a fully commercial movie theater, although this enterprise was eventually moved to nearby burlesque theaters for the more explicit material they were showing. Ultimately unhappy with the destination their Grand Lodge was headed for and paired with a decline in the downtown Washington population, the Masons decided it was time to sell the building in the early 1980s.

When the Freemasons put their temple on the market, preservationists were quick to intervene. In 1983, the site was designated as a historic landmark and Wilhelmina Holladay purchased it to house the National Museum of Women in the Arts. The building has undergone extensive renovations at various times, and was the world's first museum solely dedicated to celebrating art by women.

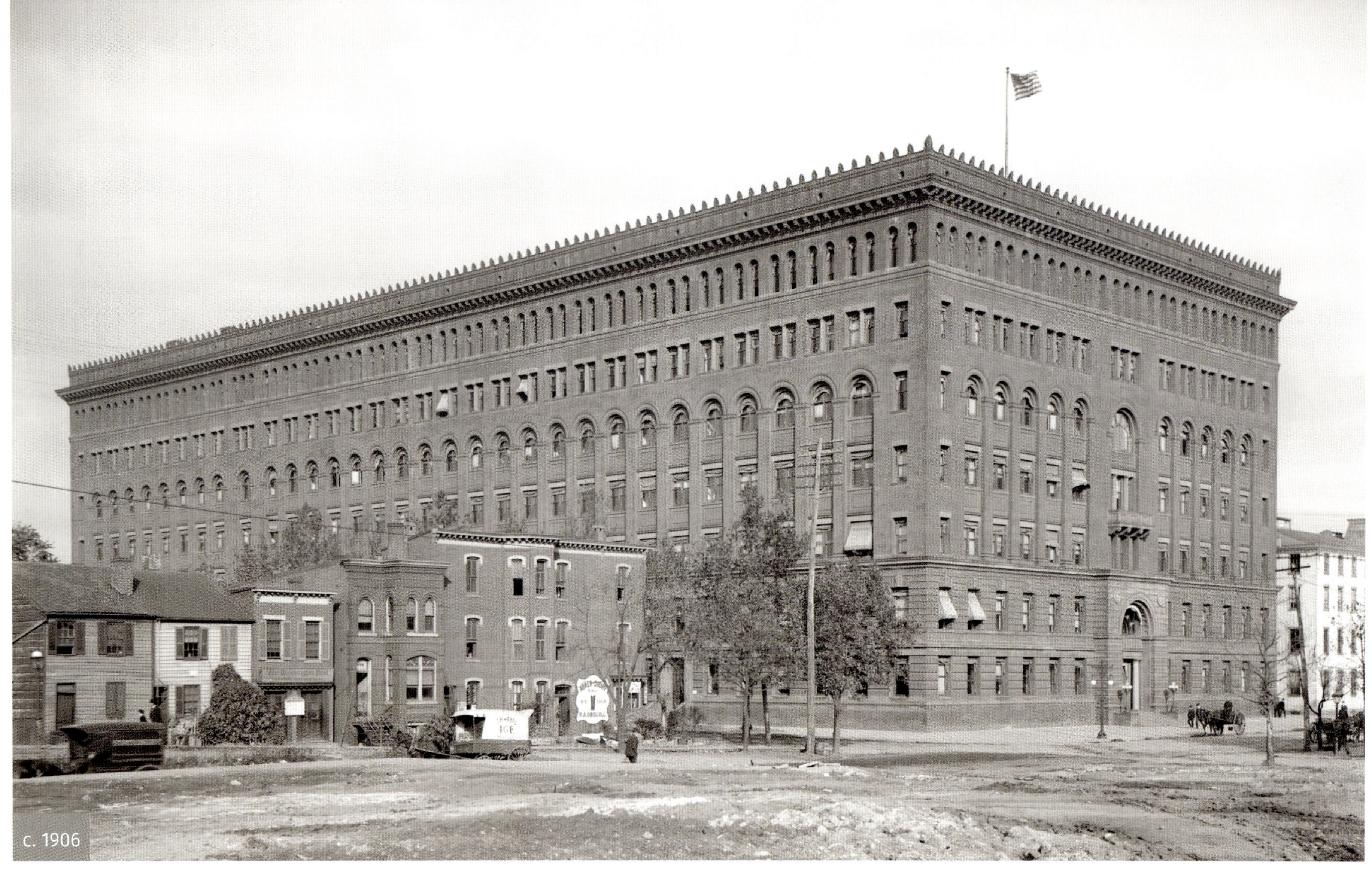

c. 1906

GOVERNMENT PRINTING OFFICE

Informing America since 1861

THEN: On the corner of North Capitol Street, near H Street and G Street, one government agency has continuously occupied the block. On March 4 1861, President Abraham Lincoln officially created what was called the Government Printing Office (or the GPO). The GPO first occupied the first printing office building in D.C., which was built by Cornelius Wendell.

The original team of 350 employees were immediately busy, as their inception coincided with the start of the Civil War. The GPO printers set the type for printing by hand at all hours of the day — ready for the next congressional announcement to arrive. Paper and ink were scarce during the years of the Civil War yet printing continued. During this period, in 1862, the preliminary Emancipation Proclamation was printed by the GPO for the War Department. It was completed before Lincoln made his official proclamation to the public.

After the war, technological improvements such as the introduction of electrical power to sustain the presses, new machinery and the introduction of machine typesetting in 1866 saw printing increase ten times over. In 1903, the GPO's consistent growth meant the agency needed a new building and architect James G. Hill designed a large steel framed structure in the Romanesque Revival style, on the corner of North Capitol Street and G Street.

Made from red brick, the building stood out against the usual white sandstone, which was overtaking Washington as the Congressional redevelopment plan pushed

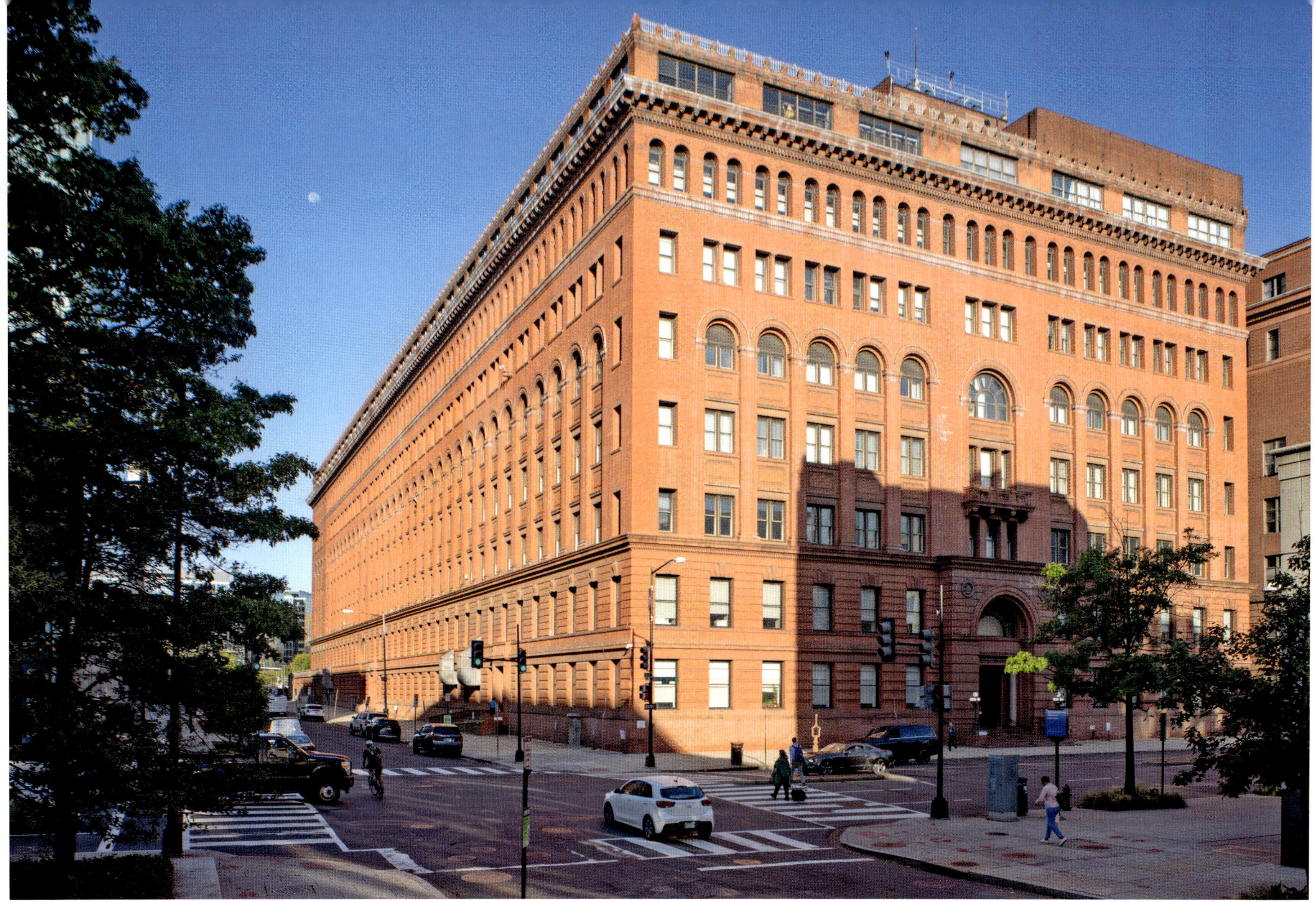

for architectural consistency. The GPO left behind the practice of setting type by hand entirely and launched the agency into its position as the world's largest printer.

The GPO did not solely report on congressional hearings, and detailed all government activity. With accounts on everything from geological surveys to agricultural research, the GPO's printing at the turn of the century nearly doubled. The onset of World War I pushed the GPO's requirements further: printing drill books for new soldiers and other military documents.

The agency hired 900 additional employees and entered a workflow system where a worker was present twenty-four hours a day, seven days a week. A second building was authorized for construction in 1926, to match the style of Building One, and Building Three followed in 1940, this time showcasing an Art Deco Influence.

NOW: In the early twentieth century, Building One underwent renovations which added a story to the structure, and also an auditorium, bowling alley, and a roof terrace with a view of the Capitol Building. Through the latter half of the twentieth century, the GPO was responsible for government reports such as the Warren Report, detailing the assassination and corresponding investigation of President John F. Kennedy, as well as transcripts of President Nixon's recordings during the 1973 Watergate scandal hearings.

By the 1980s, the GPO began to be complete work digitally and in 2014 the Government Printing Office was renamed the Government Publishing Office. The GPO still works in printing and undertakes myriad tasks including creating all American passports.

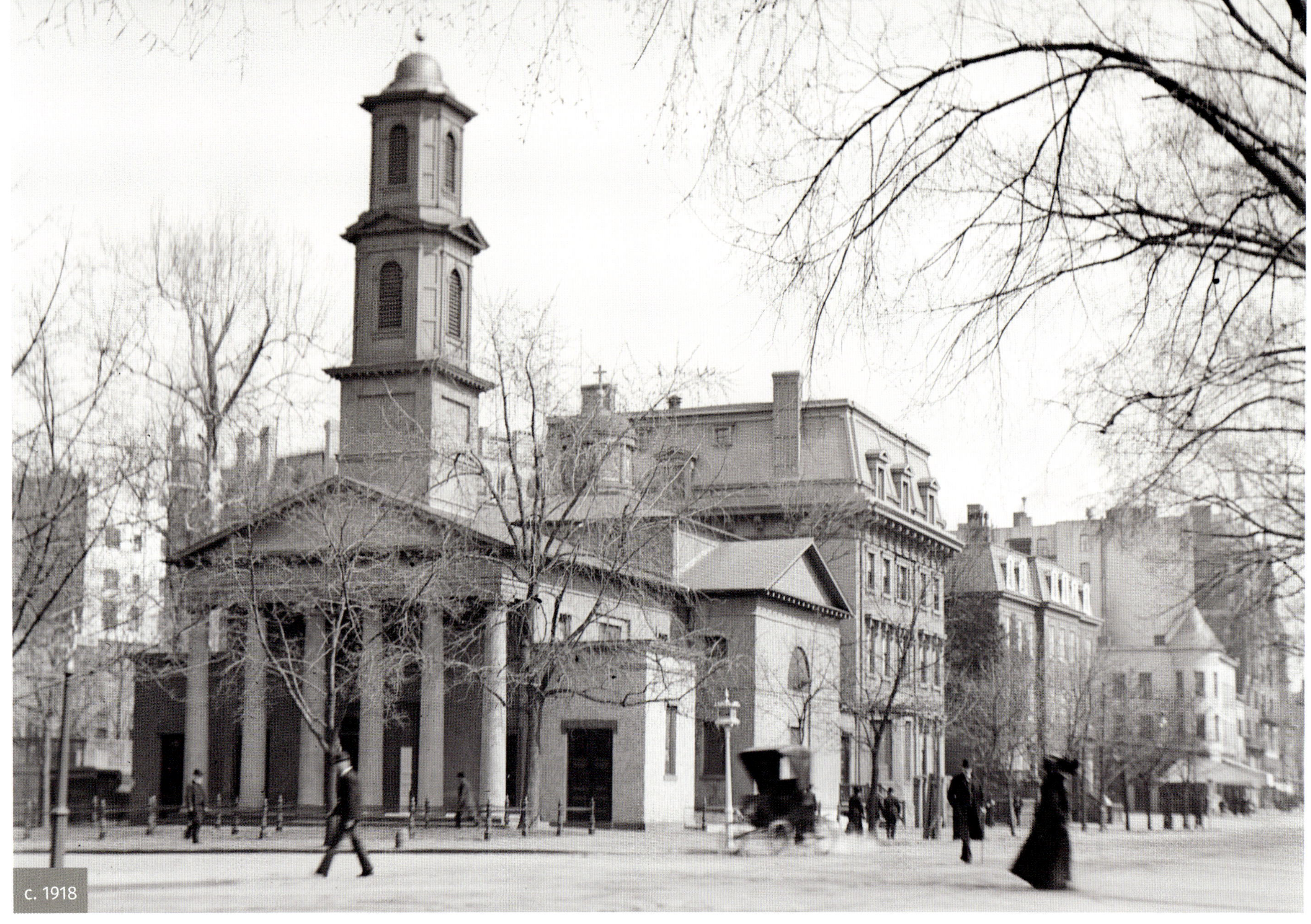
c. 1918

ST. JOHN'S CHURCH

The Church of the presidents

THEN: While the United States of America was founded with the belief that church and state should remain separate, there is one religious consistency across the various practices of almost all the presidents: attendance at St. John's Church.

In the early nineteenth century, Washington, D.C. was in its earliest years as the nation's capital city. While much of the outer areas of Washington remained an undeveloped wilderness, the downtown area around the White House was growing as those looking to gain the favor of the president stayed close by. One of these areas was the neighborhood surrounding Lafayette Park, which was once a residential neighborhood housing Washington's elite. One of the primary architects for this neighborhood was Benjamin Latrobe, who designed not only houses throughout Washington but also important features for buildings of great significance, such as the porticos for the White House. The Episcopal Church was completed in 1816 in the

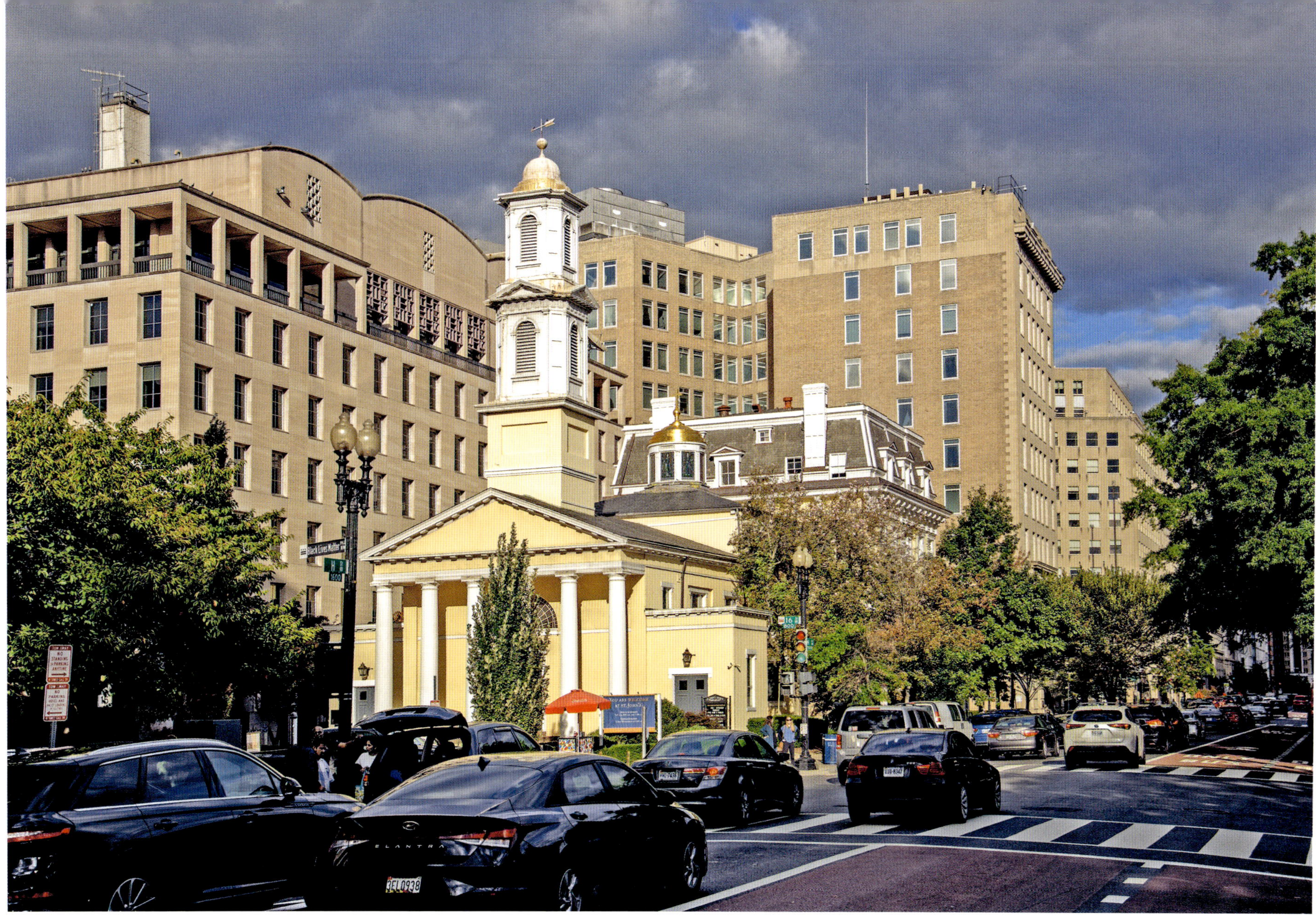

Greek Revival style and was the second building in Lafayette Square. While there were other places to worship around Washington at this time, there was not a religious institution with this proximity to the White House.

Since the building's inception, it has welcomed all Washingtonians to its pews. There are early reports of Reverend William Hawley, the second Rector at St. John's baptizing and marrying Black residents of all legal backgrounds, including those who were Enslaved. Over one hundred years later, as the Civil Rights Movement was active in Washington, St. John's church saw the need to welcome parishioners of all races, especially as the church had no Black members by the 1960s. During the March on Washington for Jobs and Freedom, an important catalyst of the Civil Rights Movement, over 700 people filled the pews of St. John's Church.

NOW: Throughout its over two century history in Lafayette Square, St. John's Church has served Washingtonians of all statuses, but the house of worship holds one title of significance, The Church of the Presidents. Despite religious preferences, every President since James Madison has attended at least one service at St. John's Church. The church boasts a prayer book that contains the signatures of every president since Franklin D. Roosevelt (excluding Richard Nixon), for their inaugural services hosted at the parish. The church itself is unassuming, with somewhat plain yellow walls and a bell tower that contains a bell made by Paul Revere's son. Despite what the church appears to be, the historical significance of St. John's Church and the stories the building could tell make it an institution in Washington, D.C.

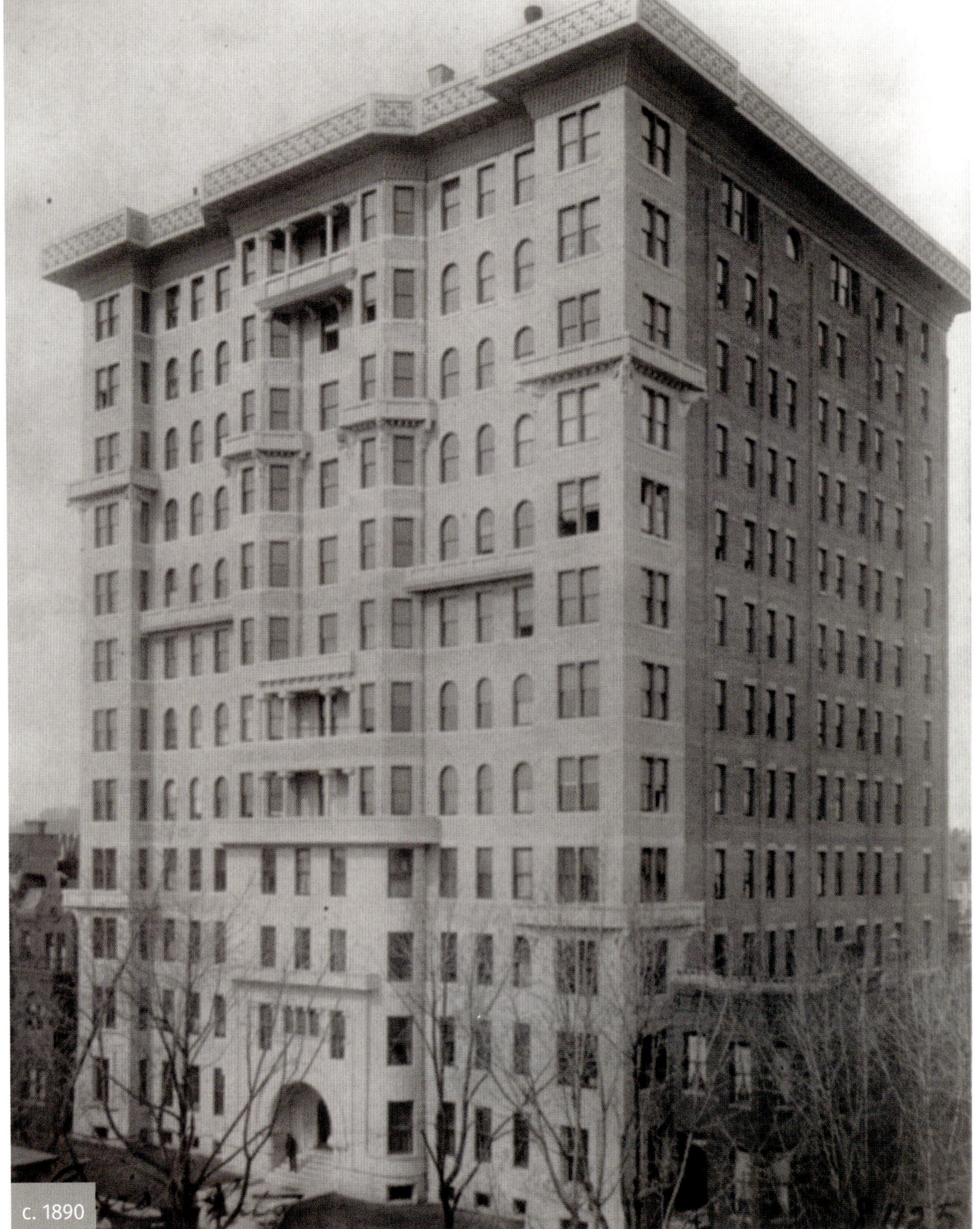
c. 1890

THEN: At the end of the nineteenth century, Washington was facing a housing shortage. Many members of D.C. society, such as government officials, could no longer afford homes that equaled their perceived status in society and instead, they became renters. A housing option originally most popular with lower class residents, renting grew in popularity in the 1890s. Architect Thomas Franklin Schneider capitalized on this popularity in Washington, constructing apartment buildings throughout the city. Considered the "Young Napoleon of F Street" due to his office location and ambition, the architect set his sights on the up-and-coming Dupont Circle neighborhood for his next endeavor.

In 1894, on Q Street NW between 16th and 17th Street, Schneider's latest structure was finished. The building was completed in the Romanesque Revival style, however was fitted with gargoyles and other gothic features not typically seen in Washington. This building was called The Cairo after the architect's inspirational visit to the World's Columbian Exposition in Chicago, where he had seen Egyptian Revival and Moorish style buildings. Despite its eclectic exterior, The Cairo's interior reflected popular styles for a Gilded Age Washington. With twelve stories, and one of the first roof gardens in the city, The Cairo stood proud as the largest non-governmental building in the city at the time of its construction.

Local Washingtonians were not as proud of their new elaborate building; they specifically disliked its height. Washingtonians nicknamed the building "Schneider's Folly" and the D.C. Board of Commissioners feared a precedent had been set for future buildings, and took action, amending D.C. building regulations to limit the height of residential buildings to ninety feet, and commercial buildings to 110 feet. This did not apply to Schneider's active project and The Cairo rose to a height of 164 feet.

THE CAIRO

Permanently changing the Washington skyline

NOW: During the peak of its popularity, The Cairo hosted high-ranking military and government officials including Thomas Edison Fitzgerald, and Queen Liliuokalani, who stayed there for six months following her removal from her position as Queen of Hawaii. Eventually, the building fell out of favor with its tenants, and transitioned into a hotel in the 1920s.

The mid-twentieth century and the years following World War II brought additional demands for The Cairo, and in the 1950s it became a facility for people discharged from St. Elizabeth's Hospital. The area surrounding the hotel began to change as well, and throughout the 1960s the once elaborate apartment building stood vacant, owing to fears of crime.

In 1972, as buildings across Washington were facing potential demolition, The Cairo became a restoration project for Arthur Cotton Moore, who had also renovated the Old Post Office Tower. Moore completed an entire overhaul of the building, from the demolished lobby to external renovations. The Cairo reopened in 1976 as a rental facility, returning to its original purpose.

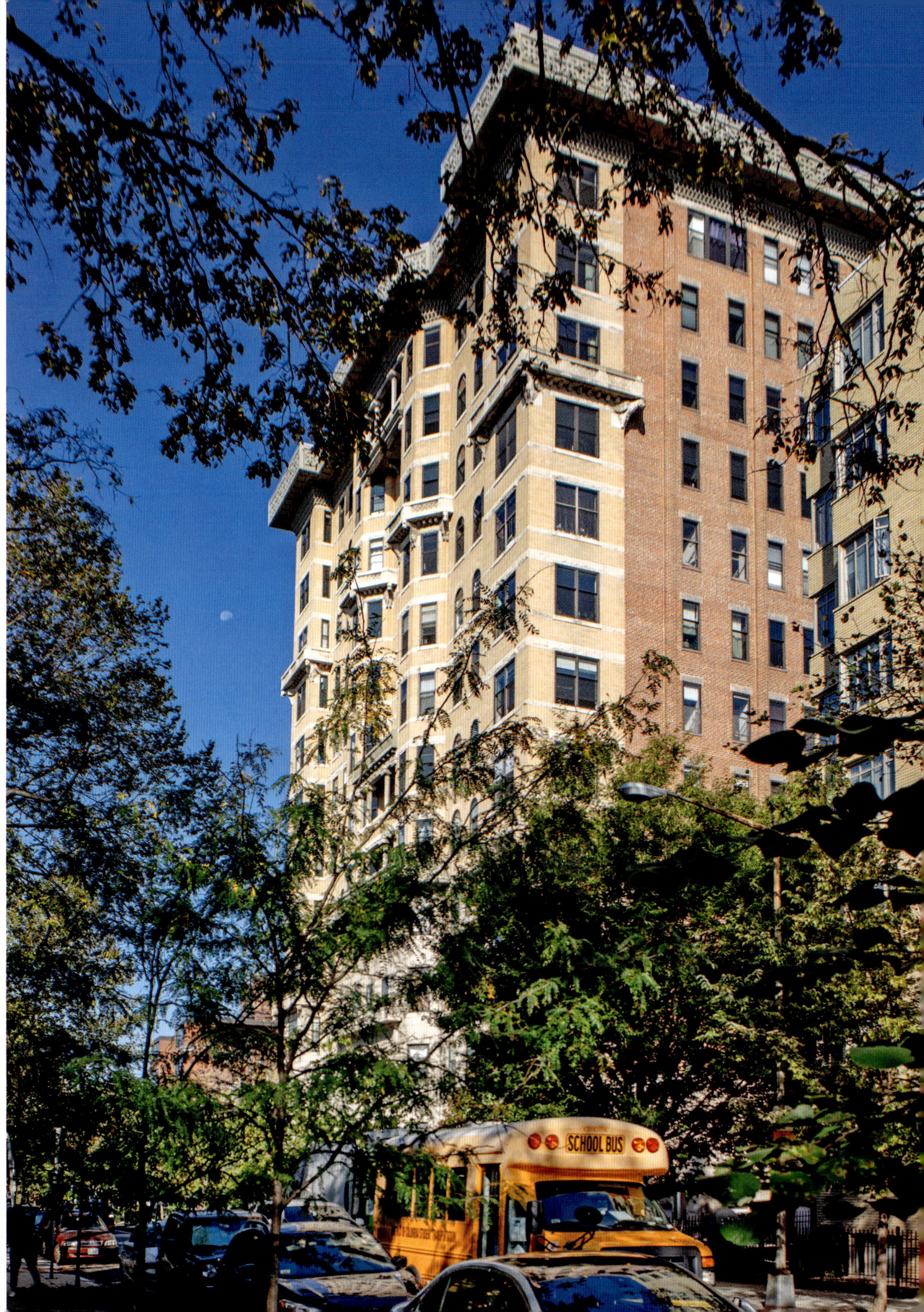

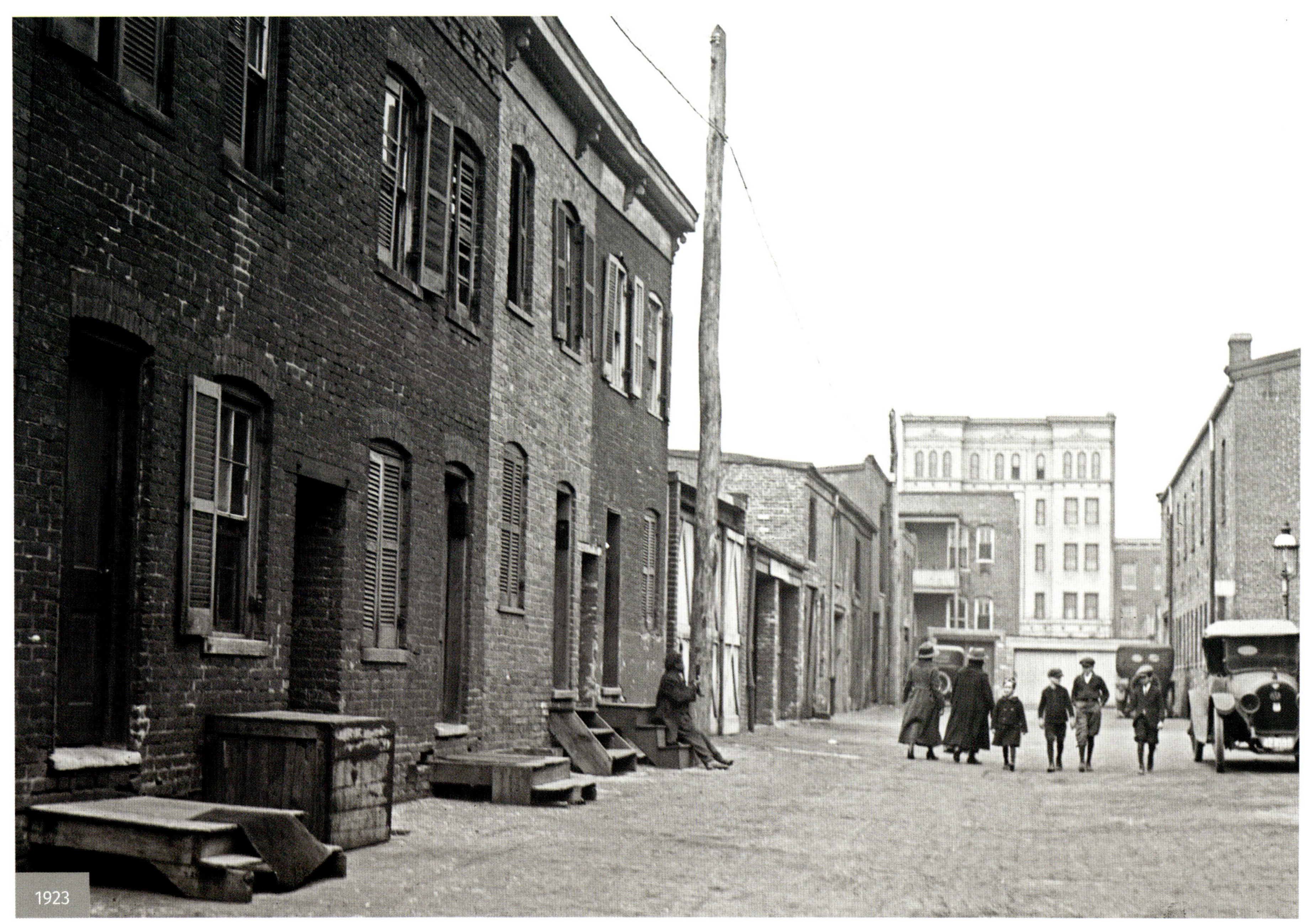
1923

BLAGDEN ALLEY AND NAYLOR COURT

The covert struggle of Washington's alley life

THEN: Washingtonian life happens not only on its primary streets, but also within the hidden connecting alleys. One of these alley systems is located between 9th and 10th street NW, around M and O street. While the alleys were included in some of the earliest designs for Washington, many did not fully develop until the mid-nineteenth century, as Washington changed from a rural farming town to an expanding metropolis.

The area, which was eventually named Blagden Alley and Naylor Court, after former nineteenth century residents Thomas Blagden and Dickerson Naylor, was initially a hub of middle-class life and represented the diversity of the city. Property owners ranged in background, and out of eighty-one residents, eleven were women. The Civil War brought a housing shortage though, and residents of the area split their existing properties into street- and alley-facing lots.

The alley and nearby court boasted a respectable group of property owners; or at least appeared to. While the external perimeter of the block appeared to be acceptable, the inside alleys of the neighborhood were packed with pieced together shanties. This crowded space included frame homes which were not structurally sound, with leaky roofs and dirt floors that were unable to protect residents from Washington's changing seasons. The system of alleys represented a growing inequality in Washington and while most residents in the surrounding area were white, those living in the Blagden Alley were mainly Black.

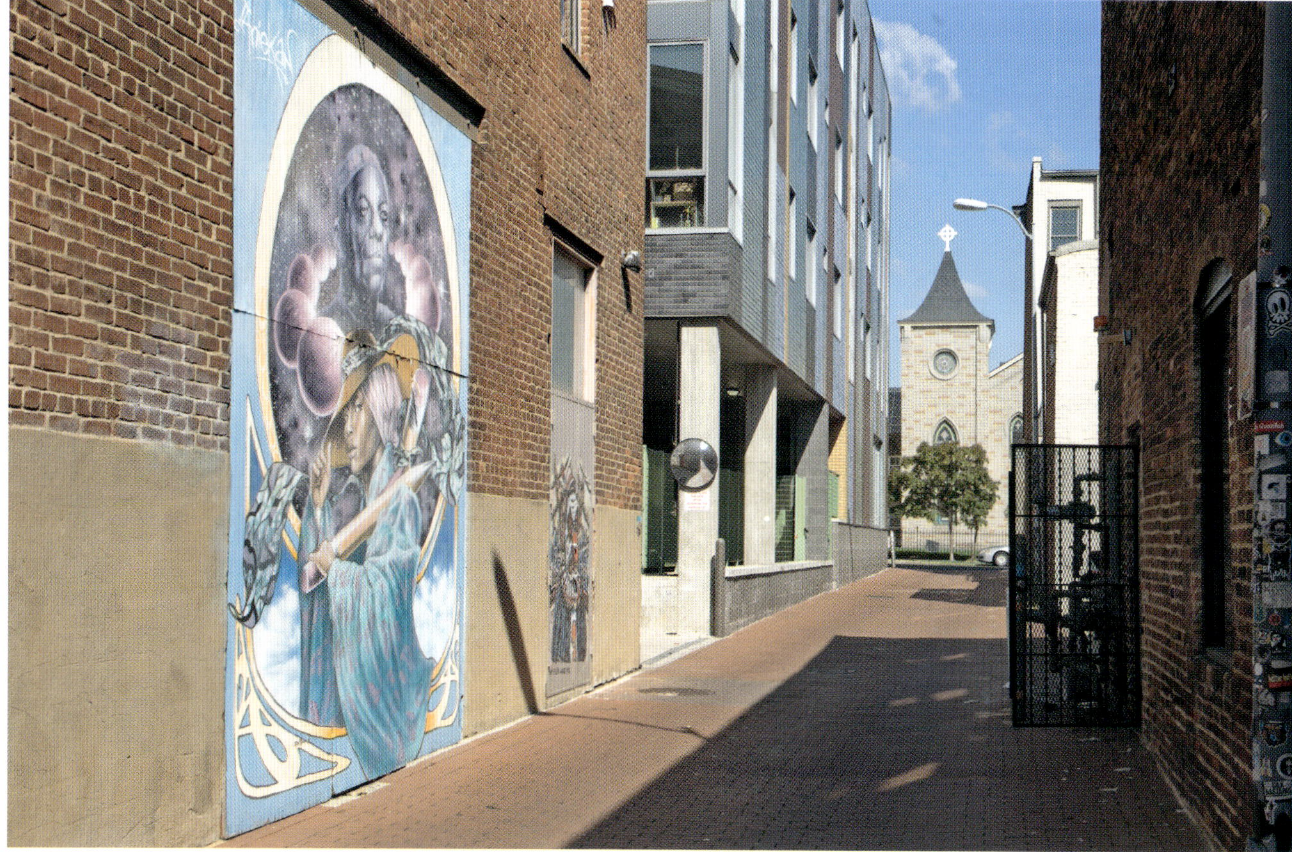

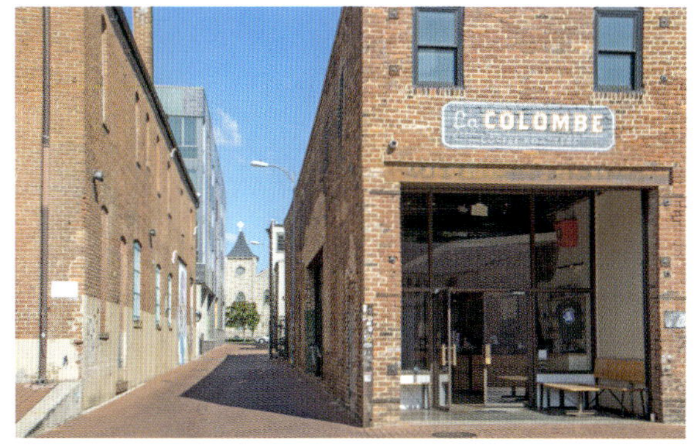

NOW: Life was hard in the alley dwellings, and crime increased as the area was continuously ignored. In 1892, Congress passed a law banning the construction of new alley dwellings, hoping to address overcrowding. Despite the passage of this law, there was little change to the existing dwellings which persisted throughout the early twentieth century. The area saw a continuing decline in conditions, which reached an all-time low in the years following the 1968 riots. Shanties and alley communities were destroyed and street facing properties once occupied by Washington's growing middle-class were abandoned for houses in the suburbs. Without its residents, the area soon saw an increased level of crime as Washington faced the crack epidemic and a wave of other criminal activities.

Not all was lost for Blagden Alley. In the 1990s, some residents saw the potential of the area in its proximity to downtown and the character of the remaining houses. Crime continued, but a movement of counterculture begun redefining the neighborhood, as art galleries and other cultural hubs opened in the abandoned buildings. The construction of the convention center nearby saw the area move from a residential area to a commercial one. Many feared that the historic character of the neighborhood would be lost and, in response, the area became a D.C. Historic Site to protect it.

LEFT: Blagden Alley no longer contains dilapidated housing structures, instead hosting restaurants and other commercial entities to work out of its old stables and back alley structures.

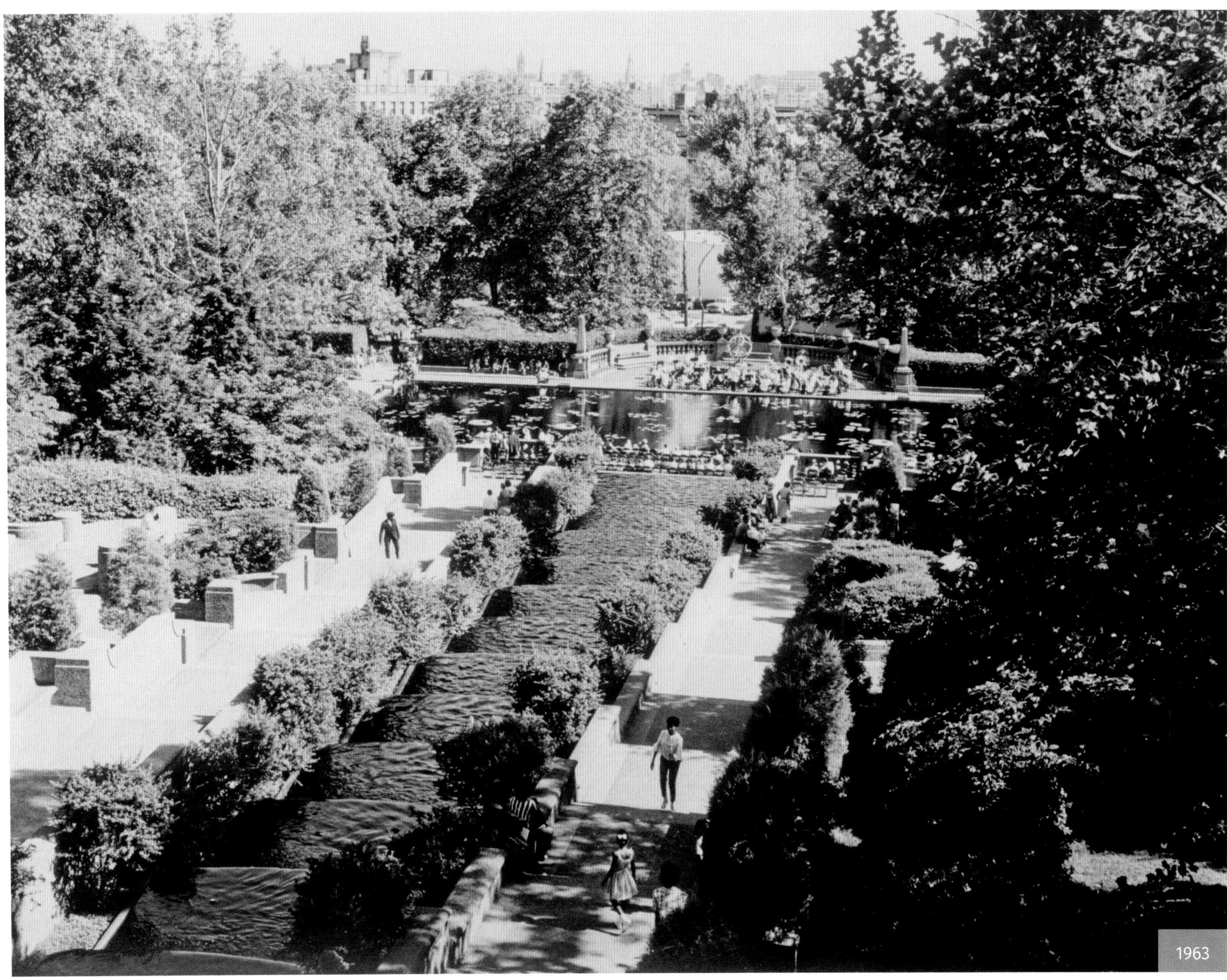
1963

MERIDIAN HILL PARK

One of America's first designated public parks

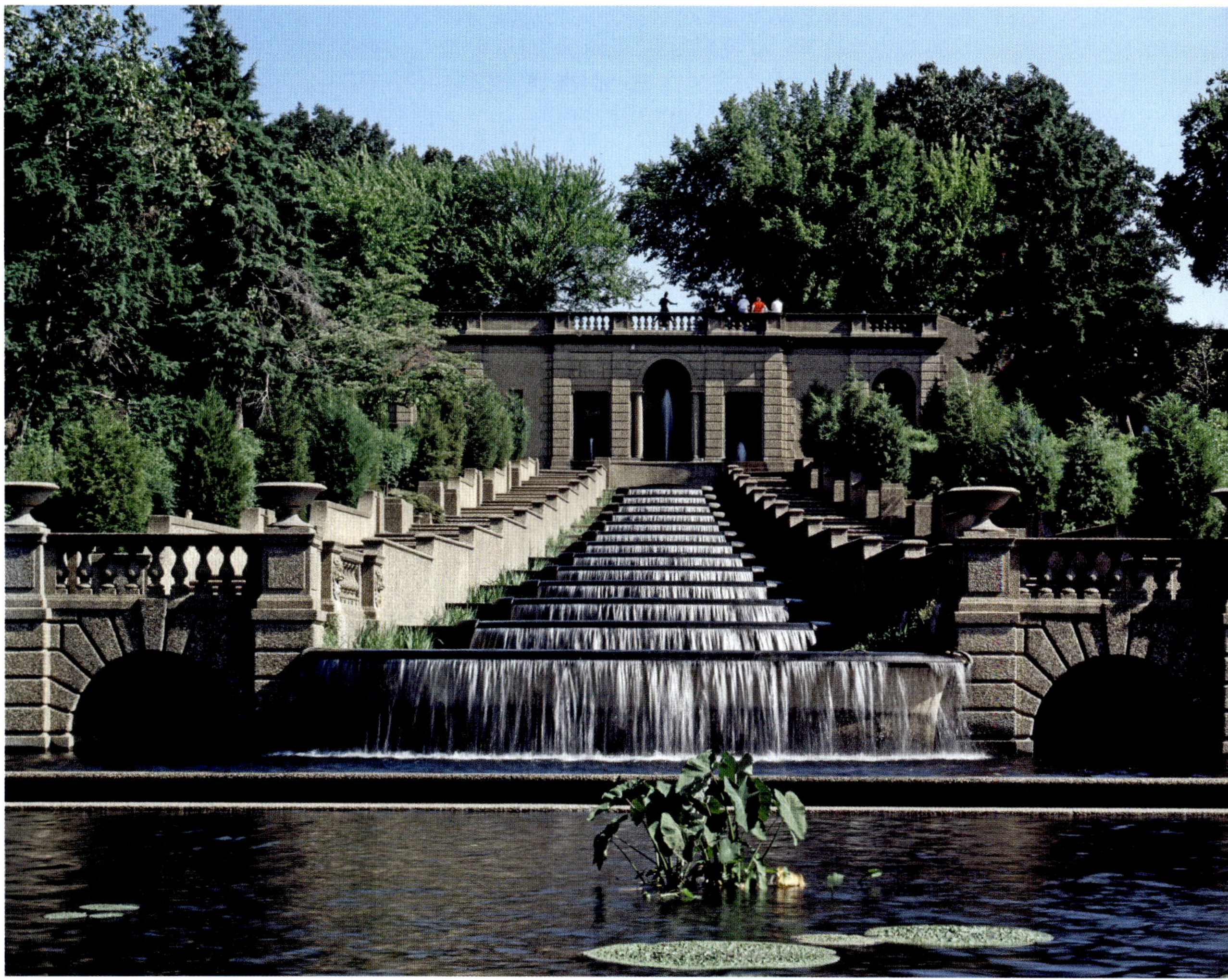

THEN: In 1814, Commodore David Porter had returned from his time fighting in the war of 1812 and needed a place to call home. Washington was still defining itself as the capital city, and while downtown had seen increased development, much of outer Washington remained untouched. Commodore Porter saw this undeveloped land as an opportunity, and purchased a 110-acre plot for his new estate. In 1818, the Commodore completed his mansion, which he called Meridian Hill as the site was situated on the longitude of the original milestone marker for the District of Columbia, and placed on top of a high hill in northwest Washington. While the Meridian later faded away, Commodore Porter's large estate was foundational in the creation of what is Meridian Hill Park today.

Since Commodore Porter's ownership, the estate changed hands several times and hosted many figures, including former president John Quincy Adams, who was a resident after his time in the White House. During the Civil War, the land was used as an encampment for Union troops, before being subdivided in the post-Civil War years.

By the turn of the century, Congress had introduced the McMillan Plan, or the Report of the Senate Park Commission, which looked to improve Washington through its parks and monuments. While the plan was largely focused on downtown improvements, it was undeniable that with Washington's growing population, people were moving further into the outer edges of Washington. In 1910, Congress bought twelve acres of land bordered by 16th Street, 15th Street, W Street and Euclid Street in the northwest with the intention of creating a park.

The Department of the Interior in 1914 hired George Burnap, a landscape architect to design the park in a style reminiscent of European garden spaces, who was later replaced by Horace W. Peaslee. Some changes were made to the original plans, however it was ultimately decided that Meridian Hill Park would emulate an Italian garden, in the capital city of the United States. Construction of the park took twenty-six years, and the area officially opened in 1936.

The park is large and divided into two primary areas: the lower park, which has a wide reflecting pool surrounded by a plaza, and an upper park that features an open green space surrounded by trees. During construction, monuments were added including statues of Dante Alighieri, Joan of Arc, and former President James Buchanan, a marble representation of serenity, and the Noyes Armillary Sphere.

NOW: Since its inception, Meridian Hill Park has served as a popular gathering place for Washingtonians, especially those in the nearby neighborhoods of Columbia Heights and Adams Morgan. It has hosted concerts by groups including the Trapp Family Singers, civil rights protests, and the longest running drum circle in American history.

Today the park, commonly referred to as Malcolm X Park, maintains its Italian garden design, serving as a place of solace for Washingtonians who desire a break from the city bustle.

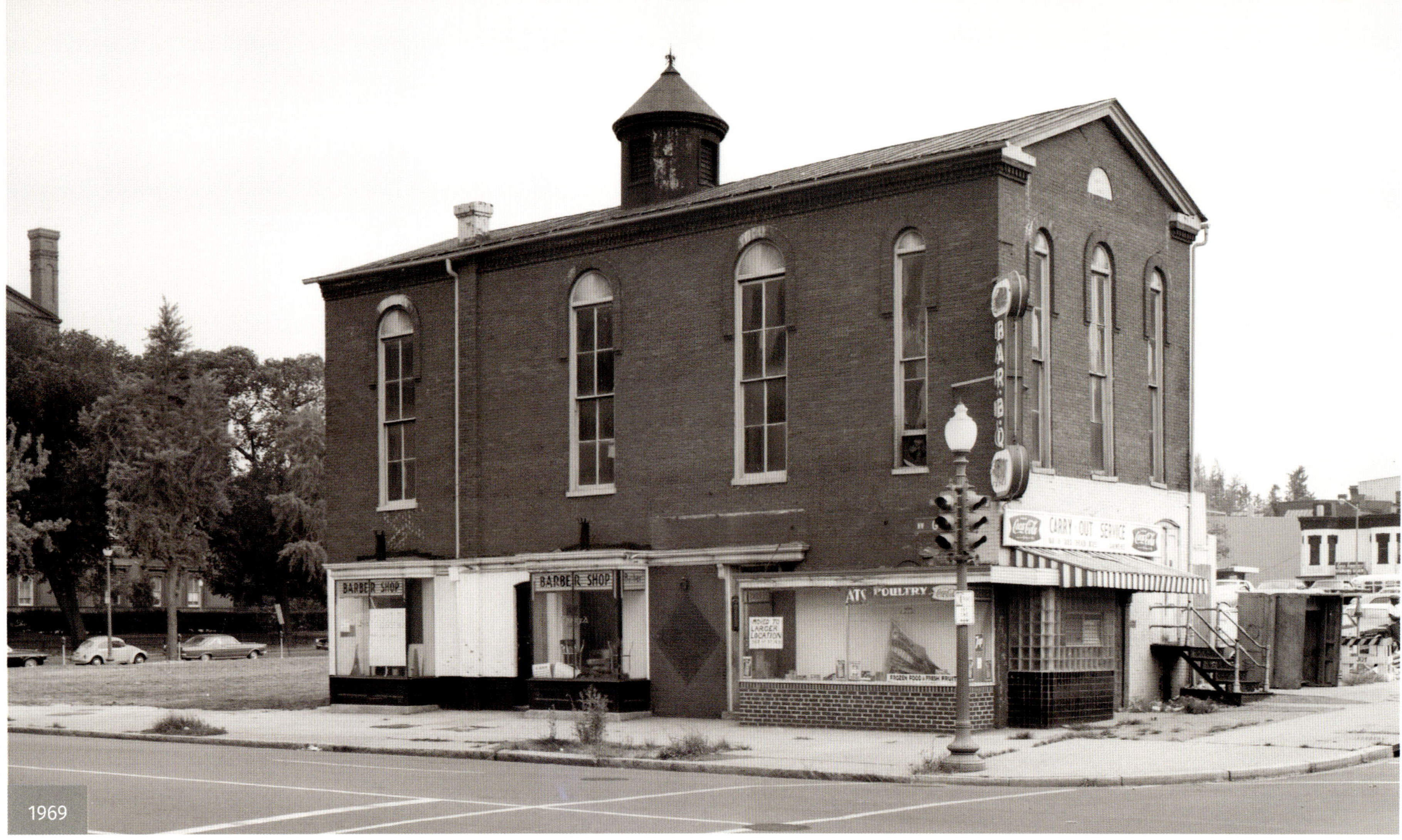

1969

ADAS ISRAEL HISTORIC SYNAGOGUE

The oldest purpose-built synagogue in the nation's capital

THEN: The US capital is made up of myriad communities, including the Jewish community in Washington, which has been a part of D.C. since its foundational years. One of the earliest Jewish congregations in Washington, D.C. was the Washington Hebrew Congregation, first established in 1852. The second was Adas Israel, which was founded in 1869. Many attendees of these first two congregations were of German descent; yet more joined from Eastern Europe, Turkey, Morocco, and other parts of the world, moving to Washington to exercise their freedom of religion. As the Jewish population grew in Washington, more congregations were added to Washington, D.C., and it became apparent that a permanent gathering space was needed.

In 1876, on the corner of 6th Street and G Street NW, the Adas Israel Synagogue was built to accommodate the growing Jewish population in Washington and the Adas Israel Congregation. A modest brick structure, the small synagogue was to become the site of moments of historical significance early in its life, when President Ulysses S. Grant attended the synagogue's dedication, making him the first sitting president to attend a Jewish service.

It seemed that the Adas Israel Congregation finally had a religious center for its growing group, however as the Jewish population increased in Washington, so did the need for a newer, larger building. In 1908, Adas Israel Congregation moved to 6th and I Street NW, into a building that could accommodate the size of the group. The small brick structure that had served as the first official gathering space for the congregation was left behind, serving as a house of worship for other religions, a retail space, and even a barbecue restaurant in the early twentieth century.

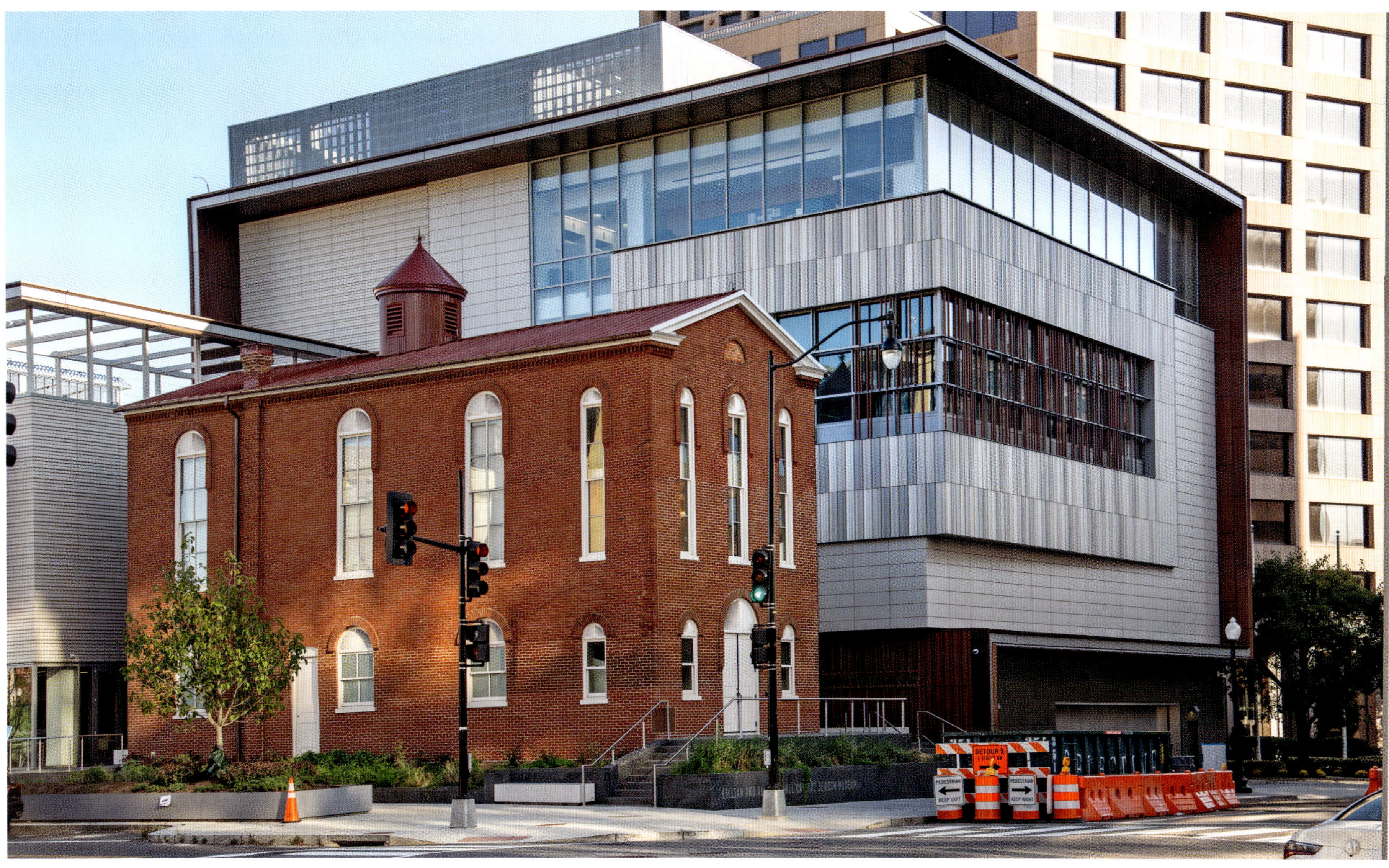

NOW: By the mid-twentieth century the former synagogue was set for demolition to make way for Washington's latest advancement, the Metro system. However, at the end of the 1960s, Jewish Washingtonians lobbied Congress to protect the building, and to save it from destruction. The path of the Metro was difficult to change once set, so Congress decided to move the entire Adas Israel Synagogue instead. The entire brick structure was picked up and moved down the street to 3rd and G Street Northwest, where it resided for over forty years.

In the twenty-first century, the building faced the problem of relocation for a second time. As construction continued throughout Washington, the building needed to be moved again to make way for the Capitol Crossing project. The building had hosted the Lillian & Albert Small Jewish Museum since 1975. In 2016, the whole building was picked up and wheeled down the street, finally reaching its new location on 3rd and F Street NW in 2019. The museum, now a part of the Capital Jewish Museum, has since reopened to the public and what is one of the oldest synagogue buildings in America lives on in Washington, D.C..

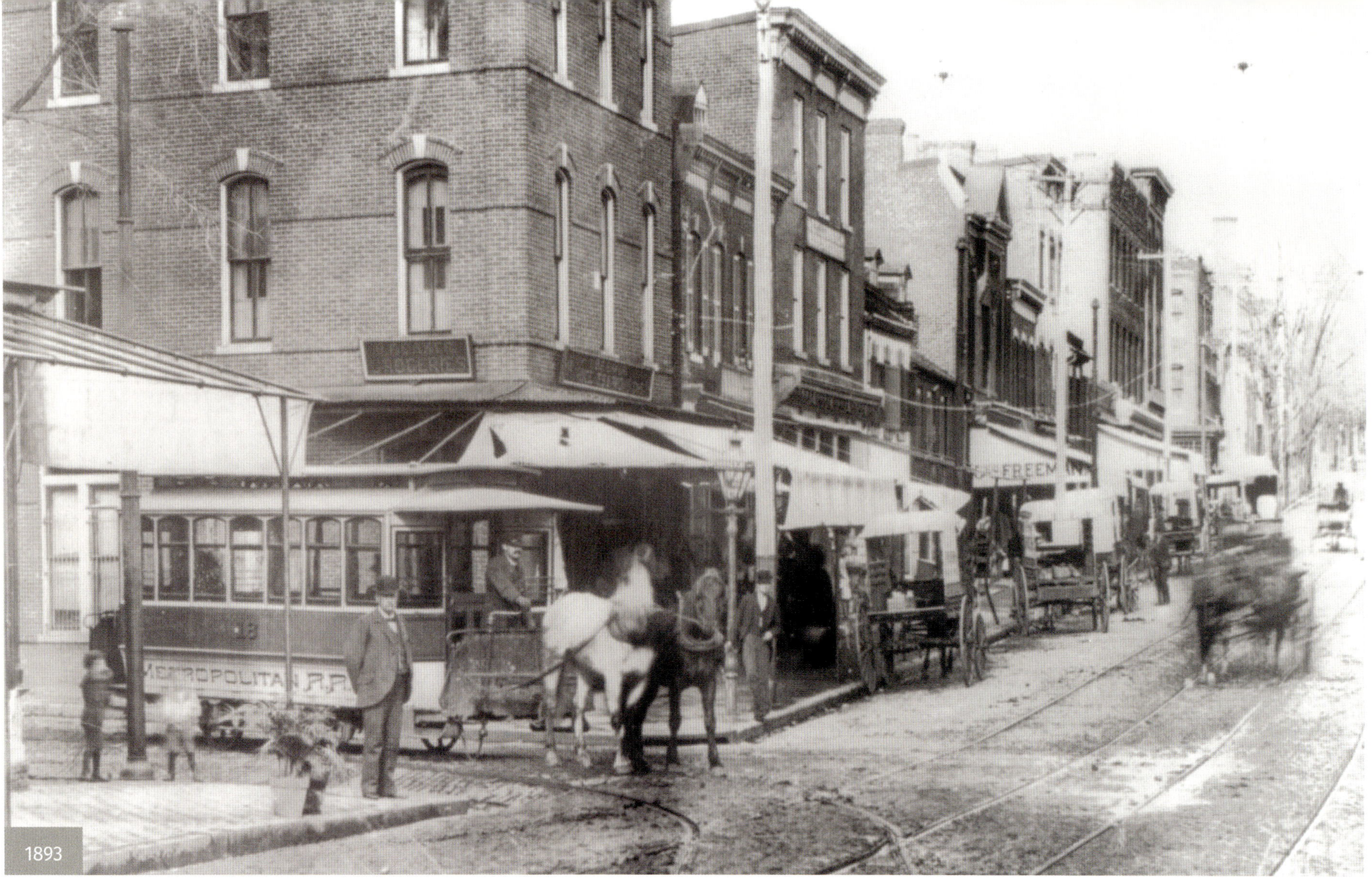

1893

GEORGETOWN DOWNTOWN

Washington's oldest neighborhood

THEN: Initially founded as its own village in Maryland in 1751, what was once Georgetown joined the soon to be new capital in 1791. Georgetown acted as a separate entity until 1871, when its charter was revoked and it officially became a part of Washington, D.C. Beginning as a Native American trading village, the arrival of Europeans altered the area's commercial nature and activity as a port town. Originating from the waterfront area, the streets began to fill with commercial buildings and businesses, which supported the imports and exports of the nearby river. The area began to thrive with new taverns and residential buildings as locals settled into their new town. By the time the District had absorbed the commercial port and growing town in 1800, Georgetown had already established itself. Many famous residents of Washington were known to make their way to Georgetown, such as America's first president, George Washington.

Georgetown was not only a commercial success, it also had a vibrant social community. Georgetown University brought students to the area, factories in the region attracted tradesmen and laborers, and the end of the Civil War increased the population of freed Black residents. Yet what was once a bustling commercial city soon faced challenges in its appeal. By the early twentieth century Georgetown was no longer popular, and it was widely viewed as outdated. The industrialization of the waterfront made the area undesirable to residents, and low rental prices brought only laborers to the area, as previous residents moved away.

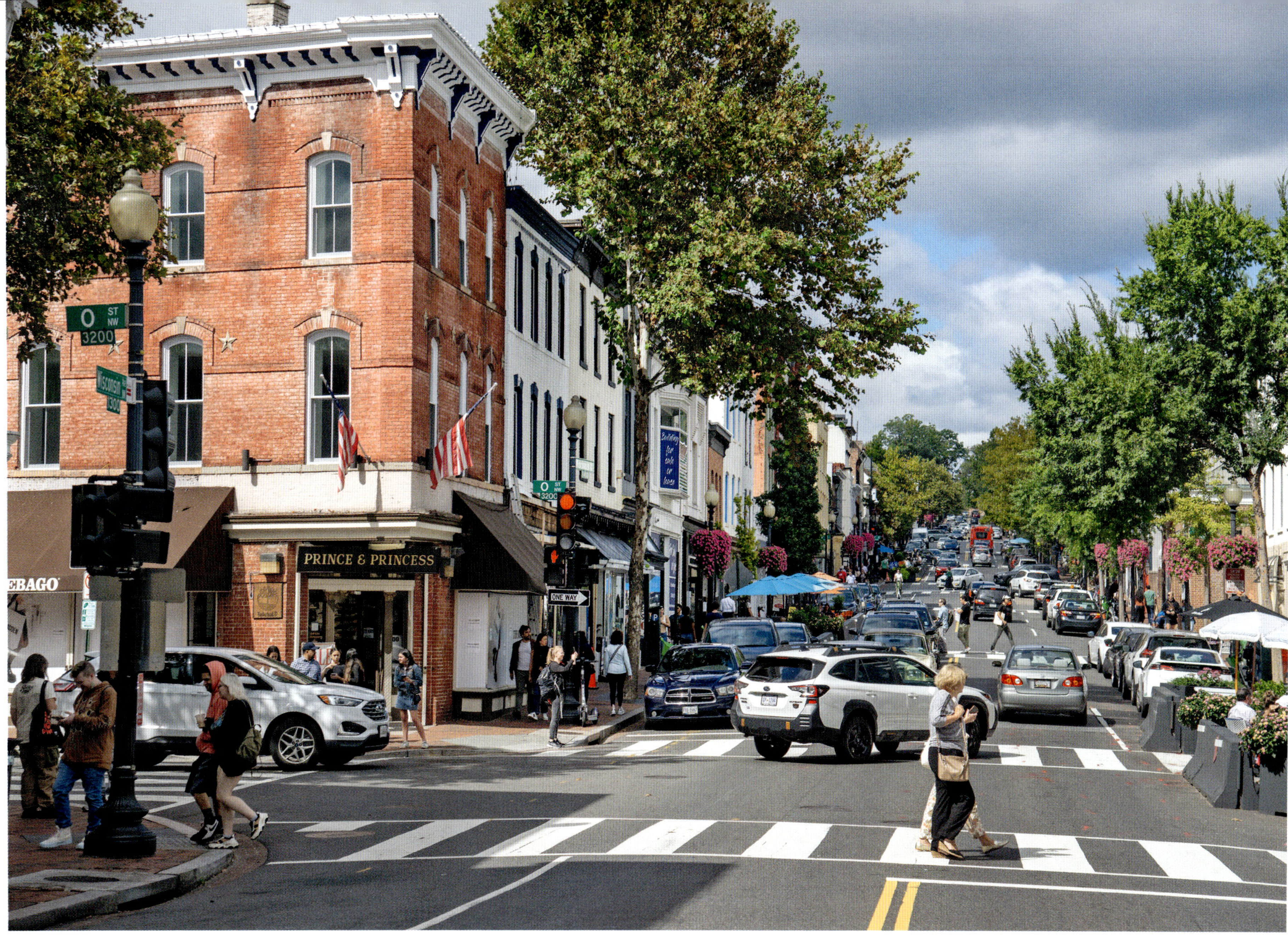

NOW: In 1920, Mr and Mrs Robert Woods Bliss started a trend that led to the eventual preservation of the entire downtown Georgetown. Their conservation of the mansion Dumbarton Oaks inspired others to save the stately and historic buildings in Georgetown from demolition by restoring them. Many incoming residents who had arrived to support the World War II effort, embraced the antiquated charm of the historic neighborhood within walking distance to the White House, bringing life back into its commercial areas. Georgetown, which had been historically diverse, lost this feature with unyielding Congressional laws that bolstered racial tensions in the area, that would persist throughout the twentieth and twenty-first centuries.

Today, Georgetown's Downtown or Historic District remains preserved and represents a window into Washington's past. A passage of a law in 1950 prevented new developments in the area, and the neighborhood has maintained its 'small village' nature. The lack of Metro access, which has been fiercely debated since the rail line was introduced to Washington, D.C., keeps the neighborhood closed off to the encroaching modernity, that has now influenced many other parts of D.C.

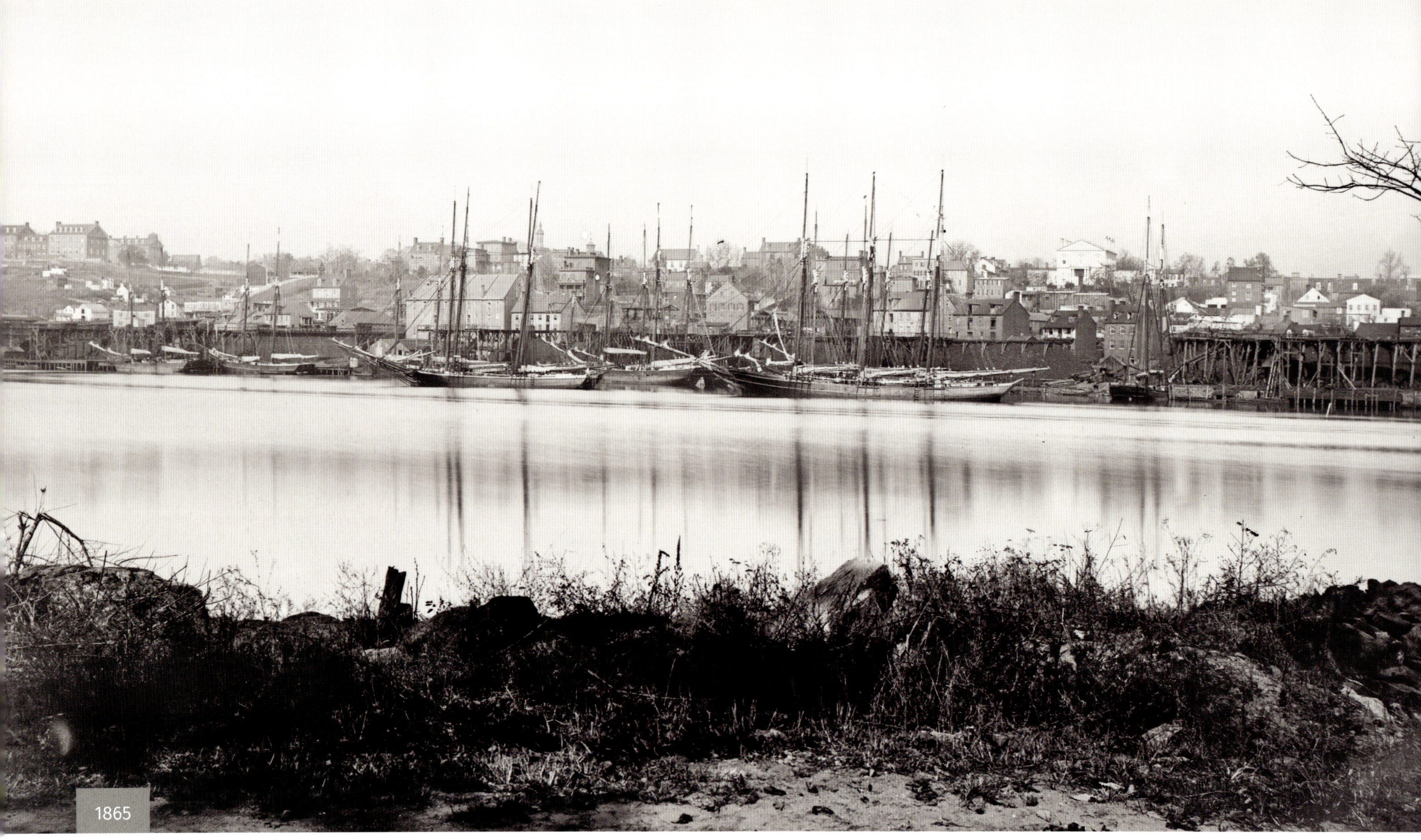
1865

GEORGETOWN WATERFRONT

Commercial port turned spot of relaxation

THEN: Founded in 1751 as its own village, Georgetown became a part of the District in 1791. The commercial success of Georgetown relied heavily on imports and exports brought in by the river, however the increased development of Washington was leading to issues in the once bustling port town. By the 1820s, the Potomac River was no longer navigable to Georgetown by boat, and the commercial income of the area was under threat. Activity was soon reinstated with the creation of the C&O Canal and horsecar lines which connected Georgetown to the main areas of Washington. Tobacco that was grown deep in the south and in Virginia was shipped through Georgetown, making it one of the largest tobacco ports in the Untied States.

Once a center for commerce and trade, the Georgetown Waterfront eventually lost its port access as large ships could no longer travel the Potomac River due to a build-up of silt. The nearby factories and commercial entities that relied on this source of income started to move away from the riverside, and the waterfront was converted into parking lots. While the rest of Georgetown began to experience historical preservation efforts, the waterfront remained largely ignored.

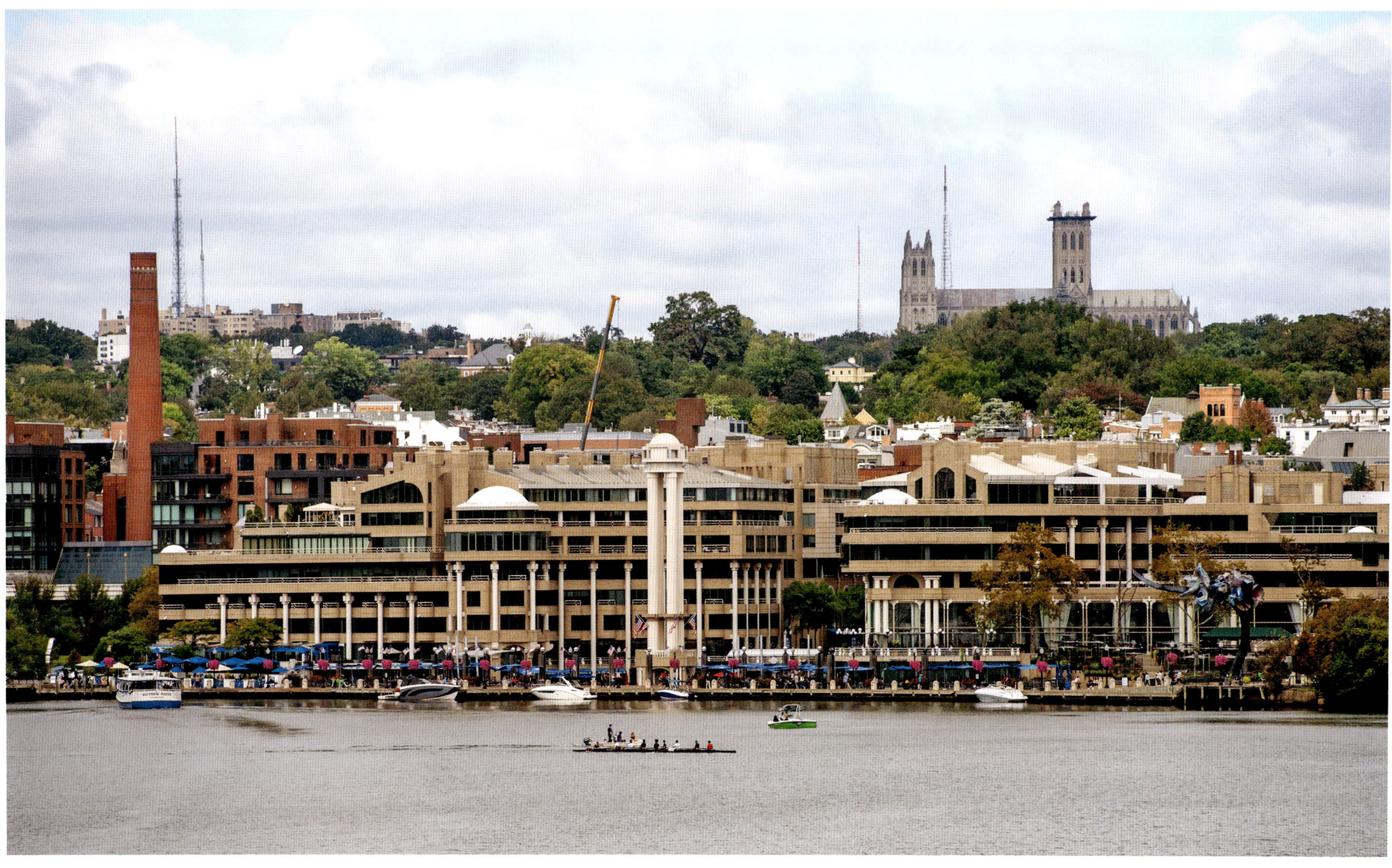

NOW: By the turn of the twentieth century, the waterfront was faced with a revival. Tall smokestacks started to rise along what was the Georgetown Waterfront as factories came back to the area. The Key Bridge was constructed in 1918, connecting the Waterfront to Virginia at a new point of access. The increased use of cars faced Washington with an ever-present problem: where to put new highways. In 1949, before Georgetown was prevented from including major developments, Washington constructed the Whitehurst Freeway, the city's first elevated road.

In the 1970s where factories had once stood, office buildings began to pop up, although the local neighborhood associations pushed against this level of development. The waterfront had always held factories and commercial buildings, but now it also held office structures. With such a beautiful perspective of Theodore Roosevelt Island and Downtown Washington, it was clear to planners that the waterfront needed a new addition to enjoy this view: a park. In 2011, the Georgetown Waterfront Park was completed, and today hosts various green spaces as well as a large walking path to take in the view of the city and the Potomac River.

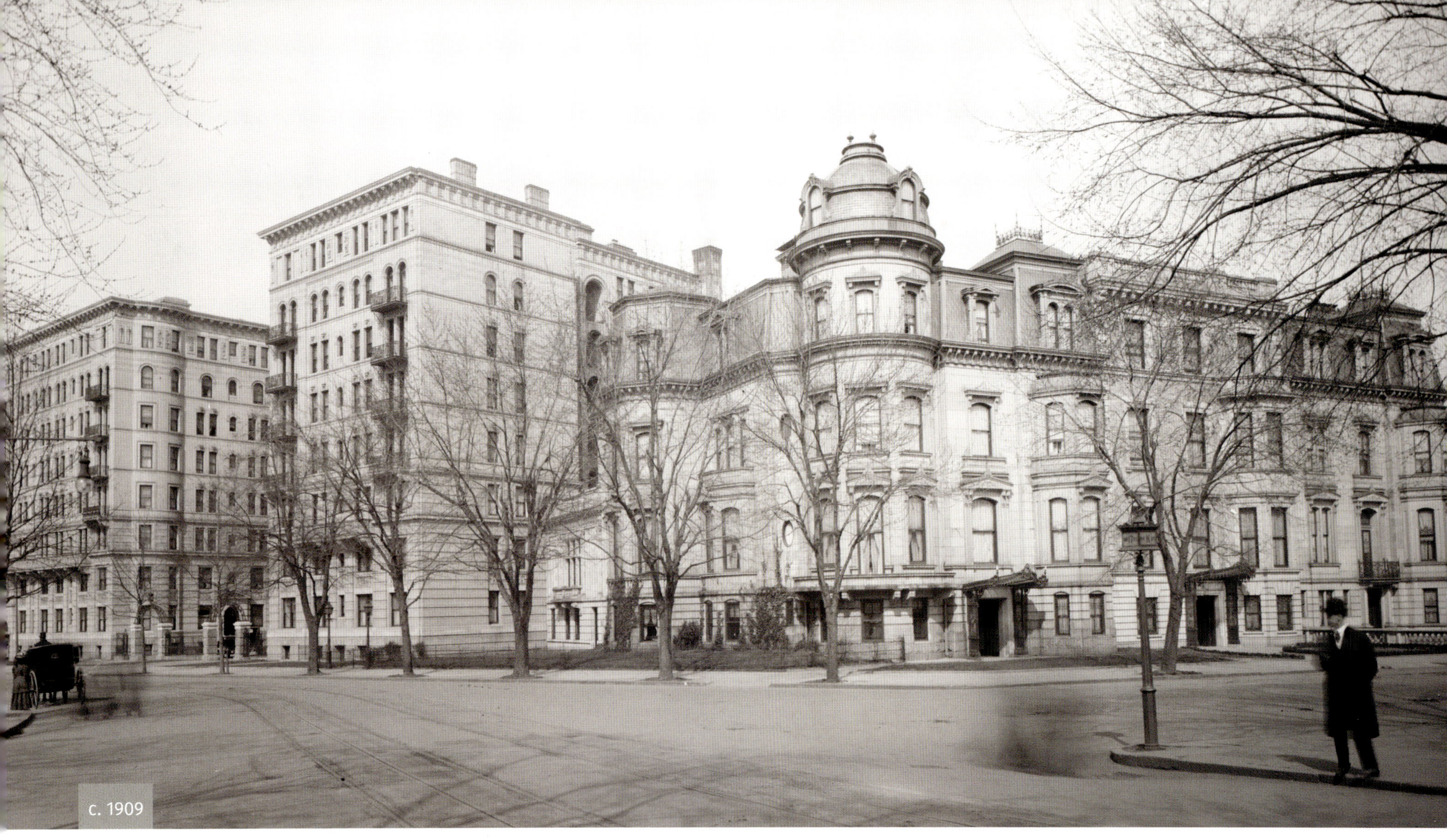
c. 1909

SHEPHERD MANSION

Washington's infrastructural improvements

THEN: In the years following the Civil War, the city's population was growing at an unprecedented rate, and new arrivals to the capital city were not greeted with the assumed metropolis, but instead met with dirt roads and a waste filled canal. D.C. needed change, and one local Washingtonian was on hand to modernize the District's infrastructure system.

Alexander Robey Shepherd was a born-and-bred Washingtonian who initially made his money through government contracts during the Civil War. Following this success, Shepherd focused his investments on constructing row houses for Washington's growing post-Civil War population and later became the head of the Board of Public Works.

Shepherd's career in Public Works had some distinctive highs and lows. Known to cut corners and incur high expenses, Shepherd was not popular with local citizens who saw his unfinished projects all around the District. The improvements he did make permanently altered the landscape of the city and its future and Shepherd was responsible for the initial paving of main roads in Washington and the installation of sewers. Ultimately, Shepherd was successful in his career with the Board of Public Works and was eventually appointed Governor of D.C.

Shepherd needed a home to represent his successes, and asked his Board of Public Works colleague and famed Washington architect Adolf Cluss to design a home. Shepherd picked a piece of land on the corner of K Street opposite Farragut Square,

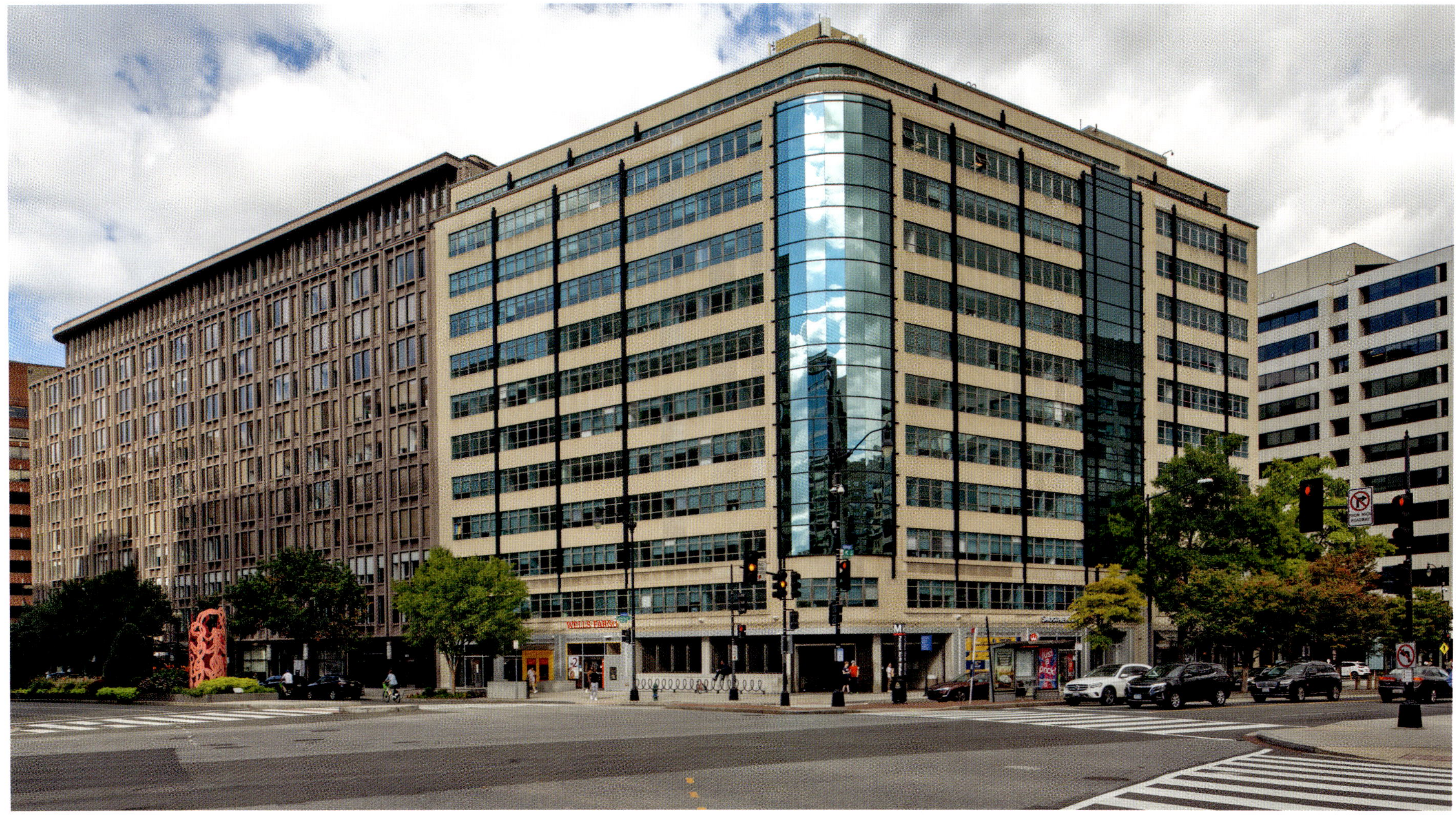

in between the White House and the up-and-coming Dupont Circle neighborhood for his residence. A corner construction, the mansion was furnished with white and gold, had a walnut paneled library, a spiral staircase, and other dramatic features. Cluss filled the entire block with Second Empire style row houses, including his own, however the largest and most elaborate one was reserved for Shepherd.

Shepherd's time in the stately mansion was limited. His family lived there only for the duration of his term as governor, when Washington eventually switched from territorial leadership to a commissioner system. The Panic of 1873 caused Shepherd to announce his bankruptcy in 1876, after hosting a reception for President Ulysses S. Grant. He then sold his illustrious mansion.

NOW: Following Shepherd's ownership, the mansion changed owners several times yet maintained high levels of social activity, hosting grand events during Washington's social seasons. At one point, the mansion hosted a wedding for one of Washington's wealthiest debutantes and the resident at the time, Margaret Draper, to Prince Andrea Boncompagni of Rome.

The building, known as the Draper Mansion, was finally sold in 1922 for commercial use, ending its long history as a residential social site. The ballroom which had been added by the Drapers became a spot for supper clubs in the early twentieth century, with the most popular being the Troika Club, an eventual destination for political and social leaders of Washington. Despite the building's success, a fire destroyed its interior in 1946, and it was later sold to developers and demolished in 1951.

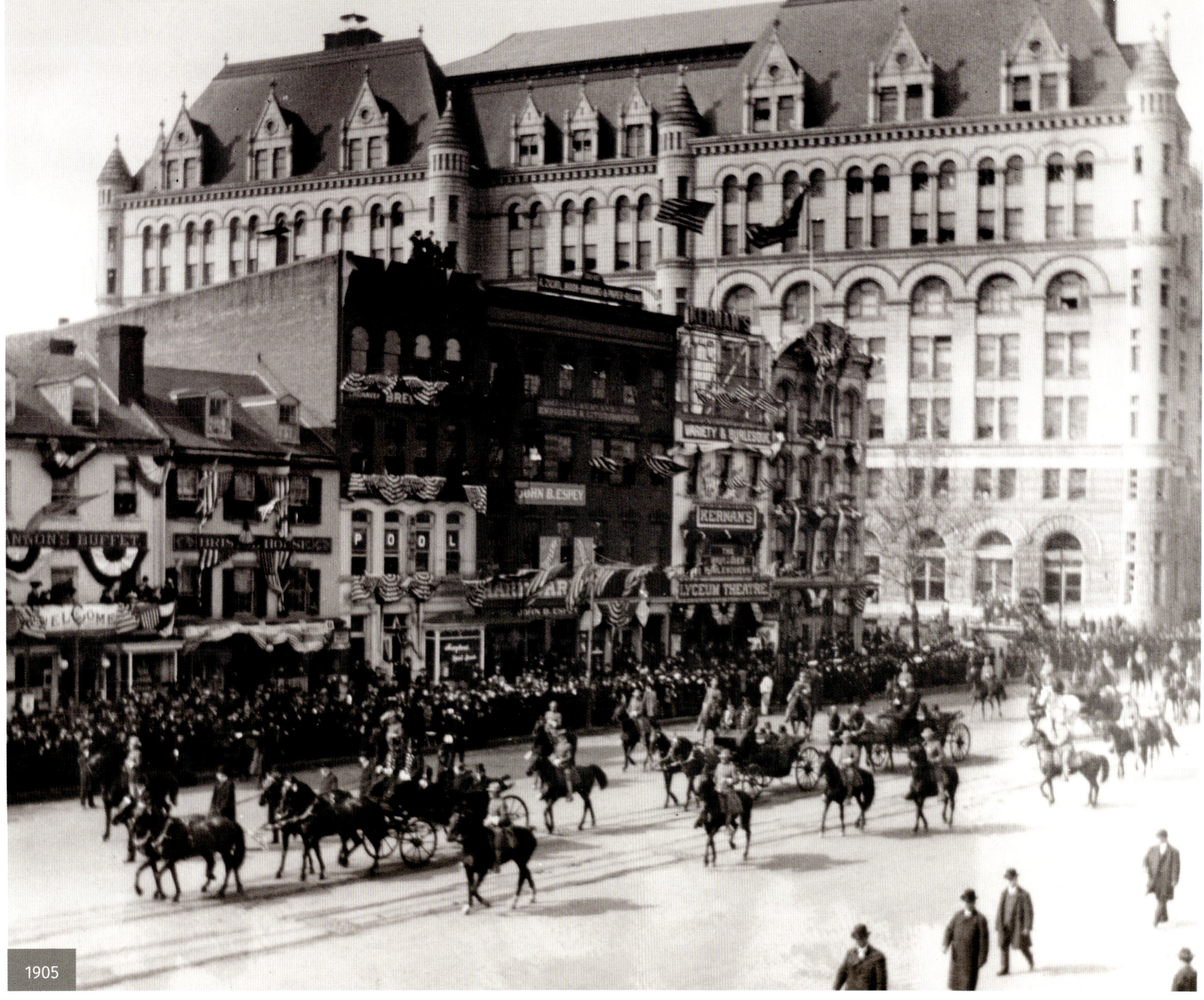

1905

PENNSYLVANIA AVENUE

America's Main Street

THEN: Since Washington's earliest days as the United States capital, Pennsylvania Avenue was a central part of the city's plan. In his 1791 blueprint for the new D.C., Pierre Charles L'Enfant included one large avenue as the shortest path connecting the Executive and Legislative branches of government. Changes to the street and surrounding area affected L'Enfant's intended plan. In a search for a new home, the Treasury Department constructed its building in front of the White House's view of the Capitol in the mid-nineteenth century, physically blocking the connection between the two seats of power.

By the early twentieth century, the neighborhood around Pennsylvania Avenue had altered again. The street was now the border of "Murder Bay," a region of Washington that saw high rates of crime and unfavorable behavior. The McMillan Plan, an urban planning effort instituted by Congress, sought to improve the central avenue and its surrounding area. Revitalization efforts continued throughout the 20th century, with the addition of different monuments and parks, such as Freedom Plaza in 1980, which was created to commemorate the accomplishments of Martin Luther King Jr.

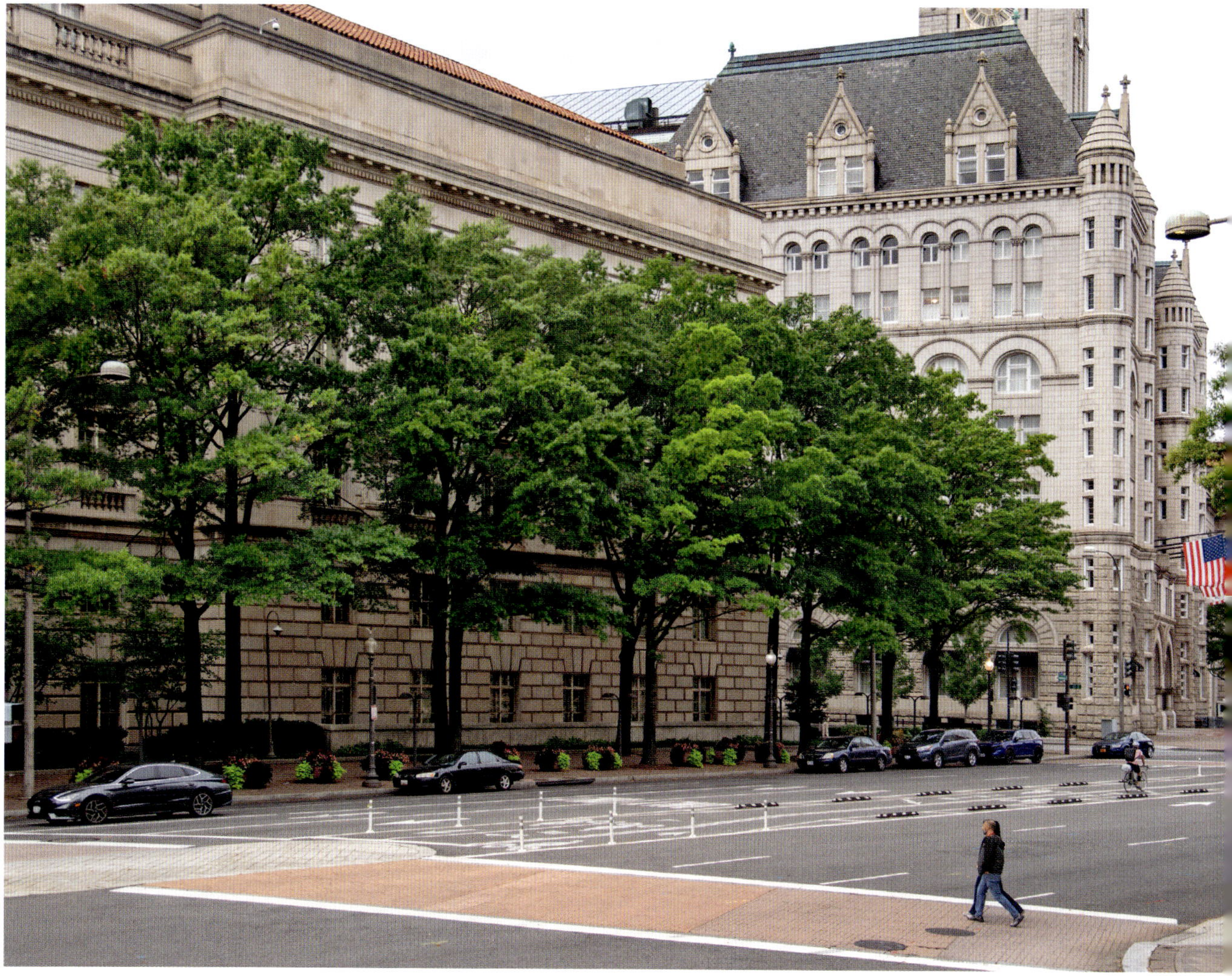

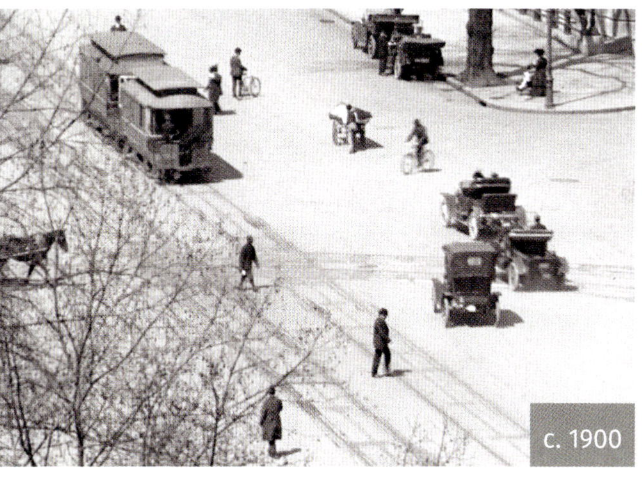

ABOVE: Following an influx of residents after the Civil War, the street was paved with wooden blocks, and tram tracks were added for more convenient transportation.

NOW: Pennsylvania Avenue spans D.C., however the most identifiable stretch of it links the Capitol Building to the White House. A fixture of the District known as "America's Main Street," this street often reflects not only the changing priorities of D.C. but also the nation as a whole. On this stretch of road, almost every president has made their way from the Capitol Building to their new home in the White House, symbolizing an era of new politics for America. The concourse has seen parades in celebration, marches in a fight for justice, and processions in honor of the fallen.

Pennsylvania Avenue continues to hold an important place in D.C. life. Bordered by historic monuments, hotels, and various federal office buildings, it has become a spot where locals can start their work day and tourists can wander down as they learn more about the nation.

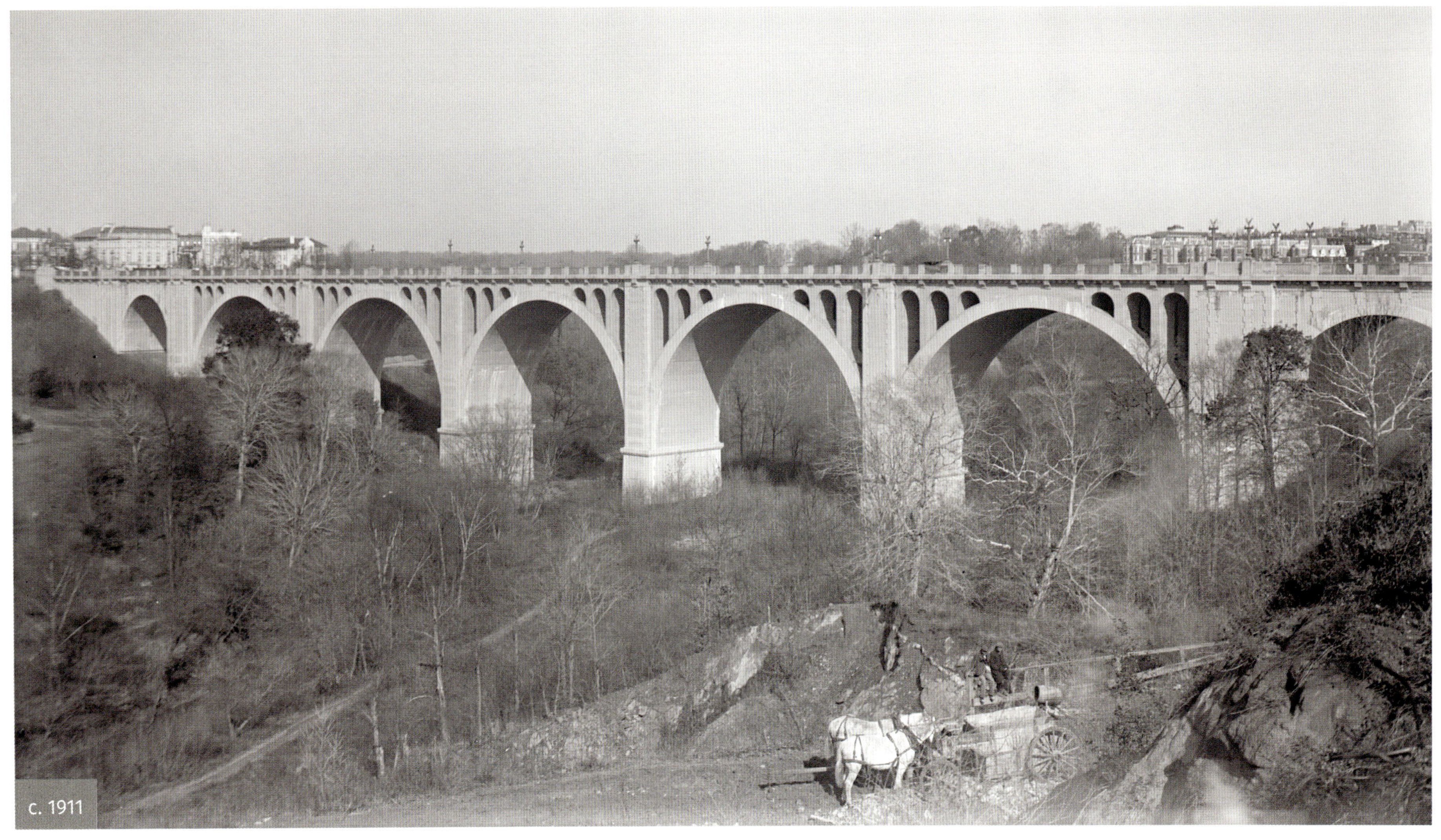
c. 1911

TAFT MEMORIAL BRIDGE

An engineering marvel

THEN: Throughout the post Civil War years, Washington, D.C.'s population was rapidly expanding. The capital city, which was once a contained downtown area surrounded by undeveloped wilderness and farmland, urgently needed new infrastructure to accommodate the growing population and their transport needs. One such piece of infrastructure was new bridges to bring those residents and visitors in and out of the District and their work and livelihoods within it.

In 1897, construction was underway for a new bridge that connected Connecticut Avenue over the Rock Creek valley. With the assistance of this bridge, Connecticut Avenue would run all the way from the White House into neighboring state, Maryland. In 1907, engineer George S. Morison completed his only masonry bridge design and revealed what was then called the Connecticut Avenue Bridge. With large concrete lions sculpted by Roland Hinton Perry, who designed the Neptune Fountain at the

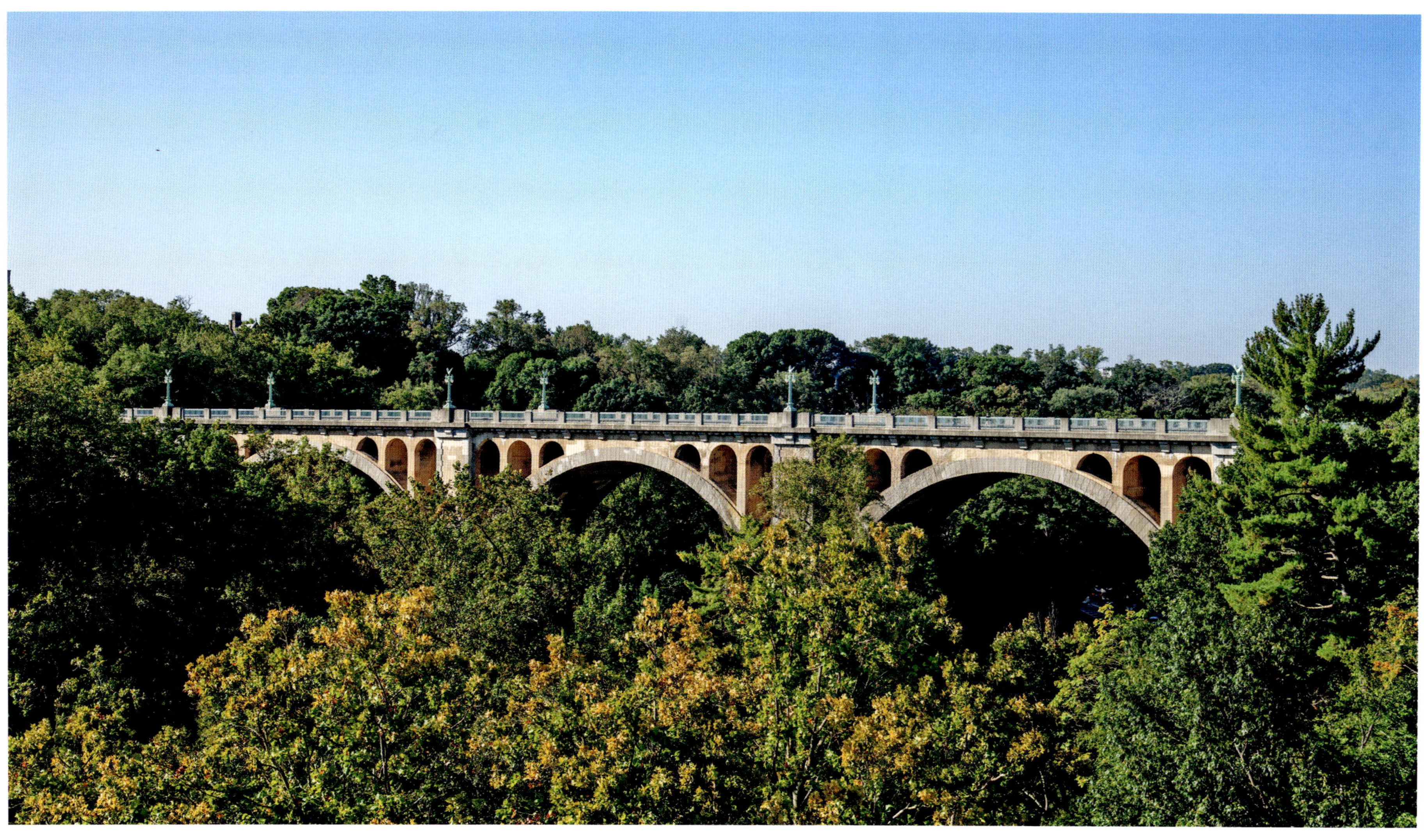

Library of Congress, what was once called "The Million Dollar Bridge" was deemed a huge success.

Following the death of former President and Supreme Court Chief Justice William Howard Taft, the bridge was renamed the Taft Memorial Bridge in 1931. The classical revival style bridge marked the transition from bridges constructed for utilitarian need to those that had specific stylistic design elements.

NOW: The bridge remains an engineering marvel. At 901 feet long, Taft Memorial Bridge is one of the largest unreinforced concrete structures in the world. What is today a commuter road that brings Washingtonians in and out of the District on a daily basis, was once celebrated as an architectural feat of clever engineering, which permanently altered the way that Washington designed and built its bridges.

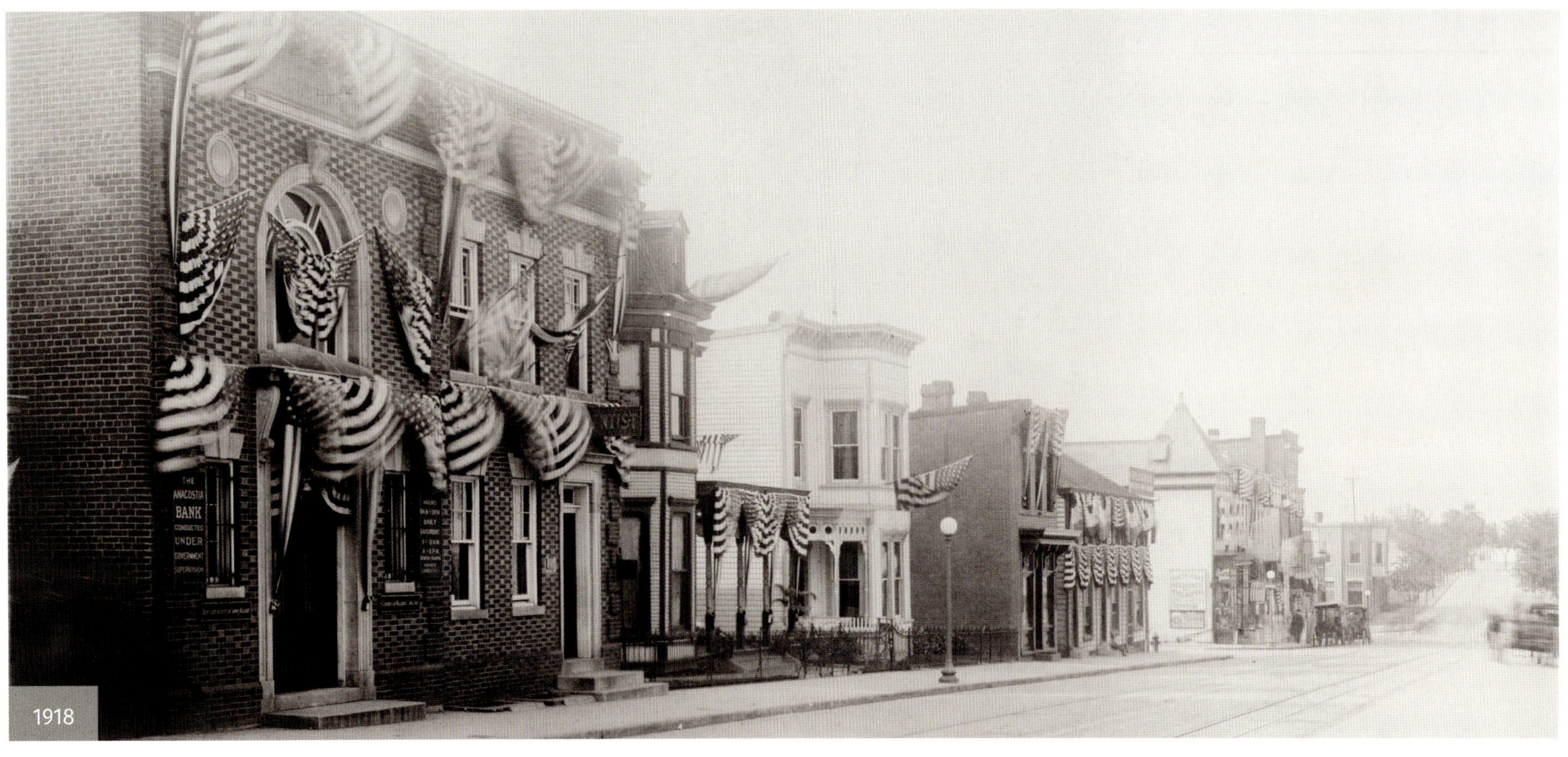

1918

ANACOSTIA

Washington's isolated neighborhood east of the River

THEN: The name Anacostia is an anglicized version of the name of the first inhabitants of the area, the Nacotchtank tribe. This Native American group were the first inhabitants of the land, and their tribe occupied the banks of the nearby river branch. With the arrival of Europeans, and the establishment of the federal city, the land east of the Anacostia River soon became its own suburb of a growing Washington.

Throughout the nineteenth century, what is now considered the Anacostia Historical District was subdivided and represented the changes of the expanding city. In 1854 what was known as Uniontown was considered an early suburb of the District, and in the years before the Civil War was reserved for select white residents. This neighborhood looked across the river into the increasingly industrial Navy Yard, and although the area was slow to develop, the introduction of the street car and connecting bridge brought laborers from Navy Yard to inhabit Anacostia.

However, early into its time as a D.C. suburb, this neighborhood had restrictive living policies and tense racial boundaries that prevented African Americans and other groups from purchasing or living in certain regions. While some parts were restrictive, nearby neighborhoods, such as Barry Farms, served as a refuge for recently freed Enslaved individuals in the years following the Civil War. Additionally, in this time famed abolitionist Frederick Douglass purchased Cedar Hill, an estate that previously belonged to the man who developed Uniontown. He defied racist restrictions and lived there until his death in 1895, and the house is now maintained as a museum dedicated to his accomplishments.

As Anacostia grew, it developed its own thriving commercial district, with different shops for locals and travelers passing through. The neighborhood was isolated from the majority of Washington, but it developed its own downtown and sense of community.

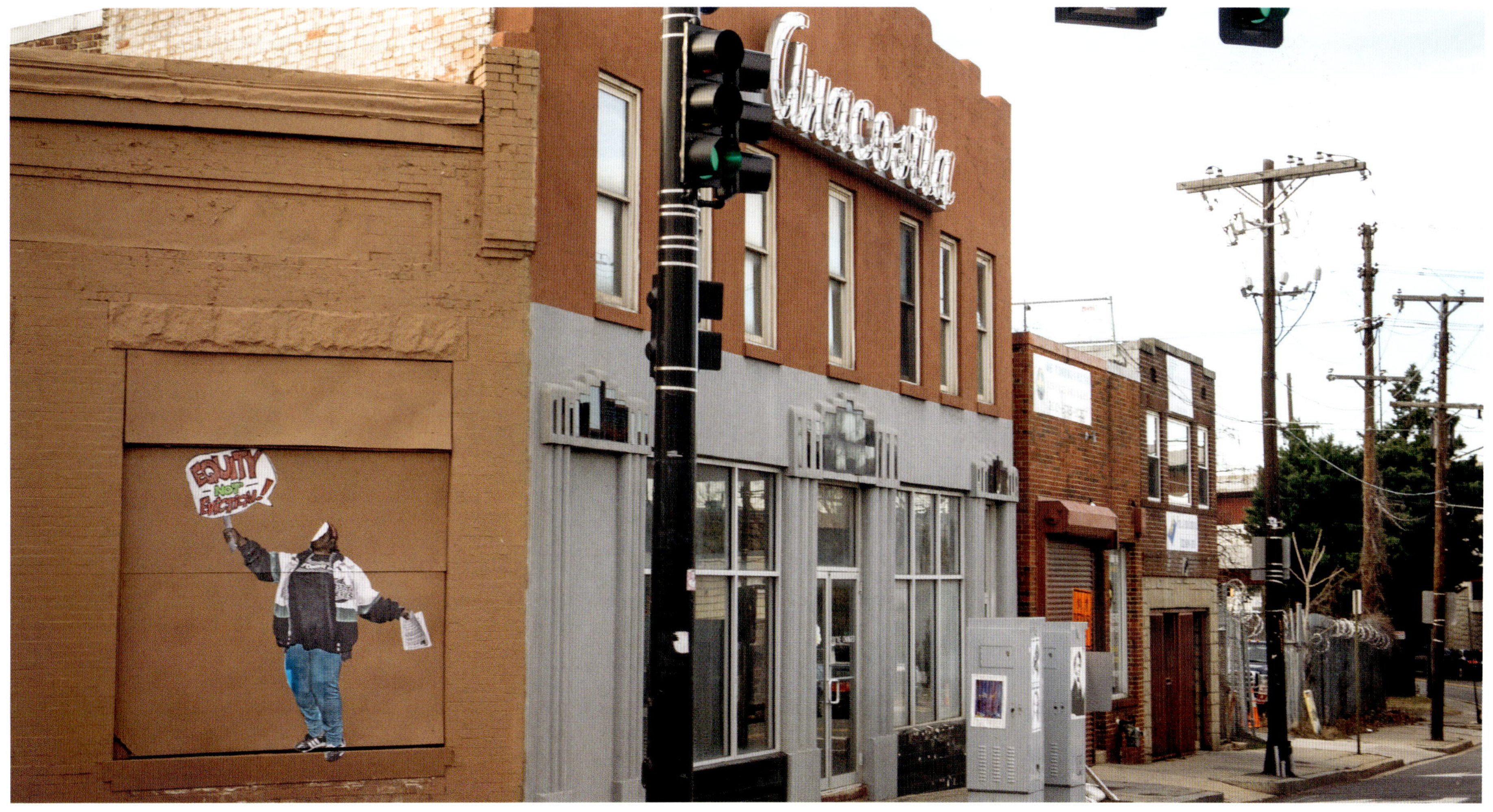

Much like the rest of Washington, a population boom following the two World Wars, as well as persistent racism, brought changes to Anacostia and its subdivided neighborhoods. The area that was known as Barry Farms was largely demolished for new public housing developments, and the addition of highways divided the once connected historic communities. What was previously a predominantly white neighborhood saw an exodus of these families into the suburbs of nearby Maryland and Virginia, and in turn the demolition of historic centers and divestment in the remaining community. Additional nearby urban development in Southwest Washington displaced residents, many of whom were African American, into Anacostia at a time when resources in the neighborhood were already limited. The remaining residents of Anacostia were moved further out.

NOW: While Anacostia saw an increase in poverty and crime as a result of these policies, the area also became an important center of civil rights and Black activism. Around twenty blocks of buildings in the central region of Anacostia were added to the National Register of historic Places in 1978, which preserved the Anacostia Historic District. Also in the neighborhood is the Anacostia Community Museum, which is the first federally funded community museum that exists under the branch of the Smithsonian Institution. Although it is physically separated by the Anacostia River, the neighborhood still represents an important part of Washington's story.